Working People
An Illustrated History of the Canadian Labour Movement

WORKING PEOPLE

DESMOND MORTON

FOURTH EDITION
REVISED AND UPDATED

McGILL-QUEEN'S UNIVERSITY PRESS

MONTREAL & KINGSTON · LONDON · ITHACA

Printed in Canada on acid-free paper

First and second editions 1980, 1984, Deneau Publishers
Third edition 1990, Summerhill Press

McGill-Queen's University Press acknowledges the financial support
of the Government of Canada through the Book Publishing
Industry Development Program for its activities. We also
acknowledge the support of the Canada Council for the Arts
for our publishing program.

Canadian Cataloguing in Publication Data

Morton, Desmond, 1937–
Working people: an illustrated history of the
Canadian labour movement
4th ed., rev. and updated
Includes bibliographical references and index.
ISBN 0-7735-1801-0
1. Trade-unions – Canada – History. 2. Working class – Canada –
History. I. Title.
HD6524.M67 1998   331.88'0971   C98-900929-7

This book is dedicated to
the men and women whose courage
and sacrifice have been the
only real assests of
Canada's labour movement,
and especially to
the late Bill Smith and his daughter,
my late wife, Jan.

Contents

Foreword to the Fourth Edition

This book was born in 1977, out of the collaboration of two historians who believed that the Canadian trade union movement needed a history that was marked less by political ideology than by a concern to locate the place of working people in Canada's history. The collaboration ended amicably in 1990. The third edition of *Working People* appeared in the same year, at the outset of the worst economic experience in Canada since the 1930s. The book was a victim of the times, as two successive publishers went bankrupt and the unsold copies found their way to Breakwater Books in Newfoundland.

This was minor on the scale of miseries experienced by Canadian working people. Hundreds of thousands of working people lost their jobs and far more lost income, benefits and retirement security as companies "downsized" or "re-engineered" in the name of global competitiveness. In Newfoundland, a quarter of the people in Canada's poorest province lost their livelihood when cod stocks failed. Real incomes for most working people had begun to fall as early as 1978, with a modest rebound in the mid-1980s. Most families adjusted by having two adult earners but, from 1990, even two-income families suffered a decline in spending power, with devastating consequences for the consumer economy and for tax revenues, to say nothing of the impact on people themselves. Governments, which had justified drastic tax cuts for corporations on the promise of future growth and higher personal incomes, found themselves with uncontrollable budget deficits. Working people became double victims when their access to health care, to education and training and to the social safety net was squeezed tight.

1990 was another turning point for labour, anticipated neither by previous editions of this book nor by any of the principal actors. Labour's party, the NDP, came to power in Canada's industrial heartland, Ontario. What seemed, briefly, to be a triumphant climax of a half-century of struggle, became in reality a demonstration of the impotence of both the labour movement and the political party it had created. Inheriting a huge burden of recession, debt and deficit, and the unfettered power of post-cold war capitalism, Ontario's NDP government brought to its task little but good will and inexperience. At a time when conventional militancy was hobbled by mass unemployment, political influence gave labour its only leverage. The Ontario experience failed, not least because unions were as bound up in the conventions of free-market capitalism as their political allies. Offered a greater partnership as the price of wage concessions, union leaders responded as they would have to a similar bid from General Motors or Peter Pocklington, with the added outrage that such an offer could have been made by their erstwhile political allies and dependents.

The value of history as experience ends only when everything is finished. Remarkably, Canada's labour movement has survived, adapted, even shown signs of strength. By the late nineties, among the American and European countries with which Canadians normally compare themselves, it was the fifth most successful in organizing a share of the paid labour force. If many of its ideas seem out of favour among current ideological fashions, the only certainty about fashion is that it changes.

This edition of *Working People* has grown out of its predecessors and is a tribute to all who assisted in earlier editions, most conspicuously my former associate in the project, Terry Copp of Wilfrid Laurier University, my colleagues, Noah Meltz and Morley Gunderson at the University of Toronto's Centre for Industrial Relations, my Erindale associates Kathie Hill and Clara Stewart, and generations of students who endured HIS 313 on two campuses of the University of Toronto and 106–405B at McGill. Since 1994, at the McGill Institute for the Study of Canada, I have had the generous assistance of Marie-Louise Moreau and Suzanne Aubin, and an understanding Board of Trustees and the wisdom of colleagues in McGill's Labour Studies Programme. Most of all, time for work on this edition of *Working People* has been jealously guarded and sacrificed by my wonderful partner, Gael Eakin.

Magog, 1 September 1998

Acknowledgements

Keeping this book in print has been a special pleasure, since it has meant continuing contact with members of the labour movement and those who study it, particularly at the University of Toronto's Centre for Industrial Relations and at McGill, once a powerhouse for Canadian labour studies and, perhaps, with a future as well as a past. Over the years, I have benefited from the wisdom of Bob White of the Canadian Labour Congress, his predecessor, Dennis McDermott, Gord Wilson of the Ontario Federation of Labour, Lynn Williams, Leo Gerard and, especially, Michael Lewis of the United Steelworkers. I can't possibly name all the CLC, federation, and union staffers who have helped with ideas, photographs, and criticisms that are much gentler than I deserve. And always there have been students, at Erindale College, at McGill, even at the Canadian Forces Command and Staff College, whose questions and ideas have helped shape this book.

Three publishers successively went out of business during production of the third edition of this book and it ended with Clyde Rose of Breakwater Books in St. John's. I am grateful to him for the terms which have restored it to print. The current edition owes much to the generosity and patience of my colleagues at the McGill Institute for the Study of Canada, Marie-Louise Moreau and Suzanne Aubin, and to Philip Cercone, Joan McGilvray and Lesley Barry of McGill-Queen's University Press. Only the author, of course, is responsible for the errors of fact and opinion, but the book has gone through enough earlier editions to suggest that the book is either helpful or opaque.

CHAPTER 1

Working People

Canada was a country that depended on workers. There were places in the world where European settlers could force others to serve their needs and produce their wealth. In most of Africa and Latin America, slavery or its second cousin, peonage, gave the illusion that work was a degrading burden from which whites must be spared. Our country was too harsh and demanding to foster such illusions.

Harold Innis, the great economic historian, suggested that Canada developed through the evolution of a series of staple trades. The cod fishery, furs, timber, wheat, and minerals — each set the pattern for exploration, settlement, and the building of transportation routes. Each trade, in turn, was shaped by the availability of human labour.

Fishermen from Portugal, Britanny, and the west of England knew the waters of North America long before explorers like John Cabot and Jacques Cartier registered their official dates of discovery. The fur trade was possible only because the marvellous Indian development, the canoe, allowed a few men to travel long distances. It was also possible because the famous voyageurs were small enough to share a canoe with almost four tons of merchandise and supplies, and because they also were strong enough to carry twice their weight across a long portage.

The workers in the staple industries were the real builders of Canada. When they are remembered, it is often in a fog of romantic legends of strength, endurance, and gaiety. The legends of Jos. Montferrand and the Chasse-Gallerie have obscured the reality of spastic backs, hernias, and thirty-year life spans which were common among the lumberers and voyageurs. For days on end

1

during the annual timber drives, the raftsmen were soaked to the skin in the icy spring run-off. Since liquor was cheap and available, it served as the best available antifreeze.

Even under the French regime, colonial policy favoured farming over every alternative livelihood. Through farming, individual families and the colonial society as a whole could achieve self-sufficiency. The one consistent attraction of moving to an uncompromising, raw land was the hope of independence. It drew rich and poor from the Old World, and probably it still does.

The essential characteristic of a worker was dependence. A worker was a *hired* person. It was a status of inferiority which, according to the claims of the people who ran business and government, needed only be temporary. Men hired for the fur brigades or the lumber gangs could use their wages to buy a farm or badly needed livestock. Work on the canals or on railway construction was advertised as a penniless immigrant's opportunity to raise enough cash to start a homestead. "Hiring out" as a farm hand was how a newcomer collected his stake and learned the farming methods of a new country.

A country of independent producers was the dreamland of every political utopian. In 1837, William Lyon Mackenzie, the Upper Canadian rebel, demanded that all industry be banned and that every business be no larger than a family could manage. That year cities and towns across North America were jammed with enough desperate unemployed people to explain Mackenzie's concern — and to show its futility.

Neither wishes nor colonial policy could make Canada a society of independent farmers and artisans. The staple trades themselves were possible only with armies of hired men. Wheat, which became a staple in its own right by the end of the eighteenth century, required a complex transportation and processing system to get it to markets. Canal building was as much a feature of the wheat staple as canoes were to the fur trade, because only when the barriers of Niagara Falls and the St. Lawrence had been conquered could bulk grain shipments reach Montreal.

Because of their scarcity, workers in the early staple trades had earned some protection for their welfare, at least in New France. In the great canal-building era of the 1840s, labour scarcity was ended by massive immigration from Ireland. Thereafter, governments felt obliged to summon floods of newcomers whenever Canadian workers showed any tendency to bid up their price.

The Irish refugees from the Great Famine formed the first major wave of newcomers to reach Canada for whom the dream of farming independence was not really available. Even the regiments of soldiers drafted to Canada to provide a dependable labour force, like Colonel John Simcoe's York Rangers, could look forward to land grants as a reward for faithful service. The Irish and many who followed them were fated to become a permanent labour force. In a series of waves, the Irish and their successors provided Canada with her construction gangs, her factory hands, and her miners. They would make possible the industrial and resource expansion that began in the final quarter of the nineteenth century.

The myth of economic independence long outlived its practical reality. Until the arrival of the Grand Trunk Railway in the 1850s, employment was almost

Canada's forests were cleared, her railways and roads were built, and her natural resources were developed by gangs of men like these. Their skill with an axe or saw, in harnessing and managing a team of horses, and in judging weather and the lie of the land were vital to Canada's economy. So was their endurance and physical strength. (New Brunswick Archives)

At the end of the season, loggers built huge rafts from the square timbers and sailed them down the Ottawa and St. Lawrence rivers. The strength and skill of workers like these made some of the greatest early Canadian fortunes. Visitors to Canada sometimes commented on the devil-may-care attitude of the French-Canadian and Irish loggers and raftsmen, but they saw the men at the end of a long, brutally exhausting season. Observers had no way of noting the short lifespan or the toll of fatal or crippling injuries in all the staple trades. (Public Archives Canada WS 2657)

always on a very small scale. Even when huge gangs of men worked on canal excavations, tasks were usually divided among small subcontractors. Some important Canadian fortunes have their roots in the skill of a sly gang boss in pocketing profits extorted from an employer or, more often, squeezed out of his workers. Those who miscalculated and went broke were likely to leave their employees unpaid after months of hard labour. Governments were more likely to meet the swindled workers with troops and police than with sympathy. Even in early factories, skilled workers resembled independent entrepreneurs, hiring their own helpers, often setting their own terms and hours of work. Glass-blowers, who were virtually artists in their craft, gave themselves a seven-hour day and two months' holidays every summer.

Perhaps that illustrated the basic problem of the worker in Canadian society. If he were not an independent farmer, businessman, or craftsman, he should either be on the way to become one or he was a failure. If he had missed the opportunities offered by the new country, a worker must accept his fate with a decent servility. Not until near the end of the nineteenth century did a workingman generally win the right to vote. Until then, political power was monopolized by people who had achieved independence or, like small farmers and skilled craftsmen, felt themselves on the verge. Like most people, the farmers and businessmen who determined law and custom in Canada believed fervently that they were being fair to all when, in fact, they were fair only to themselves.

How did our worker-ancestors live a hundred years ago? It is very hard to generalize across a century in which remarkable stability in the value of money concealed enormous changes in every other economic and social factor.

An unskilled day-labourer in 1867 might earn a dollar a day for a ten-hour day, six days a week. A highly skilled craftsman might earn three times as much. A woman's wage would be half that of a man — as little as thirty-five to sixty cents a day. A child earned as little as twenty-five cents. Employers offered no paid holidays, and they rarely felt obliged to make provision for sickness, injury, or old age except to dismiss or reduce the wages of workers who were past their prime. Until 1877, masters and servants acts allowed the courts to send disobedient or absentee workers to jail at an employer's request. There were no such punishments for employers who broke their side of the bargain. After the law was changed in 1877, Montreal and other cities and towns kept similar rules in force through municipal by-laws.

Working people in good times could afford to live in a two- or three-room cottage with a pit privy outside but usually without running water. They ate an adequate but monotonous diet heavily dependent on bread, potatoes, and cheese. Any surplus was all too likely to be spent on liquor because Canadians were notoriously a hard-drinking people.

In cities and towns, working people were almost as eager joiners as their affluent neighbours. Provident societies like the Orange Order, the Sons of England, or St. Patrick's Society looked after members in misfortune, but they also offered entertainment and a sense of importance through their banquets, picnics, processions, and political activity. Volunteer fire brigades in most Canadian cities were usually manned and organized by working people. They

Life for a Canadian working-class family revolved around some hard economic facts. No unskilled worker could earn enough to keep his family out of poverty. The earnings of a wife and children could provide modest comfort and a chance to save—if a depression did not bring general unemployment. For most families, the child-bearing years could be very hard. (City of Toronto Archives)

Inmates of the Ottawa Home for Friendless Women were expected to work for their living and the institution took in washing from hotels and the city's more affluent families. Widows, the elderly, and abandoned mothers could choose between such institutions and destitution on the streets if they had no family or savings to support them. (Public Archives Canada PA 27434)

offered competition, excitement, esprit de corps, and uniforms as well as a sense of civic duty. Canadians in mid-century were swept into a passionate excitement over sports. While the better-off turned to cricket or lacrosse, working people turned to baseball and rowing, creating a national hero in the brilliant Toronto oarsman, Ned Hanlan.

Everything depended on good times. A working-class family lived always in the shadow of disaster. Work was heavy and often dangerous. Severe and crippling injuries were commonplace in almost every trade. Epidemics swept across Victorian Canada, and medicine, even if a worker could afford it, probably did more harm than good. Winter was an annual purgatory. Prosperous Canadians might find it a season of sport, entertainment, and, at worst, boredom. To working people it was a time of reduced wages, unemployment, and soaring prices for food and fuel. As the forest retreated from major cities and towns, the price of firewood rose. In 1854, the Montreal *Gazette* reported that fuel wood took a fifth of a worker's income.

The ultimate disaster for working people was old age. The usual dispensers of useless advice urged workers to be thrifty and commanded children to care for their parents. The Victorian family did its best, and the only periods of relative affluence in a worker's life came when all or most members of a family could contribute incomes to a common pot. However, in a mobile society, economic circumstance, ambition, and hardship could scatter a family across North America. The crises of working-class life dissolved small savings. The alternatives for people too old to find work could be starvation or a prison cell with, either way, the humiliation of a pauper's grave. As late as 1892, a government inspector found most of the inmates of the Peterborough jail condemned to prison clothing and food for no other offence than poverty and inability to find work.

Did conditions for working people get better or worse as the nineteenth century advanced? Michael Cross, a social historian, insists that they got worse. A typical worker at the start of the century worked in a small shop in a small town close to green fields and fresh air. He had the pride of taking raw material and crafting a finished product. By the end of the century, the typical worker might be a factory hand, a miner, or a construction labourer, producing wealth for a huge corporation, his skill and pride in craft scorned. His home would be in an evil-smelling city slum.

Others insist that conditions improved. Early settlements might be picturesque but some, like early Toronto, were malarial swamps. Pioneer farms offered backbreaking work, loneliness, and crop failure more often than prosperity. People flooded into the towns and cities, and the most persuasive efforts of government officials, clergy, and assorted civic moralists could not keep Canadians down on the farm. Some of our unkind opinions of nineteenth-century cities and industrial life reflect this back-to-the-land propaganda. Harsh industrial discipline, low pay, and bad living conditions must be compared to rural reality, not to nostalgic reminiscences of country life.

There were good reasons to prefer urban life. The coming of railways by mid-century began to drive out the worst cruelties of winter. Employment became less dependent on the seasons. Trains could bring fuel from a greater

Much of Canada developed from a few log huts and tar-paper shacks set in the midst of a bush clearing and representing civilization to the loggers and construction crews that had moved still farther out. Early settlers often spent their first winter under canvas. The fire hazard, whether from an overheated stove or from a raging bush fire, was the greatest single risk to life and property. (Public Archives Canada WS 2644)

distance, and by the 1870s they had introduced the mixed blessing of coal. Railways also helped to make food and manufactured goods cheaper, more varied, and available year-round.

The factory system is usually presented as an evil for working people. It certainly destroyed the foundations of a number of honoured and well-paid crafts. Factory owners were often oppressive and irresponsible employers, and, at its least, factory discipline could be painful to accept. However, mechanized production made an incredible range of goods available at prices working people could afford.

Skilled workers almost certainly lost status during the period. Their proud independence was curbed by industrial employers. Casual attitudes to punctuality or productivity were curbed by factory discipline and the threat of fines and dismissal. Technology eliminated skills acquired during years of harsh apprenticeship. Trade unionism developed during the second half of the nineteenth century almost wholly to defend the status of skilled workers, not to improve the welfare of the unskilled.

One problem with our bleak view of factory and slum conditions at the end of the nineteenth century is that we don't have good comparisons with an earlier period. Observers like W.H. Howland in Toronto and Herbert Ames in Montreal responded to a social conscience that had been unconsidered in Canada half a century before. Such observers were also outsiders, noting what those who shared in the life of the working poor took for granted.

Perhaps the most important set of descriptions of industrial and working-class life in late nineteenth-century Canada was the collected testimony before the Royal Commission on the Relations of Labor and Capital, published in 1889. Historians have used the study to find evidence of cruelty and exploitation by employers. Just as striking is the matter-of-fact acceptance of conditions by witnesses who plainly believed that conditions, if not desirable, were probably inevitable.

We should not be surprised. Most of us today also accept our present circumstances as natural and, in great measure, unalterable. We can welcome modest changes; we may even be forced to accept radical transformations though we are not surprised, when the flurry passes, that most goes on as before. At the same time, we wonder how our ancestors put up with conditions that appear severe and unreasonable. Since we can learn from history how changes were finally achieved, we may wonder why reform was embraced so slowly and with such hostility, especially from those who would benefit.

Since our descendants may well ask the same questions about us, we should try to understand how and why change occurred. Working-class life in Canada a hundred years ago was a meagre, insecure, unrespected existence. Times have changed. Who changed them?

Most working people for most of their lives have accepted their position as natural and inescapable. Some have sought desperately to escape. With luck, good management, ingenuity, and sometimes a larcenous instinct, a few have succeeded. The most interesting people are those who have tried to organize workers themselves to change their circumstances. That way has been rough, frustrating, and long. Achievements have never been complete.

Yet it is those people who have done the most to transform the lives of all Canadians. They are the heroes of this book.

CHAPTER 2

Getting Organized

In the Old World and the New, working people never entirely accepted their fate. However, only rarely did they have any legal way to protest. Even peaceful attempts to present grievances became riots, mutinies, and rebellions. Leaders and spokesmen for working people became ringleaders, agitators, and conspirators to be pursued with savage vindictiveness.

Some of our own history reflects the scant sympathy our ancestors spared for people who defied authority. Perhaps Roberval was harsh when he flogged men and women at Tadoussac for indiscipline, but surely it was necessary to keep discipline? Who can sympathize with the mutineers who set Henry Hudson adrift in 1611? Thomas Scott, the young Canadian whom Louis Riel executed in 1870, owed much of his turbulent reputation to his conduct a year earlier. Scott's offence was organizing his fellow road workers to collect their overdue pay. Perhaps his eventual punishment was a fitting end for Canadian workers who protest too much. Few modern historians worry much about his treatment.

In the eyes of respectable society, working people had one duty: to labour quietly and uncomplainingly. For this, their reward might come in the hereafter since, short of escaping into wealth and independence, it would not come in this life. For working people, it was equally obvious that their only influence came through denying society their labour and, perhaps, its peace of mind.

This was exceedingly risky. No matter how pathetic the grievances, no matter what sympathy the suffering drew from influential outsiders, collective self-help by the victims has always been the fastest way to curdle charity. Sympathetic people can be amazingly patient about the afflictions of others, but workers who faced starvation for themselves and their families could be driven to desperate action.

Experts agreed, for example, that the two shillings and sixpence per day paid to Irish canal builders in the 1840s was hopelessly inadequate. It cost half that much alone to buy a man's food for a day, and most of the canallers found no more than ten or twenty days' work each month. The shanties and hovels in which the canallers and their families lived, the epidemics which swept through their tumbledown communities, and the regular reports of misery and suffering all drew sympathy and concern. Yet when the Irish put down their shovels and sent armed gangs to force others to stop work, the authorities sent magistrates, police, and troops to restore "order." Respectable opinion termed the canal strikes "riots," accepted that most of the trouble was due to old feuds between men from Cork and Connaught, and concluded righteously that the Irish were "a turbulent and discontented people...who will never be kept to work peaceably unless overawed by some force for which they have some respect."

The truth was that the Irish canal labourers were victims of supply and demand. The publicly appointed Board of Works expressed a proper concern that the canallers be suitably housed and promptly paid, but its real priority was to get the work done as cheaply as possible. When contractors left their men unpaid for months or forced them to deal at overpriced "pluck-me's," or company stores, the board deserved blame for accepting obviously underpriced bids and for delaying its own payments. Both the board and contractors took advantage of the thousands of penniless Irish who escaped the Great Famine and thousands more unemployed who fled the American depression after 1837. Even at the height of construction of the Canadian canals, contractors reported many thousands looking for work who could not find it.

Locally and for brief periods, the Irish canal workers found that they could extract wages as high as four shillings a day. By a combination of open force and a clannish secrecy, they could overawe whole neighbourhoods and intimidate the contractors. One man on the Lachine Canal workings was reported to be too terrified to go near his own site, and his men worked at their own pace. Such triumphs were rare and short-lived. The flow of new workers, the approach of winter, and the power of the authorities wiped out gains and dissolved organizations. If there were key leaders, neither we nor the authorities at the time knew who they were. Like the canallers they drifted on, perhaps to become contractors in their own right.

It is easy to assume that labour organizations have to exist when strikes occur. In fact, strikes could be spontaneous and without apparent official leadership. James Hodges, a contractor for the Victoria Bridge built across the St. Lawrence in the 1850s, complained that in Montreal "it is almost a universal custom for mechanics...to strike twice a year, let the rate of wages be what it may." Workers in a seasonal port had learned from experience that they could put pressure on employers at the beginning and near the end of the season. However, since the opportunity was seasonal, no real organization could have survived.

Labour organization in nineteenth-century Canada succeeded only when there was a durable labour scarcity. The first traces of dock labour unions can be found in Saint John and Halifax during the War of 1812. Even unskilled workers were in short supply in the ports. Longshoremen developed enough

Ship labourers, or longshoremen, were among the most militant groups of nineteenth-century Canadian workers. Their work was vital in a country that depended heavily on shipping, and in ports like Montreal and Quebec, they could use the desperation of shippers at the beginning and end of the short navigation season to win demands. Police were sent to guard any would-be strike-breakers, but the ethnic solidarity of the largely Irish ship labourers could often defeat the authorities. (Canadian Illustrated News)

strength to open an office and set wage rates. It probably helped that merchants, ship owners, and captains were too eager to cash in on wartime profits and a favourable wind to spend time fighting upstart labourers. Immediately after the war, in 1816, Nova Scotia's legislature observed that "great numbers of... Journeymen and Workmen in the Town of Halifax and other parts of the Province" had "by unlawful Meetings and Combinations, endeavoured to regulate the rate of wages, and to effectuate illegal purposes." Although such activities were banned by existing British laws against "combinations" of workmen, Nova Scotia added its own penalty of three months in jail for offenders.

Even a law could not overcome bargaining power. A carpenters' association survived in Yarmouth from 1834 to 1851, and a printers' union existed in Halifax in 1837. However, in neighbouring New Brunswick, off the beaten track of immigration and enjoying its richest era, labour had more power. According to Senator Eugene Forsey, Saint John deserves to be considered the labour stronghold of British North America, if only from the size and self-confidence of its trades processions. As many as fifteen different organizations, mustering twelve hundred or fifteen hundred members, gathered to lay the cornerstone of the Mechanics' Institute or to greet the new governor general in 1840, and to welcome the European and North American Railway in 1853. From the 1850s, the Labourers' Benevolent Association ruled the ports "with a rod of iron," loading and unloading every vessel, proclaiming wage rates by newspaper advertisement, and closing operations to attend the funeral whenever a member died on duty.

Very rarely could unskilled workers exercise such power. Prosperity, tradition, and a preference for the quiet life in an industry plagued by too many
uncertainties helped the shipping industry to accept what other employers
would never tolerate. Quebec, in the final prosperous glow of the square-timber
trade, was another port firmly controlled by its labour force. Incorporated in
1862, the predominantly Irish Ship Labourers' Benevolent Society managed to
set wages for its members, particularly after a well-managed, aggressive, and
successful strike in 1866. Shipmasters, desperate to get their vessels underway,
broke the solidarity of the merchants despite the availability of British sailors and
marines.

   Labour organizing in Canada normally depended on another kind of scarcity
— the shortage of highly skilled and experienced craftsmen. Such men could not
be recruited from the latest shipload of starving immigrants. For all the frequent
advice to learn a trade, few parents had the money or connections to obtain
indentures for a son, and many young people would not put up with the years of
deprivation, abuse, and oppression often associated with apprenticeship. Those
who did demanded both respect and income for a scarce skill and seven years of
sacrifice. If necessary, they would organize to get them.

   In Quebec, the unskilled ship labourers divided the city's shipping industry
with French Canadians who specialized in shipbuilding. The *Société amicale et
bienveillante des charpentiers de vaissaux* ("Friendly and Benevolent Society of Ships'
Carpenters") was a union of highly skilled workers who began in 1840 to protect
themselves from both the unskilled and their employers. Surviving records
suggest that skilled workers in other Canadian cities and towns also organized
unions before 1860. Most were short-lived. The commonest trades represented
were printing, shoemaking, tailoring, iron work, mechanical engineering, and
some parts of the construction industry.

   We know very little about most of these associations. Some may have begun as
convivial or benevolent organizations, offering banquets or sickness benefits.
Whatever the original purpose, most of them soon lived up to Adam Smith's
famous observation: "People of the same trade seldom meet together, even for
merriment and diversion, but the conversation ends in a conspiracy against the
public or in some contrivance to raise prices." For skilled craftsmen, the purpose
was often to keep their prices from being swept away altogether. What united
them was a desperate concern to keep up the value of their skill.

   Never before had skills been swept away with such rapidity as with the coming
of the industrial revolution. Nowhere was mechanical ingenuity more praised
and more swiftly adopted than in North America. The high cost of craftsmen in
North America brought a special challenge to displace them with machinery. As
agriculture grew more specialized and more profitable, it provided a market for
more manufactured goods. Railways and the general improvement of transportation fostered a factory system both in the United States and in central Canada.
In an age fascinated with progress and fully committed to the principle, if not
the practice, of the free market, there was little sympathy for workers who tried
to protect an investment in old and complex skills. That did not keep workers
from trying.

   Tailors and shoemakers were among the first to be hit. In Toronto, the

Journeymen Tailors' Operative Society was formed in 1852 to persuade a local firm to get rid of its new sewing-machine. After a short struggle, the machine and the girl who ran it were returned to New York. On January 26, the society showed its gratitude by marching, two hundred strong, to the Mechanics' Institute to entertain the employers. After presenting the company with a silver crouching lion, the firm's emblem, masters and men sat down to a dinner of goose and cabbage.

That was not the end of the story. In a couple of years, the employer forgot his agreements. When his tailors struck, he replaced them with women. When they drove a wagon through Toronto streets, proclaiming him unfair, he took legal action. On November 7, 1854, the tailors were found guilty of conspiracy and their society was dissolved.

That year Hamilton tailors were more successful in a similar battle. "The fiend that has come among them," reported the Hamilton *Spectator*, "is . . . none other than the steam engine, with his sewing machines and other implements of evil, seeking extermination to the whole craft. It is no wonder, therefore, that they have come out and separated themselves from the evil and have left the monster alone in his glory with his gussets and seams and skirts." The employers advertised for men who were not "afraid of machinery" and brought in fifty strike-breakers from the United States. Once informed of the situation, the American workers went home. The workers' victory was only temporary. In a few years Hamilton had even become a centre for sewing-machine manufacturing.

Without exception, skilled workers preferred to eat goose and cabbage with their employers than to risk open quarrel. The odds on success in a "turnout," or strike, were low. If economic power was not enough for the employers, the courts were dependable allies. Craftsmen also regarded themselves highly. They despised unskilled workers and dreamed of becoming employers in their own right. In the United States, where working people had become a political force in some cities, the skilled workers often bridled at association with "workies," "dirty shirts," and "rabble." Unions of skilled workers had to respond to their members' preoccupation with respectability and security.

Few union records have survived in Canada. An exception is the Toronto Typographical Union, launched in 1832 as the York Typographical Society, lapsed after 1837, revived in 1844, with a continuous existence to the present day as Local No. 91 of the International Typographical Union.

United to Support, Not Combined to Injure was the motto of the original society and of many other early unions. At a first anniversary dinner in 1833, members doubtless rejoiced to learn that employers as varied as Robert Stanton, the king's printer, and William Lyon Mackenzie, the reforming publisher of the *Colonial Advocate*, approved of their activities. Having studied the society's constitution, Mackenzie announced he could "find nothing therein but a consistent and moderate policy . . . ."

Unfortunately, the society could not avoid conflict. In the autumn of 1836, it struck Toronto's master printers to win a ten-hour day, eight dollars a week, and no more than two apprentices per shop. Mackenzie, Upper Canada's leading defender of the rights of man, was furious at such impertinence. He fired his journeymen, proclaimed that their work was "so light and easy that women could perform it," and advised the printers to study the laws of political economy. Most Toronto master printers followed Mackenzie's lead, and the typographers suffered a defeat. Their society dissolved in the aftermath of Mackenzie's disastrous rebellion in December, 1837.

When the printers revived their organization in 1844, the spur was a combination of employers bent on lowering their wages. George Brown had arrived in Toronto from Edinburgh by way of New York a year before. At the age of twenty-six, he launched the *Globe* and soon turned it into the instrument that won him personal wealth and political prestige as a leader of the Upper Canadian Reformers. A loud defender of individualism and unfettered competition for others, George Brown worked tirelessly to unite Toronto's master printers in cutting rates and increasing hours. He was at the heart of most of the trouble the typographers faced over the next thirty years.

Brown won the first round in 1845 when he forced union members, including the society's president and secretary, out of his printing shop. Two society officers responded in the best craft tradition by going into business for themselves. By 1847, the society had to accept a proposal of the master printers to "elevate the trade" by lowering the wages.

The Ottawa fire brigade in the 1860s was typical of the voluntary organizations workingmen could join. Proud of their uniforms and fiercely competitive in the race to be first to the fire, the fire brigade members were still regarded as socially unacceptable by the snobbish arbiters of Victorian Canadian society. Professional fire departments gradually supplanted one of the liveliest and most colourful organizations of Canadian working-class life. (Public Archives Canada C 20624)

However, 1848 proved a turning-point. The sociey discovered the secret of much successful nineteenth-century unionism in Canada, Britain, and the United States: the benevolent principle. Already many Canadian working people had begun turning to "fraternal" and "provident" societies to purchase what was, in effect, sickness, injury, and funeral insurance. Behind the regalia, ceremonial, and secret handshakes of many fraternal orders was a hard core of material benefit. The strength of the Orange Lodge in Canada came from its medical insurance and funeral benefits as much as from its processions and political threats. Like other unions, the typographers' society discovered that the benevolent principle was a powerful organizing tool.

Printers could afford dues which guaranteed them ten shillings a week for sickness or unemployment, and even more if they were fired for upholding union standards. What is more, they would pay on time. In turn, the society had a reserve of funds (if it managed its affairs carefully) and a firm material hold on the loyalty of its members. More and more unions emphasized their responsibility for their members. We Support Our Infirm. We Bury Our Dead — proclaimed the great banner of the Quebec Ship Labourers. There was another advantage. By offering benefits, unions could enforce better conduct. The Brotherhood of Locomotive Engineers, formed by American and Canadian engine drivers in 1864, fined members for drunkenness on duty and even expelled them for adultery. Employers and the general public were invited to note the improvement. The Toronto typographers allowed no benefits if dismissal was due to misconduct, or if sickness arose from drunkenness or debauchery. No member benefiting from the sick fund was to "remain abroad after sunset."

Employers might welcome the moral uplift sought by unions, and even George Brown approved of their provident features, but no employer would be less than master in his own establishment. However dignified and important even skilled craftsmen might fancy themselves to be, they remained servants in the eyes of the law, custom, and their employer. Even those few workingmen with the right to vote were expected to support their master's choice. Anything less deserved dismissal for disloyalty. While an enlightened few repudiated such a feudal view of their own authority, all employers solemnly believed in the presumed law of an economic order. They must buy in the cheapest market and sell in the dearest. In their own work place, they must be in control.

Since apprentices were cheaper than journeymen, George Brown and other employers did their best to hire them. When Brown discovered that women were cheaper still, he boasted proudly of his finding: "A female who knows how to read and write, can earn in a printing office twice as much as she would receive in any other employment. We have made arrangements to provide room especially for the female department of the printing office, and everything will be done to render their situation comfortable." The printers replied by referring to "Brown's harem." More conservative competitors were deterred, and the typographical society overcame that challenge to male dominance.

Like most early unionists, the Toronto printers fought lonely defensive battles against employers who were alive to developments in the neighbouring United States as well as in Canada. The printers' weapons were the conservatism of much of the rest of society and the powerful collective traditions of their own trade. Skilled workers, through the web of organizations, associations, and lodges to which they belonged, had links to respectable society and bonds with each other. Innovating employers could, for a time, be subjected to social disapproval. Fellow workers who "hogged" or "speeded up" could suffer even rougher penalties.

However, these were defensive struggles, waged only on behalf of a modestly affluent minority of the Canadian working class. They made little difference to the welfare of working people as a whole. By 1860, that fact was beginning to be recognized.

CHAPTER 3

International Ideas

The few labour organizations in Canada before the 1860s were mostly small, local, and short-lived. Yet their leaders were often in close touch with labour developments in Britain and the United States. After all, most people in Canada had come from somewhere else. For a good many of them, emigration to the colonies had been an escape from such disappointments as Robert Owen's Grand National Consolidated Trades Union or the People's Charter in the 1840s. Often they brought an idealism tinged with experience. In North America even skilled craftsmen frequently rolled up their belongings, wrapped their tools in an oily rag, and set out "on a tramp." To itinerant workers, the border between Canada and the United States was no obstacle.

If employers kept up to date with developments, so could workers. Toronto's Amicable Society of Bricklayers, Plasterers and Masons set out in 1832 to win a ten-hour day when it learned that fellow tradesmen in Britain and New York City had finally broken the old sunrise-to-sunset rule. Members of a trade believed that they belonged to a wider fraternity. The York Typographical Society welcomed a newcomer with a membership card from the Cork Typographical Society in Ireland. When the man found no work locally, the society issued seventeen shillings and sixpence to help him reach the United States.

There was another side to international connections. Both American and Canadian strikers regularly found themselves displaced by workers recruited on the other side of the border. In Toronto labour slang, the word *Buffalo* joined *rat* as a synonym for strike-breaker or scab. Doubtless Buffalo unionists had an equally low view of Canadians.

British and American worker organizations had a much longer history than their Canadian counterparts. By the 1850s, labour in both countries emerged disillusioned from several years' exposure to radical and utopian notions. In the United States, the doctrine of *pure and simple unionism* was inspired in part by the unexpected triumph of *new-model unionism* in Britain.

First of the new-model unions was the Amalgamated Society of Engineers, formed in 1851 in sober rejection of all the high-flown notions of the Chartist era. It soon became a proof of the questionable doctrine that nothing succeeds like failure. Through much of 1852, the Amalgamated fought and lost a long and merciless struggle with employers in London and Lancashire. The miracle was that the society survived, mustered its forces, and gradually won the employer recognition it had lost in its first year.

After generations of failure, the Amalgamated provided a recipe for success. A union with high dues, generous benefits, a conservative philosophy, and a strong central control could survive. The model was imitated, more or less faithfully, by "national" unions in both Britain and the United States. The Amalgamated made the model better known when a few branches developed in the United States and Canada after 1853. By 1859, branches of the ASE existed in Montreal, Toronto, Hamilton, Brantford, and London.

In the United States, the strengths and weaknesses of national unions were revealed. A broader base of membership spread the risk of such provident features as sickness, injury, or unemployment insurance, to say nothing of financial support in a strike. A broader organization shared badly needed information about wage rates and working conditions in other cities and towns. It backed up such information with an obvious desire to impose national minimum standards. The more members of a craft who were bound by union membership, the more difficult it became for employers to recruit strike-breakers.

On the other hand, the very success of new-model unionism depended on a tough, centralized authority that ran counter to local autonomy. Men like William Allan of the Engineers or Robert Applegarth of the Amalgamated Society of Carpenters and Joiners (which also crossed the Atlantic to establish branches in Canada and the United States after 1860) were rare in Britain or the United States. Few men combined a personality that inspired members with the sober qualities which kept a union solvent. Employers soon learned that an effective attack on the new unionism could be based on jealousy of union officials, who were described as "paid loafers" and "walking bosses." Union members resented money sent to a remote headquarters and they defied the directives which came back.

Like the British unions, American national unions spread into Canada on the heels of migrant craftsmen. One of the first was the National Union of Molders, established on July 5, 1859. By 1863 its first president, William Sylvis, had visited Canada and found five struggling locals. "I found that the people walked upright, and spoke the same language ...," he reported, "that the trees grew perpendicular and that the water ran downstream and that altogether it was very much the same kind of country I had left." With Sylvis's enthusiasm, the Molders changed its title to *International*, held its 1868 convention in Toronto, and elected Canadian members to senior office.

The Toronto Rolling Mills was typical of many nineteenth-century factories. It was hot, smoky, and unsafe. Skilled craftsmen often worked as subcontractors, employing their own "helpers" and apprentices. However, costs of transportation meant that many smaller and relatively inefficient operations could survive. (Metro Toronto Library Board)

In some cases, American unions reached out to bring existing Canadian organizations into their organization. The National Typographical Union, organized in 1852, accepted the Saint John printers as Local No. 65 in 1865. The Toronto Typographical Union affiliated in 1866 and celebrated by winning a pay raise from nine to ten dollars a week. The American parent organization changed its title in 1869 to International Typographical Union. The United Cigar Makers, having absorbed several locals of the Journeymen Cigar Makers of Upper Canada, broadened its name in 1867.

One of the most powerful unions to enter Canada was the Knights of St. Crispin, named for the patron saint of shoemakers. An old and proud craft, shoemakers had long observed the custom of employing readers and welcoming lecturers to provide mental stimulation during their hours of work. As a result, shoemakers provided some of the most articulate and educated early Canadian working-class leaders.

As a trade, shoemaking was ripe for mechanization. The invention of sewing-machines, first for the uppers and then for the soles, made it efficient for manufacturers to collect scattered, home-based production in factories and then to replace skilled craftsmen by women. The shoemakers fought back. A strike at Lynn, Massachussetts, in 1860 was the largest in American history before the Civil War. Born in 1867, the Crispins had developed 327 locals by the spring of 1870, 16 of them in Canada. The association included new features and old: elaborate initiation rituals, funeral benefits for members, an enthusiasm for banquets and dances, and, above all, a tough determination to preserve a proud but obsolete craft.

The mechanization of shoemaking, spurred by the need for army boots in the American Civil War, led to the destruction of a proud old craft. Through the Knights of St. Crispin, shoemakers in Canada and the United States tried to protect their status by organizing the less skilled workers. The cost of machinery drove small operators out of business and encouraged manufacturers to cut labour costs by hiring women and unskilled machine operators. The same pattern would recur in industry after industry. (Public Archives Canada WS 2197)

By no means did all American unions want Canadian affiliates. The officers of the National Bricklayers' Union issued a charter to a Toronto organization only to be repudiated by the 1871 convention of their association. A proposal to change the union's title to *international* was soundly defeated, and the Toronto charter was annulled. For this selfishness, the Bricklayers received a scolding from an American labour paper, the *Workingmen's Advocate*. Recalling that Canada had been a rich source of strike-breakers in Maine, Vermont, and in the border cities, the paper insisted, "There does not and there never has existed a valid reason why the mechanics of Canada and the United States should not co-operate in their efforts to sustain each other against the aggressions of capital."

Canadian employers preferred the attitude of the Bricklayers. Although they imported labour-saving machinery and strike-breakers from the United States, they were stout patriots when it came to American unions. Goldwin Smith, a former Oxford historian who married into Toronto wealth, managed to commute to Cornell University in New York State and later wrote a persuasive argument for Canada joining the United States, but in 1873 he was a firm nationalist on labour matters. At the Montreal Mechanics' Institute, he offered a trade union audience arguments which would stay fresh for a century:

> An American agitator comes over the lines, makes an eloquent and highly moral appeal to all the worst and meanest passions of human nature, gets up a quarrel and a strike, denounces all attempts at mediation, takes scores of Canadian workmen from good employment and high pay, packs them off with railway passes into the States, smashes a Canadian industry, and goes back highly satisfied, no doubt, with his work, both as a philanthropist and as an American.

Internationalism aroused other terrors in Bishop Ignace Bourget of Montreal. When French-speaking printers formed their own local of the International Typographical Union, Bourget insisted that the members agree to prohibit strikes and abandon the word *International*. He relented on the title only after union officials agreed to disavow any connection with Karl Marx's London-based International Working Men's Association. The union leaders meekly complied if only because one of their members had already been denied Christian burial for the offence of belonging to a "secret society."

If Bourget and Smith feared that Canadian workers might be contaminated by strange foreign ideas, they were right, although these came through literacy, not affiliation. One such idea was the demand for shorter hours of work, which swept into the industrial cities of southern Ontario in the winter of 1872.

In the United States, the idea of a crusade for the eight-hour day gave second wind to the languishing National Labor Union, a premature and short-lived organization. It offered common ground to the utopians and the pure and simple unionists who were slowly pulling the union apart. Idealists insisted that a few more hours of leisure in the day would bring a magic transformation to a worker's intellect and character. Practical men insisted that shorter hours were a way of creating labour scarcity and bidding up wages. By the beginning of 1872, only the Knights of St. Crispin had met real defeat on the issue. Elsewhere in the United States, the eight-hour day appeared triumphant.

Despite their American links, scattered Canadian unionists paid closer attention to British developments. After a five-month struggle, members of the Amalgamated Society of Engineers at Newcastle won themselves a nine-hour day. Immediately, Nine-Hour Leagues sprang up in Britain. Employers might insist that their profit lay in the last hour of toil each day, but if all employers sacrificed that hour, all would be in an identical position while workers would be richer in every way. In Canada, the first Nine-Hour League was formed in Hamilton in the wake of a packed public meeting at the Mechanics' Institute. Employers and skilled craftsmen shared the platform in a display of solidarity moderated by a warning from employers that, unless all other places adopted a nine-hour system, Hamilton could not compete.

For a few days it all seemed possible. At Brantford, a gathering of workers, manufacturers, and clergy shared uplifting arguments and promised immediate action — once the system was universal. Slowly it became apparent that the gain would only be won with struggle. Delegates who called on the management of Toronto's Northern Railway were warned that the company might employ only younger, more active men to get the most out of their nine-hour shift. In Hamilton, workers and employers moved from solidarity to separate meetings. A first strike on the issue began on February 20 when a Nine-Hour League delegate was fired at Wilson, Bowman — a sewing-machine manufacturer. The man regained his job, but many of those who had walked out with him had been replaced.

The movement spread chiefly to railway towns like Montreal, Stratford, and London, where Canadian members of the Amalgamated Society of Engineers played a leading role. In turn, they were denounced for importing the quarrels of the Old World. "There would have been no nine hours agitation at all in Canada," grumbled the Toronto *Daily Telegraph*, "but for the fact that certain individuals were sent out by the unions in England . . . ." In Halifax, the ship-caulkers won the shorter day and an increase in pay.

In central Canada, where resistance grew, the germ of a plan developed. James Ryan, the Hamilton Nine-Hour leader, proposed that the two larger centres of Montreal and Toronto would pool their resources and pour financial aid into the struggle at Hamilton. Then, at two-week intervals, Nine-Hour Leagues in each city would call out their supporters in the first co-ordinated strike in Canadian history. Meanwhile, smaller centres like Oshawa, St. Catharines, Sarnia, Ingersoll, Guelph, Sherbrooke, Brockville, and Kingston sent in exaggerated reports of their enthusiasm.

In all the planning, the weak point was Toronto. That was surprising. In 1871, the local labour organizations had banded together to form the Toronto Trades Assembly, following Hamilton's six-year lead. Labour leaders in the city had used their Nine-Hour rally to float the radical proposition that workers should enter politics. "Workingmen must become a power in the land," proclaimed John Hewitt, who alone among Canadian workers had been in touch with Marx's International. However, far from being a power, the Trades Assembly was no more than the humble mouthpiece of its affiliates, strictly forbidden to propose strikes and protests. That was the sole affair of affiliates. One of them, the powerful Typographical Union, had already made its own plans.

Early in the Nine-Hour outburst, the *Globe*'s George Brown had revealed a wholly unexpected sympathy. "It is perfectly fair and legitimate for persons to demand a reduction of the hours of labour and," he suggested, "if they feel they are now underpaid, to insist on having ten hours pay for nine hours work." After all, Brown observed, "the present is a time of great prosperity." It was entirely different when his own employees made the demand. On March 17, 1872, the Toronto printers settled on a strike date. Within a couple of days, Brown had galvanized his fellow employers into a Master Printers' Association. They would concede the wage demand, not the hours. The day the printers walked out, they would proclaim their shops non-union.

The outcome was a long, dramatic, and ultimately successful strike. The printers found impressive backing from citizens, fellow unionists, and a single

An engraving on the cover of the Canadian Illustrated News *reminded its prosperous readers of the new importance of organized labour in the 1870s. Marchers in Hamilton's Nine-Hour procession carried both the Union Jack and the flag of the United States, but their inspiration was the victory of British workers in Newcastle-on-Tyne. Hamilton's labour leaders conceived the first co-ordinated pressure strategy in Canadian labour history; unfortunately for them, it was outflanked by Toronto's more famous printers' strike. (*Canadian Illustrated News*)*

newspaper, the Toronto *Leader*, owned by a maverick Conservative, James Beaty. His obvious purpose was to pay off a score against Brown, one of Canada's leading Liberals. On April 15, a cold, snowy day, more than ten thousand people met behind the lunatic asylum in Queen's Park in a huge demonstration of sympathy. J.S. Williams, the printers' leader and president of the Trades Assembly, was in the chair. Beaty was among the speakers.

Almost beside himself at such defiance, Brown persuaded his fellow master printers to charge the twenty-four leading printers with seditious conspiracy. The men were released next day on bail, but the strike had become a political diversion. The *Montreal Star*, no friend of labour but even greedier for political capital, denounced the *Globe* publisher for intimidation. "If the printers are guilty of any offence, the managing editor of the *Globe* stands convicted on years of criminality."

The chief casualty of the Toronto printers' strike was the last faint hope of a co-ordinated Nine-Hour campaign. Just as the struggle between George Brown and his printers has preoccupied historians, it also grabbed most attention at the time. For all of James Ryan's pleadings, Toronto labour had no money for the Hamilton strike. Neither the Trades Assembly nor the printers even considered postponing their own activities to the appointed date of May 15. If the workers were disorganized and uncertain, their employers acted with impressive solidarity. In Montreal and Hamilton, employers met within a week of learning of Ryan's plans. In Toronto, metal-work masters announced that the Nine-Hour movement was "entirely unsuited to the wants of a young and struggling country like Canada." In Galt, employees of Goldie, McCullough and Company were compelled to sign a document swearing that they would not "in any way agitate or contribute pecuniary aid to such as are agitating for the reduction of the present hours of labour." In Hamilton, where two thousand men had won the nine-hour day, another twelve hundred struck on May 15. Montreal workers pledged twenty-five cents a week, and the better-paid men in the Grand Trunk Railway shops promised a day's pay. However, the support petered out by the end of June, and most Hamilton employers used the summer of 1872 as an excuse to go back to the ten-hour day. Shorter hours would take about half a century more to win in labour's "Banner City."

During the 1860s, international affiliates had given a few Canadian workers a wider horizon. The brave attempts at the Nine-Hour movement and the final failure taught some Canadians that there would also have to be national links. In the United States and Britain, the movement for shorter hours gave organized workers a glimpse of their potential strength, at least in a brief moment of high prosperity. In Canada, where even local organization was at a more primitive stage, the lesson was correspondingly modest. Out of the Canadian Nine-Hour movement had come not dreams of power but the raw question of the right of organized labour to exist.

CHAPTER 4

Political Movement

The organizers of the Nine-Hour movement had not expected to become pawns in Canadian party warfare. Except when their heads were broken in riots or when politicians hired gangs of unemployed labourers to frighten off opposition, most working people played no part in politics. Voting was a privilege for male property owners and only a few well-paid artisans could qualify. Proud of their hard-won status, they were not likely to worry about humbler working people or even to admit a common interest with them.

When George Brown of the *Globe* charged his printers with criminal conspiracy, he also thought nothing of the political consequences. As an employer, he had charged striking workers before. So had others. A year earlier, in Brantford, iron founders had won convictions against members of the Molders' Union. Brown's legal advice, from R.A. Harrison, a Conservative lawyer, had been perfectly correct. Changes in British law had made it legal for workers to organize and to strike for more pay or shorter hours. Unlike much British law, these changes did not apply to Canada. The old law against criminal conspiracy was still in effect.

Normally, the workers would not have expected much help from the Conservatives. The prime minister, Sir John A. Macdonald, warned the editor of the Tories' new Toronto paper, the *Mail*, not to annoy employers by backing the Nine-Hour campaign. "When the present excitement is over you must look to them and not to the employed for support." At the same time, with a scornful reference to labour, the prime minister added, "There is ... no necessity for your running your head against the navvies in the way that the *Globe* is doing."

There was a reason for such caution. In 1872, Macdonald faced an election

25

Sir John A. Macdonald, as prime minister in 1872, established a somewhat questionable claim to be a friend of organized workers by introducing legislation that apparently made unions legal. However, only organizations that registered qualified for protection. Contemporary workers, like later historians, did not examine the small print. (Public Archives Canada C 21290)

year and his government was in trouble. Few workers could vote but, in cities like Hamilton and Toronto, they might make the difference. Macdonald disliked James Beaty and the *Leader* had been dropped as official Conservative organ, but if the Toronto politician wanted to angle for workers' votes, the Old Chieftain would help.

Action was easy. In 1871, Britain's new Liberal government introduced a Trade Unions Act which abolished the old crime of criminal conspiracy in restraint of trade. In addition, unions which chose to register with the government won added protection for their funds and property. To pacify employers, William Ewart Gladstone also brought in a tough Criminal Law Amendment Act with severe penalties for most forms of picketing and union pressure.

Gladstone's labour legislation was a sore disappointment to the trade unionists who had worked hard to elect him, but Macdonald cared little about such details. A Canadian version of the Trade Unions Act would embarrass the Liberals, while adoption of an identical Criminal Law Amendment Act would delight employers. With little reference to the *Globe* dispute and a heavy emphasis on making Canada attractive to potential British immigrants, Macdonald hurried his legislation through Parliament. On June 15, 1872, the two bills became law.

As a political stroke, the Trade Unions Act was an immediate success. Absorbed in the struggle with George Brown, the Toronto Trades Assembly did not examine Macdonald's gift too carefully. Instead, despite the well-founded suspicions of some members and the fury of some unrepentant Liberals, the assembly set out to show its gratitude to the prime minister. On July 11, with J.S. Williams in the chair and John Hewitt working hard behind the scenes, Toronto workingmen presented Lady Macdonald with a golden jewel casket provided by a mysterious "sympathizer." The occasion allowed the prime minister, Beaty, and a number of other public figures to deliver appropriate if slightly condescending claims of devotion to the toiling masses.

The experience should have taught Toronto labour leaders that politics was a dangerous, divisive business. In his outspoken new labour paper, the *Ontario Workman*, J.S. Williams had begun to preach suspicion of both old parties and the need for workingmen to abandon blind loyalties. In practice, Williams had succeeded in tying the Trades Assembly to the tail of the Conservative party. The mysterious sympathizer, claimed the *Globe*, was Senator David Macpherson, a rich Toronto Tory. By the end of the summer, the *Ontario Workman* itself survived only by courtesy of a $500 loan from the prime minister. "I do not suppose I will ever get the money," Macdonald admitted, "but I may as well keep it over them as security for good behaviour."

What should have been most embarrassing for Macdonald's new-found friends was how little they got from the bargain. The new Criminal Law Amendment Act, with its promise of prison for such vague offences as "molesting, obstructing, watching and besetting," was as bad as the British law. The Macdonald version of the Trade Unions Act was much worse. Instead of freeing all unions from being charged with criminal conspiracy, the Canadian law exempted only those which took the trouble to register. Since no labour organization apparently ever did so, the presumed charter of Canadian labour rights was a dead letter.

The answer, visible even in the 1870s, was independent labour political action. Though their numbers were still few, labour leaders and journalists began repeating the notion that workingmen were a class. "The duty of the workingmen . . .," suggested Williams in the *Ontario Workman*, "is to be true to themselves, to look at every question from their own standpoint, to see how it affects their pockets, their condition, their morals, and having found out to their satisfaction what their duty is, to do it."

Leaders could give such directions. Would followers obey? To do so was to abandon a whole pattern of personal, ethnic, and religious allegiances which had shaped Canadian politics since the 1830s. Old ways would not change easily. They would last longer because the radical alternatives were often presented by charlatans or dreamers.

Montreal labour would remember Méderic Lanctôt, a local journalist who suddenly took an interest in labour. Between 1864 and 1867, his "Grand Association of Canadian Workingmen" grew to eight thousand members, paying dues of ten cents a month. With the proceeds, Lanctôt launched a cut-rate grocery store and promised a bakery and pharmacy to follow. Parades and processions filled the streets, and by 1866 Lanctôt was alderman for Montreal's working-class east end. His real goal was to defeat his old enemy, the co-architect of Confederation, George-Etienne Cartier. When the chance came in 1867, Lanctôt's supporters paraded, organized, and waited for the election funds their candidate had promised. After a long, fateful day, the sad truth emerged: poor Lanctôt was penniless. The Grand Association collapsed, and its leader fled to the United States.

Labour's political problem, as Daniel O'Donoghue later phrased it, was that its friends were either "foxy" or "proxy." For twenty years Sir John A. Macdonald would proclaim himself the workingman's best friend on the strength of one law that was a dead letter and another that threatened every union organizer and striker with prison. The alternative was men like Méderic Lanctôt, whose enthusiasm could be sudden, utopian, and tangled with private ambition. Was the answer to elect workingmen themselves to join the farmers and lawyers and businessmen in Parliament? Or was it, as the *Ontario Workman* argued, to back candidates who would support "such measures as the operative classes may wish to see promoted?"

By 1872, Canada's tiny labour movement was ready to do both. In Hamilton, Nine-Hour movement enthusiasm had inspired plans for a "Canadian Labour Protective Association." Nothing came of it, but the energy of Hamilton unionists probably persuaded local Tories to try the unusual experiment of nominating a mere workingman in an effort to recapture the seat from the Liberals. Their choice was Henry Witton, a painter in the Great Western Railway shops and a man who was both well read and remarkably deferential. Witton captured the seat and became the first worker to enter the House of Commons. Lady Dufferin, wife of the governor general, reçalled him as one of the curiosities of Canadian life. "We had him soon after his election when he dined in a rough coat, but now he wears evening clothes. He talked so pleasantly and was full of information."

Except as an affable clothes-horse, Witton left no record of service to working people. In 1874, Hamilton voters chose an independent-minded young lawyer named Aemilius Irving, and Witton went to his eventual reward as Dominion inspector of canals.

The alternative solution was taken up by the energetic Toronto Trades Assembly. In the United States, a National Labor Union had emerged as an ambitious attempt to unite American labour organizations. Torn by conflict between idealists and the pure and simple school, the NLU was on its last legs by 1873, but the Canadians were not dismayed. Only forty-six delegates appeared in Toronto at the end of September, but letters of regret from Montreal and Quebec allowed participants to imagine that they spoke for the entire new nation of Canada. John Carter, secretary of the Trades Assembly and a painter by trade, took the chair.

From Carter's opening message, the Canadian Labour Union breathed a spirit of cautious deference. "You do not meet with a view to confusing [*sic*] a spirit of discontent and dissatisfaction; you do not meet to create agitation for supremacy or undue power; nor to create or foster hostilities between capital and labour." Instead, Carter pleaded, delegates must show that "we are honest, earnest and prudent workers."

Carter was not disappointed. For three days delegates debated the structure and goals of their new organization, chose a slate of officers with John Carter as president, and adopted a series of policies which probably served as an accurate summary of the worries and dreams of Canadian skilled workers in the post-Confederation era.

John Carter, a Toronto painter and union leader, was chosen president of Canada's first attempt at a central trades organization, the Canadian Labour Union. Though the CLU had almost no funds and few members outside Toronto, its policies and problems were an impressive preview of future Canadian labour history. (Public Archives Canada C 38747)

Like its American namesake, the Canadian Labour Union was to be more than a political pressure group. As well as uniting Canadian locals of existing unions, the CLU could charter its own affiliates, approving their strikes only after attempts at arbitration had failed and collecting financial aid on the authority of the president. As a sidelight on the importance of mutual benefits, each directly chartered affiliate must at least provide its members with a respectable funeral "in case of death."

Among the "objects" of the new organization was to initiate pressure on Parliament and the local legislatures and to employ "means consistent with honour and integrity to so correct the abuses under which the working classes are labouring as to ensure to them their just rights and privileges . . . ." While delegates supported shorter hours and, through the secretary, John Hewitt, condemned the power of the moneyed class, their main concern was the competition of unskilled labour.

Resolutions in 1873, and at later conventions, denounced the use of convict labour by private employers and censured the employment of children under ten years of age. However, no issue was more bitter than immigration. Probably most CLU delegates had themselves been immigrants, and speakers sometimes criticized the selfishness of barring the door to latecomers. For the most part, the tone was unrelenting in its hostility. Immigration propaganda was often dishonest. Workers' taxes were used to subsidize the importation of ill-paid workers. The law allowed contractors to bring in workers at wages only a fraction of the Canadian standard. No sooner had it found a collective voice than organized labour in Canada began its long crusade against the abuses of immigration policy.

There were other demands which the CLU made on government, some of them already in effect in Britain and the United States, others still in the future. A mechanics' lien act would end the rule that stopped workers from claiming unpaid wages if their employer went bankrupt. Without an employers' liability act, a worker had to accept all the risks of the job; no frugal employer would even think of putting protective devices on his machinery. A factory act would exclude young children from factory work and enforce minimum standards of sanitation and ventilation. Government-run industrial bureaus would collect statistics on wages, hours, and conditions and do the research no hard-pressed local union could ever muster.

Other resolutions would also have a long history. Delegates opposed monopolies, approved of public education, urged arbitration instead of strikes, and hoped that the co-operative principle would "supersede the present system, as the present system has superseded the serf system of the past."

How far would delegates go to achieve their program through independent action? As in the future, the first debate was intense. William Joyce, a Toronto printer, was outspoken. Workers, he insisted, "must drill their army to fight manfully at the great battlefield — the polls — and teach the enemy that election funds are of no avail against men determined not to sell their birthright for dollars." Such speeches would be repeated many times. So would the outcome. The issue of political action was referred to a committee on legislation.

No one had travelled farther to the CLU's first convention than its new vice-president. Daniel O'Donoghue, a lively Irish-born printer, was president of the Ottawa Trades Council. That winter there was a local provincial by-election. Oliver Mowat's new Liberal government had hesitantly abolished property qualifications for candidates. It was O'Donoghue's chance. With promises to curb convict labour, a commitment to get workers a lien on a bankrupt employer for unpaid wages, and an assurance that he would work for Ottawa's vital lumber trade, O'Donoghue won by a wide margin. For the first time, a labour independent candidate sat in a legislature. In 1875, he was narrowly re-elected.

In the legislature, O'Donoghue rejected a Conservative promise of a cabinet portfolio if he would help defeat the Liberals. Instead, he became an ally of the Mowat government. Though he disapproved of its cautious approach to a mechanics' lien law which gave a worker no claim unless he was owed more than sixty dollars, O'Donoghue was no radical. He would have been content to limit the franchise to men earning more than $400 a year — a solid barrier to the unskilled and ill-paid. When he was defeated in 1879, the Ontario Liberals allowed him a succession of poorly paid government jobs. In 1883, O'Donoghue became the clerk for the Ontario Bureau of Industries. For a generation he was a Liberal agent in the ranks of labour.

Late in 1873, a disastrous world-wide economic depression slammed into Canada. Banks failed, businesses closed their doors, public works ceased. Hundreds and then thousands of men tramped the roads looking for work. Across the United States and Canada, labour organizations struggled in vain against wage cuts and dismissals. Employers took advantage of the crisis to rid themselves of troublesome unions and their spokesmen. Of an estimated 126 unions and associations in Canada in 1873, only a handful survived the decade. In Toronto, Hamilton, Saint John, Montreal, employer resistance and hard times eliminated labour organization, driving militants underground or forcing some to emigrate.

In Quebec, the end of the square-timber trade launched French-Canadian shipbuilders into fierce competition for the jobs of Irish ship labourers. In 1877 and 1878, members of the Benevolent Association fought the Union Canadienne in bloody pitched battles through the narrow streets of the Lower Town. To end the conflict, the two unions finally agreed that the jobs in the dwindling dock labour force would be shared evenly by Irish and French-Canadian workers.

Only rarely could unions retain even that much influence over working conditions. Mostly, they disintegrated or hibernated in hope of better times. Very few had funds to send delegates to so ambitious an organization as the Canadian Labour Union. Conventions dwindled until 1877 when only ten appeared, all but one from Toronto. By then, even the paternal Toronto Trades Assembly was on the verge of collapse.

For all its sad decline in strength and self-confidence, the political influence of the infant Canadian labour movement proved surprisingly durable. The defeat Macdonald had forestalled in 1872 was only postponed. Money and favours exchanged in that desperate year with would-be builders of the Canadian Pacific Railway gave Macdonald's enemies the Pacific Scandal and a decisive electoral victory in 1874.

The highly stylized and imaginative version of the bitter conflict between Quebec City's Irish longshoremen and the ship carpenters of the Union Canadienne was not produced by an eyewitness. The death of the square-timber trade destroyed the livelihood of both the major groups of Quebec workers and led to violent clashes in the late 1870s. Leaders of the strong unions on both sides helped produce a basis for work sharing. (Canadian Illustrated News)

The Grand Trunk strike of 1876-7 pitted the locomotive engineers against Canada's most powerful corporation—and the workers won. The key was the blockade of the GTR line at Belleville. When militia finally arrived from Toronto, they battered down resistance, but the company had already surrendered. (Vivian Brodie)

*Although Alexander Mackenzie, as Canada's first Liberal prime minister, had no great fondness for unions or strikes, his origins as a humble stonemason were regularly used in appeals for workingmen's votes. In fact, though Mackenzie had little to do with it, his government's legislative record for labour was far better than that of his rival, Sir John A. Macdonald. Nonetheless, though Toronto's workingmen turned out for Mackenzie in June, most of them probably voted Conservative in September, 1878. (*Canadian Illustrated News*)*

Labour's political prospects should have been as grim as the economy. In his youth, Alexander Mackenzie had apprenticed as a stonemason and sympathized with the Chartists. That was long ago. The new prime minister was a hard, self-made man, convinced that frugality and hard work were the sole secrets of his success. What saved labour's influence was the pressure of British example, Sir John A. Macdonald's willingness in opposition to trade on his image of the workingman's friend, and the tough persistence of Witton's successor from Hamilton, Aemilius Irving.

By 1875, Britain's new Conservative government had repealed the hated Criminal Law Amendment Act. Patiently but shrewdly, Irving forced the Liberals into successive amendments that finally and gracelessly stipulated that "attending at or near or approaching to such house or other place as aforesaid, in order merely to obtain or communicate information, shall not be deemed a watching or besetting within the meaning of this section." This meagre generosity was enough to win the Liberals the gratitude of the Canadian Labour Union at one of its last conventions.

The 1870s proved to be a decade of unemployment, wage cuts, disintegration, and defeat for most Canadian workers. There was one exception. Of all the new-model unions born in the 1860s, none had been more aloof or conservative than the Brotherhood of Locomotive Engineers. It was some evidence of its power and influence that not until 1876 did its members on the Grand Trunk Railway begin to share the dismissals and wage cuts which humbler workers had experienced for years. Furious at their treatment and at the disdain of the Grand

Trunk officials, the engineers struck the railway on the night of December 29, 1876. The result was a demonstration of Canada's new dependence on railways, local hatred of the arrogant Grand Trunk, and the one-sidedness of the law. Drivers who stopped their trains were arrested. At Stratford, Belleville, and Brockville, crowds of sympathizers blocked the line and attacked strike-breakers. Company officials demanded that Ottawa send troops, but Mackenzie, wholly sympathetic to the company as he was, had to confess that he did not have the authority. Although the strike quickly collapsed in Quebec and never even began on American sections of the line, the Grand Trunk management could do nothing about the blockades, particularly at Belleville. By the time militiamen from Toronto had reached Belleville and fought their way into the station, the company had surrendered. The Brotherhood of Locomotive Engineers had won.

It was a lonely triumph and it would not be repeated. When Parliament met, another of Canadian labour's long-standing demands was granted. No longer would magistrates send employees to jail because they had left their master's service without permission. Employers lost their latest excuse for jailing strikers. Henceforth, they would have to proceed through civil action, not through criminal law. That was not all. The new Breach of Contract Act also included a special reminder of the Engineers' strike. Workers in positions where public safety was involved — gas and water works and railways were examples — were excluded from the act. For them, there would be no right to strike.

For once, a labour issue divided the House of Commons and the parties. Irving denounced the exclusion as discrimination. Cautiously, Macdonald and a few leading Tories supported him. They were borne down by Liberals and Conservative backbenchers. For most M.P.'s, the Engineers' strike had been a whiff of anarchy and a threat of personal inconvenience. It must not happen again. Perhaps surprisingly, both the Canadian Labour Union and the Brotherhood of Locomotive Engineers agreed. The CLU's dying resolution congratulated the Liberals on their new law. Peter Arthur, the BLE's grand chief engineer, came all the way from Cleveland to offer his approval.

Its expectations might be pathetically meek, but Canadian labour was at least a political factor.

CHAPTER 5
Labour Reformers

The seventies proved to be a gloomy decade for working Canadians. The eighties seemed little better. If the mood of crisis lifted, unemployment remained. Most Canadians accepted recurrent problems. Some demanded reform. A labour movement which had practically vanished re-emerged.

In 1878, Sir John A. Macdonald's Conservatives regained power. In bad times, the austere honesty of Alexander Mackenzie was not enough. The Tory alternatives were hardly new. Tariffs had always been the main source of government revenue. Immigration had always appealed to politicians and businessmen as a way of settling the land and keeping down wages. The railway to the Pacific had been government policy since 1872. Packaged as the "National Policy," Macdonald's program looked like the fresh medicine an ailing Canada needed.

For working people, the National Policy had powerful consequences. Higher tariffs meant higher prices, but they also guaranteed jobs for thousands of working men — and for their wives and children too. Tory politicians could boast that they had fought the spectre of unemployment and won. Did working people really benefit? In 1881, an Ontario survey showed industrial profits of $70,400,000 for a wage bill of only $59,400,000. In knitting mills, a man earned $7.75 for a fifty-nine-hour week. Women and youths worked just as long for only $1.65 a week.

Low wages and long hours were not new problems for Canadian workers. What made them unbearable was the flood of government-financed immigration. Manufacturers had won protection for their profits behind high tariff walls. Canadian workers were still exposed to competition from hungry, desperate newcomers. Worker resentment grew when the relative prosperity of the early eighties

A rare photograph of a procession of the Knights of Labor in Hamilton, led by their banner and the band of the 13th Battalion, is a reminder that the most exciting labour development of the 1880s, like the Nine-Hour movement of the early 1870s, began in the "Ambitious City." Processions, with bands, floats, banners, and regalia, were a form of mass entertainment and a demonstration of order and respectability rather than militancy. (National Photography Collection PA 103086)

slumped and the bright promises of the National Policy were not fulfilled. Instead, the spread of factories and new industrial techniques hastened the demise of new categories of skilled artisans.

Most people thought of Canada as a rural society, and they would stubbornly persist in that myth well into the twentieth century. Industrialization under the National Policy meant that more and more Canadians, at least in the central provinces, would make their lives in cities and towns. During the eighties, cities like Toronto, Hamilton and Montreal grew rapidly without coming to grips with the basic urban problems of housing, sewage disposal and water supply. Canadians were still half a century away from admitting that the catastrophes of sickness, injury and long-term unemployment were too great to be handled by family, friends or even charitable societies.

One of Toronto's more enterprising drygood merchants made himself one of the rare businessmen to advertise merchandise by playing on sympathy for a striking union. The Knights of Labor were waging (and losing) a battle with the Toronto Street Railway for the right to represent their ill-paid and over-worked drivers and conductors. (Mail & Empire, 1886)

Yet it was in the eighties that growing numbers of Canadians began to see the interests of capital and labour as distinct and even hostile. Until then, employers often proclaimed themselves members of the labouring classes. A fraternal lodge like the Ancient Order of United Workmen was as respectably middle class as the Foresters or the Elks. Now the division between employer and employee was becoming a gulf which even skilled craftsmen would have trouble crossing.

Factory-based industry posed immense difficulties for labour organizations. Through the Knights of St. Crispin, shoemakers had tried in vain to save their trade from the factory system and mechanization. In the 1870s, the Canadian Iron Founders' Association had almost succeeded in driving the Moulders' Union from stove factories. A slow revival of prosperity brought a corresponding recovery in unionism, but only among the traditional crafts and trades where unions had thrived a decade before. Organizations of printers, metal workers, construction trades and the railway running trades had survived the seventies and now prospered modestly. In 1880, 54 union branches existed in Canada. By 1890, 240 local unions held charters, most of them in the cities and towns of Ontario, with a scattering from Victoria to Halifax.

In the intervening years, however, Canadian labour was swept by a dramatic American-based movement that ignored the rules of conventional craft unionism, inspired ideas and values that would last a century or more and transformed the lives of thousands of Canadians. Canada was experiencing the Knights of Labor.

The Holy and Noble Order of the Knights of Labor was born in Philadelphia in 1869, the creation of a thoughtful garment worker named Uriah Stephens. For each weakness of traditional labour organizations, the Order offered a new idea. Traditional craft-based unions had been destroyed by resorting to non-union women, blacks and unskilled labour; the Knights would be open to all who could claim that they earned their bread by the sweat of their brow. Only lawyers, doctors, bankers and anyone associated with the liquor traffic would be excluded.

To fight blacklists and discrimination, the Knights must become a secret society, bound together by passwords, handshakes and oaths. Even the name of the Order was concealed behind five asterisks. In an age of lodges, fraternities and romantic fascination with the mystic, the Knights satisfied a widespread taste. Stephens also concluded that strikes were futile. Most ended in disaster. At all costs, the Knights must prefer arbitration, mediation and the courting of public opinion. Better than struggle was the old utopian faith of co-operative production. Workers would create a society in which labour was treated with dignity and honour while capitalists, living on rents, dividends and capital gains, would be exposed as social parasites.

For all its beguiling mixture of prudence and radicalism, the Knights grew slowly. If there were assemblies in Canada before 1881, no record survives. In 1879, when Terence V. Powderly succeeded Stephens as general master workman, a moderation of the Order's strict principles prepared it for take-off. As a Catholic, Powderly realized that the secrecy rule alienated his church. Fresh instructions revealed the Knights, title and all, to the world. Although the Knights still remained open to most kinds of workers, individual assemblies of specific trades and crafts were not permitted. In 1879, a single assembly of the Order united all the window-glass workers of the United States. Commercial telegraphers, cigar makers and other trades soon formed their own assemblies.

International boundaries meant nothing. In 1881, the first known local assembly in Canada was formed in Hamilton. The window-glass workers crossed the Atlantic and organized the trade in England. Assemblies appeared in Britain, Belgium, Australia and New Zealand. In Canada, assemblies eventually spread from Vancouver Island to Cape Breton. In scores of communities, a Knights of Labor assembly marked the beginning of labour organization. By 1887, Canada was dotted with 168 local assemblies claiming 12,253 members. Two of the assemblies were formed by women shoe workers. During the decade, hundreds of assemblies were launched and dissolved; dozens were formed by would-be

Knights who never secured a formal charter before disappearing. Perhaps fifty or sixty thousand Canadian workers had at least a passing contact with the Noble Order.

In some respects, the Knights' organization was superbly adapted to a country of small towns and long distances. Mixed assemblies, uniting workers of many skills or none, fitted the needs of communities too small to support a local of any single craft. The idealism of the Knights could excite Canadians accustomed to uplift in Sunday sermons while the Order's opposition to strikes and conflict satisfied Canadian caution and the real weakness of working people in confronting employers.

For many, of course, the radicalism of the Knights was barrier enough. Employers in large cities and small towns, from the Masseys in their Toronto farm implement factory to a Lindsay sawmill operator, felt no compunction about dismissing workers who joined the Knights. Widespread unemployment, of course, made replacements easy to find.

What sustained the Knights, beyond a well-adapted constitution, was a growing sense of class and of injustice. Both were the products of industrialism and a sense that working people were not sharing in its benefits. The mood survived well-publicised setbacks. In 1883, the Order's assembly of telegraphers struck employers who were both greedy and unpopular. On July 19, the code message "General Grant is Dead" sent more than eighteen thousand commercial telegraphers — almost twelve hundred of them Canadian — from their keys. The Knights' headquarters promised $100,000 in aid. The strikers promised a "Co-operative Telegraph Company" to undercut the Western Union monopoly. Neither the money nor the co-operative appeared. In a month the strike was over. Telegraphers regained their jobs only by signing "the document," a pledge that they would never again belong to a union.

If skilled workers failed, what chance did other Knights possess? Dynamism, idealism and occasional freak victories like the defeat of Jay Gould's Union Pacific Railroad in 1885 allowed the Order to build a huge following. Between 1885 and 1886, North American membership exploded from 104,000 to 703,000. Swamped by floods of applications, Terence Powderly ordered recruiting halted. Instead, his followers were swept into a crusade for the eight-hour day, inspired by the rival Federation of Organized Trades and Labor Unions or F.O.O.T.A.L.U., the future American Federation of Labor.

In Canada, the eight-hour movement was merely debated, often with surprising sympathy. In the United States, the campaign unleashed years of pent-up anger. In Chicago, a focal point for labour militancy, a bitter strike at the McCormick Harvester factory boiled into a mass demonstration on the evening of May 4, 1886. Late at night, when police charged the crowd in Haymarket Square, a bomb exploded. Police survivors opened fire. Ten died; fifty more were wounded. The explosion shattered the Knights. Sympathy for factory workers curdled into fear and hate. Eight radicals, seized and savagely punished on little evidence, had no real connection with the Knights of Labor but that made no difference. In the face of business hostility and police repression, the spirit drained from the Noble

Order. By the 1890s, nothing was left but internal jealousy and the husk of an organization.

In Canada, the Haymarket explosion had little effect on the Knights but the confusion and divisions of the parent body crossed the border. As late as 1891, the Order experienced a dramatic growth in the Ottawa area but, as elsewhere, its assemblies enjoyed a brief life span. In Hamilton, the first Canadian home of the Knights, an angry dispute between the Order and local craft unions developed when the Knights accepted an assembly of strike-breaking cigar makers. Key local leaders were accused of belonging to the Home Club, a radical faction of the Knights. Local affairs were complicated when the Hamilton Knights tried to expel a pair of wandering swindlers who had gained the confidence of local members. Soon, skilled workers deserted the local assemblies for their own craft unions in major centres. In smaller communities, the mixed assemblies faded for lack of a real function.

Admittedly, the Knights survived in Canada long after they had disintegrated in the United States. Local quarrels, even in Hamilton, were patched up. In French Canada, the fading of an international link became an advantage for the *Chevaliers du Travail*, particularly after the Vatican had persuaded the Quebec hierarchy to moderate its hostility. In the 1890s, by the ironies of history, the Knights survived in Canada largely through its French-speaking and Catholic assemblies.

The enduring contribution of the Knights to the Canadian labour movement came not through organization but through intellectual influence. The emotional dynamism of the Order revived the labour press in Canada. Ideas promoted by the "brain workers" of the Order began to provide Canadian labour with a political platform. William H. Rowe, founder of the Hamilton-based *Palladium of Labor*, and T. Phillips Thompson, creator of the *Labor Advocate* and an all-purpose thinker and writer for generations of Canadian radicals, found an audience in the Knights of Labor. So did other journalists and publicists like William J. Vale, Daniel O'Donoghue, A.B. Ingram, A.W. Wright and the Toronto tailor and atheist, Alfred Jury.

While Wright and Ingram were Tories and O'Donoghue was kept on the Ontario payroll by the Liberals, the inherent radicalism of the Knights justified Rowe and Phillips Thompson in writing furious attacks on patriotism, capitalism and convention. During the Riel Rebellion of 1885, the *Palladium* took the rebel side. The *Advocate* commanded its readers to abandon both the old parties to support the cause of "Labour Reform."

Such ideas may have reached a small and reluctant audience since such papers pleaded vainly for subscribers but Canadian workers finally had access to unconventional wisdom. It is absurd to suggest a welling of class consciousness during the 1880s. The transience of the Knights in Canadian history and the lives of its thousands of members suggests the lightness of its touch. Much more important was the establishment of a radical current of thought and a few earnest disciples to promote it. The contrast with the cautious moderation of the early 1870s was striking. "We have endeavoured to enforce the doctrine," Rowe reported to *Palladium* readers, "that as labor is the source of all wealth, no man is of right entitled to what he does not earn in the sense of giving positive value for it, and that the plea of acquiring something for nothing, by which so many speculators, usurers, land-grabbers and other classes of idlers live on the labor of other classes, is a fraud and a wrong to those by whose toil they subsist."

No contemporary ideologue mattered more to the Knights than Henry George, pioneer of the "single tax." To George, all value derived from the value of land. Therefore, land values represented the only legitimate basis for taxation. Radicals turned that principle into an attack on land monopolists and, in due course, into an assault on all monopolies and unearned wealth. Support for the single tax could also, as Phillips Thompson explained, become a way-station to more revolutionary ideas. "The Single Tax movement is the Unitarianism of political economy — a half-way house where the investigator may find rest for a breathing spell but not a permanent abode. In nine cases out of ten, he will either go on thinking and apply to other social abuses arguments used by the Single-Taxer in regard to land monopoly, and so develop into a full-blown all-round Socialist, or if his courage fails him at the prospect, he will be scared back to orthodoxy." In his book, *The Politics of Labor*, published in 1887, Thompson revealed his own unconscious odyssey. It was a route many Canadian labour leaders would eventually follow.

There could only be a labour movement, of course, if there were organizations to represent and shape it. The collapse of the Canadian Labour Union and the Toronto Trades Assembly in the late 1870s was not permanent. In 1881, the presence of the International Typographical Union convention in Toronto persuaded local printers to make a fresh try at organizing a city-wide labour body. The result was the Toronto Trades and Labour Council.

In 1883 the Toronto Trades and Labour Council summoned a Canadian labour congress over the Christmas holiday. The result was an earnest, hard-working and productive meeting, and we shall return to it. However, no permanent organization emerged. In 1886, inspired by the Knights and by the election of a pro-labour mayor, Toronto unionists tried again. This time, the results were lasting. From that year the Trades and Labour Congress would ensure that Canadian unionists could count on at least one annual exposure of their hopes and concerns.

By 1886, those demands were growing in variety, extent and frustration. Macdonald's Trade Unions Act of 1872 might be a dead letter but it still allowed the Tory leader to proclaim himself the friend of the working man. It was a hollow claim. Beginning in 1879, Dr. Darby Bergin, a Conservative backbencher from Cornwall, began an annual campaign to introduce a Canada-wide factory act. How else could the hours of work be limited, children removed from factories and the terrible toll of sickness and injury be curtailed? Bergin's Conservative colleagues systematically frustrated him with a procession of investigations, consultations with industrialists, procedural delays and, eventually, constitutional obstacles. On the issue of *Capital v. Labour* in the 1880s, the Tories had plainly chosen sides.

The Liberals were less certain. The party's chief organ, the Toronto *Globe*, began by offering the doctrines of individualism. Bergin's attempt at factory legislation was state meddling. "It is of course desirable that women should not overwork themselves," the paper editorialized, "but the less the state interferes

Left

Colonel Darby Bergin, a Cornwall doctor and Conservative M.P., was an improbable figure to lead a crusade for factory legislation, but his city's textile industry doubtless offered examples of why workers badly needed protection from unguarded machinery, unventilated, overcrowded working areas, and the intensive exploitation of women and children. Bergin's defeat in Parliament owed much to his party's alliance with a new class of investors and manufacturers created by Macdonald's "National Policy." (Public Archives Canada C)

Right

Daniel J. O'Donoghue was a major figure in Canada's early labour movement from his election to the Ontario legislature in 1874 to the Berlin convention of 1902. The fact that his only surviving photographs show him with white hair and a long beard tends to underline his reputation as "the Father of Canadian Labour" at the expense of his younger reputation as a live wire. (Manitoba Archives) between employers of labour and those of the work people who have attained full growth and intelligence, the better."

Political necessity spoke louder than Liberal principles. Edward Blake, Mackenzie's successor as Liberal leader, forced a new editor on the *Globe*. James Cameron struggled hard against tradition to make the *Globe* at least neutral on "the Labour Question"; his own paper, the London *Advertiser* was virtually an organ for the Knights in southwestern Ontario. By 1885, the right to vote in federal and Ontario elections had extended to most working-class men. If Oliver Mowat's Liberals needed labour voters, *laisser-faire* was no obstacle. In 1884, Ontario's first Factory Bill passed the Legislature in fulfilment of an election promise but it was not proclaimed for another three years — on the eve of the 1886 election. Quebec's new nationalist government, under Honore Mercier, followed suit in 1887 though both governments were slow in providing inspection and enforcement.

Instead of action, Sir John A. Macdonald offered words. Facing an election in the midst of a grim recession and Quebec resentment at the execution of Louis Riel, the old Chieftain set out to rally whatever forces he could find. A hurriedly reorganized Liberal-Conservative Workingmen's Association in Ottawa became a picked audience for Macdonald's promise of a Royal Commission on the Relations of Labor and Capital. Even such a crumb was not to be sneered at, when compared with Blake's promise of the Golden Rule in labour-management relations.

The Royal Commission, chosen from loyal Conservatives in business, journalism and the ranks of labour (A.W. Wright was a conspicuous member) was dismissed by labour radicals as a typical confidence trick. It was more and less. The commission's recommendations, reported in 1889, were almost wholly ignored. In 1894, Sir John Thompson remembered to proclaim Labour Day as a statutory holiday. Legislation creating a bureau of labour statistics was passed but never implemented. The rest was forgotten.

In the history of Canadian labour, however, the Royal Commission has two reasons for significance. First, the volumes of testimony collected in Ontario, Quebec, New Brunswick and Nova Scotia are the most graphic and detailed evidence we now have of working and living conditions, attitudes and ideas in the factories, mills and mines of late nineteenth-century Canada. They testify to both the anger and the docility of Canadian workers and to the remoteness of the new kind of employer from the people who worked for him. Occasionally, even Canadians at the time could be shocked by the testimony — like the confession of J.L. Fortier, a Montreal cigar maker, that he casually beat the little boys and girls who worked for him and locked offenders in an unlighted cellar.

Second, the Royal Commission is significant because of its own divisions. The labour members were loyal Conservatives but they had minds of their own. John Armstrong, a veteran of the Toronto printers' strike of 1872, created his own majority against the employers and their journalist allies. If the Royal Commission report was ignored, it was probably because Armstrong and his rebellious group dictated the majority report.

It was symbolic of the 1880s that even Tory workingmen would no longer defer to their social superiors. The labour radicals might be a small minority in the ranks

T. Phillips Thompson was among the most durable of the radical labour journalists who worked with the Knights of Labor. He was still in the struggle in the 1930s, having steadily veered to the left in a life that began as a Liberal-leaning republican His better-known grandson is Pierre Berton. (American Punch, *July 1879*)

of Canadian labour but their influence had spread. The Knights of Labor might have passed rapidly from the Canadian scene but it had left an indelible mark. Armstrong and his supporters could now believe not merely that the interests of capital and labour were different; they were opposed.

That was the message of the 1880s.

CHAPTER 6

Hinterland Labour

For all its failures and disappointments, Sir John A. Macdonald's National Policy survived the 1880s. It lasted because the powerful central provinces of Quebec and Ontario soon came to rely on high tariffs for profits and jobs. It survived because the Liberal opposition offered no alternative except economic integration with the United States. In the 1891 election, manufacturers helped the Tory leader bury that Liberal policy of "veiled treason." Despite the ridicule of the labour reformers, Macdonald could probably count on a fair share of the working-class voters.

The National Policy did more than encourage factories and mills in the central provinces. It also defined a role for the rest of Canada — the hinterland. Beyond the industrial cities and towns, people would supply the timber, minerals, and farm produce Canada needed for use and export. In turn, they would buy the products of Canadian factories. Behind the government's fervent immigration propaganda was the promise to Canadian manufacturers that each newcomer was a potential consumer. To workers, of course, immigrants were also competitors.

This arrangement seemed logical at the time and, to some people in central Canada, it still does. In practice, it produced inequality and grievances. Raw materials, whether they are coal or wheat, are subject to world price changes. The primary producer has the least control over prices and markets. Manufacturers in the central provinces, on the other hand, could charge high prices because of the tariff, and their considerable influence in Ottawa guaranteed them an edge over foreign competition. Instead of uniting Canada in a profitable partnership, the National Policy and its descendants contributed to major strains in Confederation. Working people, whether they were farmers, miners, or woodworkers, were always the ultimate victims when the hinterland regions of the Maritimes and the West suffered.

In the Atlantic provinces, the grievance was particularly acute. Small manufacturers found that their markets were flooded by the competition from central Canada. Their misfortune followed hard on the decline of the traditional Maritime economy of wood, wind, and water. Wooden schooners sailed by hardy Nova Scotians and New Brunswickers were supplanted by iron steamships.

Among the casualties of this decline were the proud labour organizations of Saint John. In 1875, the city's businessmen met as they often had before to bemoan the unreasonableness of the Labourers' Benevolent Association and its allies. When the moaning was done, "the chairman called on Alex Gibson of Nashwaak to give his opinion, which he did in a modest and practical manner." His solution was to get workers from outside, and he calmly laid down $25,000 of his own money. Gibson had destroyed his own millmen's union the year before, and now, with a fund of $108,500, the Saint John businessmen set out to destroy the ship labourers. Although the union survived the bitter struggle, the wages of its members fell from four dollars a day at the beginning of the seventies to a dollar a day at the end. Hard times had destroyed Saint John's claim to be the labour capital of Canada.

In newer parts of the Canadian hinterland, highly skilled workers were often scarce and wages were higher than in older provinces. So were living costs. In Winnipeg, where living costs were far higher than in Toronto or Montreal, people waited impatiently for completion of the CPR, confident that the rail link would lead to lower prices. They were badly deceived. Certain of its monopoly and determined to reward its long-suffering shareholders, the Canadian Pacific continued to charge all that it could.

Most of the resource industries of the hinterland required armies of men with few special marketable skills. To speak of an unskilled worker is misleading since he had skills with an axe, saw, and shovel, an ability to harness and drive a team of horses, or to handle tools, which few present-day Canadians can boast. However, these were the skills of any farm boy and they commanded no premium in nineteenth-century Canada. Moreover, if labour was scarce enough to command an extra dollar or two a day, employers clamoured for immigrants, and the government strained to oblige. If workers would not be attracted from Britain or the Continent, companies found it possible to persuade Ottawa to admit Asians. Most of the mountain sections of the CPR were built by Chinese at enormous cost in hardship, injury, and death.

In the new cities of the West, both the traditional craft unions and the Knights of Labor found roots. In Victoria, an association of "practical Bakers" formed in 1859. The typographers soon followed. By 1885, printers, iron moulders, and carpenters all had formed local unions affiliated to internationals. In Vancouver and Winnipeg, printers led the way, with building trades close behind. Such unions were small, and they wrestled with employers who believed that being on the frontier of settlement entitled them to more than the usual rugged individualism. It took most of a decade and two different unions before Victoria carpenters won themselves a nine-hour day in 1889.

Such triumphs affected very few workers. As in previous generations, the

Robert Drummond, the founder and first head of the Provincial Workingmen's Association, created the first successful miners' organization in Canada. A cautious pragmatist, he gained prestige for himself and modest legislative gains for his members through close association with Nova Scotia's Liberal government. (Public Archives of Nova Scotia)

Most Canadians have seen the photograph of Sir Donald Smith pounding in the last spike of the Canadian Pacific Railway. The workers who built the line decided to have their own ceremony without benefit of the eastern notables but with a friendly photographer to record the event. (Public Archives Canada C 14115)

Bunkhouse life was by no means always so pleasant or comfortable, but the National Transcontinental took this photograph as part of a campaign to avert criticism of working conditions in its camps. Bunkhouses were often crowded and verminous. A standard feature was the "muzzle-loader," a bunk which could only be entered head first. (National Photography Collection WS 2627)

familiar work unit for building sections of railway or clearing forests for the lumber trade was the contract labour gang, organized for the season, paid off at the end (or sometimes stranded when the contractor went bankrupt or skipped with his money). These were the "bunkhouse men," described in a later and slightly more civilized era by Edmund Bradwin. Like the shantymen and the canallers, they were the anonymous men who built Canada. They could fight the elements and nature, but against their employers they were almost helpless.

The old regime of New France, with its regulations and notarized contracts, had protected the voyageurs as well as the fur traders. On the liberal principle that governments had no right to protect women and children, much less grown men, Canadians now accepted a romantic image of the railway gangs and lumber camps. Popular literature portrayed bunkhouse life as rough but manly, with comradeship, gargantuan meals, and big pay cheques as rewards. They ignored the harsh reality of hernias, malnutrition, endemic typhoid from bad sanitation, fetid smells, lice, and appalling rates of sickness, death, and injury. The men themselves may have had fewer illusions. Bradwin reports that work gangs taken north to work on Ontario railways often travelled in handcuffs in locked cars. Labour contractors wanted to be sure to deliver their catch.

Superintendent Sam Steele, guarding the construction of the CPR in the Rockies in 1885 with a tiny detachment of North-West Mounted Police, treated a strike of workers, desperate after months without pay, as though it was a military mutiny. The ringleaders were seized and, after a tense scene between Steele and

Workers at the Murray mine in the Sudbury district, like others in their trade, came together from many parts of the world. By the simple expedient of treating miners as individual contractors, early mining companies avoided most of the problems and hazards of underground work. They weighed and purchased the miner's ore, sold him every necessity from food to pickaxes, and made a profit on both sides of their operation. (Public Archives Canada PA 50958)

the workers, shipped off to Calgary for trial. There was, Steele proudly reported, no further trouble. For one thing, the pay car finally appeared. Perhaps striking against the "National Dream" was a kind of treason.

Strikes in Canada had never been limited to organized unions. Without such organization, however, they were sometimes violent and usually futile. Typical was the Chaudière strike of sawmill workers in 1891. For five and a half weeks, the lumber industry in Ottawa and Hull was tied up while ill-paid workers tried to stop a wage reduction. Most community opinion supported the strikers against the wealthy mill owners — Booth, Eddy, Perley, Bronson, and other familiar Ottawa names. Local assemblies of the Knights of Labor and the few craft unions in the city lent their support, leadership, and influence. The Knights' French-language newspaper, *Le Spéctateur*, became an organ for the strikers, and its editor, Napoléon Pagé, jostled for leadership with J.W. Patterson of the Ottawa Trades and Labour Council. Both urged restraint.

Angry, desperate men could not afford patience. If others would not stop work, gangs of sawmill workers would persuade them. Ezra Eddy was kicked and stoned at the entrance to his mill. Well-paid saw filers were threatened with tarring and feathering if they went back to work. The employers found ample pretext to call for militia, and four companies, composed largely of civil servants, spent a boring day guarding empty mills. (A frugal government docked them a day's pay for their absence.) What really ended the strike was the hard fact of hunger. Ottawa unionists raised little money. An appeal sent across the country brought nothing. Terence Powderly, who happened to be in Toronto, repudiated the strikers and took pains to explain that they were not really Knights. Committees of earnest citizens tried to mediate, discovered that the owners would make no concessions, and urged the men to go back to work. By the time they did so, a victory of sorts was won. So many workers had left the region that mill owners were forced to reinstate the earlier pay rate.

Among the products of hinterland Canada, none was more vital than coal. As the forests retreated, coal was the basic source of heat and energy for Canadian homes and industries. In the Maritimes, development of deposits in Nova Socita's Pictou and Cumberland counties and on Cape Breton Island was a major offset to the region's economic decline. Discovery of coal on Vancouver Island and later in the Crowsnest Pass and in southern Alberta became a vital element in western Canadian development.

Miners also were different from other hinterland workers. Theirs were not farm-boy skills. They were part of a complex, dangerous, and often inherited craft. The mines of Great Britain and later of central Europe provided the men who developed the underground resources of both the United States and Canada. There were close links in method, organization, and even ideological outlook among miners on both continents. In Britain, the United States, and Canada, coal miners played a dominant role in important phases of labour history. In all three countries, their struggles were the most violent and protracted, their employers the most ruthless, their leaders the most defiant.

Coal mining in Canada followed an oddly individualistic old-country model. Mining companies treated miners as individual contractors, selling them necessary supplies, like dynamite, and paying them for the coal they brought to the surface. This chaotic economic arrangement might be profitable for companies that could reduce their involvement with the complex, highly dangerous work underground, but it was at odds with a work situation that demanded careful teamwork and organization. Canadian mines, particularly on Vancouver Island, were among the most dangerous anywhere. Between 1879 and 1889, 326 men died in five major disasters at Wellington and Nanaimo; the work force never exceeded 2,900.

Mining companies might pretend to treat their workers as independent businessmen; in practice, they could control every aspect of their lives. In both Nova Scotia and British Columbia, mines were usually remote from existing towns. Companies built and rented houses — or shacks. They provided company stores which set prices and offered credit. Alexander McGillvray, a Glace Bay miner who testified before the Royal Commission of 1889, worked from 6:00 a.m. to 4:00−5:30 p.m. He was paid $.41−.43 a ton and earned $198.60 from April to September. There was little work in the winter in Cape Breton. In his best month, July, he earned $35.13 from which he paid $1.50 as rent, $.25 for coal, $.80 for oil, $3.24 for powder, $.40 for the company doctor, $28.49 to the company store, $.15 for school tax, and $.30 for a tallyman. That left him a balance of nothing. His house, incidentally, consisted of a kitchen and two bedrooms.

McGillvray was a skilled miner. He also had a union. Eight years before, the Springhill Mining Company had cut wages for the second time in a year at a time when coal prices were known to be booming. Angry miners met in the woods to discuss their grievance. On August 29, 1879, they met more openly to form the Pioneer Lodge of the Provincial Miners' Association. Robert Drummond, an overground boss and occasional contributor to the Halifax newspapers, was appointed grand secretary and commissioned to organize more lodges in Pictou. When the first grand council met, five lodges sent representatives. The demands showed how little the miners had. They wanted a say in mine inspection; the right to appear at coroners' investigations; a chance to organize sickness, injury, and death benefits; and the right to vote in elections, which only one miner in nine then possessed.

Soon renamed the Provincial Workmen's Association, the new organization faced a bitter struggle for survival. Like the Knights of Labor, the PWA disapproved of strikes in principle and preferred arbitration. It would gladly have become a fraternal order and legislative pressure group. It had no choice. From the first it faced discrimination, lockouts, and the frequent use of troops. An 1882 strike at Lingan in Cape Breton lasted a full year. Employers imported Scottish miners, but the newcomers bravely refused to work when they learned of the situation. There were more angry strikes at Pictou in 1887 and at Springhill in 1890, but there were also successful arbitrations. Drummond proved a cautious and persuasive moderate, talking angry miners out of midnight intimidation and convincing small mine operators that the PWA was an influence for good conduct among miners.

The Nova Scotia miners succeeded in organizing because the province's coal industry had several relatively weak employers. After an early and unsuccessful attempt to elect its own candidates, as miners had done in Britain, the PWA settled down to a quiet but beneficial alliance with Nova Scotia's long-lived Liberal government. Drummond himself was appointed to the province's Legislative Council. Slowly the legislature accepted PWA demands for better inspection of mines, the right to vote for miners earning at least $350 a year, age limits for boys employed in mines, election of check weighmen to ensure that companies were not cheating miners at the scales, and the right of miners to choose their own doctors and to prosecute managers for breaches of the Mines Regulation Act if twelve other miners agreed. In turn, these and other gains allowed Drummond to boast that his organization had won the best legislation for miners anywhere in the English-speaking world.

His pride was a little complacent. The association had won the security of automatic checkoff of union dues, and its leaders could bask in editorials praising their good sense and moderation. Drummond persuaded the PWA to endorse the 100-year lease granted to the Dominion Coal Company in Cape Breton, an arrangement that helped that early conglomerate to swallow up most smaller companies. In 1897, an internal feud developed when the PWA attempted to reduce the influence of the company store. Any attack on the pluck me's should have been popular, and it certainly pleased independent merchants. However, Cape Breton miners had become dependent on the stores to tide them over a workless winter, and they fell foul of the association majority. By 1898, only five lodges met for the annual meeting and the association was in ruins. Profiting from the disarray, in a last flickering outburst, the Knights of Labor raided the PWA's non-mining lodges.

In the crisis, Drummond and the original leaders retired. A new grand secretary, John Moffatt from Cape Breton, threw himself into reviving the association. After its brush with extinction, membership surged to five thousand by 1901 and seven thousand in 1907. Once it had abandoned the hope of organizing the steelworkers at the Dominion Iron and Steel Company mill in Sydney, the PWA appeared satisfied to collect its dues, represent miners to the provincial government, and prove to the Dominion Coal Company that it was a humble but useful partner.

Any such arrangement might have been envied in British Columbia. From the first development of coal by the Hudson's Bay Company at Nanaimo in 1849, employers on the Pacific kept miners and other employees in their place. Labour scarcity might compel them to pay higher wages, but they would allow no challenge to management prerogatives. The tone was set by Robert Dunsmuir, a tough Scot who discovered the rich Wellington coal seam in 1869 and shrewdly involved officers at the Royal Navy base at Esquimalt in his investment. During the forty-two years that Dunsmuir and his son operated mines at Wellington and Nanaimo, no union ever organized their men.

It was not for want of trying. In 1877, Wellington miners formed the Miners' Mutual Protective Association and struck. They had ample grievances. Not only did Dunsmuir cut wages and raise the price of powder, his weigh scales registered no more than 999 pounds for a load of 1,100 pounds. Dunsmuir expelled a grocer who had charged lower prices than his company store and, for good measure, drove out a butcher, a baker, and a doctor as well.

Dunsmuir did not hide his intentions in double-talk. "There is an impression in the community that we are obligated to accede to the miners' demands," declared an advertisement in the Nanaimo paper, "but for the benefit of those whom it may concern we wish to state publicly that we have no intention to ask any of them to work for us again at any price." Accordingly, he summoned strike-breakers from San Francisco. The Wellington miners collected money and paid their passages home. Then Dunsmuir ordered the miners out of their company houses. When they did not budge, his naval friends dispatched H.M.S. *Grappler*, loaded with militia, to do the deed. The expedition cost provincial taxpayers $18,000.

Dunsmuir's arrogance grated on even business supporters, but most of them took advantage of his ruthlessness. The Victoria *Colonist* could deplore the fate of "wives and little ones," but the miners had sealed their fate by daring to occupy private property and preventing its development. "What security is there in these proceedings for capital seeking investment to come to British Columbia?" asked the paper.

The Mutual Protective Association survived underground at Wellington, and in 1883 Dunsmuir again faced a strike. Once again he advertised for strike-breakers but only thirteen arrived. By now he had bought out his last naval partner, and no gunboats were summoned. Instead, Dunsmuir starved out his men and resumed business, enriched by huge land grants and secured by a partnership with American railroad barons.

Any miners' organization in British Columbia faced a single powerful employer who, after 1882, virtually controlled the provincial government. A policy of granting huge tracts of land fostered corruption, gave conspicuous

Anti-Oriental feeling among workers in British Columbia easily extended from the Chinese to East Indians when employers found yet another source of low-wage, dependable workers. Met with hostility by fellow-workers, the newcomers had little incentive to show solidarity with the province's militant union movement. (Vancouver Public Library)

fortunes to a few, and drew bitter resentment from the rest. In other parts of Canada, farming was an alternative and often, for men in the lumber camps and the railway gangs, was part of an annual cycle of work. Seeding and harvesting fitted into breaks in other employment. In British Columbia, that was not possible. There was yet another unwelcome complicating factor: Oriental labour.

Immigrants were always jealously resented rivals, but Chinese labour, with its bare subsistence needs and docility, offered competition that no white worker could match and few white employers could resist. Only the racial prejudice endemic along the entire West Coast — built on stories of opium dens, sexual perversion, gambling, and "tong wars" — united rich and poor. For white workers, anti-Oriental feeling became a central organizing principle, taken up by Canadian unionists across the country. Even the PWA's paper, the *Trades Journal*, wondered when Nova Scotia mine owners would bring in their first carload of Chinese.

In the East that was still a remote threat. In British Columbia, it was very real. The Workmen's Protective Association, a general union formed in Victoria in 1878, had no other real goal than "the mutual protection of the working class of British Columbia against the great influx of Chinese . . . ." The association soon broke up, but the Knights of Labor, in British Columbia as well as in California, flourished on anti-Oriental feeling. Elsewhere, the Knights battled prejudice against women and blacks, but on the Pacific Coast it campaigned on "the Yellow Peril." In early 1887, Knights were prominent in attempts to drive Chinese from Vancouver. When three men were arrested after an abortive assault on a Chinese labour camp on February 24, 1887, the Knights hired a lawyer to defend them.

For the Dunsmuirs, Chinese miners were the obvious answer to their labour problems. White miners forced to work alongside the Chinese hated them as aliens and strike-breakers. They also complained that the Chinese could not understand orders and complicated instructions in English. For men working with dynamite in narrow underground shafts, that was dangerous indeed.

British Columbia workers persuaded politicians to denounce Asiatic immigration and to pass brutally discriminatory laws. Systematically, the laws were disallowed by Ottawa because immigration was a federal matter. The province's workers could make common cause with middle-class citizens on one issue at least. On others, there would be a parting of the ways.

Earlier than elsewhere, British Columbia's struggling labour movement turned radical. Partly it was the existence of men like the Dunsmuirs who gave meaning to the vague socialist rhetoric. Partly it was the attraction of British Columbia to angry, impatient, idealistic men who believed that it might be easier to do in a new world what was plainly impossible in the old. British Columbia drew a steady stream of radicals, particularly from Britain but also from eastern Canada and from the United States — Ernest Jones, Parm Pettipiece, J.H. McVety, Will MacClain, and many more. Then there was the example of the American West. Beginning in the Coeur d'Alene strike of 1892, a new Western Federation of Miners had begun to show that it was possible, sometimes, to beat employers as ruthless and powerful as the Dunsmuirs. What was needed was direct action, physical force, and radical ideology.

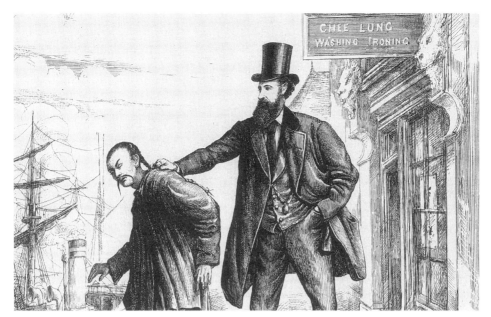

British Columbia's post-Confederation premier, Amor de Cosmos, supported an enduring tradition of anti-Asiatic racism by denouncing Chinese immigrants as unassimilable. This eastern cartoon – contemptuous, as usual, to West Coast sentiment – presumes that it is because Chinese "won't drink whiskey, and talk politics and vote like us." (Public Archives of Canada C 72064)

Below: Chinese in Vancouver outside a store. Deprived of family life and despised by their European neighbours, the Chinese introduced as much as they could of their culture to Canada, worked hard, kept to themselves, and then were accused of being unwilling to join the majority. White trade unionists could make common cause with British Columbia's middle class by denouncing the "Yellow Peril." (Vancouver Public Library no. 8056)

By the mid-nineties, British Columbia had a new mining industry. American interests and railroads had pushed the new hard-rock mining into the Kootenays, bringing out copper, silver, lead, and zinc. In 1897, the CPR, as part of its program to buy lines and open up the Crowsnest Pass route, acquired a little smelter at Trail. American mining attracted American-style unions. By 1895, the first local of the Western Federation of Miners was established at Rossland.

In 1898, a turn of the political tide left the provincial government of Charles Semlin clinging to power with less than a majority. For a tiny handful of labour sympathizers elected from Nanaimo, Vancouver, and the mining interior, it was a chance and they took it. After a couple of years of pressure, British Columbia gained a Coal Miners Regulation Act, an eight-hour day, a ban on Chinese workers underground, and other labour legislation. The experience was short-lived but memorable. It left an appetite for political organization, which other regions were slower to discover.

Mining was not the only hinterland industry where racial conflict developed. British Columbia's rich salmon fishery attracted whites and Japanese to join the traditional Indian fishermen. As in the mines, fishermen were treated as independent entrepreneurs selling their catch, although the big canneries set the prices. When the Semlin government proposed to meet an old demand from fishermen to control licences, the canners formed a Salmon Packers' Association to fight the change. The fishermen answered with unions.

Earlier attempts to organize had been destroyed by divisions among whites, Indians, and Japanese. White fishermen were even more bitterly anti-Oriental than other British Columbians, but their new leaders, Will MacClain and Frank Rogers, saw the desperate need for an alliance with the Japanese Fishermen's Benevolent Society at Steveston. By the summer of 1900, they had succeeded. With the union demanding twenty-five cents a fish and the canners bonding themselves to offer no more that twenty cents, the strike began. Union boats, with red and white flags, patrolled the rivers dumping catches. The canners answered by putting provincial police on company-owned tugs. In mid-July, led by an Indian band, a thousand fishermen marched through Vancouver. However, on July 24, militia arrived to stop the union patrols. Japanese newcomers broke ranks with their old-timers. Vancouver fishermen quarrelled with those from New Westminster. Gradually, with leaders in jail and troops on the docks, the Steveston strike collapsed. The canners had won.

For a time Rogers and MacClain kept a union organization alive, but mechanization of the cannery operations allowed the owners to offer better prices. Fishermen's individualism and the old racial hostility revived.

A stronger organization would have to wait until fishermen and most others who hewed wood and hauled water for the National Policy were ready for it.

CHAPTER 7

Trades and Labour

The explosive growth of the Knights of Labor during the 1880s proved the appetite of both American and Canadian workers for some kind of organization to assert their dignity and their needs. An economy limping out of the depression of the seventies allowed workers the hope of fulfilment without delivering it.

Part of the desire for organization was met by revived craft unionism. Hard hit in the 1870s, the printers, iron moulders, and even an occasional lodge of the Knights of St. Crispin surfaced in the early 1880s. Railway brotherhoods gradually organized most of the running trades during the decade. P.J. McGuire's new United Brotherhood of Carpenters and Joiners spearheaded the organization of construction trades in many Canadian cities, often displacing the British-based Amalgamated Society of Carpenters and Joiners.

Like the Knights of Labor, the craft unions faced bitter resistance, public hostility, and frequent setbacks. Hart Massey, faced with the threat of a Molders' local in his Toronto farm implement factory, locked out his workers until they signed an "ironclad" agreement never to join a union. Construction trades could organize more successfully because workers were skilled, possessed their own tools, and could move elsewhere. Those advantages, plus the earnest intervention of Mayor W.H. Howland, did not save the Toronto carpenters from a long and unsuccessful strike in 1887.

Unlike the Knights, the tough realism of their organizing principle allowed the craft unions to survive setbacks. In the United States, differences in philosophy and practice produced a growing and eventually remorseless conflict between the Noble Order and the craft unions. Against Powderly, the exhausted

The pride and self-confidence of solid craft unionists is displayed by these Winnipeg printers, gathered behind their executive officers, two suitably garbed "printers' devils," and two "sons of the chapel." Printers, as promoters of the enlightened "Art Preservative," did not adopt the regalia of other craft unions but they did follow the example of high dues and generous benefit plans. (Manitoba Archives)

and increasingly petulant idealist trying to keep the Knights together, the craft unions offered the squat, pragmatic New York cigar maker, Sam Gompers. Born in London of Dutch and Jewish parents, Gompers had flirted with radicalism in his youth but soon developed a clear-eyed philosophy of unionism which shaped American and, to a lesser extent, Canadian unionism ever after.

The business of unions, Gompers insisted, was not to transform society but to win more of its rewards for their members. Political goals were not merely idealistic, they were deeply divisive, and he had plenty of evidence for his argument. Against all the pressure for decentralization and local autonomy, he imposed a British model of tight central financial control first on his Cigar Makers and later on all the craft unions he could influence. Effective unionism was impossible if locals could independently launch strikes and then appeal for aid.

For Gompers and his allies, the notion of *industrial unionism* represented by the Knights — organizing all the workers in an industry regardless of skill or income — was hopelessly utopian. The only possible unionism depended on strict jurisdictional boundaries between trades with a union for each of them. *Dual unionism* — two unions fighting for membership in a single jurisdiction — was fatal to effective pressure against employers and it must be ruthlessly stamped out.

Gompers's own Cigar Makers learned that lesson in 1885 when a long strike in New York was defeated by the Knights signing an agreement undercutting the craft union and imposing their rival union label. In major urban and industrial centres in the United States, traditional unions found themselves in relentless competition with the Knights of Labor. Both sides were guilty of strike-breaking, but the Knights, with their feeble finances and their official commitment to avoiding strikes, were more often the villains.

In 1881, Gompers had been prominent in an attempt to revive a national central organization for the craft unions, the Federation of Organized Trades and Labor Unions of the United States and Canada. The weakness of FOOTALU led in December, 1886, to the first convention of a much more tightly organized body, the American Federation of Labor. Gompers and McGuire were key figures in the new organization, and Gompers became the first president. He held that office, with a one-year interruption, until his death in 1924. Starting with barely a third of the Knights' membership of 730,000, by the end of the decade the AFL was dominant, and the Knights of Labor was in ruins.

Only echoes of this rancorous struggle reached Canada. The young country had few centres where rivalry could develop. Canadian union organizers, like Daniel O'Donoghue, Alfred Jury, and Charles March, had their roots in the craft organizations. When central organizations developed during the 1880s, they brought together the Knights and craft unionists without discrimination.

The need for central organizations was as obvious as it had been a decade earlier. Except for the railways (whose unions remained aloof from all other labour organizations in the United States and Canada), employers were local. So were most issues. Whether the problem was organizing club rooms and a library for unionists or supporting a local strike, the need for a city- or town-based labour organization was obvious. Once formed, such a council could not help commenting on local political issues.

As before, Toronto led the way. On July 23, 1881, representatives of thirteen different occupations launched the Toronto Trades and Labour Council. Its founding declaration suggested an uncompromising solidarity: "We declare it the duty of every workman to use his utmost endeavours to secure the amelioration of the condition of the labouring classes generally, and to accomplish this we believe that a central organization should exist whereby all branches of labour may form allies to any particular one that may be oppressed."

Other cities followed more hesitantly. Hamilton, no longer the labour stronghold it had been, tried to launch a central body in 1882, tried again a few years later, but succeeded only in 1888. Halifax launched an Amalgamated Trades Union in 1882. Montreal's Central Labour Council, largely inspired by the Knights, began to meet in 1886. Winnipeg unionists made their first attempt in 1887, but their labour council met continuously only from 1894. Vancouver's Trades and Labour Council began its stormy history on December 5, 1889. By then more than a dozen Canadian cities and towns had similar bodies.

Locally based councils could pressure local politicians to buy union-made products, to launch public works in hard times, or to demonstrate their sympathy for workers affected by lockouts or strikes, but the real concerns of organized labour could chiefly be met only by provincial legislatures or the federal parliament. Toronto had launched the Canadian Labour Union; in 1883 the new council tried again. The call, issued in August, went to every kind of labour organization. Since the meeting was to take place during the Christmas holidays, the invitation demanded sobriety from delegates and promised them hard work.

Both requirements were met. Attendance was disappointing. Of forty-eight delegates only eleven came from outside Toronto, all of them from Ontario. However, under Charles March's presidency, the "Labour Congress" rattled through an impressive list of resolutions. Delegates enthusiastically backed March's denunciation of government programs of assisted immigration and unanimously opposed any Chinese immigration at all. They agreed to the need for factory safety legislation, renewed the old demand for effective mechanics' lien acts, and discussed how more women might be persuaded to join unions. A majority opposed grants to universities, preferring that public money be spent on school textbooks. On political action, the delegates concluded that "the working class of this Dominion will never be properly represented in Parliament or receive justice in the legislation of this country until they are represented by men of their own class and opinions."

Though the delegates were hard-working and their resolutions were a fair summary of policies espoused by Canadian unionists in the ensuing decades, the congress did not meet again. In 1886, the Toronto unionists again issued their invitations. They could boast a prolabour mayor in W.H. Howland, a brief era of support from most of the city's newspapers, and the inauguration of a "Labour Day" by the city's Exhibition Committee. On September 12, sixty-five hundred workers marched into the exhibition grounds behind seventeen bands. Office employees of the Toronto *News* and the *Globe* wore white plug-hats, while reporters from the rival Toronto *Mail* wore brown derbies.

Two days later, the first session of the Trades and Labour Congress opened with 109 delegates, 1 of them from Quebec City. An unbroken series of annual conventions would last until 1956.

Significant though it was, it is deceptively easy to write the history of Canadian labour through annual meetings of the TLC. Although it included all elements of Canadian organized labour during its first sixteen years, affiliation was casual and haphazard. So was participation. Delegate strength dropped as low as thirty-nine in London in 1895 and forty-four in Winnipeg in 1898. The time and cost of travel were decisive in determining the composition of representation. Resolutions may have reflected broad feelings among organized Canadian workers; they were more certainly a reflection of the views of the small number of active leaders who made a point of attending.

The perennial concerns of the congress resembled those of 1883 and of the Canadian Labour Union. More than American unionists, they looked to governments to legislate shorter hours, to improve safety through factory inspectors, and to provide the arbitration and conciliation which alone might bring unions and hard-faced employers together. Congress delegates denounced the mass immigration, condemned the Salvation Army for its alleged plans to unload the slums of London on the shores of Canada, and, with increasing representation from British Columbia, underlined its hostility to any Oriental immigration at all.

Although female participation faded with the decline of the Knights, women delegates were encouraged to speak of the need for female factory inspectors, in part to end the immorality that was said to accompany the mixing of the sexes in industry. "There were many instances," claimed Emma Witt of Toronto, "in which a woman among women would insist upon a closer observance of the law than would ever suggest itself to a man."

Some issues reflected the radical enthusiasms of the day. So long as the Knights were powerful in the congress, Henry George's single-tax ideas could count on a sympathetic airing. An early commitment to temperance faded with the declining Knights, the growth of brewery unions, and a developing sense that prohibition was a middle-class infringement on working-class pleasures. Banks were obvious enemies, and at a time when they issued Canada's only paper currency, the TLC was ahead of its time in proposing that only the federal government should issue legal tender. Like the CLU, the new congress waged a perennial battle against the products of convict labour.

In 1898, after years of passing similar and sometimes contradictory resolutions, the congress sensibly decided to codify its policies as a *Platform of Principles*. The sixteen points, regularly reprinted and occasionally modified, represent an important summary of the attitudes and preoccupations of the select minority of Canadian workers who had managed to form unions:

1. Free compulsory education
2. Legal working day of 8 hours and 6 days to a week
3. Government inspection of all industries
4. Abolition of the contract system on all public works
5. A minimum living wage based on local conditions
6. Public ownership of all franchises such as railways, telegraphs, waterworks, lighting, etc.
7. Tax reform, lessening taxation on industry and increasing it on land values
8. Abolition of the Dominion Senate
9. Exclusion of the Chinese
10. The union label to be placed on all manufactured goods where practicable and on all government and municipal supplies
11. Abolition of all child labour by children under fourteen years of age, and of female labour in all branches of industrial life such as mines, factories, workshops, etc.
12. Abolition of property qualification for all public offices
13. Compulsory [after 1902 "voluntary"] arbitration of labour disputes
14. Proportional representation with grouped constituencies and abolition of municipal wards
15. Direct legislation through the initiative and referendum
16. Prohibition of prison labour in competition with free labour

Equal suffrage for men and women was added in 1913 to make a seventeenth point. As a program, it was a cautiously progressive collection of ideas. It expanded the role of government through public ownership. It promoted democracy through abolition of an appointed Senate, support of proportional representation, and through fashionable American devices like referenda and the initiative. Banning child and female labour was both humanitarian for the time and usefully restrictive of the labour market.

For the most part, Canadian unionists could agree on the platform. What brought perennial division, as Sam Gompers had discovered in the United

Many people have talked about sausage factories; few have ever seen one. The George Matthews plant in Ottawa was typical of many local food-processing factories. Its male workers in 1907 would have earned less than ten cents an hour; its female employees received a little more than half as much. (Public Archives Canada PA 42288)

The first task of militant labour leaders in turn-of-the-century Canada was to launch a newspaper. In Winnipeg, Arthur Puttee's the Voice was one of the best. Wide-ranging and hard-hitting, particularly on local issues, Puttee's paper assumed that its readers would be interested in all the radical ideas of the age. Puttee himself eventually became too moderate for the Winnipeg Trades and Labour Council and the Voice was dropped as an official organ in 1917. (Manitoba Archives)

States, was how to bring it into being. In the postmortems on the Toronto Trades Assembly, which had inevitably accompanied the rebirth of the Toronto Trades and Labour Council, politics had been blamed for its downfall. Even in the new council, Liberals sat on one side of the hall and Tories on the other, with socialists, independents, and other categories perched uncomfortably in between. "It would be just as easy to move Hamilton Bay and put it upon the mountain," warned a TLC delegate in 1887, "as to get a Conservative to vote for a Reform Labor Candidate or a Reform workingman to vote for a Conservative Labor Candidate." It was an accurate prophecy.

Like its predecessor, the Canadian Labour Union, the congress learned to present its message in annual cap-in-hand sessions to the federal government. Funds were collected to allow the president to spend a few months in Ottawa during the short annual session of the House of Commons. The executive, neatly divided among representatives from Ontario and Quebec, formed naturally into committees to call on the provincial governments. For the most part, the reception was polite; it was also non-committal. The era of active (if ineffective) labour legislation had ended with the 1880s. In the nineties, the Conservatives did little more than proclaim Labour Day a statutory holiday in 1894. Among the provinces, British Columbia's Arbitration and Conciliation Act, based on American and Australian models, was imitated by Ontario. In both provinces, it proved almost wholly ineffective.

Governments of lawyers and merchants and farmers could never understand the plight of workingmen. That had been a shared labour doctrine since the 1860s. What was needed was direct representation.

As in the 1870s, politicians hurried to exploit a newly aroused trade union constituency. In an ingenious attempt to break the Tory shutout of his Liberals in Toronto, Ontario's Premier Oliver Mowat gave the city three seats but its citizens only two votes. That guaranteed the Reformers one seat, and as a running mate, the Liberals gave their support to the Trades and Labour Council's D.A. Carey. The Tories had a far stronger alternative in Ned Clarke, popular publisher of the [Orange] *Sentinel* and one of the printers imprisoned by George Brown in 1872. In the 1886 election, Carey trailed badly.

Since 1867 Montreal East had been a potential labour constituency, but not until 1887 was it won by a labour candidate, Alphonse Télésphore Lépine, a printer and journalist. Even here, party calculations made the difference. Fearing defeat at Liberal hands in the wake of the Riel agitation, the Conservatives gave Lépine their covert support. He proved a dependable ally until his defeat by a Liberal in 1896.

More than a decade later, it was the turn of the Liberals to promote a few labour victories. In 1900, Arthur Puttee, editor of the Winnipeg labour council's newspaper, the *Voice*, won a narrow by-election victory and repeated it later in the year with some discreet Liberal encouragement. He was joined by Ralph Smith, already a TLC president and a British Columbia labour M.L.A. Smith won Vancouver as a Liberal-Labour candidate.

Such a route to labour political influence was narrow and frustrating. From demanding representation "by men of their own class and opinion," some TLC delegates had moved by 1889 to calling for an independent labour party. "They ought to be tired of the old parties," insisted Patrick Jobin, "which always appealed, not to intelligence, but to ignorance." In 1893, the executive committee reported a meeting with the agrarians of the Patrons of Industry, the Dominion Grange, and the Social Problems Council. Despite an agreed program, nothing came of the meeting. The ill-attended London convention in 1895 admitted the Socialist Labor party as an affiliate, but the fire-breathing disciples of Daniel De Leon were removed a year later at a Quebec City convention.

The truth was that most of the TLC leaders, whatever their devotion to the cause of "toilers," maintained their own party loyalties. Carey, March, Robert Glockling, O'Donoghue, and Jury were devout Liberals; A.W. Wright, John Armstrong, and A.T. Lépine were equally stout Tories. In the passion of a congress session or a labour council rally, delegates might demand independent labour action or a political party for the workers. Neither their leaders nor the bulk of silent members would move in that direction.

The echo to such appeals came chiefly from the quarrelsome and tiny socialist sects. In the 1890s, socialism was a minor middle-class fad among some Canadians. "Nationalist Clubs" studied Edward Bellamy's utopian novel *Looking Backward*. A few braver souls followed Phillips Thompson into George Wrigley's Canadian Socialist League. They had little in common with the De Leonist

In 1898, the Trades and Labour Congress met for the first time in Winnipeg. The best evidence for Canada's reviving prosperity was that so many trade unionists would travel so far to attend. They included, in the front row: William Small, Winnipeg; John Flett, Hamilton; George Dower, Toronto, the TLC secretary; Daniel O'Donoghue, Toronto; an unknown delegate from Montreal; D.A. Carey, Toronto, the TLC president; Ralph Smith, Nanaimo, the president-elect; Charles March, Toronto, the first president of the TLC; and William Keyes, Montreal. (Public Archives Canada C 43179)

A German immigrant family at Quebec would soon discover that, like horse sellers, immigration agents seemed to have a special licence to exaggerate. The government wanted immigrants to settle on the land; it expected them to earn the money to develop their homesteads by working on the railways, in the mines, or logging camps. However, many newcomers headed for the cities to join an overcrowded labour market. Organized labour in Canada wanted controls on immigration and a ban on propaganda and on agencies that delivered immigrants to dockside in return for a bounty. (*Public Archives Canada PA 10254*)

Socialist Labor party, which believed that conventional trade unionism destroyed revolutionary ardour and was, therefore, an enemy of the workers. Except in remote British Columbia, where its radical message made sense to some of the victims of Robert Dunsmuir and his friends, socialism had a meagre appeal for Canadian labour in the 1890s.

Perhaps it was hard to find any reason for great hope. For all its resolutions, the Trades and Labour Congress was almost stagnant by 1898. It showed signs of neither growing nor disappearing. Canadian labour had been spared the American tragedies of the Homestead and the Pullman strikes. So far, it had also been spared the new employer weapon of court orders and injunctions, possibly because it was too weak to threaten anyone.

Except for Ralph Smith, elected president partly out of the joy of having a delegate from British Columbia at a TLC convention, the leadership was old and complacent. March and O'Donoghue were still there, but Alfred Jury was gone — appointed an immigration agent as an ironic reward from the new Laurier government.

Looking back to 1890, an aging leadership could find satisfaction. Gains exceeded losses. A few more labour councils had been chartered. In Montreal, there was a distressing conflict between the old Central Trades Council and a breakaway federated council of aggressive international locals. That would have to be resolved someday. Perhaps time would be its own medicine.

Canadian labour needed an explosion to give it life or death. It was coming.

CHAPTER 8

Gompers's Shadow

Prosperity, like most economic trends, came to Canada about a year after it returned to the United States. Much of the western world shared in the boom. Newly discovered gold deposits in South Africa may have triggered expansion. Reviving industries increased their demand for raw materials; their workers could afford more and better food. For Canadians, both developments created demand. In the United States, contemporaries mourned the filling-in of the American frontier and promptly observed that it now lay northward, not to the west. Settlement of the Canadian plains was encouraged by the development of frost- and rust-resistant strains of wheat. Grain growing became less of a gamble against the odds.

Throughout the bad years, merchants, farmers, and social critics of most points of view had denounced rings, combines, and monopolies as the source of economic stagnation. In one of those blinding transformations of opinion that are common in public affairs, the huge new corporations became the engines of prosperity. The merger movement, which had produced such gigantic enterprises as United States Steel or the Rockefeller oil empire, sent its tentacles into Canada or produced replicas like Francis Clergue's giant Consolidated Lake Superior Corporation, an integrated mining and steel producer newly created at Sault Ste. Marie.

In Canada, a scattered, feeble labour movement had no response to prosperity or to the advent of the powerful corporations. Most of the international unions represented in Canada limited their interest to the railway running trades and the construction industry. The leaders of the Trades and Labour Congress and of local labour councils spoke for a labour movement, not as people engaged in the practical business of collective bargaining for dues-paying members. Labour's issues could appeal to a wider audience and deliberately did so. Middle-class Canadians could easily be persuaded that mass immigration brought poverty, disease, and a threat to the traditional Anglo-Saxon or French-Canadian values. Even the union label, trademark of organized labour's workmanship and standards, should be sought out by a prudent customer as proof of quality and hygienic production.

In the United States, Gompers, the tough pragmatist who masterminded the American Federation of Labor, had moved past such concerns. If the corporations were organized, the AFL's affiliates must follow suit, imitating the highly centralized structure common among British unions. Central organizations could distribute funds to overwhelm locally based employers, and, with luck, they might even face the corporations. The Scranton Declaration in 1901 officially made "craft autonomy" a cornerstone for the AFL. There would be a single union for each trade and craft.

In practice, the AFL bent the rule for its more powerful affiliates, forcing the Typographers to release stereotypers, pressmen, bookbinders, engravers, and other trades, but allowing its most powerful member, the Carpenters, to swallow rivals in the woodworking trades. Gompers might denounce the rival industrial organizing principle, but the AFL's greatest success story, the United Mine Workers, was an industrial union. In a series of dramatic and largely unexpected triumphs, the ten-thousand-member UMW captured one hundred thousand bituminous coal miners in 1898. Within a year, under a charismatic young president, John Mitchell, the union broke through seemingly hopeless obstacles to add a hundred thousand Pennsylvania anthracite miners. In 1902, a long, bruising strike in the anthracite fields left consumers as far away as Ontario shivering. Finally, President Theodore Roosevelt forced the grudging operators to bargain with Mitchell. "Seldom has a single industrial disturbance in another country affected so closely the homes of the masses of the people in this country . . . ," observed a Canadian commentator in the *Labour Gazette*.

Where the coal miners led, other AFL unions followed in an organizing drive that recalled the explosive growth of the Knights of Labor, although this time the initiatives were decentralized to the federation's affiliates. If Gompers had forced changes in union structure to meet corporate power, must he not follow the corporations as they expanded their operations beyond the United States? How else could he protect American workers from cheap foreign labour? If corporations like General Electric, Westinghouse, Sherwin-Williams, Swift, and Standard Oil had begun to invest eagerly in nearby Canada, there was powerful reason for the AFL to follow.

Canadian workers might welcome the tariffs which supposedly protected their jobs. On both sides of the line, unionists pleaded for alien labour laws to discourage employers from herding strike-breakers across the line. However, unionists also complained when such laws impeded their own free flow over the border. For Canadians in particular, the labour market was continental. The newer AFL unions, like the old, welcomed Canadian locals, sometimes appointed a Canadian as fourth vice-president in hope that the honour would be repaid by voluntary organizing, and cheerfully titled themselves *international*. Sam Gompers had a healthy disdain for national boundaries and urged British,

Montreal members of the United Brotherhood of Carpenters and Joiners rally outside the Drill Hall for a Labour Day procession. The labour movement in Montreal, Canada's largest and most industrialized city, was deeply divided in the 1890s between the fading Chevaliers du Travail *and the bustling, aggressive craft unions.* (Labour Gazette)

German, and Canadian trade union congresses to exchange fraternal delegates with the AFL.

The Trades and Labour Congress had more practical concerns. Almost penniless and dependent on a wavering list of locals which might or might not pay a modest annual affiliation fee, TLC leaders knew that Canadian locals of international unions contributed automatically to the AFL essentially to support its pressure-group activities in Washington. Some of that money belonged in Canada. Unlike its predecessor, the Canadian Labour Union, the TLC had never claimed to organize Canadian workers on its own. In 1895, the same rebellious convention which admitted the Socialist Labor party took the bold step. From then on the congress would charter federal unions as well as city-based labour councils. In theory, that would place it in competition with AFL organizing; in practice, little organizing was taking place.

That soon changed. In 1897, Gompers accepted the offer of a Sault Ste. Marie businessman, P.J. Loughrin, to become the AFL's first organizer in Canada. The arrangement lapsed when Gompers discovered that Loughrin was using his position for personal and political ends, attacking TLC leaders in the bargain. However, the AFL's northward move was underway. It was confirmed in 1898. Thomas L. Kidd of the Woodworkers arrived in Winnipeg as the AFL's fraternal delegate with a promise that the federation would pay a grant if only the TLC

John Flett, a Hamilton carpenter, became one of the most phenomenally successful union organizers in Canadian history. As Sam Gompers's man in Canada, Flett laid the foundations of craft union locals from Charlottetown to Chatham. In 1902, his election as president of the Trades and Labour Congress confirmed the triumph of AFL influence in the Canadian congress. (Hamilton Public Library)

asked for it. The chief reason for compiling the Platform of Principles was to allow the Canadian labour congress to explain its policies to Gompers's organization.

The immediate return for this effort was modest: the AFL convention in Kansas City voted a mere $100 for "organizing purposes." But much more soon followed. In 1899, the AFL dispatched its first organizers, or "walking delegates," to form locals in the American south and in the Rockies. In Canada, volunteer organizers in Montreal, Ottawa, Toronto, Vancouver, and other cities accepted volunteer commissions. In Toronto, Louis Gurofsky, an energetic Jewish tailor, organized garment cutters, harness makers, cloak makers, carters, teamsters, hotel employees, and window-shade makers. By the year's end, AFL locals reported 10,457 Canadian members.

With money now pouring into the AFL's treasury in per capita dues from its growing membership, Gompers felt bold enough to choose a full-time Canadian organizer. His choice was John Flett, a suave, efficient Hamilton carpenter who had been active in the Knights and in his own local of the United Brotherhood of Carpenters and Joiners. Flett had been radical enough to support admission of the Socialist Labor party in 1895, but he had defended the AFL at congress conventions and won the vice-presidency of the TLC in 1898.

In only a couple of years, Flett compiled an incredible organizing record. In seven weeks he had formed fourteen locals in a tour of the small Ontario towns where manufacturers had often fled to escape labour organization. In two hurried journeys to the Maritimes, he found almost nothing and left a scattering of locals in every province, including Prince Edward Island. Everywhere he carried out AFL directives, settling jurisdictional fights, helping distant parent unions to resolve local difficulties, even removing charters from disobedient locals. In 1901, the AFL reported that its efforts had added eighty new locals in Canada; Flett could take credit for fifty-seven of them, and for most of the fifty locals added in 1902. In many Canadian communities, the origins of organized labour activity date from John Flett's visit.

Amazing though his contribution was, Flett's work was only part of an explosion of organization between 1898 and 1902. More than seven hundred locals were chartered in the four-year period, raising the number of organized workers in Canada from perhaps twenty thousand to more than seventy thousand. Between 1897 and 1902, the number of locals tripled; in British Columbia the growth was fivefold. For the first time, the metal trades, the garment industry, and woodworking were extensively organized. In addition to the aristocrats of the running trades, railway unions now covered trackmen and station hands. The Hotel and Restaurant Workers could boast twenty locals.

Such a phenomenal growth depended on more than Flett's dynamism or the determined work of new and old international unions. In Nova Scotia, even the Provincial Workmen's Association, devastated by internal disputes, recovered and grew. In British Columbia, the Western Federation of Miners emerged from the Kootenays to find members in the coal mines and to sponsor a radical United Brotherhood of Railroad Employees in a challenge to the old brotherhoods.

Much of the reason was prosperity. For the first time in most workers' memories, jobs were plentiful, prices were rising, and it was time to catch up. Often a single strike comes to symbolize an epoch in labour history. In 1872, it had been the Toronto printers' strike. In 1900, it was the London street railwaymen.

In turn-of-the-century North America, street railways often became battlegrounds between powerful corporations and their employees. Detesting monopolies, yet wholly dependent on the transit utilities in expanding cities, the public was torn among concern for its own convenience, sympathy with ill-treated workers, horror of violence, and helpless fury at high fares and bad service. London's streetcar system was typical. The small western Ontario city owed its original street railway to local interests, but a Cleveland corporation acquired the system in return for electrifying it. Determined to recover its investment, the outsiders gouged the employees, raised fares, and made no friends. When the railwaymen joined the Amalgamated Association of Street Railway Employees and first struck in 1898, their cause was so generally popular that the company was forced to surrender.

True to its faith, the American syndicate took its revenge slowly, firing union members, reneging on its commitments, and forcing a new strike in 1899. Once again Londoners backed the strikers. Even the mayor denounced the "un-English" behaviour of the company. However, as the strike dragged on, anger turned to violence. Strikers were arrested for sabotage. Demonstrations turned into angry protest, provoked by company attempts to run its service with strike-breakers. On the night of July 7 and on the following morning, thousands of Londoners rioted, smashing cars, beating strike-breakers, defying the police. The mayor read the Riot Act, summoned the militia, and cleared the streets. The strike was broken but its memory lingered.

When Sam Gompers visited Canada in 1900, the London strike gave him his text. American business, he told a Toronto audience, had come to Canada to oppress Canadian workers. "When the Yankee capitalist did this," Gompers declared, "it was but natural that the Yankee agitator should follow him."

It was equally natural that business, Canadian-owned or branch plant, would seize on the American connection as a patriotic weapon, and it was equally natural that Canadian workers could be persuaded to listen. In Quebec, which Flett initially regarded as ripe for organizing, American connections were as damaging as his lack of French. Workers in Quebec's large boot and shoe industry divided bitterly in the face of organizing attempts by John Tobin's Boot and Shoe Workers' International Union. When Quebec City shoe workers turned to Archbishop Begin to settle a festering dispute with their employer, a condition for his involvement was that the workers strike out all elements of conflict and materialism in their constitution. In Vancouver, J.H. Watson, a former AFL volunteer organizer, began the first verse of a long chorus when he complained of Canadian money flowing out to the United States.

In Montreal, conflict between the internationals and the older organizations like the Knights had led to a split in the city's Central Trades Council. Furious

Toronto's splendidly uniformed Governor General's Body Guard lines up at Yonge and Scollard streets during the 1902 street railway strike to escort any streetcar the company could man with strike-breakers. For once, public opinion massively favoured the strikers. (Filey Collection)

that the Knights kept control of the council by the simple expedient of spawning new assemblies, the craft locals split off in 1897 to form a new and far more dynamic Federated Trades Council. Both councils demanded recognition from the TLC.

More and more such disputes crowded in on the congress. In Nelson, British Columbia, a carpenters' local of the United Brotherhood decided to form a national union and demanded a TLC charter. That would mean war with the AFL, and the congress's new secretary, Patrick M. Draper, declined any such temptation. Flett's work in Prince Edward Island led to a new Charlottetown Labour Council — but chartered from Washington by the AFL. By now, both the TLC and the AFL had issued charters to independent, or "federal," locals. The AFL was bound to hand them over to the appropriate international; the TLC had no such obligation. The threat of dual unionism — supreme heresy in Gompers's rulebook — loomed closer. The problems could not be postponed forever.

The tremendous wave of AFL-inspired organization and affiliation transformed Canadian labour. The aging Knights of Labor, with their largely defunct assemblies, and the ineffective independent unions, with their memories and their fraternal regalia, were overwhelmed by a host of new, aggressive organizations with a clear mandate to bargain with employers and little taste for the tired political debates. The new unions were by no means the smug, conservative organizations many of them would eventually become. On the contrary, they

Soldiers of the permanent force wait, bayonets fixed, to clear a path up Main Street during Winnipeg's street railway strike in 1906. A change in the Militia Act in 1904 made it easier for municipal officials to call in troops. At the same time, a buildup in labour militancy and frustration increased the number of angry confrontations. Trade unions condemned "militarism" and urged members not to serve in the volunteer militia. (Manitoba Archives)

were the new fighting edge of a movement gone dull. They were bent on change.

For the Liberal government of Sir Wilfrid Laurier, organized labour began to acquire the significance it had occasionally possessed for Sir John A. Macdonald when he was hard pressed. With its backing slipping in Ontario, the Liberals began to woo labour. William Mulock, postmaster general and party manager for the Toronto region, presided over creation of a small new Department of Labour under his wing. To edit a new *Labour Gazette*, he chose a young graduate student with sound Liberal antecedents and a reputation as an investigator of sweatshops, William Lyon Mackenzie King. With an election approaching in 1900, Dan O'Donoghue and three other prominent trade unionists were given government jobs. The TLC convention responded gratefully by inviting Laurier and Mulock to a banquet. "If there is an aristocracy in this country," the prime minister announced, "it is an aristocracy of labour to which all belong."

When the election was over, organized labour could claim two seats in the new parliament: Vancouver with Ralph Smith and Winnipeg with Arthur Puttee. Appearances were deceiving. Both men owed their victories to Liberal aid, and Smith had so far alienated his radical British Columbia supporters that most pretence had worn off. However, Smith had also won election as TLC president in 1898 and he kept the office.

Whether it was because leading Liberals urged him to do so or whether he genuinely felt that the Canadian labour movement must respond to nationalist propaganda from senators, journalists, and big business, Smith set out at the 1901 convention of the TLC to end international unionism in Canada. In his presidential report, he announced that there must be a Canadian federation of labour and there must be national unions. Let the two national bodies deal with each other as equals.

In a single speech, Ralph Smith had charted a course for Canadian labour and issued a challenge. It was taken up. Delegates hurried the suggestion into a committee with instructions to report a year later when the TLC would meet at Berlin (modern-day Kitchener). Then the friends of international unionism went to work. Gompers increased the grant to the TLC to $300. At the time, the TLC's affiliates included a meagre 8,361 unionists. Locals of AFL affiliates could muster many times that number. So far, joining the TLC had been a matter of slight significance, dependent on the whim of a local secretary, the state of finances, or the enthusiasm of some militant member for travelling to the annual convention. Now, Flett and other AFL organizers had a powerful reason to promote affiliation.

Fighting Smith's idea was more than a concern for AFL sympathizers. Paddy Draper, the young Ottawa printer who had introduced an overdue order and efficiency into TLC affairs, was determined that Smith would not capture the congress for the Liberals. Radicals, like Phillips Thompson, wanted an end to the defunct labour politicians who used TLC meetings for an annual outing. Undoubtedly, Sam Gompers wanted a strong Canadian central body, able to organize Canada and to defeat the dual unions which threatened the AFL from the West, like the Western Federation of Miners and the United Brotherhood of Railroad Employees. There is no doubt that many Canadian unionists wanted precisely the same goals. If that meant close and even organic links to the American Federation of Labor, labour radicals could always profess a wider than national patriotism.

By the time the TLC convention opened in Berlin on September 15, 1902, much had happened. For the first time, the congress had made an extensive attempt to promote affiliation, mailing thousands of circulars, appealing to all councils (including those chartered by the AFL) to see TLC charters as well, even calling on international unions to send money. As a result, 150 delegates from 102 organizations appeared. As president, Smith was in the humiliating position of having been rejected as a delegate by his own union.

At Berlin problems postponed for years could not be avoided. Which Montreal council would be admitted? Could both international and national boot and shoe unions be recognized? Both were strongly represented. For years, the TLC had called for compulsory arbitration while the AFL, badly burned by the experience, was solidly opposed. Now the Liberals had introduced the principle in legislation governing railway disputes. Would the TLC rejoice at fulfilment of its wishes or would it change its ground?

In the four days of the Berlin convention, the issues were settled. A credentials committee, transformed into a constitutional committee, presented the details; with delegates reflecting AFL growth in Canada, the outcome was unavoidable. Henceforth, no national union would be recognized by the congress when an international union existed. So much for the Canadian Federation of Boot and Shoe Workers. In no case would more than one central body be chartered in any city or town. The two Montreal councils would have until January, 1903, to get together. In a bid for survival, the Knights of Labor demanded the right to be dual unions. For all the appeals of Daniel O'Donoghue, the motion was beaten eighty-seven to thirty-two. With railway unionists leading the debate, the TLC reversed its position on compulsory arbitration. The Platform of Principles was discreetly altered to favour only "voluntary arbitration." As the final triumph of international unionism, John Flett was elected the new president of the congress. Ralph Smith declined to stand.

In itself the Berlin convention was hardly significant. The importance of the Trades and Labour Congress, representing perhaps a fifth of Canada's modest number of organized workers, has always been exaggerated by the convenience of treating it as the incarnation of the Canadian working class. Nor is it sensible to suggest, as Robert Babcock does in *Gompers in Canada*, that the Berlin decisions were the result of strings pulled by Sam Gompers and his agents. They made sense to sensible, conscientious, and knowledgeable Canadian unionists at the time, and they may well be as defensible (or as unavoidable) today. If, by some chance, the international position had been defeated at Berlin, the immense and dynamic international presence of AFL affiliates would not have blown away. They would have done what the exiles did: they would have tried to form a rival central organization.

Misfortunes may be inevitable. Only historians can concoct painless solutions, and usually only by cooking the facts. However, misfortunes may also be mourned. The dual unions were forced out of the TLC.

Some delegates who resented the outcome promptly adjourned and organized a rival National Trades and Labour Congress on September 18. Later, in the Canadian Federation of Labour, and much later, in the All-Canadian Congress of Labour, a few enthusiasts helped Canadian-only unionism to survive in Canada without either thriving or dying. The TLC had hoped to end dual unionism; it established it on durable and particularly bitter lines. The division was all the more significant because a very high proportion of the dissenters had come from Quebec. It was far from true that the TLC or the international unions were driven from Quebec. However, in a few days, the TLC had sacrificed many of its French-speaking leaders and their locals. Almost two decades before the formal emergence of a Catholic union movement, the NTLC and its successor organizations had come to represent a conservative, nationalist, and largely French-Canadian brand of labour organization.

For the majority, enjoying the pork hocks and beer provided by the Women's Union Label League in the Saengerbund Hall, such a future could take care of itself.

CHAPTER 9

Business, Labour, and Governments

The thrust of the aggressive "new unionism" into Canada was not accepted cheerfully by business or government. Like the 1880s and far more so, the first decade of the twentieth century was a period of intense and unexpected conflict in Canada. Labour violence might not be wholly new but never before had police and volunteer militia been involved with such frequency.

At Valleyfield, Quebec, in 1900, two hundred labourers building a cotton-mill struck for a raise of twenty-five cents on their wage of a dollar a day. Strikers fought off strike-breakers, and the employers persuaded the mayor to summon militia from Montreal. When the troops arrived, three thousand mill operatives stopped work and some joined in a stone-throwing attack on the militiamen. Peace returned after a night of violence, and the strike was eventually settled by the youthful W.L. Mackenzie King. It was a fitting start to the century and the outset of eight years of violent conflict between textile workers in the Montreal area and their powerful employers.

In 1902, the year of the crucial Berlin convention, King's department recorded 123 new disputes, costing a total of 163,125 working days. That was barely a quarter of the 1901 record, but some of the strikes had a dramatic impact. Halifax longshoremen benefited from a wave of sympathetic strikes among the port's fish handlers, coal heavers, and coopers to regain some of their old influence. In Toronto, street railwaymen won their battle with an arrogant local utility when they gained the sympathy of most local citizens. Not even a force of fourteen hundred militia could safeguard company streetcars when manned by strike-breakers. The Toronto experience was repeated in Winnipeg and Hamilton during equally violent street railway strikes in 1906.

The dramatic revival of union activity encouraged Canadians to restate their views of industry and labour and to improve their weapons of defence and offence. To the ideal of union solidarity, businessmen and editors offered the virtues of individualism. It was a somewhat shopworn myth. To earn their "living profit," merchants and manufacturers had long since accepted the need to organize themselves and to pressure governments, suppliers, and consumers, much as workers had formed unions to earn their "living wage." The merger movement among businesses and the formation of huge trusts were factors which had persuaded Gompers to overhaul the AFL. The comparable development in Canada produced corporate giants like the Steel Company of Canada, Canada Cement, and the Dominion Coal Company.

However, myth outlives reality. Canadian businessmen knew the truth, but it was pleasant to pretend that they still lived in a big economic democracy, described in 1872 by the Toronto *Globe* thus: "We have no Rothschilds in Canada — no Jacob Astors, no Vanderbilts, no Tweeds, no Goulds, no Jim Fisks. But we have thousands of small investors, and these are our only capitalists. The demand for workmen of all descriptions from every corner of Ontario is constant and urgent — the supply is never equal to the demand — and as a consequence the wages are high, the employee is master of the situation, and he rules his employer with a rod of iron." In such a society, there could be no right for workers to coerce their competitors in the labour market. "While one man has the moral right to refuse to sell his labour at a certain price and on certain terms," admitted the Toronto *Mail*, "another has the same right to accept that price and to waive those terms. For a combination of men to interfere by violence or intimidation to prevent the latter is just as tyrannical as for the legislative authority to interfere to compel the former."

While monopolies, cartels, and combines were organized in discreet privacy, a labour union was an open, aggressive assertion of the right of workers to combine to improve their wages and conditions. Goldwin Smith, Toronto's wealthy and perennial sage, had preferred the business-like craft unions to the utopian idealism of the Knights, but he never overcame his disappointment that workers should prove so indifferent to his liberal principles. He had always befriended the workingman, Smith recalled in old age. "But we never thought of setting on foot a monopoly of labour in the hands of self-constituted and self-regulated associations. We never dreamed of putting an end to freedom of labour or persecuting any man for earning his bread in his own way, or making the best use of his natural powers."

Smith was sincere enough in his friendship to have helped Toronto unionists establish the Labour Lyceum as their clubhouse. His wealth financed a union-administered relief fund in the grim winter of 1907–8. Other critics had no such credentials. The *Canadian Manufacturer* raged at reports that union members had attacked strike-breakers or intimidated workers who crossed picket lines. "We do not hang, burn or drown men nowadays for their religious opinions. We claim freedom at the ballot box, and punish the men who obstruct it; in fact, all men are conscious of the danger involved in interfering with personal rights. It must be so recognized in all labor struggles and labor unions will never be what they can and ought to be so long as violence is done to the non-consenting."

Liberal individualism could sometimes be mobilized to support workers when, for example, Frank Smith of the Toronto Street Railway had denied his workers the right to associate in a union. However, business had little difficulty in answering criticism of "yellow-dog" contracts or "the document." The *Monetary Times* observed, "The condition was one which, under freedom of contract, the company had a right to make; those who did not like it had the right to prefer connection with a labour union to service under the company."

Not all employers were invariably hostile to unions. Like other forms of cartel, they could bring order and certainty to the marketplace. Railway executives conceded that the brotherhoods had done much to improve the discipline, efficiency, and moral standing of their members. Railway unions respected the sanctity of their agreements, preferred negotiation to disruption, and utterly opposed the sympathetic strike, making it almost impossible for humbler employees to organize. The Royal Commission on the Relations of Labor and Capital, reporting in 1889, assured Canadians that unions were much less dangerous than alleged. "They encourage their members to study and discuss

The Canadian Northern Railway might be heading for bankruptcy and public ownership, but at least its office employees could share in a company picnic at Grand Beach, north of Winnipeg. The vogue for scientific management in the prewar years included techniques for getting rid of unions and others for ensuring greater employee loyalty. (Manitoba Archives)

Children too young to work could help by delivering their father's dinner-pail in time for the noon whistle. The factory is in Montmorency Falls, Quebec, and the year is 1915. (John Boyd Collection)

matters affecting their interests and to devise means for the betterment of their class. It is gratifying to be assured by many competent witnesses that labor bodies discourage strikes and other disturbances in industry, favour conciliation and arbitration for the settlement of disputes, and adopt conservative and legitimate methods for promoting the welfare of the producing members of society."

Unions had their own appreciation of the merits of individualism. Craft unionism existed in large measure to preserve the autonomy and dignity of individual craftsmen. Union work rules protected the right of members to set their own pace and to safeguard time-honoured, hard-earned skills. With the new century, "scientific management" entered Canada, determined, in the eyes of its critics, to make the worker no more than a more efficient machine. Cost accounting, job standardization, time and motion study, piecework, and bonus systems became the hallmark of progressive firms. Branch plants of American corporations brought with them the ideas of Frederick Winslow Taylor, chief spokesman of the new movement. Some Canadian firms hastened to adapt. A proud showplace of the new efficiency was Toronto's Lumen Bearing Company. Workers no longer ran about to collect their own tools; simple, explicit instructions replaced the craftsman's traditional judgement; "expert advisors," stopwatch in hand, corrected "slovenly" habits and struggled for new rates or productivity. In the dehumanizing process, individualism survived only in the competition for bonuses and piecework incentives. At Hamilton's Frost Fence Company, workers could be inspired by the prospect of profit sharing.

Whether efficient or traditional, the Canadian employer was aware of a serpent in the individualistic Eden: the labour organizer. Workers, complained the Victoria *Colonist* in 1907, "are being persuaded that every man who does not take off his coat to earn his living, unless he is a labour agitator, is their natural enemy." The "jawsmith," the "walking delegate," not only put evil thoughts in the minds of workers, he also lived a life of idle luxury. Business agents — elected full-time officers in many of the craft unions — were needed to negotiate and administer the increasingly complex agreements and work rules, but employers joyfully denounced them as "leeches" and "vultures." Thomas Hood's melodramatic "Song of the Shirt," a denunciation of factory conditions, was rewritten as "The Song of the Shirk" and regularly used as filler for the business press:

> With fingers that never knew toil,
> With nose-tip swollen and red,
> A delegate sat in his easy chair,
> Eating the labourer's bread;
> Strike — strike — strike!
> Nor dare return to your work,
> And still with his swaggering, insolent air,
> He sang the song of the Shirk.

Employer indignation at anyone who interfered with their dutiful employees could become hysterical when the organizers came from the United States. During the 1902 street railway strike in Toronto, William Mackenzie, the utility magnate, appealed to loyal citizens to fight the claims of an American-based union. "So far as I can see," he declared, "there is nothing to prevent a few American labour leaders from tying up every Canadian street railway, steam railway and factory whenever it suits them to do so." Mackenzie's appeal fell flat. People knew that the union officials had pleaded in vain for the Toronto members to stay at work, and a few employers confessed that AFL influences were more often moderate than inflammatory. That did not prevent the great majority of employers from exploiting anti-American feeling. At a time when Gompers and the AFL were under merciless and effective assault by American corporations and their judicial allies, there was some irony in the repeated claims in Canada that the international unions furthered Wall Street interests. "So long as this international unionism continues," insisted the Canadian Manufacturers' Association in 1908, "there will be needless trouble in this country."

Sir Wilfrid Laurier and the Liberals shared some of the business concern. Ralph Smith's efforts to purge the Trades and Labour Congress of international links undoubtedly had Liberal blessing, and there was a distinct cooling in relations between the government and the congress in the aftermath. The

Laurier government soon had another opportunity to attack the American link. A violent, four-month strike in the spring of 1903 pitted the Canadian Pacific Railway against one of the radical new industrial unions that Gompers and the AFL feared almost as much as employers. The United Brotherhood of Railroad Employees, an offshoot of the Western Federation of Miners, was eventually defeated. One of its leaders, Frank Rogers, was shot in an ambush; another turned out to have been a paid company spy. The violence inspired Senator James Lougheed, an Alberta Conservative, to propose a prison sentence for anyone with less than a year's residence in Canada who dared to " . . . incite, urge or induce any strike or lockout, or a rise or fall in wages, or the imposition of additional or differential conditions in terms of employment, or impairing the exercise of industry, employment or labour."

Lougheed's bill easily passed the Senate. The House of Commons was saved from temptation by the Laurier government, but William Mulock chose another weapon to help prove the dangers of international unionism. "Perhaps it would assist to disillusion them," he suggested, "if an intelligent Commission, one in which the working people have confidence, were to point out the injuries that have come to them because of the interference of American unions." Mulock's commission — composed of Chief Justice Gordon Hunter of British Columbia, the Reverend William Rowe, a Methodist and former pillar of the Canadian Socialist League, and William Lyon Mackenzie King — did not quite meet the government's needs. For one thing, it could not help allowing Robert Dunsmuir to boast of his tyrannical treatment of his miners. For another, it quite exceeded itself in anti-union bias, proposing measures even more severe than Senator Lougheed's bill. While employers were asked not to be so arbitrary and "arrogant," the commission demanded a ban on sympathetic strikes, boycotts, and the circulation of lists of scabs and strike-breakers. Both the UBRE and the Western Federation of Miners were denounced by the commissioners as "revolutionary socialistic" organizations, led by "foreign socialistic agitators of the most bigoted and ignorant type."

The report of the Hunter Commission delighted employers, but the government wisely filed the document, concluding that while all internationals might be troublesome, some were clearly worse than others. The experience was valuable for Mackenzie King. Hitherto, most of his contacts with labour leaders had been with elderly, philosophical veterans like Dan O'Donoghue or Alfred Jury. In British Columbia, King had met men of a very different kind. They may well have resembled his revered grandfather, the Rebel of 1837, but he disliked them. King found their vehement radicalism almost impossible to understand. He had never placed much stock in the right to organize. If belonging to a particular union or to any union at all was an impediment to a peaceful settlement, the organization must be sacrificed. Anything else, in King's eyes, was unreasonable. The men of the UBRE and the Western Federation had been distinctly "unreasonable." The contrast with the craft unions was unmistakable. The AFL-TLC affiliates might be demanding and even aggressive but their goals were limited to realities King understood. Their leaders were a contrast to the wild idealists the young civil servant had met in the West.

Few Canadian employers shared even King's tolerance. By 1903 they were ready to launch a counter-offensive against the new unionism. Their techniques, appropriately enough, would be borrowed from the United States.

By 1900, American employers had begun to fight unions with some of their own weapons: disciplined organization and financial support. In 1899, the Chicago Building Contractors' Council had humbled the city's construction unions at the cost of a year-long strike. In 1901, the Metal Trades Association was quickly formed to beat a drive by the International Association of Machinists for a nine-hour day. The employers won. The Dayton Employers' Association, formed that year, cut union membership in the city by 85 percent. Similar organizations used even rougher methods. The Sedalia Citizens' Alliance united businessmen, factory owners, doctors, and lawyers. By denying credit and recruiting vigilantes, the alliance crushed unionism in the city. By 1903, the Citizens' Industrial Association, with David M. Parry as president, set out to glorify the open shop and to proclaim the closed, or unionized, shop as "un-American." One after another, some of the most powerful AFL affiliates reeled in defeat.

Major trade associations, like the National Founders' Association and the United Typothetae, had members on both sides of the border. In October, 1902, Toronto employers met to follow the example of Dayton and Sedalia. By 1905, the *Labour Gazette* could report sixty such associations in Ontario alone. They were backed by the Canadian Manufacturers' Association, revived and reorganized in 1900 and ready to do battle with government or labour. One of its presidents, James Murray, was the driving force behind the Toronto Employers' Association.

While employer associations in other Canadian cities scored their triumphs (Montreal's once-powerful Cigar Makers and longshoremen's union were among the victims), Toronto led the way, using divide-and-conquer tactics to exploit the limitations of craft unionism. Toronto's major stove makers, Gurney and Canada Foundry, dealt with four separate craft unions: the Stove Mounters, the Metal Polishers, the Molders, and the Machinists. Each, in turn, was confronted and defeated while the Toronto Metal Trades Council looked on in helpless dismay. Once the metal trades had been humbled, the Toronto employers turned to the construction industry. The Painters' Association proclaimed an open shop, lowered rates, and welcomed a convenient influx of immigrants. The Carpenters and Building Labourers were each compelled to surrender and wait for a better day. Meanwhile, the Employers' Association helped members by exploiting loopholes in Canada's Alien Labour Act, ostensibly designed to stop importation of foreign strike-breakers.

Unions survived the employer offensive in Toronto and other cities. In Hamilton, construction unions even succeeded in breaking up the assault. However, craft unionism in most of Canada was put on the defensive, systematically weakened, and left vulnerable to severe depressions like that of 1907−8. Union membership, as a proportion of the Toronto work force, fell steadily during the decade before 1914. "Toronto was the keystone," boasted a delegate to the convention of the Canadian Manufacturers' Association in 1908. "We have knocked the keystone from underneath and now they are civil and treat us as they should treat us, as men who have equal or even greater responsibilities."

Local victories were made easier by national organization and the benevolent neutrality of governments. Judicial harassment of unions in Canada never reached American extremes, but courts were usually ready to protect employers. In 1902, an injunction banned Local No. 30 of the Amalgamated Sheet Metal Workers from accusing the Metallic Roofing Company of unfair treatment. Toronto's famous magistrate George T. Denison frequently levied a seventy-five-dollar fine — two months' wages — on strikers who shouted "scab" at fellow workers. "I want it distinctly understood that I object to that word."

The Canadian Manufacturers' Association's most controversial intervention in labour affairs came through its deliberate promotion of immigration. The CMA sponsored a Canadian Labour Bureau in England, promising plentiful jobs at high wages in Canada's rolling-mills, machine shops, stove factories, and farm implement plants. The opening of the office coincided with the 1907–8 depression, and the association was widely discredited. In fact, the CMA was often more inhibited in its anti-union activities than some of its members wanted. In 1907, when the E.B. Eddy Company wanted a register of workers known to be "turbulent" or "disturbing," the association preferred not to take the initiative. Like good businessmen, the CMA's leaders desired the open shop and feeble unions; like other Canadians, they hoped that government would act.

In fact, federal and provincial governments had acted to establish a legal framework for the demands of workers and their unions. In contrast to Britain, where the Trades Disputes Act of 1906 set a pattern for more than sixty years of legal non-interference, Canada began building a rich body of law and of officials to enforce it. Unlike the United States, where the states played a dominant role at the outset, Canadian jurisdiction was divided, overlapping, and often confused.

The federal acts of 1872 and 1877 were assumed — perhaps inaccurately — to give workers the right to form unions and to withdraw their services without criminal penalties. Thereafter, most labour legislation timidly attempted to protect workers from their employers. Daniel O'Donoghue's Mechanics' Lien Act, adopted in Ontario in 1877, had been amended by 1896 to nullify any waiver of wages by a workman to the benefit of his employers. Presumably, hard-pressed employers had extorted such waivers in the past.

Factory legislation developed cautiously from the 1880s, caught between the more generous impulses of the age and the employers' firm grip on legislatures and party finances. By 1888, children were banned from smaller factories in Ontario, and shopkeepers could not employ boys under fourteen or girls under sixteen for longer than twelve hours a day or seventy-four hours a week. Quebec and Nova Scotia followed Ontario's humanitarian lead at a cautious distance. Enforcement in all provinces followed even farther behind. Ontario critics noted that while Toronto employed three inspectors merely to hunt for liquor offences, the entire province employed only three inspectors to enforce its Factory Act. One of them, Margaret Carlyle, a one-time factory hand from Glasgow, proved remarkably effective.

Factory legislation was a community response to the appalling toll of life and limb, often of young children. A Brantford girl was caught by an unfenced wire rope coming through the floor of her factory and torn to pieces in the

Carmen of the Canadian Northern were less satisfied than office employees. In 1914, they paraded their grievances to the old Manitoba legislative building on Kennedy Street. The company, hurt by over-expansion as one of three transcontinental systems and by a two-year-old depression, was on the verge of ruin. (Manitoba Archives)

machinery. Better known was the case of the "Farry boy," put to work at thirteen by his widowed mother. On his first morning, the boy was put on the shaper machine, a primitive tool which even veteran hands considered dangerous. Within four hours, he was under chloroform having the stumps of his fingers bound up. His employer denied any responsibility; the boy had taken the job at his own risk.

The employer was right. An employee took all the risks unless he could prove criminal negligence. By 1888, Ontario's Workmen's Compensation for Injuries Act allowed a worker to sue for up to three years' earnings, but only on proof that he had not assumed the risk or waived his claim on taking the job, and that the injury was the result of defective machinery, improper procedures, or negligent supervision. Farm workers were excluded even from this protection. Other provinces followed the Ontario example. Injury cases in the courts benefited at least the legal profession.

In 1910, James Whitney, the Conservative premier of Ontario, allowed his friend Sir William Meredith to conduct a Royal Commission of Inquiry into the problem. As chief justice, Meredith proved to be a man of rare integrity and imagination. His report was a landmark. Business and labour, Meredith discovered, were unanimous that the problem of compensating industrial injury must be removed from the courts and handed to a government-controlled mutual insurance scheme. Industrial activities must be classified according to their risks and must pay accordingly. Employers wanted labour to share in the cost; labour spokesmen stoutly refused, and Meredith took their side.

Ontario's Workmen's Compensation Act, adopted in 1914, was one of the most important labour statutes in Canadian history and, in its concept of state-run mutual insurance, a model for much to come. It faced powerful business resistance. It was "socialism of the worst kind and a most vicious measure," claimed the Canadian Lumbermen's Association. The Canadian Manufacturers' Association insisted that the benefits — basically 55 percent of previous earnings — were "preposterous." Meredith's prestige, supported by brilliant political management by Fred Bancroft, a TLC vice-president, won passage for the act. It was by no means a total victory for labour. When the new Workmen's Compensation Board was announced, labour discovered that the Conservatives had allowed no labour representation but that one of the new commissioners was a mouthpiece for the Canadian Manufacturers' Association.

Labour also turned to Ottawa for action, only to meet the opposite and more powerful influence of business. In addition to obvious and familiar issues like immigration, unions insisted that governments at all levels set exemplary standards of hours and wages both in their own departments and among government contractors. In 1900, on the eve of a close election, Laurier's cabinet issued a Fair Wages Order, compelling contractors to pay at least the prevailing rate for their locality. Alphonse Verville, president of the TLC and elected to Parliament from a Montreal constituency in 1906 as a Labour member, struggled for years to persuade the government to adopt an eight-hour day on federal works.

Caught between business and labour, governments could grant or withhold their favours. They could not escape being dragged into the conflicts of

William Lyon Mackenzie King campaigns for election in his native Berlin in 1908. The former deputy minister of labour could boast of his achievements as a mediator and as the author of Canada's new Industrial Disputes Investigation Act. As the first editor of the Labour Gazette, he had employed a good many leading unionists as local correspondents. (Public Archives Canada C 28574)

employer and employed, particularly when the community was affected or when violence spilled into civil society. Outsiders always had an answer. If the two sides could be brought together through *mediation*, surely differences could be resolved. Or, if that failed, why not *arbitration* by a sensible, independent person — or perhaps a panel of three members — to devise a solution that would be fair to all? Both the Knights of Labor and the TLC had favoured arbitration. As early as 1877, Ontario had a Trades Arbitration Act. Like Oliver Mowat's Profit-Sharing Act, it was high-minded and unused. The province's Trade Disputes, Consultation and Arbitration Act of 1894, borrowed from French, British, Australian, and other models, provided for an elaborate three-step process of councils and arbitrators, though without power to make binding settlements. The new law was almost as unused as the old even though it remained in force until 1932. British Columbia and Quebec enacted their own variants.

The problem with such legislation, and with all the optimistic claims that arbitration would ultimately render strikes obsolete, was an assumption that both sides equally wanted a settlement and merely needed to be nudged into negotiations. If both sides really had reached such a state, they could usually find the means. Otherwise, disputes were fought to the death and the union was most often the corpse.

However, in an increasingly integrated and urbanized Canada, disputes rapidly spread beyond the contenders. Coal mining had become a vital as well as a deeply troubled industry in western Canada. A nine-month strike in the Lethbridge district and in the Crowsnest Pass in 1906 left prairie settlers in danger of freezing to death. The companies, bent on wiping out unions and glimpsing victory, refused to arbitrate. Meanwhile, in the little lumbering town of Buckingham, not far from Ottawa, the MacLaren Lumber Company fired its striking workers and brought in armed guards. On October 8, a clash left two strikers and a guard dead and many others wounded. Public opinion was horrified. The government must act. Its earnest young deputy minister of labour was ready. The result of his study, honed by his experience, was a draft of the Industrial Disputes Investigation Act, soon to be known to contemporaries as the Lemieux Act in honour of King's ministerial superior, the Honourable Rodolphe Lemieux.

The act, hurriedly passed by a Parliament largely ignorant of labour problems and eager to give bipartisan approval to any ingenious solution, was to set the pattern of Canadian industrial relations for the rest of King's long life. It allowed intervention in any labour dispute under federal jurisdiction either on the request of a party involved or on the initiative of the government itself. While a tripartite board (representing employer, workers, and the public) conducted its investigation and worked out recommendations for a settlement, all conflict was suspended. There could be no strike, lockout, boycott, or picketing. Once the report was issued, the conflict could resume, but the recommendations could not help being an influence.

The IDI Act was welcomed ecstatically in an era thirsting for splendid solutions to industrial conflict. Lord Grey, the governor general, used the law as his text when he spoke to the National Peace Congress in New York. President

As a practical alternative to compulsory school attendance, many provinces were satisfied if boys of more than twelve years of age attended school after hours. Families continued to receive badly needed income and education authorities could congratulate themselves on their flexibility. As for the students, who knows? (Public Archives Canada WS 2598)

Charles Elliot of Harvard University, an old patron of King, declared the act to be "the best piece of industrial and social legislation produced in the last two decades." Even the Trades and Labour Congress convention of 1907 gave its cautious approval. The TLC gradually changed its mind.

By appearances, the IDI Act favoured labour and, where unions were hopelessly weak, it probably did so. When workers were unorganized, the act legitimized their representatives. However, experience with the act revealed that unions were robbed of their weapons during the negotiation stage; employers were not. Nothing stopped companies from stockpiling, blacklisting, discrimination, introducing yellow-dog contracts, hiring strike-breakers and private police. If the act created a kind of recognition for the workers, the form was limited, temporary, and, under King's guiding philosophy, essentially unimportant.

The potential and the limitations of the Industrial Disputes Investigation Act were apparent in a strike of Bell Telephone Company operators in Toronto in the summer of 1907. At issue were long hours of work. The company's image as a high-handed monopoly and a chivalrous public sympathy for ill-treated women guaranteed massive general support and a demand for government intervention. A Royal Commission, including the indispensable Mackenzie King, was swiftly granted. The report, when it eventually appeared, scolded the Bell Telephone Company for sweatshop methods. However, the report made no reference to issues of wages and unionization, proposed no significant alteration in working conditions, and was published only after about half the women had found other work.

Whatever others might think, King saw the outcome of the telephone strike as a triumph for his concept of industrial relations. All three parties to the conflict had been involved. Ample information had been obtained as a result of thorough investigation and its publication was sufficient to draw an expression of contrition from the company. If employees had abandoned their union or moved on to other jobs, that was, after all, an exercise of their personal freedom.

A much more serious failure of the act occurred in the strike of Grand Trunk Railway employees in 1910. The company president, Charles Hays, ignored pressure from senior cabinet ministers to reinstate employees who had sacrificed jobs and pension rights because they had followed the rules of the IDI Act and the company had not. King himself confessed to Laurier that the working of the act had proved "a tremendous handicap to the men and a no less equal advantage to the company: because it had prevented sympathetic strikes by other railway brotherhoods." The bitterness of the Grand Trunk strikers played a role in King's own election defeat in 1911.

It was a very limited revenge. Such was the hold of Liberal sympathizers on the TLC in 1911 that a motion to denounce the IDI Act failed by a narrow five votes. A year later, with the Tories in office and no Liberal friends to embarrass, a demand for repeal passed the TLC convention without a dissenting vote. It had no effect. The Industrial Disputes Investigation Act remained the dominant statute in its field until 1948. Its consequences were enormous. Stuart Jamieson, one of Canada's most respected students of industrial relations, left a harsh judgement:

> The Act . . . may well have delayed the evolution in Canada of mature collective bargaining. Particularly did this tend to be the case where King and subsequently other federal mediators and boards, frequently used the disputes settlement strategy of arranging agreements between employers and committees of their employees instead of with bona fide unions.

By 1914, some unions in Canada could look back to half a century of unbroken history; a very few could look even farther. To both business and government, however, they remained a troublesome and perhaps a transient phenomenon. That belief would generate a lot of trouble.

CHAPTER 10

Labour Radicals

For the most part, the Laurier years were comfortable for many Canadians. The economic gloom of Macdonald's later years lifted. The prosperity the Conservatives had promised coincided with the Liberal years. The prime minister's boast that "the Twentieth Century would belong to Canada" seemed no exaggeration. With the American frontier filled up, Canada offered its "last, best west," and hundreds of thousands of newcomers came from the United States, Britain, and Central Europe to find their fortune in a new country.

Like preceding immigrant waves, they discovered that the way to prosperity was brutally hard, narrow, and filled with traps. Their ill-paid labour was part of the calculation made by politicians and entrepreneurs that Canada could, for example, afford two additional transcontinental railways. Cheap immigrant labour could make it profitable to exploit the mineral wealth slowly unveiled north of Lake Huron and Lake Superior. East European workers promised profits to the shareholders of Francis Clergue's wildly ambitious Lake Superior Corporation at Sault Ste. Marie.

The influx of immigrants meant that the profits of prosperity would not extend to labouring Canadians. The old traditions of contract labour gangs could now be repeated with Poles and Galicians and Italians. The old quarrels of Connaught men and Cork men could now be extended into the quarrels of European races and cultures. American experience had taught the lesson. If workers of one language or culture protested their fate, they could be replaced by others who, at the worst, would nourish some ancient hatred of Italian against Austrian or Pole against German, or at the very least might hardly be aware that they were breaking a strike of fellow workers.

The first Dominion Executive Committee of the Socialist Party of Canada was simply the leadership of Local No. 1 in Vancouver. Toronto socialists had acknowledged the Vancouver pre-eminence as soon as the SPC had elected members to the British Columbia legislature. A tough but quarrelsome group, they and their descendants would have a lasting influence on the tone and temper of the West Coast labour politics. (Public Archives Canada C 38687)

Such ignorance need not, of course, be caricatured or exaggerated. The immigrant flood brought with it, as it always had, a frosting of articulate, discontented members. Some were refugees of the oppression of czar or emperor. Many had been trained in the mature and politically sophisticated school of the German Social Democratic party, described by Robert Michels, or in the nascent British Labour party. When Toronto socialists turned to municipal politics, their first serious mayoral candidate, James Lindala, was a Finn who had managed to acquire modest wealth without forgetting his beliefs. Even more successful was the charming, hail-fellow-well-met of labour and socialist politics, the Lancashire-born Jimmy Simpson, already by then a vice-president of the Trades and Labour Congress.

In describing historical periods, it is dangerously tempting to use metaphors drawn from human generations. Accepting all the dangers and distortions of any figure of speech, the decade before the First World War may stand as a kind of adolescence for a Canadian labour movement. It was a period of painful growth and of even more painful wrestling with authority. It was a time when ideas were tried out or perhaps, to accept the criticism of visiting British socialists like Keir Hardie, they were merely repeated as sterile slogans because of their capacity to shock. It was a period of constantly changing loyalties to ideas and organizations. It was a period when many were shouting "to the barricades," though even the shouters were scarcely moving. It was a period of excitement and ferment, of charm and frustration, and perhaps that is why it has attracted, almost from the first, such a wealth of attention from Canadian labour historians. Even when the subject was barely grasped, it was evident that exciting things had happened in the years before the First World War.

An accident of history underlined the significance of political radicalism in British Columbia. The hopelessness of organizing unions against James Dunsmuir and his fellow mining and forestry employers diverted workers to the only arena where their numbers might be made to count: the legislature. A tiny handful of labour and, later, socialist members won election. In the first years of the century, a knife-edge balance between the government of Richard McBride and its opponents gave labour and socialist politicians their chance. The achievements of men like J.H. Hawthornethwaite and Parker Williams persuaded the Toronto socialists to give their allegiance to their energetic Vancouver comrades. For good or ill, the dogmatic and quarrelsome members of Vancouver's Local No. 1 of the new Socialist party of Canada became the heart, soul, and mouthpiece of socialism in Canada.

Early Canadian socialism seemed to cultivate its own political impotence. Its doctrines rested on the literal interpretation of the contradictory teaching of Karl Marx. The working-class socialists of Vancouver, Winnipeg, Toronto, and Montreal were immensely serious, doggedly self-educated, and as immune as they could make themselves to the contradictory and confusing events of their own time. Some followed the arid guidance of the American Marxist, Daniel De Leon; more preferred the passion of Eugene Debs. All were troubled by one major element of the Marxian theory.

Surely Marx had proclaimed a law of historical inevitability. Capitalism was merely a stage, painful and certain to get worse before, as the marvellously archaic language explained, the contradictions became intolerable, the "integument was rent asunder," and the new world could be born. How far, socialists wondered, could historical processes be hastened by the intervention of mere mortals? Could the Second Coming be hurried by earnest Bible-thumping? On the contrary, the revolution might be delayed by successful reformism. If the misery of the proletariat was eased by political reforms or successful trade unionism, the cause of true socialism would not be served. To the disciples of De Leon or to ardent members of the SPC, union leaders were self-evident charlatans, propping up the capitalist order.

If these were beliefs of a tiny sect or of a handful of middle-class intellectuals, socialism would hardly have mattered. In fact, socialist ideas attracted some of the most articulate and effective leaders of Canadian labour. Marx's ideas made sense of their struggles with remote and powerful employers. H. Parm Pettipiece, the brilliant editor who inspired the Western Federation of Miners in interior British Columbia, J.H. McVety, James Watters, Bob Russell, Richard Johns, Jimmy Simpson, John Bruce, Fred Bancroft — men like these were drawn to socialism, and the list goes on and on. In Montreal, Gustave Francq, the scrappy little Belgian atheist and TLC vice-president, was a socialist. So were many more. Yet all of them were also active unionists.

Were they hypocrites? In the eyes of J. Wesley Wrigley or Wilfred Gribble, guardians of the socialist flame, they might be. Yet such men were also in touch with the "toiling masses" for whom the SPC claimed to speak. Socialists routinely denounced the twin heresies of *meliorism* (trying to achieve modest improvements) and *revisionism* (daring to challenge the official version of Marxian canon). Yet could working men and labour leaders stand by when strikes broke out? Some did; most could not. Could they resist the opportunity of election campaigns to spread their message? Would they, if they were Jimmy Simpson and vastly popular with all who knew him, from the Methodists' Epworth League to the Typographers, escape election? Both Left and Right sneered that Simpson lived on the real estate earnings of his wife, but they used his leisure to make him organize the Labour Lyceum, to sit on countless boards and commissions, and to use his reports in the *Star* as rallying propaganda for the cause.

If socialists wanted to leave the narrowness of their Marxist faith, they had the powerful example of Britain, where the socialist wing of the new Labour party managed to combine elected office and ardent support of principle. Keir Hardie, the bearded, saintly Scottish socialist, was a frequent visitor to prewar Canada. He enjoyed assaulting local monarchists with the promise "The King of England will never be blown up by a bomb; he is too insignificant to notice." Hardie even defended suffragette violence, proclaiming: "The Russian people rose in revolution and the whole world applauded them. Why should not the women rise in revolution for the very thing the men in Russia wanted — the vote?" Hardie was one influence; the bald, emotional Eugene Debs was another. From Ontario to British Columbia, the American socialist spoke passionately for his beliefs. The disciples he attracted could sustain their new faith with a subscription to *Appeal to Reason*, a brilliantly written socialist periodical from Kansas, or, more locally, by reading *Cotton's Weekly*, a periodical distributed from Cowansville, Quebec, by a brave, crippled writer named W.B. Cotton.

As a political force in the scattered ranks of Canadian labour, socialism came to matter during the 1900s. Locals of the Socialist party of Canada, sustained by a few valiant, eccentric souls, had spread from coast to coast by the end of the decade. Socialism even claimed a few scattered adherents in New Brunswick, Nova Scotia, and in the wholly autonomous Dominion of Newfoundland. Immigration strengthened its ranks, with newcomers from Britain and, increasingly, from recalcitrant ex-subjects of the Russian czar or the Hapsburg emperor. For a few Canadian union leaders, socialism was a vibrant alternative to the bland labourism of the Platform of Principles or the condescension of Liberal or Tory politicians.

Within the ranks of the Trades and Labour Congress, socialism and labourism were increasingly at odds. In 1906, delegates to the annual TLC convention voted to launch the congress into politics. A cautious executive handed over the responsibility to the provinces. In British Columbia, the only province where labour could conceivably muster real political forces, the attempt to launch a purely labour party was swiftly and effectively sabotaged by the socialists and their allies.

Those allies included a growing number who denounced any form of electoral politics, socialist or labourist. The Industrial Workers of the World (Wobblies),

Local No. 145 of the Western Federation of Miners was the pioneer union organization in Porcupine—later renamed Timmins. The Western Federation had emerged from tough and often bloody struggles in the American Rocky Mountain states to win a foothold in the hardrock mining districts of British Columbia. A colourful and often radical organization, its successor was the International Union of Mine, Mill and Smelter Workers. (United Steelworkers)

formed by remnants of the American Labor Union and the Western Federation of Miners, set out to fight the "pure and simpledom" of Sam Gompers's American Federation of Labor. The Wobblies denounced craft unionism in all its forms and organized on industrial principles. Thanks in part to the plottings of that perennial stormy petrel, Daniel De Leon, the IWW's parents split and the infant almost died. It was rescued when the remaining leaders, chiefly Bill Haywood, sidestepped the socialist ideologues and set out to take the Wobblies directly to the "bindle stiffs" and roving unskilled labour of the American and, by extension, the Canadian West. These were the men who wandered from mines to lumber camps to railway construction or wherever there were labouring jobs. Conditions were often appalling and the treatment as brutal as employers could get away with, but such men were not angels and they could respond, like the Irish canallers of the 1840s, with violence of their own. Certainly the "stiffs" had no commitment to an established order and they would be the last men to settle down to the care and tending of a mortgage. They were, to a romantic eye, the proletarian embodied. That has undoubtedly been their fascination.

Not all theories are invented by philosophers. Big Bill Haywood was fed up with the interminable haggling of the socialists. Surely the suitable weapon for labour was not the ballot but the strike. If all workers were organized, regardless of skill or wage differentials, then workers would control society. Otherwise, by withdrawing their services, they could bring the whole creaking edifice to a halt. Unknown to Haywood, a French thinker and radical named Georges Sorel had come up with a more sophisticated version of the same idea. He also invented a label for this theory of the general strike — *syndicalism*.

Once organized in a huge industrial army, workers need only cease work altogether to command the state and to control capitalist society. The owners and their middle-class allies would be helpless. Not a wheel would turn. There was no need to win power through elections or, for that matter, by armed revolution. In pre-1914 Europe, socialist and labour leaders talked seriously of calling a general strike to prevent the impending world conflict. In North America, Bill Haywood harboured no such grand illusions.

And in Canada, where did the Wobblies stand? As in the United States, they won respect from labour and even some liberals because of their courageous free-speech fights in Victoria, Edmonton, and other western towns, and because they were the first labour organization positively committed to welcoming Oriental members. The openness of the Wobblies to all races and forms of work made them attractive, and the IWW halls in many cities became mail-drops, employment agencies, reading-rooms, and shelters for men on the road. They clearly defended men's dignities more adequately than the rival hostels of the Salvation Army.

However, the IWW in Canada was like the socialists. It might, in quiet times, denounce politics as futile, but when elections came its sympathies were firmly expressed. More seriously, it was an organization with a revolving door. The critics of its organizing principle were in effect right. Transients could not be organized for long or effectively. The greatest Wobblies' strike in Canada, on the Fraser Valley division of the Canadian Northern, lasted almost a year, but it was essentially broken early. While it served to inspire one of Joe Hill's famous labour songs, the outcome was hardly in doubt. The Wobblies survived chiefly to give organized labour a healthy jab of unrespectability. It was, insisted the probusiness *Canadian Annual Review*, "a pestilent body of undefined anarchist principles from the Western States." No more needed to be said.

Compared to the messy turbulence of the West Coast and its occasional incursions in the immigrant-bursting cities and towns blossoming on the Prairies, Atlantic Canada seemed an island of tranquillity. Only in Nova Scotia was there a substantial labour organization in the Provincial Workmen's Association, but it was as eager as ever to earn the respect of its employers and to win modest but continuing gains for its miner members.

Not that history was uneventful in the PWA. The union outlived internal schism over the issue of company stores and external raiding by a last gasp Knights of Labor. Revived under John Moffatt, a new grand secretary, the PWA made a resolution to stick to mining and then, incautiously, reversed itself by accepting the workers in the Sydney mill of the Dominion Steel and Coal Company. The outcome was a disastrous strike in 1904, which cost most of the mill workers their jobs and left the union, at the end of the seven-week struggle, financially broken and discredited.

That was very much how Dominion Steel and Coal wanted it. As one of the innumerable mergers of the period, the company had gradually acquired almost all the coal-mining capacity of Nova Scotia, to say nothing of mills, shipping, and the provincial government. Instead of facing a variety of small employers, the PWA must now deal with a giant. Provided it stayed in its place, made no demands, and kept the men in order, Dominion Steel and Coal was sensible

Soldiers from Halifax spent most of the winter of 1909–10 guarding strike-breakers at the Dominion Coal Company's Cape Breton mines. The experience was so unmemorable that most of the men refused to re-enlist. They, at least, had a choice. For their temerity in supporting the United Mine Workers, most of the strikers lost their jobs, homes, and savings. (Beeton Institute, College of Cape Breton)

enough to be grateful and to express that gratitude in a compulsory checkoff of dues for the union.

Such a situation was tailor-made for a raid by another union, and the ebullient, aggressive United Mine Workers of America were ready for the attempt. With three hundred thousand American members, the UMW was by far the biggest union in the United States and a loyal pillar of the AFL. Faced with the challenge, the PWA leadership fought back. Convinced that the UMW was an evil foreign bully, the Nova Scotia association felt entitled to resort to even highly questionable political and procedural manoeuvring to keep them out. Both the company and provincial government naturally gave their backing, while a majority of the miners, certainly in Cape Breton, wanted a change. A Board of Conciliation and Investigation found for the company and PWA on the grounds that the United Mine Workers was a "foreign organization . . . having power to call sympathetic strikes."

The outcome was one of the longest and most bitter strikes in Canadian history. In Cape Breton, it was a civil war as much as a strike. Because it controlled checkoff, the PWA could insist that men who joined the United Mine Workers be dismissed. Because many miners lived in company-owned houses, strikers and their families were evicted to spend most of the piercingly cold winter of 1909–10 in tents on the barren hills overlooking Sydney and Glace

Bay. Families and friendships were torn apart. To guard the mines and the strike-breakers, most of Canada's small permanent militia was obliged to spend that same dreary winter in Cape Breton. Scores of men were arrested.

Despite the obvious preference of its employees, the Dominion Steel and Coal Company could proclaim its patriotism in fighting the UMW. "Our company will never consent to be dominated by a foreign labour union, whose interests may be allied with those of our competitors in the United States and we will, in the interests of the preservation of our mines and property, in which the people of Nova Scotia are jointly interested with us, stand firmly in the decision." In vain could the UMW insist that its officials had been on hand only to distribute relief or that the strike was controlled from start to finish by Nova Scotians. After a million dollars had been poured into the conflict, the UMW conceded defeat. The company promptly announced its new agreement with the PWA and regretted that, since production was up to 9,000 tons a day, no new employees would be needed.

The story was not finished. In Cape Breton, the support for the United Mine Workers simply went underground. In 1917, under the pretext of creating an entirely new and more effective provincial organization, the key supporters of the UMW captured the miners' leadership. By 1918, the eleven thousand Cape Breton miners were de facto members of the United Mine Workers. The PWA was dead and little lamented.

If the UMW's District No. 26 in Cape Breton had proved a temporary disaster, its District No. 18 had captured the Alberta coalfields from the divided and failing Western Federation of Miners. It was and would remain a district infected with the fashionable western Canadian radicalism. In 1909, it not only declared that Chinese and Japanese must be admitted to membership, proposed to desert the TLC, and denounced the Western Coal Operators' Assocation, but it also announced that it would quit work the moment the contract expired. This threat brought J.E. Morgan of the UMW international board to Fernie to force obedience and a more conciliatory attitude. "In this case," confessed the *Canadian Annual Review*, "internationalism has been the peaceful influence as in Nova Scotia it had been the provocative force."

However, this half-hearted endorsement did not mollify the traditionally hostile mine owners of British Columbia when the United Mine Workers became the latest organization to try to crack the Vancouver Island mines. The outcome was the long and relentless Nanaimo strike of 1913–14, permeated with violence, mass arrests, large contingents of aggressive militia, and a bitterness which did not subside until war broke out in August, 1914.

The radicalism that permeated Canadian labour and finally came to dominate the Trades and Labour Congress, particularly under the presidency of James Watters after 1910, was an expression of frustration and weakness. While numbers of unionists grew impressively during the period, the prevailing impression was one of confrontation. The issue was almost always the same: recognition of a union. Arbitrators, conciliators, and the new machinery of the Industrial Disputes Investigation Act could make little headway with such an issue, and perhaps only rarely did they try. It was enough that the workers should work and be paid. To demand more was to challenge the prerogatives of

During the Vancouver Island coal strike of 1913 – 14, hundreds of miners were rounded up by the militia and herded into barbed-wire concentration camps. Towns like Nanaimo and Ladysmith were under virtual military occupation for almost a year before the outbreak of war in August, 1914, summoned the soldiers elsewhere. When companies could call on the government for soldiers to overawe their workers, why should they negotiate? (Provincial Archives of British Columbia)

Hardrock miners at Kimberly wait for their shift to begin. The mine, originally purchased to bring more business for the CPR's line through the Crowsnest Pass, rapidly became one of the company's most profitable operations. The miners, drawn from veterans of labour battles all over the Pacific Northwest, brought a radical tradition to British Columbia's interior. (United Steelworkers)

capital in an era when capital was not only defended but almost worshipped. That, in itself, could explain the desperate but unfocused radicalism of the few and the futility of the majority.

Members of the Cobalt Miners' Union line up for a chilly procession during the winter of 1913–14. One of the easternmost outposts of the Western Federation of Miners, the Cobalt union helped organize a large number of sister locals across northern Ontario in the period between 1900 and 1920. To succeed, the union had to overcome ancient ethnic and racial hostilities, which were sometimes deliberately exploited by employers. (Ontario Archives — Lawrence Collection)

Workers at Plessisville were part of a rapidly industrializing Quebec. Despite images and myths of a conservative, rural society, French Canada was more urban than English Canada by 1941. (Public Archives Canada. PA 24660)

CHAPTER 11

Labour and the First World War

The four years of the First World War involved Canada in her most drastic period of economic and social change. Hardly an institution or value remained unaffected. The impact of war forced Canadians to accept votes for women, prohibition of liquor, and the income tax. Thanks to a munitions industry that grew from perhaps a thousand workers to more than three hundred thousand men and women, Canada staked her first real claim to become an industrial nation. Wartime inflation and the well-documented evidence of business corruption and profiteering made Canadians more critical than they had been for generations of the philosophy and practices of business.

The war years were as traumatic for Canadian labour as they were for any other sector of society. A prewar depression, beginning in 1912, dragged through the first year of war, decimating union ranks and leaving an army of unemployed that furnished the first huge wave of recruits for the Canadian Expeditionary Force in August, 1914. Slowly, wartime contracts pulled the country out of recession. By 1916, Canada faced a serious labour shortage as munitions factories and CEF recruiters scrambled for manpower. Full employment amidst factory conditions encouraged a massive growth in union membership — from 166,163 in 1914 to 378,047 in 1919.

However, war proved an embittering experience for Canadian workers and for their union leaders. Price increases appeared to outpace wartime wage increases. Official propaganda demanded a total national effort and a sharing of sacrifices, but businessmen managed every significant aspect of Canada's industrial mobilization and they appeared determined that labour would gain nothing from the national struggle. Excluded from consultation and influence, union leaders became increasingly open and virulent enemies of the government of Sir Robert Borden and, in time, of the political system. Radicalism before 1914 had been localized, verbose, and transient. By war's end, the widespread sense of grievance allowed radicals to shatter the unity of the Trades and Labour Congress. A protest movement was born that the traditional, sober, cautious labourism of the congress could not contain.

Radicalism, of course, was not entirely new to labour or to Canada. Prewar May Day rallies drew crowds of thousands in Montreal and Toronto. James Simpson, who had broken with his more doctrinaire socialist comrades when he served on a federal Royal Commission on Technical Education, won a city-wide election to Toronto's Board of Control in 1914. In 1911, delegates to the TLC convention in Calgary deposed William Glockling, a Liberal, and chose J.C. Watters, a British Columbia socialist, as the new president. Seizing on the current touchstone of labour radicalism, the delegates at Calgary also endorsed industrial unionism and called for a general strike in any country contemplating war "so that the workers may see the pitiful exhibition of fighting by those capitalists who seem so fond of it." The same mood led delegates to denounce militarism and the newly arrived Boy Scout movement.

The other feature of the war years, inflation, was also apparent before 1914. The incredible price stability of the nineteenth century gradually vanished, and the causes were as complex as they were much discussed. The wealthy blamed a taste for luxury among the lower orders; the lower orders condemned the greedy profiteering of their masters. In Montreal, the Child Welfare Exhibition Committee determined that an unskilled worker could earn $555.00 a year — by working six days a week, fifty-two weeks a year, without illness or holidays. Provided he spent nothing on drink, entertainment, sickness, furniture, education, church contributions, or savings, such a workaholic paragon could barely provide for a family of five. In Toronto, the *Star* calculated a tight budget that required $931.00 a year, or $17.90 a week. The old familiar wage of $1.00 a day was now equivalent to starvation.

Militancy and inflation combined to increase the number of strikes. In 1912, the government reported the worst record since 1901. Liberals could blame the new Conservative administration. Borden's minister of labour, Thomas Crothers, was a small-town lawyer from western Ontario. Unlike Mackenzie King, Crothers brought little more than a kind of affable ignorance to his portfolio. The TLC met the new government with a blunt demand for repeal of the Lemieux Act, reasoning that the Tories might be willing to eliminate a Liberal law. Crothers ignored the request, lectured British Columbia unionists on the benefits of immigration, and announced to Cape Breton, still seething from the 1909–10 strike, that he found "a contented and comfortable people with entire agreement between employers and employed." No wonder that even Crothers's colleagues took no notice of him.

When war came on August 4, 1914, Canada was emotionally, economically, and militarily unprepared for what would follow. The declaration of hostilities came at the end of a hot holiday weekend. Canadians stumbled into weeks of anxiety, euphoria, improvisation, and confusion. Colonel Sam Hughes, the strutting militarist who served as Canada's minister of militia, scrapped careful

The Working Class Candidate ~1917

Vote

SIMPSON for CONTROLLER

It was not a good year for working-class candidates. Despite his ardent socialism, Jimmy Simpson's personal charm and wide connections with Methodist and temperance forces had won him a city-wide election to Toronto's Board of Control for 1914, but labour's wartime opposition to conscription outraged the city's patriots. Trade union ventures into politics in 1917 virtually all failed—except for a handful of candidates who waved the flag and backed the government. (Author's collection)

mobilization plans and personally organized an expeditionary force from more than thirty thousand Canadians brought by train to a camp near Quebec City. For many of them, hunger had rivalled patriotism as a recruiting sergeant.

At Guelph in 1912 and Quebec in 1913, the Trades and Labour Congress repeated its 1911 resolution against war, but so had labour and socialist organizations in most of the powers that found themselves at war. Those who preached a general strike against war found, to their chagrin, that workers had joined the packed, cheering throngs that greeted the war news in most European capitals. Both the French and British governments acted early in the war to bring union leaders and socialist politicians into at least a consultative role, recognizing however dimly that the war would demand a total national effort. No such consultation occurred in Canada. Meeting in September, 1914, the TLC dropped its antiwar sentiments, pledged its loyalty, and drew the line only against any form of conscription. Since Sam Hughes had loudly proclaimed that no conscript would be allowed in the CEF and that a married man needed his wife's permission to enlist, the TLC position was hardly controversial.

Neither Borden nor his labour minister paid any heed to the British and French example. Besieged by swarms of businessmen seeking contracts and colonelcies, it never occurred to the prime minister that organized labour had the slightest claim to be consulted on wartime policies or problems. Certainly, in the first year and a half of the war, few unions were in any position to assert

When leaders of the Trades and Labour Congress met in Vancouver in 1915, their opposition to the war effort had wilted badly in the light of union members' obvious willingness to enlist and to support patriotic appeals. Most of the smiles were rather forced. The four key figures were, second from the left: *Gustave Francq (Montreal), Jimmy Simpson (Toronto), Paddy Draper (Ottawa), and James Watters (Vancouver). (Public Archives Canada C 53612)*

Members of the painter's union, Local No. 732, proudly marched down Winnipeg's Portage Avenue on Labour Day, 1914. Winnipeg unionists faced suspicious employers and their own disputes about radical and moderate tactics, but they also lived in Canada's richest, fastest-growing city. Despite a depression and a war that would surely be over by Christmas, men of the building trades could feel plenty of confidence that September. (Manitoba Archives)

either radical or economic demands. Some local unions were decimated when their members enlisted in the CEF or returned to their British homeland. Others fell victim to an economic slump, which grew sharply worse when the outbreak of war further disrupted business. Between 1913 and 1915, union strength in Canada fell by 20 percent, and 134 locals ceased to exist.

Canadian manufacturers had been confident that the war would bring fresh orders and profits. Unfortunately, the ill-designed, shabbily produced uniforms, equipment, and weapons of Canada's soldiers did nothing to encourage Britain to place orders in Canada. Neither did the flurry of promoters and confidence men, often armed with endorsements from Canada's minister of militia, who descended on wartime capitals. In an early move, Hughes mustered cronies, confidants, and metal fabricators in a Shell Committee, primed to bid for British artillery contracts. When eventually the orders came, the performance was shameful. Inexperienced and incompetent manufacturers, more avid for profits than productivity, failed to deliver. Politicians insisted on spreading the contracts to a host of tiny enterprises, few of them competent to fulfil their promises. By the end of 1915, Britain's new Ministry of Munitions refused to give Canada any more work until the munitions industry was totally reorganized. The outcome was an Imperial Munitions Board, a British agency operating solely in Canada under Canadian officials and staff but immune from Canadian political interference.

The new board was not an immediate success; old problems and jealousies took months to clear away. Nevertheless, under the management of Joseph Flavelle, a Canadian businessman who had made his fortune in the tough, competitive bacon export business, the board worked through its problems. By 1917, the board had become an effective and even efficient enterprise employing more than three hundred thousand Canadians, sixty thousand of them women.

For Canadian organized labour, however, the Imperial Munitions Board became an early enemy. In 1900, in the wake of Mackenzie King's revelations about the sweat-shop conditions in which government uniforms were manufactured, Ottawa had agreed to a fair-wage clause in future federal contracts. With the wartime profusion of government contracts, Crothers spent much of his time in feeble efforts to remind ministerial colleagues of the order. Flavelle, pointing to the fact that his was a British organization, deliberately ignored fair-wage provisions. The British, who had a similar rule, refused to enforce it in Canada. The truth was that Flavelle, like other senior businessmen who dominated Canada's war effort, had no intention of conceding anything to union demands. Workers, he declared, should be glad of a job.

As chairman of the Imperial Munitions Board, Flavelle was as furious at greedy, inefficient manufacturers as he was contemptuous of trade unions. However, there was a distinction. As an employer and manager, he regarded union leaders as meddling busybodies. As Canada's labour surplus turned into a serious shortage, the IMB pressed for dilution of its skilled metal workers by women. Employers and even some of the board's staff resisted such a shocking innovation, but the most vehement resistance could be expected from the craft unions. *Dilution* was a threat to strict apprenticeship rules and hard-earned skills.

Loading cordite charges into the brass cartridge case was a delicate but unsophisticated job. Although shell manufacturing gave Canada experience in large-scale manufacturing, it did very little to improve the technological potential of the country's branch plant industry. Generous profit margins made big fortunes for contractors, but the benefits were rarely plowed back in new plants or more efficient processes. Low quality often hurt Canada's manufacturing reputation. (Public Archives Canada PA 24562)

Women factory workers were nothing new in Canada but handling a drill press or a lathe had always been men's work. The Imperial Munitions Board hired a special adviser to help it attract women employees and even ordered press censorship of any incident that might have harmed its image. More that thirty thousand of the IMB's quarter-million employees were women. (Ontario Archives)

For the Maid, Here Are Uniforms, Smartly Efficient

In Striped Galatea, Blue Percale and Black Alpaca, They Are Trim and Well Cut.

A. Cool blue percale with comfortable open neck would be excellent as a morning working frock. A pocket and white pearl buttons down the front make it practical and easy to get into. The same model can also be had in Oxford grey and pink. Sizes 34 to 44. Price, $3.50.

B. The regulation black alpaca with white collar and cuffs. This, with a dainty white apron, is the smart and pleasant person that opens the front door of an afternoon. Sizes 34 to 44. Price, $6.95.

C. A workaday dress of striped galatea that is also admirable while the morning duties are going on in a well-ordered household. Sizes 34 to 44. Price, $3.75.

One group of workers particularly affected by job opportunities in the wartime munitions factories were domestic servants. Apart from low pay, long hours, few holidays, and tyrannical mistresses, most of the horrors of being a housemaid are neatly summarized in this advertisement. (Mail & Empire, 1916)

The major union in the growing munitions industry was the International Association of Machinists, a once-conservative craft union going through a radical phase. Flavelle's main weapon against unionization was the Lemieux Act, formally extended to all munitions factories in March, 1916. Strikes that were not preceded by the long process of investigation and arbitration would now be illegal. The Machinists had other grievances, from failure to uphold the fair-wage clause to a strong suspicion that the IMB kept a blacklist of union activists.

The inevitable confrontation developed in Hamilton. Whatever its past history as a labour town, Hamilton's employers were among the most harshly anti-union in Canada. One IAM member, reporting his employer's response to the union demands, explained, "We went in and he asked us if we were in about that 'thing', pointing to our schedule, and when we replied that we were, he said that we must be in the pay of the Kaiser, and that the men who drew it up should be decorated with an iron cross." Faced by a stubbornness from Hamilton employers and from Colonel Frederic Nicholls of Canadian General Electric in Toronto, the government ordered Judge Colin Snyder to investigate. Snyder bluntly endorsed the IAM's demands. A strike was unavoidable.

The union itself tried to prevent the stoppage. IAM officials pleaded desperately with their members to stay calm — and were furiously denounced by Hamilton newspapers for stirring up trouble. Even Flavelle advised employers to accept Judge Snyder's report. Crothers urged Flavelle to cut off orders to the Hamilton plants. That was going too far for Flavelle. A walkout ensued.

For the Machinists, it was a disaster. By insisting on following strict legal processes, union leaders had forfeited the confidence of their members. At the same time, the IAM officials were denounced as "paid labour agitators." An employers' association advertised for workers, but Flavelle invoked government censorship to prevent the union from publicizing its case. Only the *Industrial Banner*, published by Jimmy Simpson, defied the ban, but it preached only to the existing sympathizers. By the end of July, 1916, Hamilton munitions plants were back in full production and the striking machinists had drifted elsewhere. Their only ally, the Amalgamated Society of Engineers, had withdrawn from the strike on curt orders from its British head office.

The Hamilton machinists' strike confirmed the foul relations between Canada's labour leaders and the IMB and Borden government. Crothers was further discredited with cabinet colleagues and the TLC. In 1917, Mark Irish, a Conservative M.P.P. from Ontario, joined the IMB to help with labour relations, but his chief role was securing more attractive conditions and opportunities for women munition workers. Across Canada, thoughtful employers filed away some important lessons. However strong their grievances, craft-based unions could be isolated and destroyed. Skillful propaganda, of the type the Hamilton employers had distributed, could win public sympathy for business.

While the war continued, the Hamilton defeat could be absorbed. Skilled machinists could easily find other work. Union membership continued to grow. However, the same manpower shortage that made jobs available posed a growing threat to the overall rights and freedom of Canadian workers.

The appalling casualty lists of 1916, combined with Sam Hughes's silly

The Women's Lunch Room at the British Munitions Supply Company in Verdun, Quebec. Despite the spartan atmosphere, such special facilities were considered unusually generous by Canadian employers. The Verdun factory, owned by the IMB, saw itself as setting an example of enlightened conditions. It was part of the price of attracting women workers. The cost was offset by women's lower wages. (Public Archives Canada PA 24439)

recruiting policies, left the CEF increasingly desperate for men. Sir Robert Borden's promise, almost casually included in his New Year's message for 1916, that Canada would send half a million men to the field, could only be honoured by some form of conscription. To that prospect, the Trades and Labour Congress was publicly and inalterably opposed. It might forget its opposition to capitalist war, but since its 1915 convention it was committed to "unchangeable opposition to all that savours of conscription either here or in the empire."

The government tried a compromise. A National Service Board under a Calgary Tory, R.B. Bennett, organized a national registration based on all adult males submitting a postcard. Union leaders were divided. In the West, not even a visit from Borden or Bennett could soften the opposition. In Ottawa, assured by the prime minister that this was not the first step to conscription, J.C. Watters and the TLC executive gave an official endorsement. Besides, Watters reported, the government had promised that, henceforth, wealth would "bear its due proportion of contributions and sacrifices in the war."

Unfortunately for Watters and his colleagues, the westerners were right. After

Put in those terms, no wonder soldiers voted for Sir Robert Borden's Union government. Labour leaders tended to forget that most Canadian soldiers were workers too, and that they wanted solidarity from their fellow-country men. They also wanted a fair deal from the government and help in finding postwar jobs. Canada's unions missed an opportunity when they showed little interest in the problems of returned soldiers. (Public Archives Canada PA 8158)

a long and agonizing visit to Britain and France in the spring of 1917, Borden returned convinced that he could not keep faith with the CEF without imposing overseas conscription. On May 18, 1917, he announced his military service bill. Betrayed and discredited, the TLC leadership immediately made common cause with the western militants. In June, affiliates and non-affiliates alike were summoned to a special congress meeting to lambaste the Borden government, the IMB, and other labour enemies, and to swear resistance to conscription. Only five of the eighty unions represented dissented.

Labour's protests had no more impact on Borden's conscription policies than they had had on Sir Joseph Flavelle. When he formed his Union Government of Tories and proconscription Liberals in October, 1917, Borden ignored the congress and appointed Gideon Robertson, vice-president of the Order of Railway Telegraphers, and two other officials from the highly conservative Brotherhood of Locomotive Engineers to be the government's advisers on organized labour. By no means the labour Quisling of some portrayals, Robertson was a fair representative for a good many older, paunchy unionists. Neither he nor his union had ever joined the TLC.

Snubbed by the appointment of Robertson, the TLC leadership turned to the painful task of opposing conscription. Against heavy bombardment from virtually all of Canada's English-language press, the labour leaders could offer only the shrill, radical voices of their western members. "If I have to shed my blood," proclaimed Fred Dixon in Winnipeg, "I would prefer to do it here where I know it would be for freedom." When the congress met in convention, it reluctantly voted 134 to 101 that it would not try to resist the implementation of the Military Service Act. Immediately, it was the target for a furious blast from the *B.C. Federationist.* "There is nothing at present in common between the labour movement of the east and that of the west . . . The labour movement of the east is reactionary and servile to the core . . . If there has been any advance and progressive thought, it has, as a rule, come forth from the west . . ."

This was a stirring claim and most of the 101 dissenters had come from British Columbia and the Prairies. Unfortunately, it was easier to find leaders than followers in the anticonscription campaign. For all the trumpeted hostility of western union leaders and their newspapers to the government's policies, western compliance was perhaps even more complete than elsewhere. Western radical and labour leaders could preach a doctrine of brotherhood and reform unfashionable in wartime; official records are spotted with demands from humbler westerners for the internment of foreign competitors for their jobs.

The 1917 election gave Canadian labour its first real opportunity to test its strength at the ballot box. Nowhere were expectations higher nor the results correspondingly more humiliating than in the West. Even with endorsement from Laurier Liberals, none did better than the Reverend William Irvine in Calgary, with 32 percent of the vote. R.A. Rigg, who resigned his seat in the Manitoba legislature, won only 26 percent in Winnipeg North. In Winnipeg Centre, which four years later went solidly labour, R.S. Ward did not win a single poll.

The TLC involvement in the 1917 election was necessarily hurried and almost wholly unfinanced. Outside British Columbia and Alberta, it could not turn to organized provincial federations. In Ontario, a Labour Educational Association, founded in 1903 for more tranquil purposes, was forced into service. Led by Jimmy Simpson, London's Joseph Marks, and Sam Hughes's radical niece, Laura Hughes, the LEA did its utmost. Walter Rollo served as party leader and won 30 percent of the votes in his Hamilton constituency. In Temiskaming, Arthur Roebuck, a young lawyer, ran as both Liberal and Labour and won 40 percent. Elsewhere, anticonscription labour candidates failed miserably.

The truth was that Canadian workers had heard both national and union leaders. While the war continued, patriotism would come first. In the United States, where the AFL had become a full partner in the war effort from the moment of declaration, Sam Gompers had been transformed into an influential and even popular national figure. Amidst Canada's wartime election campaign, the American union leader descended on Ottawa and Toronto, deposited $10,000 of AFL money in Canadian war bonds, and lectured Canadian unionists on their patriotic duty. In some eyes, Gompers's interference was unforgiveable, but the old union chief knew where real support lay. So did some of labour's own candidates. Several hurriedly endorsed conscription, and one of them, Charles Harrison in Nipissing, was elected as a Unionist.

Industrial action had failed at Hamilton in 1916. Political action had proved disastrous almost everywhere in 1917. What tactics remained? The question was put and answered most clearly in the West. Even in advance, the western radicals had predicted failure for the TLC's election tactics. If Ontario had been keen on them, it must be because Ontario unionists were either raw or reactionary. The West's answer must be more radical and uncompromising.

By 1918, the consequences of a dramatic struggle in Russia were slowly becoming apparent around the world. The ancient, hideous tyranny of the Romanovs had come tumbling down. A compromising, corrupt, middle-class regime had followed it to the scrap-heap within months. The Bolsheviks had triumphed. Accurate details were desperately scarce. Yet it was apparent that the workers had seized power and the results, at least from a distance, looked admirable. Westerners might perhaps be excused a mildly perfervid view of their own situation. All around them, the established order seemed to be flailing and failing to keep order.

In the East, when a prominent Toronto socialist, Isaac Bainbridge, was arrested for sedition, even Magistrate Denison felt compelled to release him for lack of evidence. For Ginger Goodwin, fiery vice-president of the British Columbia Federation of Labour, there was no such legality. Near the mining town of Cumberland, he was caught as a draft dodger and shot — allegedly while trying to escape. In Vancouver, a mob of soldiers smashed the premises of the Vancouver Labour Council, dragged the secretary, Victor Midgley, into the street, and forced him to kneel and kiss the Union Jack.

Throughout Canada, organized labour grew in numbers and frustration as the war continued. Almost alone among the Allied powers, the Canadian government had refused to take labour into its confidence. Left outside as a faction, it behaved factiously. Whatever its occasional claims, Sir Robert Borden's administration expected Canadian workers to be obedient, respectful, self-sacrificing backers of a war effort that was all too plainly making some people very rich. Working-class families contributed most of Canada's sixty thousand dead. Canada's overseas forces confirmed and accentuated the barriers between classes. While other politicians almost automatically became captains and colonels, Winnipeg's R.A. Rigg enlisted as a private after his 1917 defeat. He returned from the war a corporal. At home, soldiers' families lived on charity from the Patriotic Fund while the government reluctantly adopted a timid wartime income tax on the rich.

The foundations of postwar bitterness were well built.

CHAPTER 12

Western Revolt

The final year of the First World War was remorselessly dreary. Organized labour had been humiliated by the failure of its pathetic resistance to conscription. Farmers were furious when the exemptions for their sons were cancelled in March, 1918, just when the boys would be needed on the land. News from the front was grim as German offensives rolled back the Allied lines. Wartime economies had far outlasted the dire prophecies of 1914, but the strains were now almost unbearable.

Despair and defeatism were apparent in the rash of strikes and disruptions which marked the year. Sir Joseph Flavelle and his fellow industrialists insisted that the most patriotic men had long since enlisted. His labour relations manager, Mark Irish, cursed "the cupidity of the manufacturer and the stupidity of the workman" with equal force. In fact, workers were now believing the message of their leaders that war sacrifices had not been shared equally, even in the great cause of "saving the world for democracy." The highly publicized profiteering of Flavelle's bacon-exporting business became a universal public symbol for all the claims, real and fancied, of injustice and mismanagement.

Everywhere war had encompassed workers with restrictions. Perhaps only their leaders worried when socialist and radical organizations were banned in mid-summer and when foreign-language newspapers were first ordered to print in English and then, under patriotic fire, were closed altogether. A government Order in Council banned strikes in July, and Sir Robert Borden boasted of the joy his "Anti-Loafing Law" had given him. Both orders had little real effect, but they were symptomatic of a billowing flood of regulations and restrictions, which even some judges refused to enforce.

Paradoxically, the growth of regulations was accompanied by increasing defiance of government and corporate authority. The year 1918 was one of strikes and many of them were successful. The reasons were obvious. Inflation had boosted prices 40–60 percent and, in the workers' view, had been even more extortionate. In the wake of a century of price and wage stability, inflation was particularly unsettling. Nervous employers, under pressure to deliver, were often compelled to be conciliatory. David Bercuson gives convincing evidence that munition workers' wages in the metal trades — by far the most militant — kept well ahead of inflation during the war years. In 1918, both Labour Day and the civic holiday were conceded for the first time since 1914. Universal prohibition of liquor prevented serious absenteeism the next day or the morning-after productivity losses which normally followed holidays.

Nowhere were tempers higher in 1918 than in the Canadian West. It was perhaps only a continuation of the militancy which had been evident from the turn of the century and which had even captured the TLC presidency for J.L. Watters since 1911. The tough labour radicals who fought for the IWW and the SPC met employers who were just as hard and ruthless. For them and their workers, the West had been a land of opportunity, and there were some similarities between R.B. Russell, the Glasgow-bred machinist and socialist who emerged as the eloquent leader of the Metal Trades Council in Winnipeg, and local employers like T.R. Deacon, the self-made engineer, or the Barrett brothers of the Vulcan Iron Works.

While membership in the International Association of Machinists grew in the munitions factories, other trades and occupations, particularly in the public sector, also organized. For the first time, policemen, firemen, clerks, telephone operators, elevator hands, and other such categories joined unions en masse to press for bonuses and pay increases to match inflation.

To Flavelle and the Imperial Munitions Board, the West had been a nuisance from the start, demanding and receiving munitions contracts purely for political and regional reasons, delivering slowly, poorly, and at high cost. Winnipeg ranked thirtieth among cities where contracts were placed. One problem was labour conflict. In 1906, Vulcan Iron Works, Deacon's Manitoba Bridge and Iron Works, and other contract shops had beaten unions with a ruthless combination of lawsuits against leaders and injunctions against picketing, and the technique was adopted by other Winnipeg employers, like F.W. Woolworth. On May 1, 1917, yet another round of this struggle was started and lost by R.B. Russell. The presence of a reform-minded Liberal government under T.C. Norris made no difference to the rules of the game.

The militancy of western labour leaders and radical leaders, in contrast to that in eastern Canada, was an obvious consequence of the losing struggle western workers had often waged against their employers, to say nothing of the suspicion that the West might be the last stop for the discontented and the utopian. In turn, the extremism of their language and tactics created a class rift already visible long before the events of 1919 exposed it to national view. When labour M.L.A.'s in Manitoba like R.A. Rigg and F.J. Dixon were vilified and, in one case, savagely beaten for their anticonscription stand, there was no need to invent a class war.

With a banner urging workers of the world to unite, members of Local No. 23 of the
Social-Democratic party of Canada meet in Transcona, outside Winnipeg. The prosperous citizens of
Winnipeg's south end were convinced that groups like this were responsible for the turbulence that
culminated in the 1919 general strike. In fact, Ukrainian and other non-English-speaking groups
had little contact with the city's labour movement. (Public Archives Canada WS 31)

During 1918, after years of defeat and frustration, some Canadian workers
won victories which suggested the merits of fresh tactics. In April, a dispute
between the Winnipeg city council and some of its employees burst into a strike.
As city opinion makers debated the right of public servants to strike, other city
workers and soon thousands in private employment joined the strike in
sympathy. Employers and civic leaders divided before the threat. From Ottawa,
on Borden's orders, came Senator Gideon Robertson, the government's new
labour voice. With a Citizen's Committee of 100 serving as conciliatory representative of respectable Winnipeg, Robertson produced a settlement. In turn,
this apparent triumph of sympathetic strike tactics discredited moderates in the
city's labour council like the aging Arthur Puttee. Militancy obviously worked.

The lesson was confirmed in July when the Letter Carriers' Union struck the
Post Office. While the strike in the East was soon ended, the postmaster general
and Crothers had to come all the way to Winnipeg and make fresh concessions
before western postmen would go back. It was another triumph for militancy. In

Ottawa, it was Crothers's downfall and Robertson's chance. For the first time, Canada had a trade unionist as minister of labour. There were other strikes. One of Robertson's first duties was to mediate a shipbuilding strike against IMB contractors in British Columbia. To the outrage of R.B. Butchart, a West Coast employer who called Robertson "unprincipled, a liar and worthless," the workers got parity with American workers. So did Canadian shopcraft workers in Division No. 4 of the Railway Employees' Department of the AFL. The Canadian workers were given the same wage settlement as U.S. railroaders to avert a strike. In Winnipeg and the West, however, the concession that gave Canadians the American "McAdoo Award" seemed inadequate. They felt themselves freshly aggrieved even by parity. Their appetite seemed uncontrolled.

Not every struggle was a victory. Russell's Machinists had a new battle with the Winnipeg employers in August, 1918, and a fresh defeat. However, Russell could place the blame on a labour member of an investigating commission. By condemning Russell and the union for striking while the investigation was in progress, the labour representative had betrayed the workers. Another respected moderate was deposed.

When the Trades and Labour Congress met in Quebec City in September, both the East and the West were ready. Instead of welcoming the westerners, the easterners treated them as tiresome nuisances whose power over the congress must end. Denounced as a sellout by fellow westerners, Watters was defeated, but the victor was Tom Moore, a Niagara Falls carpenter and proven moderate. When Bob Russell challenged Paddy Draper for the secretary-treasurership, he was trounced. The westerners faced defeat in resolution after resolution. Finally, before they left for home, they met in caucus under Dave Rees, an Alberta UMW official, to lick their wounds and plot a comeback. They would meet in Calgary in March, not to break from the TLC but to plan for a radical comeback.

Before March, much happened. On November 11, the Germans accepted an armistice and, eventually, a one-sided imposed Allied peace settlement. For the Borden government, peace only brought fresh crises. Half a million soldiers and three hundred thousand munition workers must somehow be found other work. A huge debt and the cost of more than sixty thousand dead and as many permanently disabled veterans must be absorbed by a country of less than eight million. Returning soldiers were unsettled, impatient, difficult. As during the war, they could turn against socialist agitators, and many of them carried on a bitter vendetta against the so-called enemy aliens. However, they wanted jobs, incomes, security, excitement, a rich bonus payment, and appreciation. Once the cheering was over, they found themselves regarded as troublesome strangers.

Some soldiers were also suspected of bringing home the "bacillus" of bolshevism. Certainly it entered the country in some form, although any accurate information about the Russian Revolution and its aftermath was scarce to non-existent. Radicals apparently believed that the "soviets," or committees, which allegedly ran Russia, were formed out of the unions. This, in turn, provided a fine working model to those unionists who had exhausted their patience with elections and preferred syndicalism. Windy theorizing, whether syndicalist or socialist, mattered to very few, but it provided slogans for steadier working men and food for the terror of middle-class alarmists.

Radicals of all kinds were on hand in Calgary on March 13 when the Western Labour Conference convened in the little labour temple. By then the idea behind David Rees's small caucus was long since supplanted by a core of radicals. Far from plotting tactics within the TLC, the goal of men like Jack Kavanagh and R.J. Johns (chairmen of the resolutions and policy committees respectively), Victor Midgley, William Pritchard, Joe Knight, and Bob Russell was to create a wholly new industrial union structure. To help win their point, Midgley arranged for the annual convention of the British Columbia Federation of Labour to be held in Calgary just before the conference. That guaranteed a tough core of supporters. Others did their bit. Of 239 delegates, only 2 came from Ontario.

The conference was completely managed, and some delegates, like Elmer Roper, later CCF leader in Alberta, were indignant at being railroaded. Such scruples troubled a minority. Among the resolutions was a call for a nation-wide vote for a national general strike to demand a six-hour day and five-day week as a measure against postwar unemployment. Other resolutions denounced censorship, upheld the Bolsheviks, and called for an end to government by Order in Council. A major resolution, sprung on delegates and hurriedly passed, was a

Left

*Symptomatic of a world turned upside down after the 1914–18 war was the horrifying discovery that both policemen and housemaids would consider joining unions. Despite the benign view taken by Marland, a Toronto cartoonist, respectable opinion took a dim view of any organization of the twin pillars of middle-class security. The formation of police unions in Quebec City, Winnipeg, and other cities led to mass dismissals. Maids' unions never really got started. (*Mail & Empire)

Right

Another business response to the unusual labour militancy of the postwar years was strike insurance. Since Canadians were already one of the most insurance-conscious people anywhere, why not add a new form? (*Mail & Empire)

W.MARLAND 1919

CRUSH IT.

The Toronto Mail & Empire's *cartoonist offered Canadian unions some familiar advice in 1919. In fact, there was almost nobody in Canada at the time who knew what bolshevism was about, although there was a growing number prepared to believe that it must have some merits if it had such enemies. The Trades and Labour Congress had, in fact, crushed its own radical wing at the 1918 convention but earned no rewards for its efforts. (*Mail & Empire)*

call for a referendum to lay the foundation for a new labour organization to secede from the AFL and the international unions. The details would be worked out by a central committee led by Johns, Midgley, Pritchard, Knight, and Joe Naylor of Cumberland.

The new organization, already to be known as the One Big Union, would not exist for some months while the referendum and the planning continued. Only one condition was imposed — political involvement by the new body would be superfluous. This was absurd. Farmers and the rest of the union movement were more engaged in politics than ever, and, in 1919, major gains would be made in Ontario and Alberta. The Calgary radicals opposed the tide, infuriated or worried socialists and moderates alike, and did not, in the event, keep to their own doctrine. Most would run in elections in a couple of years. The reason for the position was a triumph of syndicalist theory among men who barely understood it. It was also a typical gesture by the Socialist party of Canada, which included Johns, Knight, Kavanagh, and Russell. Theirs was a chiliastic faith. The great revolution was coming; there was no need to encourage it. To create a militant and class-conscious union would be enough.

There was another problem, afterwards soon apparent. The rhetoric and the organization at Calgary in March concealed profound differences among the sponsoring leaders, and equally profound confusions. Did they want to follow the Wheel of Fortune model suggested by Father Haggerty, the American labour agitator, and transmitted via the Australian One Big Union? Midgley and Pritchard tried their own hand at an organizational plan and gave it up. Did the Canadian OBU plan to supplant older organizations? Midgley said no. Carl Berg, a fiery Edmonton syndicalist, published a local OBU bulletin to prove that all the past would be swept away. Embarrassed SPCers found that they were among the moderates.

The trouble was that time did not stand still to allow the western labour philosophers to spin their plans. Across Canada and chiefly in the West, workers were restless and worried. Inflation continued. The returned men demanded jobs. Where were the gains working people had expected for their sacrifices? In Winnipeg, the building trades' council pressed wage demands on the employers. Rebuffed, they planned a strike. In the metal trades, employers would not even meet with the workers' representatives, who were intent on a resumption of the old hostilities. There was only one answer: a strike. By the beginning of May, both groups were prepared to walk out. On May 2, the building trades struck.

However, thanks to the 1918 experience, it seemed logical for both groups to ask for the kind of help that had worked for the civic workers. The Winnipeg Trades and Labour Council, its moderates in the discard, was easily persuaded. On May 6, the council voted to poll its affiliates. A week later, the results were announced — eleven thousand for the strike, five hundred opposed. At 11:00 a.m., Thursday, May 15, 1919, the Winnipeg General Strike began.

The goal was obvious and the tactics appeared to be brilliantly successful. Though the city boasted perhaps twelve thousand card-carrying unionists, between twenty-five and thirty thousand workers obeyed the strike call, from operators for the government telephone system to militant mailmen, from teamsters and delivery men to firemen and employees at the waterworks. The police would have come out, but the strike committee urged them to stay on duty. Only the leaders were divided. Russell and Johns were angry that the strike would pre-empt their own organizing work. It was premature. George Armstrong, a socialist, felt that it was all wrong in principle. As official leaders, they could show no hesitation. As the best speakers and most respected unionists in the city, their role was at the head of the laughing, joking strikers, convinced in their own minds that a day or two would make the city's employers see reason.

Normally, they might have been right. However, the city's leaders, particularly in business and on the city council, had vowed that the 1918 humiliation would never be repeated. An organization called the Citizens' Committee of 1000 rapidly emerged. Unlike its conciliatory predecessor, the new committee was bent on organizing resistance, providing essential services, and demonstrating, once and for all, who ruled Winnipeg.

To the strike committee, hurriedly formed by the labour council, that was not at issue. Its main concern was to keep the peace and prevent provocation. It avoided any production of banners, badges, or buttons. "Do nothing," ordered its newspaper. "Just eat, sleep, play, love, laugh, and look at the sun." With Winnipeg entering its hottest spring in recent memory, strikers headed for the

Leaders of the Winnipeg General Strike deliberately refused to organize pickets and processions for fear of provoking a clash with authority or with strike opponents. Instead, they ordered supporters to go to the parks and enjoy the unusually hot spring weather. Orators like R.E. Bray, a returned soldier, provided some of the entertainment for bored, restless workers. (Manitoba Archives)

Special constables are sworn in at Winnipeg. The decision of the City Council, urged on by the Citizens' Committee, to dismiss the police force gave an opportunity for those who had been yearning to crush the strike with physical violence. The passions and prejudices have been recorded in Douglas Durkin's novel, The Magpie. *(Public Archives Canada WS 1650)*

Gideon Robertson served as minister of labour in the Union government and returned briefly in the 1930s. He was typical of the solid, dignified leaders who rose to lead the older craft unions. Proud of their skill and even prouder of the wealthy and influential friends they made, men like Robertson had no understanding of the impatient radicals of western Canada (Public Archives Canada PA 33996)

parks and away from the growing stench of uncollected garbage.

While the official government of the city and of Manitoba did little, offering mediation only if all the workers went back to their jobs, the Citizens' Committee played an increasingly active part. So did the strike committee. To protect vital services, the strikers issued letters and placards to prove that workers were not betraying the strike. In turn, these assertions of strike committee authority were seized on by hysterical critics as evidence that the strikers were pretending to govern Winnipeg. A selection of labour leaders' speeches could be offered to prove that men like Russell, Bill Ivens, and others would not think it a bad idea.

Two groups particularly mattered in the developing propaganda war: the returned men and the large foreign-born population of north Winnipeg. The veterans probably split evenly between the sides, but their common desire was for action and excitement. They wanted parades, demonstrations, and perhaps a fight, and the strike committee could not curb them while the Citizens' Committee hardly tried. On the other hand, the "enemy aliens" took little or no part in any phase of the strike. Some were active in socialist and radical organizations, but all of them became victims as the Citizens' Committee portrayed the conflict as the work of conspiratorial foreigners out to destroy the institutions of their adopted country. It was an effective if shabby technique for drawing support away from the strike, particularly among returned soldiers. It did not help that the returning Fort Garry Horse marched through the streets amidst jeering prostrike crowds, convinced that the men were sent to fight them. In fact, like other overseas units, the cavalrymen marched to their armouries and immediately disbanded.

Two events precipitated both violence and the end of the strike. In Ottawa, the Borden government hurried through legislation drastically increasing both the extent and the penalties for the crime of sedition, and warrants were made out for the arrest of strike leaders. The other event was the dismissal of the city's police force for its prostrike leaning and its immediate replacement by a large crowd of untrained but enthusiastic special constables mobilized by the Citizens' Committee. The first result was an inconclusive riot on June 10. On June 17, before dawn, twelve supposed strike leaders were seized and hurried to a jail outside the city. Six were "aliens," none of them really connected with the strike, two were aldermen, one a returned soldier, and three (Russell, Johns, and Pritchard) had to varying degrees tried to avoid the affair. Johns, who had been absent raising funds, was arrested on his return; one man escaped.

Winnipeg labour was outraged. On Saturday, June 21, prostrike veterans defied the mayor's ban on parades and filled the street in front of City Hall. A streetcar was stopped and its windows shattered. A contingent of Royal North-West Mounted Police formed at the south end of Main Street, charged into the crowd, and repeatedly, sometimes firing revolvers, worked to clear the streets. An army of special constables backed them up and drove the crowd into back streets. By late afternoon, downtown Winnipeg was deserted. Two civilians were dead or dying; dozens were arrested; almost a hundred on both sides bore injuries. Winnipeg labour would remember June 21 as Bloody Saturday.

The strike was nearly over. New editors, Fred Dixon and the Reverend J.S. Woodsworth, took over the strike newspaper and commented on "Kaiserism in Winnipeg." They promptly joined the other strike leaders in jail. On June 25, the forty-second day of the strike, it was over. Its leaders facing trial, its members hungry and penniless, the Winnipeg Trades and Labour Congress surrendered.

The defeat in Winnipeg changed much. The myth of the general strike as a practical labour weapon died almost before it was born. Sympathetic strikes in other western cities flickered briefly and went out. Only in Toronto and in Vancouver was the attempt seriously carried through, but the consequence was a devastating and humiliating defeat in both centres. In the midst of the Winnipeg conflict, the would-be leaders of the OBU finally met in Calgary, this time in great secrecy. The referendum had been almost all they could have wished. The role of the internationals and of the TLC during the Winnipeg conflict — doing their utmost to bring their members and affiliates back to duty — was further ammunition for OBU speakers. However, even if the differences and the dilemmas could have been solved, the OBU leaders had not done so, and the new organization was launched amidst substantial confusion among leaders and followers alike about its organization, tactics, and relationships with existing unions.

As a result, the One Big Union lasted about a year as an effective organization, growing like a mushroom among frustrated, humiliated western workers and

Mounted police break into a gallop as they charge down Winnipeg's Main Street. The crowd, gathered in holiday mood on Saturday, June 21, 1919, suddenly realizes that the fun is over. By evening, two men will be dead, dozens more injured, and the day will be remembered as Bloody Saturday. (Manitoba Archives)

collapsing as quickly under the joint assault of employers, governments, and the pragmatic organizers sent west by Tom Moore of the TLC and by the major internationals. The organization was torn by splits, systematically defeated in the coalfields of Alberta when mine owners insisted on preserving a United Mine Workers closed shop, and in other industries by refusal of employers to negotiate. Slowly, the western labour councils came back to the TLC. The OBU was left with Bob Russell, some faithful Winnipeg locals, and the *Bulletin*. For a few years, it became the most popular paper in Winnipeg by adapting the enormous gambling potential of the British soccer pools to the possibilities of a North American market. The organ of a movement pledged to production for use, not profit, was handing out seventy thousand dollars in profits before Manitoba courts ruled it all illegal.

There were other aftermaths of the Winnipeg General Strike. For those arrested in the predawn raids of June 19, there were trials and sentences, ranging from two years for Bob Russell to six months for lesser lights; J.S. Woodsworth was not brought to trial at all. By then the brilliant former Methodist clergyman, who had lost his job for his pacifist views, was on his way to election as a Labour member for Winnipeg Centre. He and William Irvine, another former clergyman elected in Calgary, represented the most durable consequence of the western labour revolt — a commitment to electoral politics that led slowly to the CCF and the New Democratic party.

Another aftermath was the report of the Mathers Commission, an attempt by Royal Commission to come at the roots of the labour ferment in postwar Canada. With strong dissent from the business members, Senator Smeaton White and François Pauzé, the majority offered a series of relatively progressive recommendations as a social code for a reconstructed Canada. There should be state insurance against unemployment, sickness, invalidity, and old age; a maximum eight-hour day and a weekly day of rest; a minimum wage, especially for women and girls and for the unskilled; a recognition of unions and the right to organize; and a bureau to promote industrial councils on the then-fashionable British model of "Whitley Councils" in industries where unions had gained no foothold.

Manitoba's counterpart, a commission to investigate the causes of the Winnipeg General Strike, was the work of only one man, H.A. Robson. Far less sympathetic to labour than Mr. Justice T.G. Mathers and his supporters, Robson anticipated history by giving little weight to the theories of revolution and subversion which had fuelled the Citizens' Committee. No admirer of hot-tongued labour leaders, he insisted that the stubborn refusal to accept basic collective bargaining, combined with the flaunting of class wealth and privilege, had kindled the anger and provided a radical minority with more than enough backers.

To give the Mathers Commission an audience, the government followed an American example and summoned a National Industrial Conference on September 15–20, 1919, in Ottawa. A month earlier, the Liberal party had found a new leader, William Lyon Mackenzie King, chosen at least partly on his assumed grasp of modern industrial problems as demonstrated in the much cited, rarely read publication, *Industry and Humanity*. Whether or not his party realized it, King had committed the Liberals to working for an eight-hour day, a forty-eight-hour week, and the "introduction into industrial government of principles of 'Labour and Community' representation and part control." Such notions were representative of the more generous-spirited members of a nation that, for the most part, was still bewildered and outraged by industrial action.

There was little sense of reconciliation at the National Industrial Conference, billed as a sounding board for the Mathers Report as well as a basis for preparing Canada's membership in the brand new International Labour Organization. Beyond welcoming further discussions and an additional Royal Commission or two on minimum wages, the conference broke up in futility. The TLC delegates, appropriately moderate, did not imitate Sam Gompers who simply walked out of the counterpart gathering in Washington.

The western revolt was an act of desperation from weakness. A minority in the Canadian labour movement and almost systematically defeated by the employers in their region, the western workers had taken advantage of a brief moment of market power in 1918 to make gains. By crediting radical aggressiveness and not market opportunism, an understandable error of judgement was made. Bob Russell used to say that you could make a poodle look like a lion, but that it was a long way from the real thing. He and his friends had talked of revolution; his followers had sometimes felt that they were performing the necessary work. None of them had really worked out the consequences.

CHAPTER 13

Unroaring Twenties

In fashionable imagery, the twenties stand out as a decade of prosperity, loosening morals, climbing skirts, and dull politicians like William Lyon Mackenzie King. The image of an era is usually set by the middle class. They provide both the journalists and the historians. The decade looked a lot less like paradise to working people. In 1929, before the Crash, the Department of Labour judged that a Canadian family of four needed between $1,200 and $1,500 for the minimum comforts of life. Its own figures showed that 60 percent of men and 82 percent of working women earned less than $1,000 a year. Life hardly roared for them.

It seemed a poor reward for people who had struggled so hard for victory in the Great War. The undoubted prosperity of Canada, the huge fortunes made in mining and speculation were kept by very few. Only 13,400 Canadians in that year reported incomes larger than $10,000.

A decade earlier, the future had promised much more. True, the Winnipeg strike had been defeated; in the United States, a massive strike by steelworkers had ended in defeat. But these could be blamed by old and established unionists as the folly of radicals. Across the United States and Canada, union membership rose. In 1919, it reached 379,000, more than twice the prewar figure. In Ontario and Alberta, labour members sat in government and held cabinet office. In Manitoba, when provincial elections came, many of the leaders of the strike won election. However, the promise of 1919 and early 1920 was not fulfilled.

For Canadian workers, organized and unorganized, the twenties turned out to be a decade of torpor and defeat. Union membership fell sharply until almost the end of the decade, reaching a low of 240,000 by 1924. Some unions, like the

Machinists, which had made substantial gains in wartime, were shattered, but even old unions, like the Typographers, suffered stinging defeats.

There were reasons why the twenties should have been dreary for working Canadians. The economic catastrophe of the First World War could not be easily overcome, even in a country thousands of miles away from enemy action. By May of 1920, the dismantling of wartime controls in most belligerent nations caused a collapse of international trade. The inflation of prices, begun in wartime and a major cause of protest in 1919, suddenly reversed. Consumers rejoiced, but the consequence was rising unemployment from coast to coast. When recovery was observed in 1923, the Canadian Manufacturers' Association claimed that the relief was due to a mass exodus to the United States. In the spring of 1921, a quarter of Quebec unionists were out of work. In British Columbia, where Russell's One Big Union had tried to organize the lumber industry, unemployment defeated the attempt. Wage rates fell. In 1921, the Department of Labour reported eighty-five strikes against wage cuts. Most were lost.

Throughout the twenties, the TLC met in annual convention, solemnly re-electing Tom Moore and Paddy Draper, passing resolutions, planning lobbies, and settling into the complacency of middle age. It would have been

J.B. McLachlan emerged in the 1920s as the intransigent leader of Cape Breton's embattled miners. At war with his own union almost as much as with the owners and managers of BESCO, McLachlan proved that Cape Breton workers would "stand the gaff." A prominent Communist, he left the party rather than compromise his own integrity. (Paul MacEwan)

Members of Ernest Drury's farmer-labour government meet in the cabinet room at Queen's Park to see whether Ontario's new government can find a common program for its rival elements. In fact, the farmers and their two labour colleagues maintained unexpected harmony and produced some solid reforms, but militants outside the legislature helped destroy the new regime to the delight and benefit of Ontario's Conservatives. (Ontario Archives)

hard to perceive, from the TLC's own minutes, that Canadian labour as a whole was in difficulties. Suspicious critics might have pointed to the $50,000 offered the TLC by a powerful group of businessmen pressing for high postwar tariffs. In fact, nobody needed to persuade the congress to favour tariffs; what was needed was for the government to listen to labour. The money undoubtedly was useful to fight the OBU and to put the TLC on a sound business footing. Perhaps that seemed the most appropriate policy for such businesslike times. It did not foster resistance to the systematic elimination of all the promises, real and implied, that had been held out as rewards for wartime sacrifices.

If there was resistance, it came from the hinterland and, above all, from the United Mine Workers in Cape Breton. Mine wages had risen during the war. By 1921, rates were such that miners finally believed that they had a decent standard. However, their company was now the British Empire Steel Corporation, headed by a ruthless, driving executive from Britain named Roy Wolvin, who was determined to make the company profitable. The task was almost hopeless since Cape Breton coal was expensive and the mines were old-fashioned and inefficient. Wolvin's solution was a series of pay cuts. Conciliation boards failed to budge him, and the outcome was a "100% strike." Half the cut was given back, and twelve hundred soldiers sent to the scene withdrew.

The miners saw this as a partial victory. More radical leaders denounced the union for "selling out." James McLachlan, a fine orator and red-headed radical who had first appeared in the 1909 strike, emerged as a leader in District No. 26, displacing the more cautious ex-Newfoundlander, Silby Barrett. Under McLachlan, the UMW members were drawn into supporting a desperate strike by steelworkers in Wolvin's Sydney mill. This proved to be the most violent strike in Nova Scotia history. Masked strikers stopped maintenance workers from entering the plant. A magistrate was knocked unconscious when he tried to read the Riot Act. Permanent troops and an ill-trained provincial police force rushed to the town. Troops fired over the heads of strikers. This violence and counter-violence helped McLachlan bring out the coal miners at the end of June, 1923.

This was a double disaster. It was the pride of the UMW and a basis for its strength that it kept its contracts. John L. Lewis, president of the union, withdrew District No. 26's charter, appointing a new executive under Barrett. The Sydney steel strike collapsed, and when the miners went back to the pits, they were faced by a fresh wage reduction of 20 percent. A third strike ended in a slight restoration of wages. In 1925, another drastic wage cut brought another bitter five-month strike. It ended with the wage cut in place, a blacklist of union activists enforced, and miners and their families living in starvation. Jimmy

The conflict between the Cape Breton coal miners and their absentee proprietors was expressed in a contemporary cartoon. Many Canadians resented the arrogance of BESCO officials, and discontent over the provincial government's eagerness to back the company helped explain the unexpected Conservative victory in the Nova Scotia election of 1925. (Beeton Institute, College of Cape Breton)

THE MILITANT COAL MINERS

The Coal Barons: "Trouble with you people is, you want the earth."
The Coal Miners: "Trouble with you is you've got it."

In 1921, J.S. Woodsworth was elected as member of Parliament for Winnipeg North-Centre. He would hold the seat until his death in 1942. Except for a brief period when he was obliged to earn his living as a Vancouver longshoreman, Woodsworth had had no direct experience of manual labour, but in Parliament he showed how effective even a small Labour group of M.P.'s could be. (Ontario Woodsworth Foundation)

When nine miners died in a fire at the Hollinger mine, Finnish socialists in Timmins refused the company offer to pay for the funeral and used the occasion not to mourn but to organize. Some socialist miners, on principle, had no more that a common-law relationship with their wives. Since the marriages were not legal, the company refused to pay relief benefits to the widows. (Multicultural History Society of Ontario)

McLachlan, arrested, tried, and imprisoned for alleged "seditious remarks" during the 1923 strike, remained the hero of the unionized miners, but he had little to lead.

The ugly battles of Sydney steel and Cape Breton coal revealed the divisions and ambiguity of public attitudes in the rest of Canada. It was obvious that the miners were starving, and unions and church organizations sent relief. Wolvin, who had boasted that the Cape Breton miners couldn't "stand the gaff," was disciplined and finally removed by powerful shareholders (including Sir Joseph Flavelle) because his intransigence was hurting the company. However, it was also easy to claim that McLachlan and his followers were serving Red interests. Indeed, Communist influences were all too apparent in the demands of District No. 26 for affiliation to the Red International of Labour Unions, based in Moscow, and the increasingly bitter assaults on Lewis, the UMW, and the local Mine Workers official, Silby Barrett, continued.

Besides, with prices falling and world markets weak or erratic, wage cutting was in style at least until the end of 1926. In the United States, American employers adopted aspects of the Mackenzie King strategy for employee representation that had been worked out for the Rockefellers. As the "American Plan," it became a demand for the open shop and the "right to work," without being bound by any union restriction. Canadian employers were much less systematic, but they were determined to bring their employees to heel and to put a stop to the kinds of attitudes fostered by wartime labour scarcity.

Less dramatic than the terrible Cape Breton strikes, the struggle between the International Typographical Union and the major eastern Canadian employers was just as significant. In 1921, the ITU decided to enforce a demand for the forty-four-hour week. Originally, in 1919, the union had agreed to accept a forty-eight-hour week only on condition that the shorter week come in 1921. In the tougher times, employers insisted that they would concede the demand only if wages were cut accordingly, and if the open shop was introduced. To the ITU this was anathema, and the strike developed.

For once, the employers were as well organized as the men, a result of belonging to the United Typothetae. The chairman of the Toronto employers' committee was the manager of the Methodist Church Publishing Company, an organization prominent in printing social gospel tracts and demands for political reform. That did not inhibit him or his fellow employers from using all the familiar devices of strike-breaking. The ITU was presented as a foreign conspiracy, controlling innocent Canadians. The open shop was vital to an employee's freedom. The strike-breakers were patriotic citizens. No compromise was allowed on either side until the ITU was forced to surrender in 1924. The three-year battle virtually ended effective collective bargaining in most of the Canadian printing trades.

More positive than the pure open shop was a further application of the Mackenzie King labour relations philosophy, the industrial council. This device, endorsed by the Mathers Commission and inspired by the example of the so-called Whitley Councils in Britain, encouraged formation of "plant councils" in which workers chose half the delegates; the company chairman and the other half came from management. The goal was to give workers "a voice" in discussing production and grievances, without the power to make change. Such councils were used by firms like Massey-Harris, Imperial Oil, and the big meat packers. Some companies introduced recreation clubs, pension plans, savings systems, even profit sharing on a modest scale. This was a Canadian version of scientific personnel management, the latest triumph of American know-how.

With organized workers in a desperate and losing struggle with management, it did not help that Canadian labour was more divided than ever. The split in Canadian labour, which began in 1902, had never really mattered much. The nationalist fragment, the Canadian Federation of Labour, was weak and discredited. By 1917, the PWA had ceased to exist. Even the One Big Union, after reaching impressive heights in late 1919 and early 1920, collapsed to near insignificance. By 1921, Tom Moore and Paddy Draper of the Trades and Labour Congress could survey the Canadian labour scene with some confidence.

The first important sign of a rival was in Quebec. French-Canadian labour had developed predominantly in international unionism and in the TLC. It would continue to do so. However, members of the Catholic hierarchy in Quebec had intervened directly to settle strikes over the heads of union leaders as early as the 1900 boot-and-shoe strike in Quebec, or the 1903 tramway strike in Montreal. In 1907, the first Catholic union, or *syndicat*, had been formed among paper workers in Chicoutimi as a deliberate challenge to the secularist, international unions. In 1909, Quebec bishops had denounced the idea of religious neutrality in labour organizations as "false and dangerous."

Catholic unionism was a slow growth, at least until the war gave an impetus to all unionism in Quebec, as elsewhere. In 1918, Catholics in Montreal deliberately began to train potential union leaders, concentrating on the building trades in a shrewd awareness that, as a major contractor, the church could best exert its influence in that industry to favour Catholic tradesmen over members of "neutral" unions. Alfred Charpentier, once an ardent craft unionist, was a typical convert, his Catholicism and his French-Canadian nationalism aroused by the war and Henri Bourassa's passionate crusade against conscription. In 1921, an organizing conference at Hull laid the foundations for a Confederation of Catholic Workers in Canada. The next year, at Montreal, a first convention chose Pierre Beaule as president, claimed twenty-six thousand members in ninety-six syndicates, and won the blessing of both the church and the provincial government of Quebec.

Catholic unionism, in the open and increasingly aggressive, was a deadly challenge to the TLC and to the internationals in Quebec. Backed by the political power of Catholicism and by employers delighted to have an alternative to the monopoly of the construction trades, the Catholic confederation was quick to embarrass the government. Senator Gideon Robertson, still minister of labour, rejected the confederation's demand for an official place in the National Building Conference, convened by the industry and the international unions. "If it once gets in the mind of the people that in your Province for a man to get along in his work he must accept a certain religious guidance, it will not be conducive to the improvement of relations between your Province and other parts of Canada." For this comment he was denounced by the opposition and by the strongly conservative Montreal *Gazette*.

Catholic unionism developed independently of the TLC; the congress was more directly to blame for the emergence of an even more dangerous rival. In 1908, A.R. Mosher and other employees of the government-owned Intercolonial Railway had formed the Canadian Brotherhood of Railway Employees. This organization claimed jurisdiction over all but the running trades and, for a brief period, even extended its sway into the United States. In 1917, Mosher, as president, moved his headquarters from Halifax to Ottawa, affiliated with the TLC, and proceeded to expand his organization through the entire system of railways by then collapsing into federal control. It was by far the strongest of any unions with their headquarters in Canada. However, in the Brotherhood of Railway and Steamship Clerks, it found an implacable rival; and in the BRSC's Canadian vice-president, Frank Hall, Mosher found a formidable opponent.

Unfortunately for any hope of reconciling the two, the TLC's constitution, adopted in 1902, gave it no flexibility. By congress rules, Mosher's CBRE was a dual union. When it would not surrender its autonomy to Hall's union, the CBRE was expelled in 1921. Five years later, Mosher gathered in the pathetic remnants of the Canadian Federation of Labour, the One Big Union, and a varied assortment of Canadian breakaway unions and in March, 1927, led the formation of the All-Canadian Congress of Labour.

The new congress was a sworn rival to the TLC. Its first paid employee, W.T. Burford, promptly launched a congress monthly magazine which was distinguished by its extravagant venom against all forms of international unionism. The employer propaganda of the 1900s could not match Burford at his most vitriolic. The congress was also committed, in rhetoric if not resources, to the OBU's demand for industrial unionism. If it did not insist too much on action, it was because many of its tiny Canadian affiliates were as committed to the craft principle as Sam Gompers. The ACCL was also committed, from the first, to the doctrine of labour political action and the development of a labour political party in Canada. These were interesting notions, but they could not drag the craft unionists of Canada away from their unions or from the TLC. The ACCL remained merely an outcropping from the Canadian Brotherhood of Railway Employees, an extra platform for A.R. Mosher with his hundreds of fresh ideas and desire to expound on them. At best, it could claim perhaps fifty thousand members, a third of the TLC's normal total.

The third split was in some ways the most infuriating and destructive. There had always been radicals and socialists in the TLC, at least since 1895. Sometimes, as in 1911, they had been a significant influence at conventions, but time and experience had worn the most ardent of them, like Gustave Francq or James Simpson, into pragmatic acceptance of reality. Some, like Hawthornethwaite or Watters, had become despised moderates even by the TLC's standards. However, the formation of the Communist party of Canada in a barn near Guelph in 1921 brought Canadian labour its first effectively conspiratorial radical movement. Canadian unions were familiar with international directives, but they had come from a known and comprehensible source, the United States, not from Moscow in a new and revolutionary Soviet Union.

The advent of communism split the Canadian Left. The lines were not simply those of moderate and radical. The solemnly doctrinaire Socialist party of

Canada refused to admit that the Russian Revolution had followed Marx's rules — an ideologically correct but possibly irrelevant conclusion. A minority of its members, inspired by the Bolshevik triumph, decamped. The small majority stuck by their arid faith. Among non-British Canadian socialists, who had drifted into the more moderate and electoral Social Democratic party, wartime harassment and the apparent triumph of socialism in or near their homeland made them ardent recruits. The new Communist party depended on a small cadre of English-born leaders like Jack MacDonald, Tim Buck, and later Tom McEwan, but its members came overwhelmingly from Jewish, Ukrainian, Finnish, and other new Canadian stock.

Within the labour movement, Canadian Communists took their strategic direction from Moscow and their example from the United States. In both countries, the first orders were to "bore from within," to capture the AFL and TLC from conservative leaders and transform them into radical forces. This strategy cost the Communists the support of Bob Russell, since it meant the liquidation of his OBU. In 1924, Tim Buck opposed Tom Moore for the presidency of the congress. The outcome was 156 to 44 for Moore; a year later Buck won only 29 votes.

Under the watchful eyes of Lenin and Marx, serious-minded Communists and sympathizers gathered for their photograph at the Sholom Aleichem School in Winnipeg around 1926. Union organizing in the garment industries of Winnipeg, Toronto, and Montreal was paralyzed for most of the 1920s as Communists and socialists struggled for control of the major unions, the ILGWU and the ACW. (Multicultural History Society of Ontario)

Toronto's union label league meets under the patronage of Jimmy Simpson, now an elder statesman of the city's labour movement. The union label on printing, clothing, shoes, and other products or a union shop card in the window allowed union members and sympathizers to use their purchasing power to support the labour movement and to boycott its enemies. (Milton Adamson)

Faced with this threat, the TLC response was angry and defensive. It launched a monthly magazine, the *Journal*, explicitly to combat "those who would bring about the disintegration of the organized labour movement and the substitution of a 'dictatorship of the proletariat'." Their anger had some grounds. Communists were ingenious and tireless in exploiting discontent among union members, splitting, dividing, agitating, inspiring and very occasionally winning strikes that more conservative unionists condemned. In both the American and Canadian union movements, Communists like Buck and MacDonald were finally expelled amidst torrents of bad feeling and unpleasant publicity.

In one of the constant tactical changes dictated from Moscow that frustrated their work, the Canadian Communists in 1927 were commanded to abandon boring from within the TLC and to turn their attentions to the new ACCL and to developing their own unions from a number of radical unions, particularly in the mining districts. The Mine Workers Union of Canada had inherited many of the members and much of the radicalism of the fading Western Federation of Miners (now a feeble International Union of Mine, Mill and Smelter Workers). By bringing these affiliates to the ACCL, the Communists hoped to destroy Mosher and capture a new federation easily. Instead, the tough railway unionist expelled them.

The chief Communist triumph was the penetration, domination, and early destruction of that feeble but hopeful by-product of the TLC's involvement in the 1917 election, the Canadian Labour party. Supported by some TLC activists, immensely decentralized among provincial federations and city labour councils, the CLP could boast of few triumphs in the 1920s. In 1926, it claimed ten thousand members in Ontario unions, but in that year, Buck, MacDonald, and the Reverend A.E. Smith, the Communists' all-purpose front man, managed to deny Jimmy Simpson his customary endorsement in a race for the Toronto Board of Control. The result was a violent debate, a split, and a decision by the losers — the non-Communists — to revive the Ontario Independent Labour party. The Communists were left with the shell and soon abandoned it. By then, so had most unionists.

The effect of the Communists, therefore, was to freeze the TLC in its conservative, unenterprising stance, to shatter and dissolve the Canadian Labour party, to weaken the ACCL, and to exclude the OBU. It had run through a number of its own more appealing leaders as well, expelling Maurice Spector, a serious intellectual, and Jack MacDonald, its most attractive unionist, because they had failed to see the merits of Stalin in time.

Photographs designed to teach immigrants the rules of North American life gave a mildly idealized picture of a "typical" worker's breakfast and what a dutiful wife would load in her husband's lunchbox. However, it is hard to get a better view of what life was supposed to be like. (Public Archives Canada WS 2019 – WS 2028)

After the First World War, most women were forced out of the jobs they had filled in factories and
service trades to make room for returning soldiers or unemployed munitions workers. The proportion
of women in the work force did not fall, but they found their way back to their traditional, low-paid
occupations. Loading olives in a bottle might be monotonous, but it resembled women's work in the
home and could therefore be almost as ill paid. (Public Archives Canada C 36971)

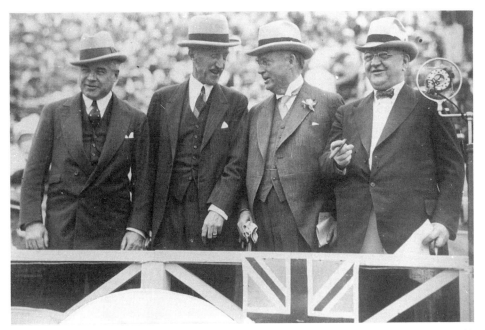

The 1920s did not roar for a great many ordinary Canadians, but they were years of comfortable prosperity for businessmen and their political friends. With prosperity already cracking under them, Sir Edward Beatty of the CPR, Lord Willingdon, the governor general, R.B. Bennett, the new Conservative prime minister, and his Ontario ally, Howard Ferguson, look amazingly confident. (Ontario Archives)

At the same time, by testing the rather narrow limits of Canadian tolerance, the Communists had fought and lost a number of battles for free speech, particularly in Toronto where open conflict had become endemic by the end of the decade between Communist speakers and the Toronto Board of Police Commissioners. In 1928, the Toronto police commissioners banned the use of Yiddish at a meeting and commanded that no reflection on the government or on constituted authority be uttered. In Sudbury, Aarvo Vaara, editor of the Finnish radical paper, *Vapaus*, was arrested and jailed for seditious libel under the laws hurriedly enacted for the 1919 Winnipeg General Strike.

The one creative thing that the Communists did came out of necessity. Forced out of existing unions as people of dual loyalty, they were obliged to form their own union organization, the Workers' Unity League. Even this step was dictated from Moscow and followed a model set by the Trade Union Education League, a Communist organization in the United States. With the shadow of the depression already advancing across the country, the WUL set out to generate an amazing array of organizations run with interlocking directorates of reliable members and taking on organizational challenges the traditional unions had no intention of tackling. However, this heroic phase was still in the future when the twenties ended.

It was not wholly a decade of defeats and divisions. The prosperity of the times at least persuaded some governments to introduce reforming legislation. This was a decade in which old age pensions were finally forced past the Canadian Senate, when provinces gave allowances to blind persons, to mothers left as widows, and to orphans. The majority of provinces had minimum wages for women and children by the end of the decade, and the Canadian Manufacturers' Association had to muster all its resources to keep Alberta from adopting an eight-hour day as a maximum. To be sure, governments carefully inserted loopholes. In Ontario, for example, a minimum wage of $12.50 a week need only apply to 80 percent of the workers. Employers used piecework rates and, in the case of Eaton's, fired workers who could not earn enough to keep up the scale.

Part of the pressure for reform came from Canada's membership in the new International Labour Organization, established to ensure that all signatories to the Treaty of Versailles lived up to its somewhat imaginative commitments to better wages and working conditions. Canada's membership in the ILO was something of a triumph for a country asserting its independence from Britain, but this was not sufficient to make Canadian employers or their political representatives hasten to honour her signature. The eight-hour day just happened to be one of those commitments. W.L. Mackenzie King might be prime minister from 1921 to 1930 — with a brief interval — and his heart might bleed for working Canadians, but there were practical limits to his charity.

Perhaps the cruellest cut came when his famous Industrial Disputes Investigation Act, the triumph of his earlier career, fell victim to constitutional revision. In the case of *Snider* v. *Toronto Electrical Commissioners*, which finally reached the Judicial Committee of the British Privy Council in 1925, Lord Haldane decreed that the federal government had no right to meddle with labour relations in other than a strictly federal sphere. As a result, provinces would develop their own separate systems, and, while the Mackenzie King model would be dominant, the special enthusiasms, influences, and politics of each province would begin to pull them in different directions. For Canadian unionism, the benefits were not easy to perceive.

CHAPTER 14
Surviving the Depression

People usually date the Great Depression of the 1930s from the Wall Street crash of October, 1929. In fact, the stock market disaster had little to do with the economic situation in Canada. The direct cause was a failure to sell the West's huge wheat crop of 1928. The reality of a depression dawned on Canadians when the heavy winter unemployment did not vanish with the spring of 1930. In Ottawa, the Liberal government of William Lyon Mackenzie King refused any special measures. Relief was a provincial matter. If Conservative provincial governments demanded federal dollars to spend in an election year, they would not get five cents from him.

King's uncharacteristic bluntness soon cost him a general election — and saved his Liberal party from being blamed for the worst economic depression anyone could remember. Unemployment grew worse. World prices for raw materials collapsed. Canada's traditional exports of wheat, lumber, and minerals were almost unsaleable. A grim cycle of layoffs and wage cuts paralyzed sector after sector of an integrated economy.

Statistics, however primitive and incomplete, told part of the story. The value of Canadian exports fell by a quarter. By 1933, new investment was a mere 11 percent of the 1929 level. In 1930, unemployment almost doubled from the previous year to 11 percent. By the end of 1933, one Canadian wage earner in four was looking for work. More than 1.5 million Canadians — out of 10 million — depended on direct relief for their existence. To get it, they had to prove absolute and humiliating destitution. In relatively affluent Ontario, that could mean living on thirty to forty dollars a month, meat twice a week, and chopping the toes out of welfare shoes to make them fit. In rural Saskatchewan, devastated

139

With the city's furniture workers on strike and chicken pluckers in the local packing plant about to join them, Stratford's unionists prepare to march. Discretion has effaced what the marchers will be no longer, but the argument that higher wages might cure the depression remained a shocking heresy to almost all Canadians. (Ed Seymour)

by drought, rust, and grasshoppers, as well as by depression, relief was a standard ten dollars a month and a bag of flour.

In Ontario, some of the unemployed could go home to the family farm, and the rural population actually increased. Across the Prairies, the double disaster of climate and falling prices reduced whole regions to the edge of starvation. In British Columbia, northern Ontario, and New Brunswick, thousands of seasonal jobs in the woods vanished in the face of glutted markets. The railways, with too little to carry, watched freight and passenger revenue collapse. Their employees, once the envied aristocrats of labour with pensions and lifetime security, suddenly faced wage cuts and massive layoffs just like lesser mortals.

Within a year, the disaster in Canada's primary industries had spread to manufacturing. Both major railways cancelled orders for engines and rolling-stock. Automobile manufacturing, the glamour industry of the twenties, cut production by two-thirds. Industrial cities like Hamilton, Montreal, and Windsor struggled to provide relief for as many as a third of their male workers. Government and business centres like Ottawa and Toronto suffered far less.

Even in the same community, the depression affected people very differently. Middle-class people with secure jobs might suffer salary reductions, but the cuts were more than matched by a 30 percent drop in the cost of living. Wage rates fell during the depression but far less than the level of employment or prices. On

Meeting in 1933, the TLC renewed its call for unemployment insurance and rejoiced privately that strict craft union principles had allowed it to survive hard times. From left to right: Percy Bengough; Jimmy Simpson; Paddy Draper, the durable secretary-treasurer; Tom Moore, the president; R.J. Tallon, who had come a long way from convening the Western Labour Conference in 1919; Fred White, M.L.A.; and John McLeod, a fraternal delegate from the British Trades Union Congress (National Photography Collection C 28340)

the other hand, young people leaving school faced a hopeless job market. Single men were laid off in favour of family men. Most Canadian provinces had legislated minimum wages for women. Employers replaced them with boys.

Denied employment, the single men were then sent packing by welfare officials who reserved their bounty for destitute breadwinners. Once on the road, the unemployed found that municipalities restricted relief to their own local citizens. Strangers were neither welcome nor eligible. One of the first, obvious symptoms of the depression was a growing army of young drifters, swelling the ranks of the traditional hoboes, following rumours of employment wherever they led, and finding, like the veteran bums, that winters were better in British Columbia.

In the economic crisis, unions could do little enough for their own members and nothing at all for the armies of the unemployed. Beaten, divided, and rendered nervously conservative by the battles of the twenties, the TLC, the ACCL, the Catholic syndicates, and the OBU seemed to have energy only to fight each other.

The previous decade had cost the unions their wartime gains, driving them back to the customary strongholds in the railways, construction, mining, and some traditional service industries. Now even these industries were under attack. Soon construction was almost at a standstill. In 1931, Toronto building trades offered to accept a cut in their hourly rates only to be informed by contractors that it would make no difference. The railway brotherhoods could boast only that they had kept their wage cut to 15 percent.

In the circumstances, most unions imitated their clientele — tightening their belts, reducing expenses, hoping for better times. In 1930, the nationalistic ACCL cancelled its annual convention as an economy measure. The TLC met in Vancouver and called for unemployment insurance, a tariff commission, and an advisory commission on immigration — its essential program throughout the worst of the depression years. The aging Tom Moore and Paddy Draper, now re-elected almost automatically as congress president and secretary, reflected their members. They, too, wanted to conserve their jobs and had no incentive to explore radical alternatives.

It is fashionable to denounce the craft unions, both national and international, for their conservatism and complacency during the terrible depression years. By their own rather narrow standards, they demonstrated the strength of the craft principle. Not even in the 1870s had organized labour faced such an economic disaster, yet union membership in Canada fell by less than 15 percent, and at least some of that loss may have been due to the dubious figures some of the fringe organizations had submitted to the Department of Labour. The traditional unions, for the most part, recognized their limits, devoted their resources to maintaining their own members in good standing, and avoided quixotic temptations. It may have been inglorious but it was sensible.

Conventional wisdom argued that strikes and organizing were impossible during a depression. Experience confirmed the principle. In 1930, there were only sixty-seven strikes in Canada — fewer than in any year since 1915. Only twenty ended in favour of the employees. In the years between 1930 and 1935, most strikes occurred in mining and the clothing industry. The cause was not so much employee militancy or employer repression, though both were present. The real reason was the continuing acrimonious rivalry between conventional unionism and the Communists.

Only the Communists could take comfort from the depression. For them it was history unfolding as it should. The economic collapse of bourgeois capitalism had come far sooner than anyone might have expected. It was their opportunity. In the Workers' Unity League, the Communist International had given them a well-adapted weapon.

In 1929, the Comintern had directed an end to the boring-from-within strategy which had sent North American Communists on the hopeless errand of capturing control of the AFL and TLC. By December, 1929, the WUL was born as the Canadian affiliate of the Red International of Labour Unions. Within months, Communist leaders and sympathizers had brought in the Lumber Workers Industrial Union, a former ally of the OBU. Even more important was the Mine Workers Union of Canada, affiliated in 1931. Until his arrest in 1931, Tom McEwan, a Scottish-born blacksmith, led the league whose real strength was its core of tireless, disciplined organizers. Many were of Ukrainian or Finnish background, able to talk to workers in the tough resource industries in their own language.

Though it published the usual elaborate constitution and structure of decision making, the WUL was a tightly controlled organization, managed by the Communist "fractions" who directed the tactics of its proliferating affiliates. By 1933, the league boasted eleven industrial unions covering woodworkers, shoe and leather workers, furniture workers, textile workers, the needle trades, fishermen, auto workers, and a variety of other jobs.

Organizers worked fast, secretly, and with dedication. A nucleus of sympathizers would be found, grievances formulated and presented to an employer before he knew what was happening. A strike usually followed with as little notice as possible. Thereafter, the WUL used every imaginable device to publicize the strike, deluging the strikers with telegrams of support from innumerable front groups, sending gifts of food and money. By 1933, the Communists claimed responsibility for three-quarters of the strikes in Canada.

In the summer of 1931, organizers from the Mine Workers Union of Canada answered an appeal from coal miners in the Estevan-Bienfait area of southern Saskatchewan. The miners had tried in vain to interest the TLC in their miserable circumstances, and they had even appealed to a provincial government mine inspector to find them a union organizer. The MWUC did not need a second call.

The Bienfait miners shared all the familiar evils of mining-camp life, from company-owned houses and stores to dishonest weigh scales and flagrant disregard for safety. Since the coalfields produced low-quality lignite, the owners matched their losses with short time and wage cuts. By 1931, men opened their pay envelopes only to find out how much deeper in debt they were to the company.

When Mabel Marlowe wanted to prevent Flin Flon miners from voting themselves back to work after a month of hungry waiting, she mobilized some of their wives, blocked the steps to the community hall, and challenged the RCMP to attack. In a more chivalrous age, the police held back and the few voters who braved the blockade had their clothes torn off. (Manitoba Archives)

By September, the MWUC had signed up virtually every miner and demonstrated its strength by a two-day strike for the reinstatement of one of its members. On September 7, the real strike began. The employers, organized as the Saskatchewan Coal Operators' Association, struck back, rejecting any recognition of a revolutionary body affiliated to the Red International. Respectable Canadians heard little about the miners' desperate circumstances and a great deal about the Communist threat. To publicize its case, the union proposed to take the miners and their families to nearby Estevan.

Hurriedly, the mayor of Estevan banned any demonstration in his town. Local police and firemen were reinforced by RCMP. Well aware that a clash was likely, the MWUC organizers did nothing to warn the Bienfait miners. Men, women, and children rode into an angry and deadly battle with the police. By the evening of September 29, three miners lay dead and many more were injured on both sides. Dozens of miners were arrested. In the aftermath, a Royal Commission forced a settlement on both sides, but the Mine Workers Union was beaten from the Bienfait mines. Not until 1945 did a union succeed in organizing the fields. However, the Estevan tragedy made excellent propaganda.

The WUL had more success in Ontario, winning agreements in the Toronto garment and furniture industries. In September of 1933, organizers turned to the sleepy railway town of Stratford. With the usual speed, secrecy, and fervor, the Chesterfield and Furniture Workers' Industrial Union signed up workers at Stratford's seven small furniture factories and took them out on strike. Employers, as usual, fought back, offering improvements for their "loyal" workers, rejecting Communist conspiracies, and threatening to leave their factories closed forever. Trouble began when strikers tried to stop employers from removing partly built radio cabinets to be finished elsewhere. It grew worse when the WUL also organized ill-paid chicken pluckers at the nearby Swift plant. An all-day battle erupted outside the plant when strikers besieged local and provincial police. Prompted by Colonel W.H. Price, Ontario's attorney general, city authorities demanded troops. Two weak companies of the Royal Canadian Regiment arrived from London and Toronto accompanied, as an act of unwitting folly, by their brand new machine-gun carriers.

The Stratford strike demonstrated both the strength and the futility of the Workers' Unity League tactics. The little, tracked vehicles, promptly described as "tanks," symbolized the "iron heel of ruthlessness" which Prime Minister Richard Bedford Bennett had promised the Communists. Fortunately, neither they nor the soldiers could be used. Ontario's Liberal leader, Mitchell F. Hepburn, on the verge of victory, used the Stratford affair to demonstrate Tory stupidity and his own sympathy with the workers. The Communists had scored a brilliant propaganda coup. However, the furniture workers gained nothing from the publicity victory. By November, they had been starved back to work.

For all the romantic appeal of their campaigns, that was the familiar outcome of Communist union organizing. Occasionally, as in the Kitchener and Waterloo furniture factories, the tactics succeeded. In the great majority of cases, they failed, leaving a heritage of violence, martyrdom, and misery. Employers could be all the more certain of government and community support because they were doing battle with "revolutionary communism." In 1934, Manitoba's pre-

Marching against Ontario's Liberal government did little to soften Mitchell Hepburn's heart, but it gave unemployed Torontonians and their allies a sense of purpose and something to do. Organizations like the East York Workers' Association did more than march. They lobbied municipal officials, organized mass pickets to prevent evictions, and helped elect the township reeve. (Ontario Woodsworth Foundation)

mier, John Bracken, sent in a powerful RCMP detachment when Communist-led strikers prevented a back-to-work vote at the big Hudson's Bay Mining and Smelting operation at Flin Flon. At Corbin, in British Columbia, another MWUC strike collapsed in failure after a brutal episode when police drove a bulldozer through a picket line of miners' wives.

From the first, the Bennett government and its provincial allies were se ious about their iron-heel approach to the Communist threat. Much of Cana lian opinion agreed. When University of Toronto professors appealed for the right of free speech for Communists, they were pilloried in the press and by their own chancellor, the venerable veteran of the Laurier cabinet, Sir William Mulock. In August, 1931, at the behest of the Ontario attorney general, the Toronto headquarters of the Communist party was raided and eight leaders were arrested. By the end of the year, seven of them faced long prison sentences. Mulock, as chief justice of Ontario, confirmed most of the verdicts. Other Communists were seized, rushed to Halifax, and ordered deported. Laws, hurriedly enacted at the time of the Winnipeg General Strike, found a new use.

The prime target for Communists, and the chief concern for the government, was the army of single, unemployed men, the worst victims of the depression. The new Conservative government responded with more energy than it has been given credit for to the unprecedented economic disaster. By any previous standard, the expenditures authorized for unemployment and farm relief were huge. To meet the cost without borrowing, the government doubled its income and corporation tax revenues and increased its sales tax income sevenfold. When public works grew too expensive for provinces and municipalities to meet their share of the cost, Ottawa authorized direct relief. However, little of this help reached the single unemployed.

By 1932, some provinces and the federal Department of the Interior had opened work camps for the unemployed, single men. In October, on the inspiration of Major General A.G.L. McNaughton, the chief of the General Staff, the Department of National Defence assumed responsibility for creating a whole system of relief camps on the promise that the men could be fed, housed, clothed, and paid an allowance of twenty cents a day at a cost to the taxpayer of no more than a dollar per man per day. With military control wrapped in civilian clothes, but all too apparent in the strict rules about grievances and agitation, the camps were intended by McNaughton to quarantine young men from Communist influence, build up their physiques and self-confidence, and ensure that a generation of young men was not lost forever to the nation. In almost all respects, the relief camps resembled the highly praised Civilian Conservation

Workers in the Bennett government relief camps complained of primitive conditions in the bunkhouses and resented the absurd pocket money allowance of twenty cents a day, but their real fear was that the government had packed them off to wilderness construction sites to forget about them. A short-term makeshift became intolerable when the depression dragged on for years. (National Photography Collection PA 35676)

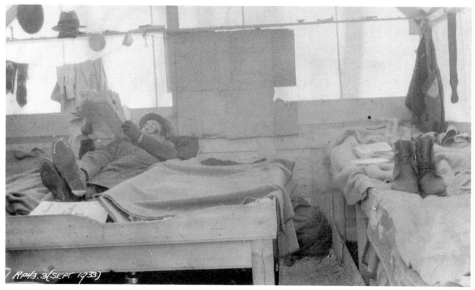

Corps of the American New Deal. One difference was that the American CCC wore uniforms. The Canadians were issued shapeless cardigans and cloth caps, so that charges of militarism could be avoided.

As an expedient for a short-term emergency, the relief camps could have been a brilliant success. When one year stretched into a second and a third, the relief camps became a hotbed of frustration and despair. In theory, men could leave whenever they chose. In practice, local relief officials had sent them to the camps without option. Conditions were comparable to any civilian bush camp, and the administration was probably more efficient. What was intolerable was that young men realized that, because their society had no better use for them, they had been condemned through no fault of their own to labour forever on a humiliating pittance of twenty cents a day. They satirized their wages and their military administrators by calling themselves "the Royal Twenty Centers."

In the cities, the Communists had rapidly overcome the loss of their leaders and had turned to organizing the jobless. Unemployed associations sprang up, almost all of them carefully controlled by their Communist fraction, affiliated to the Workers' Unity League. Their processions, demonstrations, and meetings gave the unemployed a sense of purpose and something to do. Confrontations with police, politicians, and sheriffs' officers gave members a sense of dignity and a feeling that they were not helpless victims.

The next stage was to organize a Relief Camp Workers' Union. Organizers evaded the vigilance of camp officials, survived expulsion, changed their identity, and kept moving. Many of the camps, like the single unemployed, were in British Columbia. Early in 1935, several thousand of the Royal Twenty Centers descended on Vancouver, demanding work at fifty cents an hour and supporting themselves by "tin-canning" on the city streets. There were clashes with the police, an occupation of the city art gallery, and a rapid erosion of local sympathy. Even local unionists pleaded with the men to go back to the camps. Instead, their leaders decided to lead them on an "On to Ottawa" trek.

More than a thousand men left Vancouver on east-bound freights. The usual small cadre of Communist organizers maintained an impressive discipline, well aware that the project depended on public sympathy. At Calgary, city officials were virtually compelled to grant food and shelter. The trek leader, "Slim" Evans, was a former mine union leader from Alberta. Faced with a snowballing movement from the West, the Bennett government decided to summon Evans and his lieutenants to Ottawa to negotiate. While Evans and Bennett traded sneers and insults, the trekkers were halted in Regina, conveniently close to the big RCMP training depot and far away from the next centre of left-wing agitation and unemployment, Winnipeg. On Dominion Day, police and workers clashed on Regina's Market Square. A police officer was killed, scores were injured, and more than a hundred trekkers, including Evans, were arrested. The next day, most of the men returned to their camps.

The July 1 tragedy was an embarrassment to the Bennett government. For all its efforts, the depression had not been curbed. The relief camps, with their hopeless inmates, became a popular symbol of the government's failure. In 1931, Bennett had exploded when a largely Communist delegation had demanded unemployment insurance. "We will not put a premium on idleness," he had shouted. In 1935, unemployment insurance was one of the major elements of his "New Deal." So was a national minimum wage and a law imposing a minimum of one rest day a week. The legislation merely enacted commitments Canada had long since made to the International Labour Organization, but all would have been unthinkable only five years earlier. In 1934, in a little-noted step, Bennett's minister of justice, Hugh Guthrie, finally amended the Criminal Code to make informational picketing legal. It had, in fact, been against the law since the 1890s, and police had enforced that law when and how they chose.

However, Bennett had not blasted his way into the markets of the world; he had not defeated unemployment; and, despite jailing and deportation, he had not crushed the Communist party.

In 1935, Canadians had other alternatives than to return to the familiar embrace of the Liberals. In Alberta, William Aberhart, a gospel preacher with a curiously persuasive manner, had mesmerized a desperate, frightened province and created the world's first Social Credit government.

In the 1930 election, J.S. Woodsworth had been joined in Parliament by only two Labour members, his Winnipeg colleague, A.A. Heaps, and a Vancouver socialist, Angus MacInnis. The tragedy of the depression only increased Woodsworth's impatience for an effective labour party in Canada, but it could come, he insisted, only by patient building. In Saskatchewan, a school principal named M.J. Coldwell had carefully created an alliance between a provincial labour party and the provincial wing of the Progressives. In Winnipeg, Woodsworth's own Independent Labour party was strong enough to elect federal and provincial members. In eastern Canada, political support was limited to the fading United Farmers of Ontario and a lone labour member from Hamilton, Sam Lawrence. Still, something must be tried.

In Calgary, in 1932, the small, scattered western labour parties met for their annual conference. This time they were joined by representatives of farmer political organizations from the western provinces and by a few uncomfortable purists from the aging Socialist party of Canada. The result was an agreement to attempt to merge differences in an awkwardly named "Co-operative Commonwealth Federation (Farmer Labour Socialist)." In June of 1933, it met again, provided itself with an elaborate program in the Regina Manifesto, and set off under its new leader, J.S. Woodsworth, on a long and winding road to power.

The CCF's claim to *Labour* in its title was tenuous. Some unionists came as spokesmen for their local labour parties, but none of them professed to speak for the TLC. Aaron Mosher, of the Canadian Brotherhood of Railway Employees and the All-Canadian Congress of Labour, made the trip to Calgary to show his support for Woodsworth, but his presence damned the new party even among strong socialists in the craft unions. The years of propaganda from W.T. Burford and Mosher himself had left scars. Mosher prudently decided not to attend the Regina convention in 1933, but the damage was done. That September, Jimmy Simpson led a delegation to the TLC convention at Windsor, determined to win endorsement of his new party. The question was not even put to a vote. Spurned by Canada's major labour organization, Woodsworth had to build the CCF on its cantankerous farmer and socialist foundations.

The March of the "Resoluters"

They have passed resolutions covering all sections of the glob e—Ireland, Russia, Poland, etc.—and are marching to Windsor to again "Resolve." But Canadian Trades Unionists would probab ly die from heart-failure were these "Resoluters" to resolve to live like good patriotic Canadian citizens.

When James Simpson led delegates to Windsor in 1933 to try to persuade the Trades and Labour Council to endorse the brand new CCF, respectable craft unionists may very well have regarded Simpson and his supporters as tramps and troublemakers. They were even more indignant that A.R. Mosher, head of the rival ACCL, had had the temerity to endorse the new party. (Toronto Telegram, *1933*)

However, in 1935, Canadians did not turn to the CCF nor Social Credit. With the Conservative vote fractured by the breakaway Reconstruction party, voters listened to the Liberal slogan King or Chaos and the promise of balanced budgets, strict economy, and an end to reckless experiment. The victory turned into a Liberal landslide. In Alberta, the Social Credit magic translated into federal votes. Without a base, the CCF emerged with only six members of Parliament, two each from Manitoba, Saskatchewan, and British Columbia.

Much conspired to accentuate the Liberal victory. Recovery, denied by the Liberals and invisible to most Canadians, had in fact been in progress. By early 1936, the Liberals could close the relief camps and transfer the remaining inmates to construction work for the railways. Meanwhile, one of labour's divisions was apparently healed. Suddenly eager for "popular fronts" in the face of a Nazi Germany and a Fascist Italy, the Comintern commanded the liquidation of the Workers' Unity League. Within a few months, Canadian Communists had wound up their most romantic and famous institution. One casualty was the veteran Cape Breton radical, J.B. McLachlan. In a final battle against his detested foe, John L. Lewis, he had thrown his huge prestige behind the WUL campaign in the Cape Breton mines. Now the latest command from Moscow directed him to wind up his organization and make his peace with the UMW. McLachlan refused. The penalty was expulsion and an early, embittered death.

The Workers' Unity League left little behind but a myth of confrontation and imaginative defiance of authority. Throughout its history, most of its members were among the unemployed, and, by definition, a union of the unemployed is composed of members who want to get out. The WUL and its Communist activists played a role out of all proportion to their strength and numbers, but a careful analysis of their achievements suggests that boldness and sacrifice did not overturn the realities of the depression. Courageous but erratic leadership could produce violence and publicity, but it left little in the way of self-sustaining labour organization.

Such developments could only come with different economic circumstances and a new framework of legislation. The example came from the United States: Franklin Delano Roosevelt's New Deal. The 1933 National Industrial Recovery Act promised that "employees shall have the right to organize and bargain collectively through representatives of their own choosing and shall be free from interference, restraint and coercion." For the first time, a United States law not merely permitted collective bargaining but asserted that it was a positive goal. When the section proved unenforceable, Senator Robert Wagner helped to push the National Labour Relations Act through Congress. Rhetoric became hard law. Unions which could win majority support from workers could be certified as legal bargaining agents. They could be protected from management interference in their activities.

The Wagner Act made possible the explosion of union organizing in the United States after 1935. For Canadian workers, it provided the model legislation they desperately needed in order to share in the gains of unionism. However, through the re-election of Mackenzie King in 1935, Canadians could expect nothing more than fusty reiterations of the merits of the Industrial Disputes Investigation Act.

CHAPTER 15

Industrial Unionism

During the depression years, Canadians were regularly assured that recovery was just around the corner. For many that notion became a mocking slogan. Afterwards, they would remember the thirties as a decade of unrelieved misery and frustration.

That was by no means true. For Canadians in the Maritimes or those who worked in ill-paid, marginal industries, the thirties were grim — but so were the twenties. People with secure jobs and comfortable incomes suffered little more than a sense of insecurity and a twinge of guilt during the thirties. For them times were bad only in contrast with the unprecedented affluence of postwar Canada. For farmers in Saskatchewan and Alberta, the thirties saw an almost unbroken run of terrible crop conditions, coinciding catastrophically in a world-wide collapse in wheat prices.

In general, economic conditions in Canada reached their lowest point in 1933. By 1934, a slow, hesitant, and ill-distributed recovery was in progress. Employment opportunities began to improve. The prices, which had fallen sharply since 1929, began to climb back to earlier levels. Wages, which had been slower in falling, were also slower in recovering.

Some industries were barely affected. Farmers still scarcely covered production costs. Construction remained slow. The chief gains were in business, manufacturing, and metal mining. By 1936, both Canadians and Americans could believe that the economy had, as their politicians insisted, turned the corner. In 1937, Canadian automobile production was almost back to predepression levels. Factories were busy producing toasters, radios, refrigerators, and the other new domestic gadgets of the electric age. The iron and steel industry,

The Noranda strike at Rouyn, Quebec, in 1934 attracted national attention when airplanes were used to bring in police and take out prisoners. For those directly affected, the strike showed the enthusiasm of the Quebec government and the ultra-nationalist Canadian Federation of Labour for exploiting prejudice against the largely foreign-born members of the Mine Workers Union of Canada. The strike ended with recruiting of English- and French-speaking workers and the importation of provincial police to protect them. (Multicultural History Society of Ontario)

rubber, textiles, and a tiny chemical industry all reported big gains in sales and profits.

The 1937 boom was only a recovery in contrast to 1933. Even industrial cities reported 10 percent unemployment. The return to 1929 levels ignored the population increase during the thirties when a bulge of youngsters had pushed into the work force only to find nothing open to them. Moreover, the recovery passed suddenly. By the second half of the year, the economy was in trouble again. Unemployment rose. Investment fell off sharply. The politicians and experts who had boasted in both the United States and Canada that they had beaten bad times had to find fresh remedies.

Throughout the thirties, Canadians had followed events in the United States more closely than ever before. Although Britain had reluctantly assumed responsibility for a bankrupt Dominion of Newfoundland, it was clear to everyone after the Imperial Economic Conference that the British Empire could no longer pretend to be an economic alternative for Canada. In the twenties, Canadian prosperity had been fuelled by huge American investments in branch plant manufacturing and in the resource industries. In the thirties, the Canadian economy's dependence on the United States was underlined by the shared misery of the depression. Through radio and film newsreels, ordinary Canadians also acquired a direct experience of politics and legislation during the crucial New Deal era. Canadians could compare the cool, aristocratic elegance of Franklin Delano Roosevelt with the blustering of R.B. Bennett or the shapeless fatuity of his Liberal successor, William Lyon Mackenzie King. They could also follow the extraordinary surge of militancy which suffused American labour between 1934 and 1937.

To their own surprise, American unionists had found a friend in President Roosevelt. Until 1932, the Democrats had had no better claim on labour allegiance than the Republicans and, in some respects, even less. The Progressives, like Senator Robert LaFollette and his son, had been drawn from the Republican ranks. However, labour soon found a vital role in the New Deal coalition. A central cause of the depression, according to some of Roosevelt's advisers, was that too few American workers could afford the products of American industry or find the leisure to enjoy them. Building strong unions had been a key feature of the National Industrial Recovery Act. By 1934, as the National Recovery Administration set out to develop a series of industry-wide codes, including union recognition, American workers began joining and creating unions at a rate unprecedented since the heyday of the Knights of Labor.

Their optimism was premature. Union organizers might claim that "F.D.R. wants you to join a union," but the hidebound reactionaries who ran the American Federation of Labor by no means agreed. The new unionists were left in weak, ill-run "federal unions" until the old craft unions could sort out their jurisdictional disputes. Employers struck back, crushing the new organizations and substituting their own "company unions" when necessary to meet the NRA codes. William Green, the aging AFL president, and his chief lieutenants, "Big Bill" Hutcheson of the Carpenters and Dan Tobin of the Teamsters, felt that their judgement had been confirmed.

Other major union leaders were furious at the lost opportunity. John L. Lewis was a big, bushy-browed tyrant with a powerful voice and a taste for biblical oratory. His union, the United Mine Workers, had almost been annihilated in the struggles of the twenties and early thirties. He had seized his chance in 1934 to recapture most of the losses. So had Sidney Hillman of the once-powerful Amalgamated Clothing Workers and David Dubinsky of the International Ladies' Garment Workers' Union. Their rage at the futility of the AFL leadership broke into an open shoving match between Lewis and Hutcheson at the federation's 1935 convention at Atlantic City. Immediately afterwards, Lewis, Hillman, Dubinsky, and their supporters formed a Committee for Industrial Organization, determined to take advantage of the fresh organizing opportunities offered by Senator Robert Wagner's National Labour Relations Act.

At the heart of employer hostility to unions was the loss of managerial omnipotence, not simply the fear of higher wages. A union prevented an employer from hiring, firing, setting wages, demanding overtime, or, for that matter, granting a half-holiday as his own whim or judgement dictated. Behind the strikes and violence, the yellow-dog contracts, the company unions, the goons and vigilantes, there was usually one brutal struggle: whether or not a union could force recognition from an employer. In industries with small or scattered employers, as in construction, and in industries vulnerable to sabotage or disruption, like railways, recognition had been extorted. What barred mass unionism in the United States and Canada was the power of major employers who were resolutely determined never to deal with any union.

At one blow, the Wagner Act created a legal procedure which forced an employer to accept an orderly, legal process by which workers could choose their own bargaining agent. While unions were compelled to prove that they had the allegiance of a majority of employees, management was barred from a long list of unfair and oppressive anti-union practices, from firing union sympathizers to promoting a company union.

The Wagner Act was not immediately effective. It took time to develop effective machinery and to make both unions and management familiar with its working. Above all, American employers were convinced that it would soon face the fate of most New Deal legislation: it would be thrown out by the Supreme Court. Until April, 1937, when the Court made an unexpectedly favourable decision in the case of *National Labour Relations Board* v. *Jones and Laughlin Steel Company*, the Wagner Act really had no more than an encouraging influence on union organizing. For Lewis and the Committee for Industrial Organization, that was enough.

The CIO, as it soon became known, began with the steel industry, the closest to Lewis's own United Mine Workers. A trusted lieutenant, Philip Murray, headed a Steel Workers Organizing Committee which, by the end of 1936, had signed up one hundred thousand members. It was on the verge of a brutal confrontation with the huge United States Steel Corporation when the company suddenly backed down. Business was too good for a disruption. It was cheaper to recognize the union, give a wage increase and a forty-hour week. By May, Murray's SWOC had three hundred thousand members.

Other organizing committees fanned out into the rubber, glass, textile, electrical, and packinghouse industries. None was more significant than the auto industry, dominated by the bitterly anti-union "Big Three" — General Motors, Ford, and Chrysler. Auto workers had responded more than most to the apparent opportunity of 1934. They had been brutally defeated. The remnants, still under the AFL, rebelled in the spring of 1936, chose a visionary ex-Baptist minister named Homer Martin as president, and resumed organizing as the United Automobile Workers.

A series of flash strikes forced Martin's hand. The first target of the UAW would be the biggest, the huge General Motors body plant at Flint, Michigan. On December 30, 1936, the GM workers simply sat down at their benches. The corporation was desperate. By their occupation, the workers controlled the dies for all the GM cars but the Chevrolet. The company cut off the heat and sent in the local police. The workers met them with a shower of missiles. Again the police attacked. The workers met them with fire-hoses. General Motors demanded that Michigan governor Frank Murphy send in the National Guard. Murphy, a Democrat in a Republican state, refused. Instead, he and President Roosevelt demanded that the company negotiate. On February 11, the huge corporation recognized the UAW.

Workers all over the United States and Canada watched the progress of the CIO with growing amazement and delight. An organization which could humble two of the most powerful and arrogant corporations in the world in quick succession could obviously defeat any lesser obstacle. A romantic mythology rolled across the continent. Businessmen and editorial writers might rage at a

General Motors strikers settled down to find heat from a makeshift stove and to read headlines reporting that Oshawa's mayor Alex Hall had found no reason to send police against them. That was good news for them and infuriating for Ontario's premier, Mitchell Hepburn. He wanted any pretext to crush the strike. (Archives of Labor and Urban Affairs, Wayne State University)

new, radical, Communist conspiracy to undermine freedom, but the old admiration for corporate management had been badly eroded by the depression and a great many people rejoiced that the workers had come into their own. Auto workers, long the victims of discrimination, wage cuts, and the physical trauma of assembly line speed-ups, chanted a new defiant song:

> When they tie the can to a union man,
>   Sit down! Sit down!
> When they give him the sack, they'll take him back,
>   Sit down! Sit down!
> When the speed-up comes, just twiddle your thumbs,
>   Sit down! Sit down!
> When the boss won't talk, don't take a walk,
>   Sit down! Sit down!

Top
Premier Mitchell F. Hepburn had won over Ontario voters by his promise to "swing left where few Liberals would follow" and on being a simple onion farmer from Elgin county. As premier, Hepburn liked to help people, and few were more eager for help than wealthy Toronto businessmen with profitable visions for a depression-ridden province. Private aircraft and powerful companions were pleasures of political power. (Public Archives Canada PA 52470)

Ideas about the causes and cure of the depression were a dime a dozen, but some members of the crowd in this Regina park would have had a hard time finding ten cents to reward the speaker for his efforts. For many Canadians, the thirties offered a strong incentive for an economic education and too much enforced leisure to absorb it. (Public Archives Canada C 29310)

Top

Strikers at Courtaulds, a British-owned textile plant in Cornwall in 1937. Although union leaders could regard the General Motors strike in Oshawa as a victory, the CIO could boast of few other triumphs in the prewar years. Lacking federal and provincial legislation to match the U.S. Wagner Act, the CIO letters were an inspiring but ultimately frustrating symbol to Canadian workers. (National Photography Collection C 80188)

Charles Millard, leader of the Oshawa strikers, Homer Martin, president of the UAW, and Hugh Thompson, an international organizer for the union, inspect a cheque for $100,000. Since the union was penniless, the cheque would have bounced, but it impressed the press. (Archives of Labor and Urban Affairs, Wayne State University)

In Canada, the New Deal had been watched and, after a time, imitated. In British Columbia, a new Liberal government, closely watched by an aggressive but inexperienced CCF opposition, introduced a flutter of social and labour legislation as its "New Deal." The term was immediately applied to the rich package of legislation unveiled by R.B. Bennett in a series of radio addresses in the winter of 1935. In Quebec, the Liberal government of Alexandre Taschereau listened to the Catholic syndicates and followed French and Belgian examples. In 1934, a Quebec law allowed industry-wide meetings of employers and workers to establish wages and working conditions, which could then be enforced by government *decree*. In Ontario, the provincial government tried to help industries establish *codes* of wages and conditions so that generous or humanitarian employers would not be victimized by ruthless competitors. In 1936, Mitchell Hepburn's Liberal government codified these arrangements with an Industrial Standards Act. Unfortunately, codes, decrees, and standards all meant little in the absence of powerful worker representation. Employers' standards of generosity were meagre, and enforcement was almost impossible. As for the new government of William Lyon Mackenzie King, its chief achievement was to enable the Judicial Committee of the Privy Council to dispose of virtually all of R.B. Bennett's belated reforms. In Canada the sound of Roosevelt's New Deal was little more than an echo.

During 1936, Canadian unionism had begun a major comeback. A year before, membership stood at its lowest point since 1914 — 280,704 workers. By the end of 1936, union strength stood at 322,473, its highest point in sixteen years. Most of the gains were in the internationally linked craft unions. With employment picking up, skilled craftsmen could renew their memberships. The breakup of the Workers' Unity League meant that existing central organizations acquired most of its units. Even the Catholic syndicates grew by 7,500. Communist unionists had initially concentrated on rejoining A.R. Mosher's All-Canadian Congress of Labour — with such effect that two of his colleagues, W.T. Burford and R.B. Russell, promptly broke away to form a tiny Canadian Federation of Labour in protest against the influx of "anarcho-communists." Mosher's organization was spared, however, when fresh orders from Moscow directed the Communists to transfer their support to the Trades and Labour Congress.

In the United States, the emergence of the CIO came at an ideal moment for Communist unionists and their sympathizers. Barred from the AFL (though not from the TLC) by William Green and his henchmen, young, tough-minded Communist organizers had plenty of scope in the industrial organizing drive. Lewis, Murray, Hillman, and Dubinsky, all veterans of their own anti-Communist drives, were confident that they could both use and control their militant agents. Indeed, their main concern was to find organizers and funds enough to do what demanded to be done in the United States; Canada was, at best, a distant priority.

Canadian workers were not so patient. In 1936, there was a long strike at the Courtauld plant at Cornwall. Without official CIO backing but with the magic letters always available as a symbol, organizing pushed forward in northern Ontario, in Kitchener's rubber and tire plants, among steelworkers in Hamilton, and auto workers in Windsor. Late in 1936, John L. Lewis announced that his Mine Workers would take the lead in organizing workers in the big Sydney steel mill. Lewis's man in Cape Breton, Silby Barrett, became the CIO's only official in Canada.

More often, workers took the initiative. At Point Edward near Sarnia, workers at the Holmes Foundry appealed to the SWOC for help. An organizer found every imaginable grievance from pitiful wages to dangerous working conditions, but he also found that the CIO enthusiasts were largely Slovak, Ukrainian, and Polish and despised by the English-speaking majority. On March 2, excited by the success of sit-downs in the United States, seventy of the workers sat down at their machines. Soon a mob of furious Sarnia citizens, armed with crowbars, bats, and steel tubes, invaded the plant. As Sarnia police watched with ill-concealed satisfaction from their side of the town line, the battered, bleeding sit-downers fled from the building to be arrested and charged with trespass. In the legislature, Premier Mitchell Hepburn jumped up to declare: "My sympathies are with those who fought the strikers....There will be no sit-down strikes in Ontario. This government is going to maintain law and order at all costs."

A month earlier, workers at the General Motors Oshawa plant had met an announcement of a production speed-up with a sudden strike. Soon the workers were in communication with the UAW, and Hugh Thompson, fresh from the Michigan sit-downs, arrived to organize Local No. 222. In a month, more than four thousand GM workers had signed on. Charles Millard, a former small businessman and active Anglican layman, was elected president.

General Motors in Canada was an easy target. Company pension plans were accompanied with medical inspections which weeded out most men over fifty. Announcement of a record $200 million profit was accompanied by notice of the fifth wage cut in five years. However, with the example of its American parent, the Canadian branch plant showed every sign of coming to terms with the UAW. Then Premier Hepburn intervened. From his vacation in Florida, he commanded his colleagues to keep Thompson under surveillance, and he rushed back to Toronto at the first hint that the company might settle. When a strike followed, on April 8, the Ontario premier proudly announced his "showdown" with the CIO. He was, Hepburn boasted, meeting "the first open attempt on the part of Lewis and his CIO henchmen to assume a position of dominating and dictating to Canadian industry."

Hepburn, whose single term as Ontario premier had been marked by flamboyant failure, had undoubtedly discovered a popular cause. Actually, he was intervening on behalf of some of his wealthy business friends (Sir James Dunn, J.P. Bickell, and George McCullagh) to keep CIO organizers out of Ontario's rich goldfields. However, his crusade against invading Americans and Communists struck a responsive note. Mosher's ACCL joined in denouncing the CIO interlopers, and the TLC kept quiet about some of the most blatant anti-union politicking in modern Canadian history. Hepburn's chief hope was violence. Millard's union failed to oblige. Liquor stores and taverns were closed. The Oshawa mayor, Alex Hall, refused to provide the Liberals with a pretext, and the local police force stayed neutral.

A furious Hepburn mustered his provincial police, demanded RCMP reinforcements from Ottawa, and, when too few were sent to satisfy him, replaced
the federal policemen with his own force of specials. Recruited largely from
university students, "Hepburn's Hussars," or the "Sons of Mitches," bedded
down in the basement of the legislature and awaited the call for action.

The striking auto workers at Oshawa resisted Hepburn's provocations, but
they might well have collapsed for more traditional reasons. Whatever Hepburn
believed, the CIO had trouble enough of its own without attacking Ontario's
greedier employers. The UAW itself was penniless. The best the union could do
was to organize an elaborate bluff that it had deposited $100,000 to the credit of
its striking local. Hepburn's performance included firing two of his cabinet
ministers, Arthur Roebuck and David Croll, for failing to share his hostility to
the CIO. "My place is marching with the workers," Croll announced, "rather
than riding with General Motors."

In the end, the strike was settled. By an elaborate subterfuge, the agreement
made no reference to the UAW or the CIO, and both Millard and the union
lawyer, J.L. Cohen, had to declare that neither of them represented the CIO.
Well aware that they were penniless and that the militancy of their members was
eroding fast, the Canadian leaders would have accepted almost anything. In fact,
they won every substantive demand from a forty-four-hour week to a clause
promising no discrimination against union members. On April 23, General
Motors was back at work.

While Hepburn claimed victory, most people believed that the magic letters
had won another triumph. That was hardly true. If GM had not signed earlier
with the United Auto Workers, it might have been much tougher in Oshawa, but
the Canadian workers had managed and supported their own strike without real
help from the United States. Moreover, in the absence of the kind of legal
backing represented by the Wagner Act, industrial unionism in Canada was as
hard as ever to establish. At St. Catharines, MacKinnon Industries, a GM
subsidiary, kept an open shop against determined organization attempts. In
Brantford, despite a long tradition of labour sympathies, a UAW local lasted
only a month.

The United Rubber Workers of America, another offspring of the CIO, also
entered Canada through a quick agreement with a branch plant, the B.F.
Goodrich factory in Kitchener. Other American subsidiaries were soon
organized in Kitchener, but when the Rubber Workers tackled Kaufman
Rubber, a local firm, it met a crushing defeat. A.R. Kaufman, well known for his
support of early birth-control organizations, was ruthlessly anti-union. He
stonewalled his employees, scorned provincial mediation efforts, and drove the
URWA out of Kitchener.

Thanks to the 1925 *Snider* case, it was unlikely that a national equivalent to the
Wagner Act was possible in Canada. In Nova Scotia, Silby Barrett's organizing
efforts, aided by Moscow directives to his mortal enemies, the local Communists,
resulted in the revival of District No. 26 of the United Mine Workers and the
establishment of Local No. 1064 of the Steelworkers of America by December,
1936. Two surprising political results followed. To the astonishment of the
struggling CCF, word arrived that District No. 26 had decided to affiliate to the

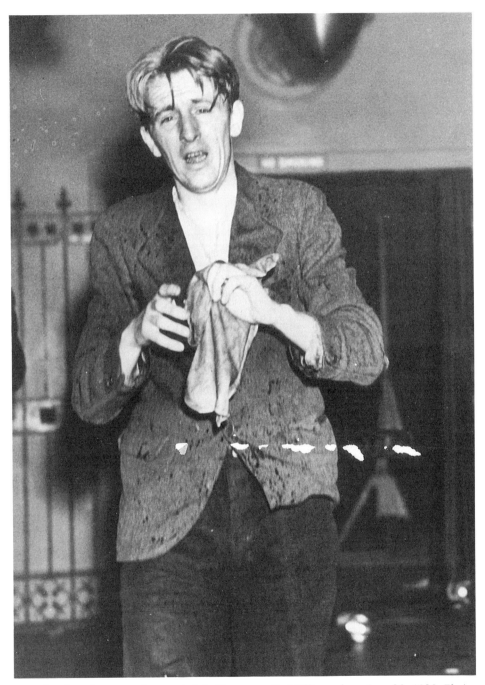

On orders from Ottawa, police attacked the Vancouver Post Office early on June 20, 1938. Fleeing occupants, eyes streaming from tear gas, had to run a gauntlet of police batons and truncheons as a penalty for their defiance. (Provincial Archives of British Columbia)

On June 20, 1938, an enterprising Vancouver photographer was up early enough to see city police and RCMP get ready to clear unemployed demonstrators from the city's main post office. As tear gas drove the occupants from the building into a gauntlet of baton-wielding policemen on the street outside. (Provincial Archives of British Columbia)

party. Two senior party officials had to travel to Sydney to discover whether it was true and then how it might be managed. Just as important was the provincial government's decision to enact the Nova Scotia Trade Union Act of April, 1937. For the first time, a Canadian province asserted that workers had the right to form a union, bargain through its officers, and collect a payroll checkoff. Unfortunately, like other provinces which followed suit, no satisfactory mechanism for certification of unions or enforcement of the act was included.

Another critical success for the Steelworkers came unexpectedly in Sault Ste. Marie. Having created their own Unemployed Workers Association in the depth of the depression, local citizens went on to create an Algoma Steel Workers Union. By January, 1937, the independent union had won recognition and checkoff from management. Even before the ASWU affiliated to the Steel Workers Organizing Committee in September, 1940, it had become an important factor in Ontario union organizing.

In Quebec, the CIO's biggest triumph came in Montreal's garment trade. In

1934, the Needle Trades Industrial Union of the Workers' Unity League had fought and lost a bitter month-long strike. Community support for the ill-paid, ill-treated French-Canadian women in the Jewish-run industry was counter-balanced by horror at the Communist backing for their union. The WUL's defeat was an opportunity for Bernard Shane of the International Ladies' Garment Workers' Union. By the simple device of concentrating on the skilled cutters and then extending their gains to unskilled workers, Shane had organized the coat trade in Toronto and Montreal. The dressmakers, after their 1934 experience, were much harder to organize. Moreover, when Shane once again concentrated on the cutters and pressers, the employers announced that they had signed an agreement with the Catholic League of Needle Industry Workers.

Shane refused to give up. Neither did the ILGWU, well aware that its American employers were making plans to move to the cheap labour market of Montreal. The union hired Claude Jodoin, then president of the Quebec Young Liberals, and persuaded Raoul Trepanier, president of the Montreal Trades and Labour Council, to be chairman of the strike committee. Without warning, at dawn on April 15, 1937, the strike began. More than four thousand workers answered the call.

The conflict was long and brutal. Spokesmen for the Catholic union demanded that the government arrest Communists and foreign agents in the ILGWU. Gerard Picard, secretary-general of the Canadian and Catholic Confederation of Labour, claimed that the CIO union was illegal. Maurice Duplessis, premier of Quebec and already an open foe of active unionism, proclaimed that he would have Shane and Trepanier arrested without bail for conspiring against public order. While the two men waited nervously over a weekend for their trip to the notorious cells of the Quebec Provincial Police, a sympathetic member of the Liberal opposition, Candide Rochefort, rushed back to Montreal in case he was needed to take over the strike.

In fact, Duplessis did not carry out his threat. From the first the unity of the employers had been fragile and fraying. For the most part small operators, a lengthy strike was as disastrous to them as to the workers. On May 4, a marathon bargaining session began. At 2:00 a.m. on May 6, an agreement was found. The ILGWU had won recognition. Shane had won a forty-four-hour week, grievance procedure, a closed union shop, and a wage increase. Women who had earned eleven dollars for an eighty-hour week went back to work for sixteen dollars for a forty-four-hour week.

In the strike of the Montreal *midinettes*, the Catholic union had found itself in a spoiling role. It soon faced its own test in Quebec's old-fashioned textile industry. In Canada and the United States, no industry fought unionism more consistently or brutally. By fleeing to low-wage, one-industry towns, textile plants had secured favourable ground. Government reports of starvation wages and long hours did nothing to soften their attitude.

The most dramatic struggle in 1937 occurred when the National Textile Federation of the Canadian and Catholic Confederation struck Dominion Textiles. The company president proclaimed that he didn't "care if the plants remained closed until Christmas"; but he did not have to wait so long. The

More than a thousand young Canadians served in Spain with the International Brigades. Almost half of them never returned. A lucky one hugs a younger sister at Toronto's Union Station in late 1938. The Canadians were mobilized by the Communist Party and many were veterans of relief camps and protest marches. (Public Archives Canada C 74970)

strikers, among the worst-paid people in Quebec, had no strike fund and nothing but public charity to keep them going. After three weeks, the big Montreal mills opened their doors, and with police protection, desperate workers broke ranks. Archbishop Villeneuve, determined to salvage something for the prestige of Catholic unionism, extracted an agreement from the company that, in fact, gave the workers less than the province's minimum wage for women. Even that agreement was broken in four months, and the union faded away.

As late as 1937, more unions shared the experience of the National Textile Federation than of the ILGWU. Except for Oshawa and the Montreal dressmakers, the CIO could boast of no real victories for all its efforts across Canada. In Hamilton, the Steel Workers Organizing Committee was defeated. In British Columbia, the International Woodworkers of America became one of the few internationals with a president and the bulk of its members in Canada. It was a small achievement. In a brutal strike at Blubber Bay, police and strike-breakers attacked union members and beat one organizer so badly that he died. The IWA was almost destroyed.

Even gains could be temporary. Shane's achievements for the ILGWU in 1937 came unravelled under the joint assault of employers and internal dissidents. By a year after the strike, the union was disintegrating. In Oshawa, in a local reflection of the turbulent UAW politics that had deposed Homer Martin and given the union Communist leadership, Charles Millard was defeated as president of Local No. 222 by his financial secretary, George Burt. Quickly hired by Barrett to take charge of the Ontario operations of the SWOC, the pro-CCF Millard arrived in Toronto to find his office staffed and guarded by active Communists.

After only a couple of years, the CIO in Canada appeared to be stillborn, and most of the corpse was owned by the Communists. Yet another moribund fragment had been added to the long list of Canadian labour organizations.

CHAPTER 16
Fighting Hitler and Management

On September 10, 1939, Canada officially found herself once again at war. Even a year earlier, it would have seemed impossible for a united Canada to involve itself in another European war. The Left had warned frantically of the fascist menace. The Communists had mobilized more than a thousand of the country's youthful unemployed for the war in Spain, but the great majority of their countrymen were scornful of the Mackenzie-Papineau Battalion and some muttered "good riddance" when reports returned of murderous casualties. Canada was disarmed, isolationist, and reluctant to go crusading against Herr Hitler.

With brilliant political skill, Mackenzie King had brought people around. Both he and the Conservative leader, R.J. Manion, swore that there would be no conscription. The small CCF was torn between the pacifism of its revered leader, J.S. Woodsworth, and the conviction of younger M.P.'s like T.C. Douglas that the Nazi menace had to be faced. The government made plans for a war which would cost the minimum of Canadian lives and achieve the maximum possible recovery for a sagging Canadian economy.

When the war began, Canadian labour was as weak as it had been in 1914 and even more divided. Long after the American Federation of Labor had expelled the CIO unions, the Trades and Labour Congress had delayed and deferred the deed. Early in 1939, the Canadians finally got the ultimatum. If the CIO unions stayed in, the AFL affiliates would leave. Tom Moore, still president of the congress, grimly obeyed orders. It was easier because the CIO drive in Canada was as stalled as it had been since the Oshawa triumph. Its organizing committees and their few scattered local unions served often as fronts for

165

C.D. Howe visits the International Nickel Company on February 16, 1942. The general manager of Canada's economic war effort looks as awkward and uncomfortable as the workers dutifully assembled to hear his words. As a politician, Howe was a fine engineer. (Public Archives Canada C 19378)

veteran Communist organizers and battlegrounds for contending political ideologies.

Until only weeks before the outbreak of war, the Communists had been almost frenzied in their efforts to build a popular front against Hitler and fascism. No issue mattered more. Suddenly, with announcement of the Nazi-Soviet pact, no issue mattered less. Never had the contradictory orders from Moscow demanded a more humiliating change of line. In hours the popular-front slogans were forgotten. Loyal Communists, open and secret, accepted a fresh directive: the war with Hitler was the last gasp of a decaying bourgeoisie and should be sabotaged in any useful way.

Certainly the opening months of Canada's war effort had a somewhat enervated look to them. In the earlier war, Sir Robert Borden had committed Canada to victory at any cost; for King, the war was to be a limited undertaking in which the interests of Canada (always identical with his Liberal party) would ever be paramount. It was a view most Canadians fervently shared. The government had only one basic plan: avoid the errors of the previous war. Avoid commitments of fighting men that might lead to conscription. Use the war to develop durable and profitable Canadian industries by emphasizing air-crew training. Stop profiteering before it began by creating a powerful Wartime

Once again, women flooded into wartime factories. Again the government encouraged the move by emphasizing the pleasures of the work place. However, the government also included women in its selective service regulations. If women wanted to leave their jobs in this Winnipeg propellor factory, they had to get official permission. (Public Archives Canada C 81418)

Prices and Trade Board and using the War Measures Act to control the economy.

King was sure that he would not repeat Borden's habit of ignoring organized labour. In large measure this was due to the prime minister's confidence in his own expertise as an industrial relations specialist and to his belief in himself as a devoted friend of at least those workers who were "responsible." Certainly the aging president of the TLC, Tom Moore, the former carpenter from Niagara Falls, was in that category. Thanks to King's approval, a long-standing private bill from J.S. Woodsworth had finally become law at the first 1939 session of Parliament. For the first time, it would be a criminal offence to fire an employee for the simple offence of favouring a union. (It took a very stupid employer to fail to find another pretext.) Such kindness, King believed, would allow Moore to swing his members behind the Liberals in the forthcoming federal election.

Labour had other preoccupations. While the TLC counted its losses from the CIO expulsion, the industrial unions looked for new allies. They found them in a surprising place — A.R. Mosher's All-Canadian Congress of Labour. The ACCL had led the vituperation at the CIO invasion, but its nationalist principles proved costly. For all the backing Mosher's own Canadian brotherhood could bring, the ACCL was bankrupt and floundering. The CIO would bring fifty-five

Top

J.A. "Pat" Sullivan was one of the founding forces of the Canadian Seamen's Union. A Communist who was interned when the war got serious in 1940, he was released, officially forgot his politics, and was promptly elected vice-president and then secretary-treasurer of the TLC. No Communist rose higher in Canada's labour movement and no unionist ever fell faster when, in 1947, Sullivan left the Communist party and told all. (Public Archives Canada The Gazette, 1947)*

Throughout the war, Mackenzie King was acutely conscious of the judgement Canadians would pass on his Liberal government when they went to the polls. The swing of organized labour to the CCF, reflected in opinion polls and election victories, finally pushed the prime minister to agree to family allowances and to authorize P.C. 1003, creating national machinery for union recognition and certification. (Public Archives Canada C 22001) thousand members, energy, and prospects. The most frantic nationalists had left with W.T. Burford; the rest were content when the CIO unions promised generous autonomy for their Canadian districts. In return, anti-Communist CIO leaders wanted both the ACCL's legitimacy and its powerful anti-Communist bloc vote, while the Communist's union expert, J.B. Salsberg, insisted that his side could spread its influence through a larger organization.

The bitter internal struggle was evident when the 1940 ACCL convention turned into the founding meeting of a new Canadian Congress of Labour. CCF supporters elected four of the six members of the CCL executive — Aaron Mosher; Silby Barrett, the coal miner who had headed the CIO in Canada; Charles Millard, who was in a desperate fight with Communist organizers in his new job as Canadian head of the SWOC; and Sol Spivak from the Amalgamated Clothing Workers. The secretary-treasurer of the new congress was a youthful-looking UMW leader from Alberta, Pat Conroy. He and M.M. Maclean from the Canadian Brotherhood of Railway Employees were unionists long before they supported the CCF and they resisted the trend to political battling, but there was no doubt that the Communists would never have their backing in a clinch. The Communists fought hard, but their voting strength was tested when Nigel Morgan of the British Columbia-based International Woodworkers ran against Mosher for the presidency. Morgan collected 175 votes to Mosher's 283. Delegates also passed a resolution condemning nazism, fascism, and communism as equal evils.

Communist influence always far outweighed mere numbers. Party members, totalling no more than a couple of thousand, used their organizing skills and the prestige available at all times for outspoken militants to win union office. In the early months of the "phoney war," many Canadians could forgive the Communists for their lack of enthusiasm for the war and forget the dramatic switch of August, 1939. The government declared the party illegal and banned its papers, but suppression, like much of the war effort, was half-hearted. King had no wish to imitate Borden by creating labour martyrs.

Mackenzie King's political luck was never more in evidence than in the spring of 1940. Having led his Liberal party to an unprecedented landslide on the basis of a cautious war effort, he was safely home when the Nazi blitzkrieg swept into Norway and then across the Low Countries into France. Within weeks, the Allies were battling for survival. In two months, Britain and her dominions stood virtually alone against Hitler and German military might. The phoney war was over.

In rapid succession, legislation and Orders in Council transformed the war effort. The National Resources Mobilization Act gave Ottawa total control of manpower, including conscription for home defence. The near tolerance of the Communists ended abruptly, and by mid-1941, ninety-eight active members found themselves in internment camps along with Canada's fringe of Fascists, Nazis, and outspoken dissenters, like Montreal's Mayor Camillien Houde. Others left Canada or went underground. In due course, the Communists could claim a special martyrdom at the hands of a tyrannical wartime government. J.A. Sullivan and other officials of the Canadian Seamen's Union were arrested in the midst of contract negotiations. Clarence S. Jackson, the former accountant who headed the United Electrical Workers, claimed that he was interned for leading a strike by employees of Canadian General Electric.

As in the previous war, the outbreak did not lead to immediate union growth. Among organized workers, the early winners were the long-established organizations. The United Mine Workers immediately recovered the membership losses of the thirties. Thanks to uniform contracts, the Amalgamated Clothing Workers and the International Ladies' Garment Workers demanded and won solid union shop agreements across Canada.

With British war production desperately needed for home defence, Canada again had to develop her own arms industries, this time for airplanes, vehicles, tanks, and artillery, as well as shells. This time the czar of Canadian munitions was not a private businessman like Sir Joseph Flavelle but an American-born engineer and Liberal cabinet minister, Clarence Decatur Howe. Howe and the dollar-a-year businessmen who commanded his exploding industrial empire had no love of unions, but politically labour organizers could not be resisted.

As in the earlier war, the biggest winner was the International Association of Machinists. Forgetting its strict craft principles, the IAM concentrated on the brand new aircraft industry, supplying trainers for the British Commonwealth Air Training Plans. Workers in factories at Vancouver, Winnipeg, Fort William, Toronto, and Montreal joined lodges and won union recognition and big wage increases. The International Brotherhood of Electrical Workers, a pillar of the craft principle, overlooked its beliefs and set out to organize production workers. The International Brotherhood of Boilermakers, Iron Shipbuilders, Welders and Helpers made slow progress in the shipyards, which were plugged with contracts for merchant ships and escort vessels to meet the growing U-boat threat in the Atlantic.

Craft unions made big gains because they had experienced organizers and bargainers, because they had a legitimacy with employers and the government that the CIO unions had yet to win, and because the Trades and Labour Congress's political neutrality allowed Communists, CCFers, Liberals, and the politically indifferent to function without overt conflict until the end of the war.

In Ottawa, the government faced a host of unfamiliar problems as Canada found herself promoted to the status of a major ally to hard-pressed Britain. One critical factor was labour; another was inflation. Not only was price stability a necessary element on the home front, it was essential if the Canadian dollar was to maintain its standing on world exchanges. Wartime needs gave a push to a long-standing political promise: unemployment insurance. Bennett's 1935 scheme had been abandoned for constitutional reasons. The defeat of Quebec's Union Nationale government in 1939 and the advent of a more pliable Liberal government under Adelard Godbout softened provincial resistance. The clincher was the wartime benefit of siphoning off spending power through premiums. Unemployment insurance in the war years was another form of taxation.

With rival labour organizations scurrying for members, labour peace was much harder to achieve. An early government measure was to extend the Industrial Disputes Investigation Act, with its delaying effect on strikes, to all national wartime industries. Another step, Privy Council Order 2685, declared that fair and reasonable standards of wages and working conditions *should* be observed and the right of workers to form their own unions *should* be recognized. Greeted with pleasure by Canadian union leaders, it soon proved to be an empty gesture. When the Canadian Congress of Labour complained that employers ignored the order, Norman McLarty, King's minister of labour, blandly explained that P.C. 2685 was not supposed to be coercive.

Much worse followed. On December 16, 1940, P.C. 7440 imposed a peculiar kind of wage control on workers. Some unions had won spectacular gains for their members in aircraft factories, machine shops, and other key war plants, and the government was worried. The new order directed the boards appointed under the Industrial Disputes Investigation Act to limit wage settlements to rates established during 1926–29, a period of "reasonable wage levels." A cost-of-living bonus of $1.25 a week might be paid as an addition.

How the measure worked soon became apparent. Peck Rolling Mills in Montreal, a subsidiary of Dominion Steel and Coal of Cape Breton fame, was compelled to recognize the Steel Workers Organizing Committee to represent its workers. However, a board appointed under the IDI Act refused any wage increase on the argument that the current rate of thirty cents an hour was higher than the 1929 level. J.L. Cohen, already the CIO's most popular lawyer and a member of the investigating body, issued a forceful minority report. The company preferred the majority view, and a harsh two-month strike did not change its mind. Employers had found a fresh weapon against unions and wage demands.

For all the prime minister's protestations of affection for the workers, his government soon appeared to be vigorously anti-union. By July, 1941, the CCL's research director, Eugene Forsey, insisted that "the government's labour policy is as thoroughly and consistently anti-union as it dares to be." To C.D. Howe, unions were a disruptive and potentially dangerous nuisance. In a dispute at the General Motors engine plant at St. Catharines, Howe promised RCMP protection for workers who broke a strike. At Arvida in the summer of 1941, a simmering dispute between the Aluminum Company of Canada and a Catholic syndicate flared up when workers occupied the huge plant, switched off the furnaces, and allowed the enormous pots of molten metal to *freeze*. Acting on excited claims that an "enemy alien" had inspired the sabotage, the government rushed two companies of troops to the scene, too late to do anything. Howe, himself, offered his resignation on the argument that colleagues had worried about legality and jurisdiction before acting. The prime minister pacified him with fresh powers to order in troops. No evidence of enemy sabotage was ever found. The real problem was broiling heat and unilingual English management.

A major source of trouble was King's long-standing indifference to union recognition and his preference for the traditional unionism represented by the TLC. At Hamilton's National Steel Car Company, a strike followed management refusal to consider an employee vote on union recognition. A controller, appointed by the government to get the vital factory running again, allowed the vote but then refused to deal with the Steelworkers when the union won. A second strike was necessary before the government appointed a more conciliatory controller.

The story of Kirkland Lake was much more tangled and bitter. As Mitchell

In 1937, Mitchell Hepburn fought the CIO in Oshawa because he wanted to keep union organizers from penetrating the gold mines of Northern Ontario. When workers were finally driven to strike in 1941, the Liberal premier sent most of the province's police force to Kirkland Lake. The miners answered with their own march through the town and the long, grim struggle was underway. (Public Archives of Canada PA 121252)

Hepburn had long feared, the CIO eventually did build a union in Ontario's goldfields through the International Union of Mine, Mill and Smelter Workers, the heir of the Western Federation of Miners. The inevitable IDI Act board was necessary. Labour's nominee was J.L. Cohen, but for once the chairman, Mr. Justice C.P. McTague, a former Toronto Tory, joined him in his views. Union recognition, insisted the board majority, was justified. When the employers bluntly refused even to meet the board, the employer representative was angry enough to make the report unanimous.

That did nothing for the union or the miners. In a strike vote, workers in eight of the twelve mines voted two to one to walk out. On November 18, 1941, the strike began. It was almost exactly what the mine owners wanted. Gold markets were slow in wartime. From Toronto came words of encouragement and hefty contingents of provincial police, forwarded by Premier Mitchell Hepburn. The newly joined Globe and Mail, owned by gold-mining interests, led a newspaper chorus of outrage at workers who dared to strike in wartime.

Mosher and Pat Conroy had seen it coming. They had urged Mine-Mill leaders to put their organizing priorities on Sudbury's nickel mining, a vital war industry where Ottawa would have to force a settlement. Mine-Mill had its own priorities, determined by Reid Robinson, the union's Communist international president. Stuck with a suicidal plan, the Canadian union leaders did their best to save the Kirkland Lake strike, raising help from unions, clergy, and just plain citizens. Two freezing months later, the strike collapsed. The miners left the area, joined the army, or made what terms they could. The Canadian Congress of Labour was bankrupt. Mine-Mill's organization was swept away all over northern Ontario. In Sudbury, hired thugs smashed the union office and badly injured an organizer.

Organized labour and its sympathizers were furious at King. George Grube, a Toronto CCF supporter, wrote in the Canadian Forum: "To interpret the attitude of this government . . . as weakness before powerful financial interests is to miss

Top
The Kirkland Lake strike produced a number of effective organizers for both Mine-Mill and the Steelworkers. One of the best was Larry Sefton. A rare combination of idealist and shrewd tactician, Sefton gave an imaginative flair to his union's organizing drive.

Humphrey Mitchell, Canada's wartime labour minister, welcomes Trygve Lie, Norwegian socialist and future U.N. secretary-general, to Ottawa. A Hamilton trade unionist and a Labour M.P. from 1931 to 1935, Mitchell made few friends in the labour hierarchy and earned little respect from his Liberal colleagues, but some of Canada's most important labour legislation was adopted in his time. (Public Archives Canada C 29838) the whole point. It was completely consistent and unscrupulously deliberate. Never has Mr. King more clearly shown the murderous power of his talent for inaction." To be fair, King deplored Hepburn and the powerful mining interests behind the *Globe and Mail*, but he kept most of his opinions for his diary.

Seeking to reassure labour, he decided to displace the ineffectual Norman McLarty and sought to persuade Tom Moore to become minister of labour. The elderly TLC chieftain urged instead that King appoint Humphrey Mitchell, a Hamilton electrician and TLC stalwart who had served from 1931 to 1935 as a Labour M.P., without ever leaning to the CCF. Mitchell, a ponderous, amiable man who had filled a number of government jobs since his defeat in 1935, was acting as secretary to the National Labour Supply Council. He was easily elected for Welland on February 9, 1942. On the same day, in the apparently rock-ribbed Tory riding of York South, the Conservatives' new national leader, Arthur Meighen, was decisively defeated by a CCF high school teacher named Joe Noseworthy. Experts pondered the significance. In Ottawa, King could rejoice in the defeat of a hated rival, but obviously some profound changes were building in the heart of Canada.

Mackenzie King remained confident that he could keep change firmly within the Liberal party's orbit. In the summer of 1941, the war had entered a new phase. Suddenly, the huge German panzer armies rolled over the Soviet border and destroyed much of Stalin's Red Army. In Canada, Communists performed as dramatic a switch as in 1939. Suddenly the war became a desperate struggle for democracy against fascism. In the unions, Communists now denounced strikes and disruption. In the Steel Workers Organizing Committee, Silby Barrett and Charles Millard were condemned by Communist-controlled locals for permitting strikes at Peck Rolling Mills and other war industries. The only crime of the King government was in keeping patriotic Communists behind barbed wire. Public pressure compelled release of leading figures like Jackson and Sullivan, while other Communist leaders, like the party secretary, Tim Buck, came out from hiding or returned from the United States.

The Soviet involvement in the war and the consequent switch of Canadian Communists became an enormous asset to the government in ensuring labour peace. In the autumn of 1941, while inflation appeared in danger of spiralling out of control, King turned to labour leaders for support of a policy of rigorous wage and price controls. Moore, Mosher, Alfred Charpentier of the Catholic syndicates, and J.B. Ward, representing the railway brotherhoods, promised their support. In sweeping measures adopted barely a week after their first formulation, prices were frozen at current levels, wages could not be increased without written approval from a new National War Labour Board, and the cost-of-living bonus was made compulsory.

It was a policy which could perhaps have only been imposed on a divided labour movement, conscious of its weakness and eager, as it had not been in a previous war, to prove its patriotism. As for the government's goal of controlling inflation, it would prove a remarkable success. The cost of living, which had risen 20 percent in the first two years of war, rose less than 10 percent from 1942 to 1945. However, the policy stirred up controversy within labour and government and, in time, unconsciously paved the way for the greatest advances in Canadian trade union history.

CHAPTER 17
"People Coming into Their Own"

By 1943, the outcome of the war was no longer really in doubt. A long, bitter struggle remained, but Hitler and the Axis powers would be defeated. Canadians could so far count themselves very lucky. War in the air and on the North Atlantic had brought tragedy to many homes, but only at Hong Kong and Dieppe had soldiers perished in large numbers.

By 1943, Canada's wartime economy edged toward its peak. Thereafter, manpower shortages and swelling inventories of the weapons and equipment produced in Canada led to the first cutbacks in the new war industries. After a slow start, Canada had reached the unprecedented state of absolutely full employment. With workers in desperately short supply, their bargaining power and that of their unions must necessarily increase. Membership in unions grew by a hundred thousand in 1941, and another hundred thousand were added in 1942.

In fact, the claims were misleading. Membership figures were supplied by unions themselves, and they included tens of thousands who had signed up in hope of recognition. In the first three years of the war, only two mass-production industries were newly organized in Canada, the aircraft plants and the shipyards. In both cases, manufacturers had powerful financial and moral pressures to increase production. In the aircraft factories, the International Association of Machinists signed agreements which included no provision for union security or even for checkoff. That would make it easier for employers in the postwar world. On both coasts, shipyards worked around the clock to turn out freighters and the small, unsophisticated escort-vessels known as corvettes. Jurisdictional disputes complicated labour relations in the yards, but unionization was rapid and wage rates were among the highest in Canada.

175

Governments during the depression refused to accept responsibility for ensuring that Canadians were adequately fed and housed. Suddenly in wartime, Ottawa controlled prices and wages, directed when and where men and women would work, restrained rents, and, through this friendly postman, issued ration books to each citizen. If this was the socialism politicians had denounced in the 1930s, a good many Canadians now felt that it might not be so bad after all. (Public Archives Canada C 26110)

There was a brutal contrast between improvised wartime industries and companies with long-established patterns of labour relations. The Steel Company of Canada stoutly refused to deal with the Steel Workers Organizing Committee. Elections for a works council, set up in 1935, were swept by a solid union slate in 1942. H.G. Hilton, the self-made Stelco president, refused to discuss any form of union representation. When the worker representatives resigned in protest, Hilton simply filled up the council with their defeated opponents.

Most Canadians worked for small companies in small towns. The history of unionism in Canada is the story of countless little struggles, some of them successful, most of them frustrating failures. Take the example of metal workers in the little Ontario city of Galt. Between November, 1942, and January, 1943, Arthur Williams had tried to organize them. A staff member of the Canadian Congress of Labour, Williams had started with textile workers and moved to the metal trades because of backing from Charles Millard's Steelworkers. By the end of January, he had two thousand signatures and a majority of workers in nine establishments.

From Toronto, Millard mailed each company a proposed collective agreement and an invitation to start bargaining. The companies, led by Galt's largest firm, Babcock-Wilcox, and by Goldie-McCullough ("Goldie's" to locals), flatly refused to meet the union. Millard arrived in Galt, presented charters to the new locals, and promised support in what he claimed was part of a "world-wide struggle to ensure better postwar conditions for labour." Provincial conciliation officers failed to persuade the companies to negotiate, and the union, armed with a strike vote, called for an Industrial Disputes Investigation Act board.

A month passed before a federal investigator agreed to a board. Meanwhile, one of the companies fired two union activists, provoking a brief strike. Conciliation finally began in April, although employers had long since helped non-union employees to set up "associations." The chairman of the IDI Act board was sufficiently impressed by these organizations to adjourn hearings and go off on vacation. Tension mounted steadily until, on May 21, exasperated workers at seven Galt plants downed tools and set up picket lines.

The strike was surely excusable; it was even more certainly illegal. Spurred into action, a majority on the conciliation board issued its report dismissing the Steelworkers' application in all but two small plants, where it could bargain for its members only. The union had, insisted two board members, only a "slight majority" of the employees and it had used "tactics of persuasion which were not commendable." The minority report, written by Andrew Brewin, a Toronto lawyer and CCF leader, argued in vain that the principle of majority rule might be applied in industry as in other areas of society. Most of the strikers lost their jobs, and the employee associations ruled the roost.

Martine Malti, a shipyard worker at Pictou, solves her child care problem in a way traditional to her Micmac people as she poses during construction of a wartime corvette. While a few highly-publicised day-care centres were established in wartime factories, most women workers had to solve their own problems. (National Archives PA 116154)

When the Canadian Congress of Labour endorsed the CCF in 1943, it could list plenty of grievances with the Liberal government. However, the real reason was that CCFers in the Congress organized the endorsement. They then organized a Political Action Committee to deliver support without realizing how swiftly they would be checkmated. The members were, from the left: Fred Dowling (Packinghouse Workers), R.J. Lamoureux (Steel), Andy Andras (congress staff), Bob Carlin (Mine-Mill), Charles Millard (Steel), Louis Palermo (Clothing Workers), and Joe Mackenzie (Rubber). (Newton, Ottawa)

The members of Canada's National War Labour Board were probably as unconscious as anyone that they were going to make lasting changes in the country's industrial relations system. They were probably much more conscious of the bitter personal and political differences between labour's nominee, J.L. Cohen, left, and the chairman, Mr. Justice C.P. McTague, centre. (Public Archives Canada PA 112763)

Employer-sponsored organizations still proved effective anti-union weapons. J.S. Maclean, president of Canada Packers, boasted a reputation of liberalism and enlightenment on the "labour question," but when his company union was challenged by Fred Dowling's Packinghouse Workers' Organizing Committee, he fought back hard and fast. The minister of labour, Humphrey Mitchell, served as mediator, proposing a "plant council." Mitchell's department arranged a representation vote for all Toronto plants of Canada Packers although the union had sought to represent only two of them. The plant council won by a small margin. The PWOC won smaller plants in Vancouver and Moose Jaw, but the key Toronto operation was protected. In Kitchener, a town notorious for tough employer resistance, the Burns Company eliminated the Packinghouse Workers by lockouts, firings, and a stated willingness to shut down for the duration of the war.

The United Auto Workers, still boasting of the 1937 settlement at Oshawa, had to be content in most places with the so-called Niagara Formula, with shop committees composed of union and non-union representatives. The Ford Motor Company in 1942, conceded a feeble recognition to the UAW, with no provision for checkoff or maintenance of membership. In British Columbia, the International Woodworkers of America organized 90 percent of the loggers in camps on the Queen Charlotte Islands. The companies bluntly refused to bargain. Instead, union organizers were routinely run out of camps, and one company posted a sign — Not All Saboteurs Are Japs. The IWA claimed ten thousand members in British Columbia — and a single agreement!

In some Canadian centres, wartime politics helped promote unionism. In Montreal, seething with indignation at the Mackenzie King government's conscription referendum of 1942, appeals to endorse the national war effort fell on thin soil. Not only was Montreal's Mayor Camillien Houde interned for his anti-war statements, but the city's administration, bankrupt after the heavy depression spending on relief, had been placed in trusteeship to the province. In a series of dramatic confrontations, municipal employees — beginning with outside workers and finishing with office employees, and including police and firemen — won the right to organize and improve their depression-level wages. Such a radical development would have been impossible without substantial public support, cheering from the sidelines by frustrated city politicians, and the inevitable weakness of a government-appointed administrator.

In the rest of Canada, the political climate was less favourable to organized labour. Thwarted by organizing failures and hindered by wartime constraints on collective bargaining, labour leaders began to lead their members in the same direction as in the previous world war: political action. In the Canadian Congress of Labour, CCFers dominated the senior positions and controlled a number of powerful affiliates, but even the Trades and Labour Congress began to sway from its Liberal or non-partisan allegiances.

In the West the CCF had grown steadily. By the end of 1941, it formed the official opposition in Saskatchewan and faced a nervous Liberal-Conservative coalition in British Columbia. However, the CCF's most dramatic breakthrough came in February, 1942, with its by-election victory in York South. Thousands joined the party. In April, Ontario CCFers chose a leader, E.B. Jolliffe, and adopted a program. In July, 1942, a CCF–trade union conference began the slow process of affiliating unions to the new party. By fall, money raised by the conference paid for a tough, eloquent Cape Bretonner named Clarie Gillis to come to Ontario to lead the campaign.

By the end of 1942, a poll indicated that the CCF could claim support from 27 percent of Ontario voters and 23 percent of all Canadians. Both federal and Ontario Liberals began working frantically to divert workers from the dangerous new allegiance. An Ontario Select Committee on Collective Bargaining met large delegations of workers and listened patiently to reports of the delays and frustrations caused by existing labour law. Weakened by internal rivalries following Mitchell Hepburn's unexpected departure, the Ontario Liberals summoned up the energy to pass the first Canadian version of the Wagner Act. It did not save them. The provincial election of August, 1943, ended in a narrow victory for the Ontario Conservatives. The Liberals were swept out of office. The real surprise was that voters in the industrial cities of the south and in the mill towns and mining camps of northern Ontario had turned to the CCF. Overall, the turnout was the lowest in Ontario history, but workers had for once flocked to the polls. The CCF won 32 percent of the popular vote, 40 percent of the urban vote, and thirty-four seats in the legislature — just four less than the Tories.

All of this was a very serious concern to the federal government. Desperate to keep the country united behind his Liberal party, King had given his chief attention to his French-Canadian supporters, but he retained a conviction that somehow working people held him in special esteem. That mood was not apparent in 1943. Full employment and higher wages also encouraged displays of boldness which might have seemed impossible a few years earlier. In January and February, 1943, the Steelworkers struck the huge mills at Sydney and Sault Ste. Marie to win a fifty-five-cent minimum wage rate. Government ministers, led by C.D. Howe, fumed and threatened, but it was apparent, at least to King, that locking up strikers or their leaders would not produce steel. The workers won their point and their example was imitated. Two of the major strikes of 1943, a ten-day illegal walkout of nine thousand coal miners in Alberta and British Columbia and a ten-day "summer holiday" of twenty-one thousand aircraft workers in Montreal, were based on money issues.

For other workers, economic issues took a back seat to the struggle for union recognition. Many workers were persuaded that only a solidly entrenched union could possibly protect their rights on the shop floor and sustain the fight for a living wage. Just as employers wanted no entangling commitments that could limit their postwar freedom, union members came to believe that only a durable organization could cushion a postwar depression. And durability would be impossible in Canada without a legislative foundation like the Wagner Act in the United States. If the federal and provincial governments would not act, support for the CCF made sense.

Concern about the postwar world had spread to government, if only as a morale-building device for war-weary Canadians. The Atlantic Charter of August, 1941, symbol of the historic meeting between Roosevelt and Churchill off Argentia in Newfoundland's Placentia Bay, proclaimed war aims in terms of

Provincial treasurer Clarence Fines, Saskatchewan premier Tommy Douglas, and labour minister Charlie Williams meet the Trades and Labour Congress in Regina in 1951. Though they took over one of Canada's poorest and least industrialized provinces, the CCF promptly gave provincial employees free collective bargaining, made it easier for unions to organize, and presided over an endless series of pay-as-you-go reforms that made Saskatchewan the home for social reform in Canada for twenty years. (Archives of Saskatchewan)

the *four freedoms*. In addition to *freedom from want*, the charter specified *social security* and *fair labour standards* among its goals. In late 1942, Sir William Beveridge released a report which called for a massive overhaul of British social legislation and proposed many of the elements of the postwar welfare state. In Canada, a committee of wartime civil servants headed by a McGill professor and former CCF sympathizer, Leonard Marsh, produced a *Report on Social Security for Canada*, a comparable blueprint for comprehensive social security for Canadians from infancy to old age.

Marsh's report made recommendations designed not simply to prevent a postwar depression but to ease some of the enduring problems of working-class poverty. He called not just for continued unemployment insurance but for occupational readjustment training programs and a reserve of public works projects as well. Not only did he recommend national health insurance but also a system of cash benefits for the sick, universal contributory old age pensions, and maternity allowances. In a modern society, it was simply unrealistic to expect children to assume financial responsibility for aging parents. Poverty, he suggested, was a family phenomenon. A wage which could support a single worker was hopelessly inadequate for a family with a growing number of children. Employers could hardly be expected to pay workers more if they had children; a family allowance, based on the number of children, was the answer. The Marsh Report horrified business leaders and their editorial allies. The price tag of $900 million, $500 million of it from federal coffers, would have sounded like national bankruptcy if Canada had not been spending many times as much on the war effort, and thriving in the process. Walter Gordon, a future Liberal cabinet minister, noted that Marsh had spent just a week to think out his proposal. He scoffed that if the professor had spent thirty hours thinking how to spend a billion dollars, what would he have done in a longer period? Other Liberals were more imaginative — or worried. The *Canadian Forum*, sympathetic to the CCF, noted that the Marsh recommendations were "the price Liberalism is willing to pay to prevent socialism."

Labour leaders could argue that unions were as essential to the welfare of workers as plans for health insurance and children's allowances. As CCF strength rose through 1943, governments began to revise their approach to labour problems. In British Columbia, the Conciliation and Arbitration Act was amended to require companies to negotiate with union representatives when the minister of labour was satisfied that the union represented a majority of employees. There was still no labour relations board to supervise the legislation, but the concept of certification had at least arrived. The International Woodworkers of America could finally convert its strength in numbers into collective agreements with the major firms during the autumn of 1943, though recognition was grudgingly conceded and with no concessions on such questions as the checkoff of union dues.

In Quebec, the most immediate pressures for a certification procedure emerged from the intense rivalry of the international and the Catholic national unions in the pulp and paper and the aluminium industries. The International Brotherhood of Pulp, Sulphite and Paper Mill Workers had held union shop contracts with Price Brothers' mills in the Lac St. Jean region since 1939, but by 1943 a determined organization drive had won the majority in three mills over to the Catholic confederation. The company then fired workers who refused to join the international, and an angry dispute developed. The provincial government annulled the union shop provision in the contract and appointed a Royal Commission to report on the specifics of the dispute. A similar struggle at Arvida, where the raid was launched by an international union, was referred to another commission.

The Quebec Labour Relations Act of 1944 was based on the report of the Prévost Commission and introduced yet another variant of the Wagner Act to Canada. Quebec's new certification procedure was eagerly embraced by all unions in the province, and the law contributed to the organization of tobacco workers, shoe workers, and electrical workers in Montreal as well as locals in other parts of the province.

In Ottawa, the federal cabinet, at Mackenzie King's urging, asked the National War Labour Board to inquire into "Labour Relations and Wage Conditions in Canada." Hearings began in April, 1943. In the next two months, nearly every major trade union leader in the country appeared as a witness, along with dozens of business leaders and government officials. Labour's message was clear: wage control must be lifted for lower-paid workers, with fifty-five cents an hour set as a national basic wage rate. Equally necessary was a national labour code based on the Wagner Act.

Public sessions of the inquiry ended in June of 1943, and by the fall both minority and majority reports were in the hands of the government. The majority report was written by the board chairman, Mr. Justice C.P. McTague, a veteran conciliator and former active Conservative. Despite his politics, McTague had struck the prime minister as a fellow spirit, and labour remembered his sympathetic if unavailing report at the time of the Kirkland Lake gold miners' strike. McTague earned his reputation: Canada should have a labour code which met the demands of the labour movement, and the best way to meet the demands of the ill-paid workers was a system of family allowances. Only in that way could the burden on families with many children be relieved without starting a general wage scramble. "If the authorities . . . do not see their way clear to remove during the war emergency the control of wages below the level of 50 cents," McTague argued, "then we can think of no other solution . . . than a system of family allowances."

The minority report was written by J.L. Cohen, a labour lawyer who was close to the Canadian Congress of Labour leadership. Cohen backed the proposal for a national labour code, but he also argued that wage controls on lower-paid workers must be removed and a national minimum wage of fifty cents an hour established. He faithfully echoed both the CCL and the TLC positions, argued at their 1943 conventions, that a family allowance was simply a substitute for a living wage.

The King government found both reports embarrassing — and kept both reports secret. Liberal desperation grew, heightened by a humiliating by-election setback in August, 1943. Four hitherto safe seats were lost, two to the CCF in western Canada, one to the Communist-controlled Labour Progressive party, and one to Quebec's antiwar group, the Bloc Populaire. In October, Mr. Justice McTague resigned from his federal position and, to King's rage, promptly became president of the freshly titled Progressive Conservative party.

Earlier, Mackenzie King had shared the horror of many of his cabinet members at the alleged prodigality of the Marsh Report recommendations. "To tell the country that everyone was to get a family allowance was sheer folly," he told his diary. "It would occasion great resentment everywhere." The idea, put forward by J.S. Woodsworth in 1929, slowly began to gain in appeal. It would satisfy workers' demands for more money. Moreover, it was popular with King's Quebec ministers and, accordingly, aroused fury from the Conservatives' new welfare critic, Dr. Charlotte Whitton. Social reforms, Dr. Whitton insisted, would "weaken the fibre of the nation."

The four by-elections in August, 1943, made the difference. "In my heart," King wrote in his diary, "I am not sorry to see the mass of the people coming a little more into their own, but I do regret that it is not a Liberal party that is winning that position . . . . What I fear is that we will begin to have defection from our own ranks in the House to the C.C.F." There was still something that he could do.

Parties in power, as the Liberals were accustomed to argue, could always do what oppositions could only promise. When the Department of Finance's experts, now largely converted to the new orthodoxy of John Maynard Keynes, agreed that family allowances could help overcome a postwar recession, one obstacle was overcome. Humphrey Mitchell's officials finally agreed to the need for a labour code. In January, 1944, the speech from the throne committed the government to what were promptly christened "baby bonuses." In February, the cabinet approved an Order in Council, P.C. 1003, which restated the principles of the American legislation and provided the machinery to give them effect. McTague could take whatever private comfort he could that his ideas had finally been implemented, without credit, by a Liberal government.Those provincial governments which had not already adopted their own version mostly now followed suit, and by the end of 1944, unions had access to formal certification procedures in virtually all sectors of the economy.

Since the beginning of union history, the most critical, conflict-ridden step had been to secure employer recognition. The significance of P.C. 1003 and its provincial variants was that, for the first time, there was not only legislative backing for the principle of orderly collective bargaining but also rules, procedures, and supervising agencies to ensure that workers could choose a bargaining agent and enter into negotiations. That by no means exhausted the grounds of conflict, and employers and even unions found ways of subverting or distorting the apparent intentions of the legislation. However, a dramatic step had been taken.

Thanks to P.C. 1003 and similar legislation, certification led to first agreements with scores of companies that had resisted unions for generations. The Steel Company of Canada was finally forced to the bargaining table after Local No. 1005 of the Steelworkers won certification by three to one in a supervised vote. However, many new agreements lacked another vital safeguard — union security. The Steel Company resisted any agreement, and a conciliation board refused to endorse any form of maintenance of membership or checkoff. In Kirkland Lake, the Mine, Mill and Smelter Workers won certification in some mines, but the sole concession to union security was a voluntary, revocable checkoff.

Union security mattered in the last years of the war for at least two reasons: stringent wage controls, imposed from December, 1943, left little prospect of winning wage increases; and labour feared, with good reason, that many employers who had been forced to recognize unions had no intention of continuing the relationship once the war was over. Both sides believed that the key to union survival in a postwar period of high unemployment and reconversion to peacetime production would be some form of union security. Like other human beings, industrial workers would be tempted to avoid or postpone paying their membership dues. Local leaders would lose valuable time in the chore of collecting the money. As a minimum, unions needed a voluntary and irrevocable (for the term of the contract) checkoff at source to place the organization on a solid financial footing and to allow planning of future activities.

The classic Canadian battle for union security was waged on the picket lines outside the Ford Motor Company plant in Windsor, Ontario, during the autumn of 1945. Ford had been notorious for its anti-union policies, and nearly eighteen

Top

At Windsor, the Ford strikers adopted a form of picketing that seemed ironically suitable for the motor industry. UAW members simply drove their cars to the streets around the plant, turned off the engines, locked the doors, and walked home, creating a colossal traffic jam. It was, said Mr. Justice Rand, "an insolent flouting of civil order." It was also dramatic and non-violent. (Archives of Labor and Urban Affairs, Wayne State University)

Ford workers in Windsor benefited in 1945 from powerful support from American auto workers across the river in Detroit. While the Canadian branch plant of Ford was free to pursue its hostility to unions so long as it did not cause trouble to the parent company, the UAW in the United States not only sent marchers to Windsor and carried Canadian messages on the Detroit media but threatened more pressure than Ford wanted. (Archives of Labor and Urban Affairs, Wayne State University) months of fruitless negotiations preceded the strike. A federal conciliation board reported that the "issues of the union shop and the checkoff . . . are at the root of all difficulties between the company and the union" and urged agreement on at least a voluntary, irrevocable checkoff.

Neither side would accept the compromise, and on September 12, 1945, the strike began. At first the strike enjoyed widespread support in the city, and Mayor Arthur Reaume promised that "imported police" would not be used to break the strike. Then, after six weeks of peaceful picketing, the Windsor Police Commission ordered the police to open the picket lines to allow employees into the powerhouse. A brief shoving match was enough to dissuade the city policemen, but, over the mayor's protests, the police commission demanded reinforcements from the Ontario Provincial Police and the RCMP. The workers responded by surrounding the plant with an enormous automobile blockade. The factory buildings were completely isolated.

The Ford strike ended when both sides agreed to binding arbitration of outstanding issues. The sole arbitrator, Mr. Justice Ivan Rand, was called to settle the union security issue and did so in one of the most important decisions in the history of Canadian labour. After condemning the union for its lawlessness and the company for its intransigence, Rand went on to reject the union shop on the grounds that it "would deny the individual Canadian the right to seek work and to work independently of personal association with any organized group." However, he also concluded that it was " . . . entirely equitable that all employees should be required to shoulder their portion of the burden of expense for administering the law of their employment, the union contract; they must take the burden along with the benefit."

Mr. Justice Rand's formula was that all members of the bargaining unit would have union dues checked off but no one would be required to join the union. This solution to the heated question of union security was widely approved by Canadian union leaders, though employer enthusiasm was notably restrained. The Rand Formula became a celebrated contribution to Canadian labour practice and an historic milestone.

CHAPTER 18

No Falling Back

Canadians greeted the end of the war with a mixture of joy and apprehension. The loss of forty-five thousand men and women, however tragic, was smaller than the toll from the previous world war. The rewards were far greater. By 1945, Canada had the third largest navy in the world and the fourth largest air force. The economic expansion of the war years and the devastation of most of Europe and Japan made Canada, at least for the time being, a major industrial power. The country's financial strength had allowed the government to finance most of the war effort from taxes and the savings of ordinary Canadians. Strict control of wages and prices had curbed inflation.

Now, with peacetime, workers and employers alike feared that the country would rapidly revert to the misery of the prewar depression. That was the experience of the previous postwar era, and the same pattern began to emerge as the government cancelled war contracts, closed shipyards, and appeared determined to abandon a host of new industries generated by war needs. Women workers began to be squeezed out of the labour force, and by the end of 1945, unemployment was a problem in major centres of war industry like Montreal, Toronto, Fort William, and Vancouver.

However, the Liberal government of W.L. Mackenzie King also remembered the foreclosures and unemployment of 1919–20, and the punishment that voters had imposed on Arthur Meighen and the Conservatives. The remedies offered by John Maynard Keynes may have seemed too radical for the thirties; by 1945 they had become almost conventional wisdom among government advisers. If Canada was headed for a postwar depression, the Keynes answer was massive government stimulus to purchasing power. Family allowances and a new

After the Second World War, the breakdown of the old craft barriers and bitter memories of the depression years made it easier for unions to appeal to veterans for support. At the same time, these Vancouver marchers were denounced as unpatriotic because disruption of the salmon canning industry hurt Canada's foreign trade. (United Steelworkers)

National Housing Act, designed to make home ownership easier, were first steps. A million returning service men and women received half a billion dollars in war-service gratuities and rehabilitation credits, and a substantial clothing allowance. For the first time, most of them had a considerable lump sum to buy a home, a car, furniture, and appliances they could only dream of in the depression years. Through programs of vocational training and university education, the government kept a hundred thousand veterans from entering the labour market immediately.

By 1945, the Liberals had campaigned for their "New Social Order" and they had accepted Keynes. But they were not socialists. C.D. Howe, the American-born engineer who had managed the wartime economy like a giant corporation, saw to that. King made him minister of reconstruction. Howe's policy was "orderly decontrol." The government kept its controls in the postwar period, but management of the economy was handed back to businessmen. Donald Gordon, chairman of the powerful Wartime Prices and Trade Board, stayed at his post, but his mandate looked increasingly lopsided. "We will permit price increases only when they are needed," declared the prime minister, "and may not rule out some gradual and moderate increase in wages and salaries." King's announce-

In postwar Canada, the Liberal government's policy of "orderly decontrol" appeared to mean that prices could rise but wages were still held down to 1929 levels. Anger at inflation was fuel for the record number of strikes in 1946. (Public Archives Canada PA 93674 Canadian Tribune)

ment came as the board released three hundred items from price control. There was no mention of wages.

Most Canadian union leaders had accepted wage control as the price for P.C. 1003. During 1945 the majority of strikes had arisen from "union" issues, not from the traditional demands for more money or shorter hours. The vital Ford strike in the autumn of 1945 was waged for the dangerously theoretical issue of union security. By 1946, workers and their leaders would no longer accept wage levels based on those of 1926–29. Unionists, fearing an early recession, decided to take while the taking was still possible. It was time to prove to union members, many of them new and inexperienced, that a union card could bring results. It was time to prove to management that unions were not a wartime affliction. The new CIO-backed unions were determined to win for Canada the industry-wide settlements that had become familiar in the United States.

With the war over, Communist union leaders could bury the memory of their no-strike pacts by demonstrating that they could be even more militant than their detested CCF rivals. Tactical support for King and the Liberal party, a strategy dictated by the Yalta Conference, dissolved with the Gouzenko spy revelations and the sudden, shocking arrival of the cold war in Canada.

Most union members needed no prodding from union leaders. After the stability of the thirties and the war years, price increases after 1945 alarmed most Canadians. Family incomes, swollen by overtime bonuses and frequently by a wife's wages, suddenly fell. For the first time, many workers had built savings and now they found them threatened. Meanwhile, even for people bred to regard a job as a blessing to be cherished, the evidence of full employment brought courage. The release of pent-up purchasing power meant that manufacturers could sell almost anything they could find labour and resources to produce. They were scrambling for both.

Circumstances made 1946 an even worse year for strikes than 1919. There were differences. Although employers and the new unions were really testing each other's strength, they now followed the rules set out in P.C. 1003. Shrill, irrational scare-mongering was generated by employers and answered in kind by the unions, but for the most part, the postwar strengths were tests of economic, not physical strength. The victories, defeats, and compromises of 1946–47 were vitally significant in the history of Canadian organized labour because, in a number of major industries, they set the pattern for generations.

The first major strike of the year began in the lumber camps and sawmills of British Columbia on May 15. The International Woodworkers of America was the latest of a long series of unions to fight its way into the West Coast forest industry. As elsewhere, employers were convinced that it was a shotgun wedding, imposed by P.C. 1003 and due to break up when wartime regulations ended. When the union demanded a twenty-five-cent-an-hour increase, the employers answered with twelve and a half cents, confident that the shaky new union would be forced into a hopeless strike and the woods would again be union free. Instead, thirty-seven thousand workers stayed out. A federal conciliation report proposed a compromise — fifteen cents and a forty-hour week for part of the year. The IWA did not budge. As the "spearhead" for the nation-wide CCL campaign, both the congress and the union desperately wanted a picket-line victory.

Within ten days another Communist-led union, the Canadian Seamen's Union, had joined battle. A TLC affiliate, the CSU had fought a shrewd battle to win recognition from shipping employers on the Great Lakes and St. Lawrence during the late thirties. In wartime, union leaders had imposed a no-strike pact, and their members had gained little. Now it demanded substantial wage increases and an eight-hour day. When employers fought back with strike-breakers, strongarm men, and antiquated merchant-shipping laws that made strikes akin to mutinies, the union won powerful public backing by emphasizing its twelve-hour working day. Were these reasonable conditions for merchant seamen who had won the Battle of the Atlantic?

The seamen's strike provoked violent clashes between police and CSU members at Thorold on the Welland Canal and at Cornwall, where strike-breakers with iron bars waged a pier-side battle with strikers. The violence and the stubbornness of shipowners who refused to negotiate forced the government to intervene. Under wartime regulations, a controller took over twenty-nine shipping companies. On June 22, the strike ended with a 20 percent increase in pay and concession of the three-watch, eight-hour day. However, trouble was stored up for the future when the American-based Seafarers International Union expelled the CSU on the grounds of its Communist leadership. As the union set out to organize Canada's deep-sea sailors, such worries seemed remote.

Both strikes were in progress when another Communist-led TLC union, the United Textile Workers, called a walkout of six thousand millhands in Montreal and Valleyfield. Under Quebec's complex labour law, interpreted by the unsympathetic government of Maurice Duplessis, the strike was illegal. It was also inevitable. Since 1942 the two chief organizers, Kent Rowley and Madeleine Parent, had wrestled with a recalcitrant veteran of union-busting, Dominion Textiles. The provincial and federal labour boards backed the company. In Montreal, where the union had painfully secured certification, the strike ended after five weeks of picketing. The gains were meagre — seven to eleven cents an hour increase and a forty-five-hour week, but at least the textile trust had been forced to negotiate. At Valleyfield, where the union was not even certified, the struggle was violent. Provincial police broke picket lines and used tear gas to disperse strikers. Rowley and a local organizer were arrested and held without bail. However, the Valleyfield workers held firm and went back only when a certification vote was promised. The union easily won. In several Ontario textile towns, the UTW's Quebec victory encouraged certification.

Clarence Jackson of the United Electrical Workers had been a strong advocate of the CCL's co-ordinated push to break the wage freeze. It was ironic that his own union became engaged in a succession of uncoordinated battles across southern Ontario. A strike at Phillips Cables lasted from February 18 to April 15. The UE's key local at the big Westinghouse plant in Hamilton staged several false starts before walking out on July 5. Other locals followed, but it was not before November 1 that the union members returned to work.

Unions with Communist leadership had been first into the 1946 campaign. The chief enemy of the Communist bloc in the CCL was Charles Millard, national director of the United Steelworkers. His industry was critical to the postwar boom in consumer buying. Two of the three big Canadian steel producers, Algoma in Sault Ste. Marie and the Dominion Steel and Coal Company plant in Sydney, had been organized since before the war. However, the huge Stelco works in Hamilton had only narrowly favoured the union in a wartime vote, and its president, H.G. Hilton, firmly believed that a tough struggle would rid himself of a temporary impediment. When the government in April approved a five-dollar-a-ton increase in steel prices, Millard's union asked what its share would be. The answer, endorsed on the spur of the moment by the minister of labour, Humphrey Mitchell, was ten cents an hour.

The union had very different ideas: nineteen and a half cents an hour, a forty-hour work week, two weeks' vacation with pay, union security, and a nation-wide agreement. That summer the steel industry became the crisis point of the whole union struggle. A week before the strike deadline, Ottawa appointed a steel controller, F.B. Kilbourn, and proclaimed heavy fines and prison terms for those who ignored his orders. The union refused to be impressed. "If they arrest five on the strike committee," replied a local leader, "five more will take their place 'til all the union members are in jail." On July 15, the strike began.

Top

Charles Millard counts the votes as Local No. 1005 members decide to strike the Steel Company of Canada. The vote was important because the local seemed like the weak link in the 1946 bargaining strategy. Millard's prestige and that of non-Communist leaders in the CCL was on the line because the effectiveness of each faction would be tested by practical results. (Public Archives Canada PA 120499)

The Stelco strike in the summer of 1946 would have collapsed if the company could have maintained production. The union blockaded roads around the plant, hired a launch to patrol Hamilton Bay, and even dropped leaflets from the air. City police looked the other way as long as picketers avoided violence. The company was not well pleased. (National Photography Collection PA 120521)

At the Algoma plant and in Sydney, company and union settled down to the routine of peaceful picketing, mild abuse, and endurance. In Hamilton it was different. Hilton crowded a thousand non-strikers on to Stelco property, fed and housed them, and set out to keep the plant working. Outside, Local No. 1005 laid virtual siege to the big plant, using a motor launch to watch the harbour approaches and a light plane to drop leaflets.

The Steelworkers faced a double battle: against Stelco and its two allies, and against a government which had staked its reputation on a ten-cent maximum increase. Both Hilton and Millard appeared before the House of Commons Standing Committee on Industrial Relations. Millard may not have converted hostile M.P.'s, but his appeal for a minimum guaranteed wage of $1,750 a year cut to the core of the dispute. Mitchell, his dignity caught up in his insistence on his stated increase, tried to persuade the striking steelworkers that only a minority blocked a return to work. The clumsy device only bolstered strikers' morale. Donald Gordon, of the Wartime Prices and Trade Board, was a more articulate champion of the ten-cent maximum, but unionists and even many other Canadians had grown tired of his pronouncements.

Finally, it was an exasperated prime minister who forced a settlement. Fed up with his minister and other government officials and incensed by Hilton, King summoned Mosher and Conroy of the CCL and then Millard. Shrewdly, the old politician recognized that Millard dared not settle for less than the fifteen cents his Communist enemies had won for the IWA in British Columbia. At the same time, with the strike running into October, funds and patience were exhausted. At the critical moment, King arranged for Kilbourn to raise the company wage offer to thirteen and a half cents and Millard compromised on other demands to get a settlement. When DOSCO management put the settlement in jeopardy by claiming it could not afford the increase, Ottawa hurriedly promised a higher subsidy. On October 1, the great steel strike ended. For all its intransigence, Stelco had been forced to bargain, and the basis for a mature relationship had been established.

Despite the seven hundred thousand man-days lost, the steel strike was not the biggest of 1946. The Canadian locals of the United Rubber Workers determined to win a more modest version of the industry-wide agreement that the "Big Four" rubber companies in the United States had been forced to concede a year before. The Canadian branch plants were unimpressed. Although weak locals at Dunlop in Toronto and at A.R. Kaufman in Kitchener hurriedly settled, eleven Ontario locals walked out on June 23 and stayed out until October 17. Once again the union faced not only the companies but ham-handed attempts by Humphrey Mitchell to coax members to accept the ten-cent standard increase. The union answer was to ignore federal government meddling and to look to the provincial Department of Labour for help. It was Louis Fine, Ontario's brilliant mediator, who finally brought the two sides together, winning a compromise settlement that closely resembled the Steelworkers' contract. The real result was twenty years of peaceful industrial relations, steady but not spectacular wage increases, and, in time, a reasonable pension plan. The 1946 rubber strike established union credibility and taught both sides that the price of conflict, eight hundred thousand man-days of production and wages, should not be exacted often.

Top

Percy Bengough, TLC president, speaks on behalf of a jailed Kent Rowley, organizer of a bitter 1947 strike against the Valleyfield operations of Dominion Textiles. Rowley and his wife, Madeleine Parent (on Bengough's right), were later fired by the United Textile Workers and organized their own nationalist union organization. (Kent Rowley–Madeleine Parent Collection)

In postwar Canada, almost everyone, including Montreal tavern waiters, appeared willing to organize and go on strike. However, with legal procedures for union certification, negotiation, and going on strike, the violence of the past rarely surfaced. Of course, it was still necessary to remind employers and the police that the law had changed. (Public Archives Canada PA 80753)

Top

Packinghouse workers waged one of the longest and most difficult of the postwar strikes because their union had to deal simultaneously with nation-wide companies and provincial jurisdiction. Tough-minded leadership and crucial support from Saskatchewan's CCF government made the difference between victory and defeat. (Fred Dowling)

A Montreal restaurant owner found his own way to protest the postwar round of strikes, particularly one by the Montreal Tramway Commission. Some merchants, particularly in union towns, came to realize that increased purchasing power for workers brought benefits to them as well. (Public Archives Canada The Gazette, Montreal)

During the winter of 1946−47, other strikes followed. At Noranda, Quebec, members of the Mine, Mill and Smelter Workers stayed out from November 22 to February 10 before they were granted the "steel formula" wage increase. Not all unions won. On December 20, five hundred Nova Scotia fishermen tied up their boats to force recognition of the Canadian Fishermen and Fishhandlers Union. Despite impressive solidarity, the strike collapsed when the Supreme Court of Canada ruled that fishermen were not eligible for collective bargaining rights.

At the end of January, it was the turn of the once-militant District No. 26 of the United Mine Workers to launch its first real strike since it had been forced to "stand the gaff" in 1925. As usual, DOSCO pleaded poverty, but this time Ottawa bluntly refused to increase its heavy subsidies. A Royal Commission on Canada's coal industry released its gloomy report just as the strike began. The miners found themselves pleading for a living wage in what was officially proclaimed to be a dying industry. The strike started on January 31, stopped for two weeks on a company promise of fresh negotiations, and resumed when it was apparent that DOSCO had used the time to stockpile and to save its customers from the threat of a cold winter. The strike, like so many of its predecessors, was a defeat. When the men returned on May 26, it was for the company's original offer of a dollar a day with the promise of forty cents more, all of it tied for the first time to an increase in productivity. Bitterness and anger at the company interpretation of the rules and victimization of union militants led to a further two-week strike within a couple of days. It made little difference. In the picture of union victories, Cape Breton remained the grim exception. The reason was obvious. Even in 1947, a quarter of its people were out of work. Few of its veterans could qualify for government training and education grants; such was the depression poverty, claimed Clarie Gillis, the CCF M.P., that few boys had had clothes to attend school and reach the minimum qualifying standard of a Grade 8 education.

The biggest strike of 1947 was a victory. Launched like other CIO unions by a fervent organizing committee, the United Packinghouse Workers had struggled to certification in an historically ill-paid, anti-union industry. Moreover, it presented incredible organizing difficulties. Though dominated by three national companies — Swift, Burns, and Canada Packers — meat processing was provincially regulated and closely watched by powerful farm lobbies in each provincial legislature. Because it was national, a major company could easily switch production from a struck plant to a plant in an adjoining province. Because labour laws differed widely from province to province, a legal nation-wide strike was virtually impossible.

Fred Dowling, the UPWA director in Canada, decided to plunge ahead. On August 22, the strike began in British Columbia and rapidly spread eastward. Federal emergency legislation, which might have stopped the movement, had lapsed on May 15, 1947. Like it or not, provincial governments had to cope. In Prince Edward Island, farmers persuaded a willing government to seize the only packing plant, man it with strike-breakers, and break the union. In Quebec, the Duplessis government cancelled UPWA certification on the grounds of an illegal strike. That did not reopen the plants. Provincial officials gathered in Toronto to set up a united front; Saskatchewan's CCF government braved farmer wrath by refusing to go along. In the end, Dowling had what he wanted. The companies were forced to bargain. When Swift settled on October 18, its two competitors followed within a week. Once again a new and enduring labour relations pattern was established for a major Canadian industry.

The postwar pattern had been possible for two reasons: a structure of labour law and practice had been created through P.C. 1003; and union leaders had shown not only that strikes could be long and tough but that the ensuing settlements could be realistic compromises. In this, there was no real distinction between the Communist-led unions and those headed by leading CCFers like Millard and Dowling. On the other hand, federal labour officials like Mitchell and Donald Gordon had left the continuing impression that wage controls would always favour management and make unions the public scapegoats for inflation.

For all its significance, P.C. 1003 was no more than a wartime regulation, bound to lapse when the war emergency officially ended. For Mackenzie King, establishing a durable national labour relations system became the legislative monument he sought to crown his long career. Ideally, it would be legislation to which all provinces could subscribe and so the disintegrative effect of the *Snider* decision could be forgotten. Mitchell and King's minister of justice, Louis St. Laurent, set to work in 1946, flattering their master by building changes on to the structure of his beloved Industrial Disputes Investigation Act. The product of their labour, altered little by cabinet discussion, provincial ministers, and fervent lobbying by labour and employers, was the Industrial Relations and Disputes Investigation Act of 1948.

Neither labour nor employers were very pleased. Eugene Forsey, the CCL research director, complained that the act was neither new nor national. The act excluded civil servants, avoided legislative guarantees of union security, allowed old time-wasting tricks in certification and bargaining, and said far less than the American law about unfair labour practices. Employers grumbled that unions could not be sued for damages. Provinces retained their freedom to go their own way and, if most imitated the pattern of the new act, all of them developed enough peculiar differences to give full employment for labour lawyers.

There was one great Canadian industry which had escaped the pattern of strikes. The railway brotherhoods, most conservative of Canadian unions, had loyally done the government's bidding through the war years and after. By 1948 the pressures from railway workers had become intolerable. The non-operating unions, headed by the veteran TLC stalwart, Frank Hall, had determined on a settlement of twenty-five cents an hour; the companies offered ten cents. By July, 1948, a national rail strike appeared inevitable.

For the old prime minister, the crisis was a last opportunity to display his skills as a mediator. Technically, the government could take over the railways. The prime minister refused. Instead, he summoned Frank Hall to his home, Laurier House, for tea. Conversation turned on the writings of William James and the Count de Mortigny, on King's retirement, on his fondness for the brotherhoods. Finally, King took Hall to the library and sat him facing the portrait of the prime minister's mother. Only then did they turn to the dispute. Gradually, King introduced the figure of seventeen cents:

I said 17 cents had come into my mind because of associations of the past. We had been looking at a picture of Old Pat [his dog]. He had asked me how long Pat had been with me, and I had told him, seventeen years to the day. I also mentioned that my birthday was on the 17th. 17 seemed to be a number that was mixed up with my life in different ways.

The strike was averted by an increase of seventeen cents. N.R. Crump, the president of CPR, was brought around by the argument that only Communist Russia could benefit from a Canadian rail strike that summer.

At seventy-four, King retired as prime minister. He lived on in retirement for only two more years. Yet the labour relations system he had created, with its favours for prudent, reasonable men like Frank Hall, its hostility to passionate, uncompromising leaders like J.B. MacLachlan, would long survive him, permeating the values and expectations of an entire labour movement. Perhaps its most striking impact came where it might least have been expected — in Quebec.

Under Duplessis, re-elected in 1944, Quebec had promptly asserted its independence from the Industrial Relations and Disputes Investigation Act and even from the modestly prolabour legislation of the short-lived Godbout government. The tradition of codes to protect the unorganized, of endless processes of mediation, of inexplicable delays in certification allowed discretion and discrimination. For those who troubled the peace of mind of the province, the Padlock Law survived, ready to condemn as Communist whatever ideas might shock the government or its policemen. Perhaps, claimed a 1948 commentator, the Duplessis government offered no special protection to national corporations, but Quebec-owned companies threatened by aggressive unions might count on a sympatic hearing from the minister of labour and full enforcement of laws against illegal strikes or turbulent picketing.

The other proof of Quebec's difference remained its Catholic unions, driven perhaps to more militancy than was wise by the competition of materialistic and atheist unions, but still securely tied to Quebec and its values. As late as the winter of 1948, earnest village priests managed a campaign to drive the International Brotherhood of Paper Makers from the mills of the Lac St. Jean region.

Yet there were differences. In 1945, a diminutive Catholic social activist, Gerard Picard, replaced the aging and conservative Alfred Charpentier at the head of the Canadian and Catholic Confederation of Labour. As union membership doubled to 93,370 by 1948, Picard chose staff from Father Georges-Henri Levesque's school of social studies at Laval. Among the ablest was an aggressive young organizer named Jean Marchand.

How great the changes in Catholic unionism were became dramatically apparent early in 1949, when contract negotiations between workers in the big asbestos mines of the Eastern Townships and their American employers collapsed. The industry had a long record of unions, strikes, and conflict, but it had few memories of the kind of prosperity that wartime and postwar demand for asbestos had generated. It was also apparent that workers had shared very little in the gains of companies like Asbestos, Bell, Flintkote, and Canadian Johns

Flanked by a policeman and politicians, Maurice Duplessis and Archbishop Joseph Charbonneau symbolized the union of church and state that many people regarded as characteristic of Quebec. In fact, Duplessis had no intention of having his will challenged. Though Charbonneau was no radical, his open sympathy for the asbestos strikers in 1949 alarmed fellow bishops and raised fears that the government would curb funds to Catholic institutions. (Public Archives Canada The Gazette, *Montreal)*

Manville. The union negotiators, headed by Marchand, made it clear to the members that they could wait for the usual delays and compromises of arbitration or they could launch an illegal strike. They demanded a strike. He suggested a day to think about it. "No, no," they shouted. "On with the strike."

The angry mood among the asbestos strikers was not new. Neither was the immediate government declaration that the strike was illegal, nor the arrival of provincial police and the fluttering of court injunctions and writs. What was different was that the union was solidly part of a deferential Catholic system and that it soon could claim the backing not merely of local clergy but of the powerful archbishop of Montreal, Joseph Charbonneau. The strike became violent. When the companies attempted to keep going with non-strikers, union members responded by kidnapping and beating company officials and dynamiting company property. From Quebec, Maurice Duplessis and his ministers denounced the union for anarchy and violence as well as for defying the law. More police arrived.

The strike bewildered and divided Quebec opinion. While many shared the indignation of the Duplessis government, even conservative nationalists, like the aging Canon Lionel Groulx, saw the strike as a struggle of Québécois against big foreign companies. Archbishop Charbonneau, who had never forgotten his years among the poor workers of northern Ontario, proclaimed that it was the church's duty to intervene and ordered collections for the strikers at every church door. Almost as significant was support from CCL and TLC unions. For once, a single impressive strike broke down the barriers between Canada's rival labour organizations.

Neither prayers nor money would necessarily win the strike. After two months, the companies refused to drop prosecutions. Two were back in production, and Canadian Johns Manville announced that one shift was working and that, for the sake of older workers, the strike should end. Angry strikers packed a big parish hall in Asbestos. On the night of May 4–5, they surged out to attack the mines. Police manning barricades were seized, beaten, and shoved into the Iroquois Club's basement to be beaten again. Union leaders and clergy stood by apparently helpless. Early on the morning of May 6, provincial police counter-attacked. A powerful force collected at Sherbrooke and drove through the night to Asbestos. This time it was strikers who were herded into the basement of the club and savagely beaten. By nightfall, two hundred workers had been arrested.

The violence at Asbestos, fully reported, hit the world news. Divisions over the strike grew even deeper. Somehow it dragged on into June with support slowly falling away as miners, their savings exhausted, left the region or slipped back to work. Finally, it was the archbishop of Quebec, Maurice Roy, who presided over negotiations to end the strike. By June 27, after five bitter months, full production resumed. The union was recertified. The men gained a ten-cent raise and re-employment without discrimination, save for those convicted. Other issues would be arbitrated.

The union called it a victory and there was dancing in the streets. The truth was soon apparent. The strike-breakers kept their jobs. A hundred active strikers waited in vain for recall notices. The eventual arbitration gave little that the companies had not conceded. However, the Asbestos strike served notice to the world that Catholic unions were no less militant than their secular counterparts. Increasingly, they would share common goals and values as well as tactics. The church in Quebec had learned the high cost of its union involvement. Under pressure from Duplessis and the more conservative bishops, Joseph Charbonneau was abruptly deprived of his archdiocese and banished to Victoria, British Columbia. A pastoral letter on February 1, 1950, removed the church from its leading role in the syndicates. Henceforth, chaplains would be little more than figureheads.

To all appearances, the Asbestos strike had pushed the CCCL into the mainstream of the Canadian labour movement. Appearances might be deceiving.

CHAPTER 19

Struggle for Allegiance

After the dramatic struggles of 1945–47, some of the heat went out of the Canadian union movement. Wartime gains had been confirmed; so had their limits. Public resentment at strikes, a modest recession from 1949 to 1950, and the difficulty of organizing workers in the service and office sectors of the economy stalled the growth in union members.

Perhaps union leaders had some reason to rest on their laurels. For the first time, the share of union members among Canada's non-agricultural workers was as high as in the United States. Passage of the IRDI Act and corresponding legislation in the provinces offered stability to a labour movement that had existed too long on the margins of respectability. Most Canadian workers in major manufacturing plants, in mines, and in the forest industry were now organized. If they were not, it was because employers, like Dominion Foundry and Steel in Hamilton, had discovered that union wage rates and enlightened personnel policies could keep union organizers at bay.

There was another reason for the slowdown in union growth: Canadian union leaders were busy with a remorseless internal struggle whose outcome would determine the political direction of the entire trade union movement.

Sam Gompers had warned that mixing unionism and politics produced bad feeling and divisions. His critics answered that only political direction saved unions from becoming mere business organizations; only political action could bring vitally needed gains. Both sides were right. During the forties, the threat of labour backing for the CCF helped force the King government to deliver progressive social legislation. Even more important, labour's political influence compelled the government to accept a postwar commitment to full employment

During the war, Communist labour leaders became fervent patriots once the Soviet Union was attacked, preventing strikes in their own unions and denouncing them in others. One reward was a wartime visit overseas for Pat Sullivan, left, C.S. Jackson of the United Electrical Workers, and Nigel Morgan of the International Woodworkers, far right. They and J.A. Whitebone of the New Brunswick Federation of Labour (by no means a Communist) are offered a battlefield briefing by Brigadier C.C. Mann. (National Photography Collection PA 94333)

and economic expansion. On the tide of that expansion, the union movement had consolidated its wartime gains. But Gompers was right, too. Politics were divisive.

At the simplest level, there was the distinction between the Trades and Labour Congress and its younger rival, the Canadian Congress of Labour. Badly burned by its experiment with the Canadian Labour party in 1918, the TLC stubbornly refused any partisan adventures. In 1932, it rejoiced when a Tory newspaper flattered it on its "conservatism." A year later, a convention resolution to endorse the infant CCF was withdrawn for lack of support. An obvious contrast was the CCL. In its ancestry was the Communist-run Workers' Unity League and the All-Canadian Congress of Labour, whose venerable president, A.R. Mosher, had been a founding member of the Co-operative Commonwealth Federation in Calgary in 1932. From its inception in 1940, the CCL was wracked by the merciless rivalry of Communists and CCFers.

On most issues the CCF was divided. There were always CCFers who responded to every Communist appeal. There were CCFers who disdained a trade union connection for fear of selling out socialist doctrine for mere political gain. Such people remained a minority. The CCF's first leader, J.S. Woodsworth, was uncompromising in his conviction that communism and socialism were as compatible as dictatorship and democracy. When Woodsworth was gone, David Lewis, the CCF's national secretary, and Charles Millard, its leading unionist, remained to remind the CCF that Communists were its most implacable enemies. Woodsworth and his political heirs also insisted that the CCF could only grow in Canada as a movement backed by organized labour.

Since the Communists shared that determination, the CCF rapidly became an obstacle to be destroyed by any means. In the United States, Communist infiltration had destroyed the remnants of the Socialist party during the thirties; the CCF would suffer the same fate. Meanwhile, Communists worked tirelessly to organize unions, to wrest control of them into their own hands, and to use them for a variety of party goals, from funding Communist causes and hiring Communist organizers to endorsing appropriate political resolutions.

The war years heightened the CCF-Communist rivalry. Abrupt shifts in Soviet policy, obediently followed by Canadian Communists, caused only temporary embarrassment. After years of demanding a united front against fascism and sending six hundred Canadians to die in Spain during the civil war, the Canadian Communists switched into noisy opposition to Canada's war effort against Hitler when the Nazi-Soviet pact was signed on the eve of the war in 1939. In June of 1940, more than a hundred leading Communists, including Pat Sullivan of the Canadian Seamen's Union, had joined Fascists and Nazis in internment camps.

No sooner had Hitler's armies invaded the Soviet Union in June of 1941 than the Communist line shifted. Communist leaders now clamoured to be released. Once liberated, Clarence Jackson led his United Electrical Workers' Union in a no-strike pledge. Other Communist-dominated unions dared not go quite so far, but their leaders ensured labour peace and denounced rivals, like Millard's Steelworkers, that did dare to press for wartime gains.

Patriotism brought rewards. Jackson's union reached a peak of thirty thousand members by 1944. Communists came to dominate not only the Electrical Workers and the Canadian Seamen's Union but the British Columbia district of the International Woodworkers of America, the Shipyard and General Workers Union, and much of the United Auto Workers and the International Union of Mine, Mill and Smelter Workers, heir of the old Western Federation of Miners. Within the CCL, at least a third of the members were organized in Communist-run unions, and their voice, carefully rehearsed and reinforced by Communists in other unions, was even more dominant. Within the TLC, Communists ran fewer unions, but in 1942 the Seamen's leader, Pat Sullivan, won election as a vice-president, and in 1943 he secured the powerful post of secretary-treasurer, denying throughout that he was any longer a Communist.

During the war years, the CCF could boast even more spectacular gains. Thanks to Millard's Steelworkers, the democratic Left retained a margin of support in the CCL, but its main gains were among voters. Despite the temporary unpopularity of Woodsworth's pacifism and the CCF's support for Japanese Canadians, the party spoke directly to the anxiety many Canadians felt about the postwar world. In February, 1942, the CCF won a spectacular by-election in the Toronto constituency of York South. In July of 1943, it captured thirty-two seats in an Ontario provincial election, almost enough to make it a government. A year later, it swept to power in Saskatchewan. Party supporters could indeed believe that the stars in their courses were working for a CCF victory.

The CCF's gains were accompanied by evidence of union support. It was only in 1938 that the first labour organization affiliated with the party. However, the action by Cape Breton's District No. 26 of the United Mine Workers led in 1940 to the election of that tough, eloquent miner, Clarie Gillis, who soon stumped the country looking for union support. In the summer of 1942, a CCF Trade Union Committee made a serious start in Ontario with both CCL and TLC union backing. A year later, in June, the groundwork was prepared when the Canadian Congress of Labour formally endorsed the CCF and urged its affiliates to study the party's program.

Or was it all hopelessly premature? The CCL's secretary-treasurer, Pat Conroy, obviously thought so. When Millard, whom he regarded as a domineering rival, set up a CCF-dominated Political Action Committee, Conroy deftly frustrated its activity. Compared to the Communists, his hostility was mild. By 1944, their threats and pressure had almost annulled the impact of any CCL endorsement.

By now the Communists had renamed themselves the Labour Progressive party, but Soviet directives ordered them to support the wartime Liberal government. Communists who had poured vitriol on King (and who would do so again) now rhapsodized about his virtues and raged at the CCF as "utopian socialists." By 1945, Communists were in the ironic position of endorsing Mitchell Hepburn in Ontario and campaigning publicly for the election of the Liberal candidate, General A.G.L. McNaughton, in the Grey South by-election.

Federal and Ontario elections in 1945 were crucial to the future of the CCF. Persuaded by recent triumphs, the party approached the contest with high confidence, certain that voters would ignore the savage propaganda campaign waged against it. On June 7, Ontario voters gave the CCF a mere eight seats. A week later the bewildered party won only twenty-six federal seats. Clarie Gillis was the only CCF M.P. east of Winnipeg. The CCF bid for major status had been stopped in its tracks.

There were many reasons. The bitter propaganda campaign against the CCF had sent nervous voters to the polls in unusual numbers. King's New Social Order promised much of the CCF program without the threat to familiar institutions. Even among unionized workers, only a minority believed that the CCF offered more than the traditional parties. However, there was yet another cause for the CCF humiliation: the Communists. Had the votes not been drawn away by Labour Progressive candidates, at least eight more seats would have been won by the Ontario CCF and as many more by the national party. In the Trades and Labour Congress, a Right-Left team of Percy Bengough as president and Pat Sullivan as secretary-treasurer had emerged from the war. The combination of Sullivan's pressure and Bengough's periodic golf games with Mackenzie King had worked a miracle. The congress had hurriedly formed a political action committee and, for once, directed its members how to vote — for the incumbent Liberal government.

Pat Conroy, the CCL secretary-treasurer, flanked by David Lewis and Stanley Knowles, could be depended upon to give the 1948 CCF a blunt message. An Alberta coal miner, Conroy preferred the CCF to the Communists in the ideologically torn CCL but not by very much. He bitterly disliked Charles Millard, leader of the rapidly growing United Steelworkers. (National Photography Collection PA 120719)

Across Canada, the Communists had good reason to rejoice. Their voting strength might be tiny, but by cleverly exploiting their union influence they had broken the CCF drive. However, if the Communists celebrated, CCFers in the union movement planned vengeance. Long before the cold war, the CCF had concluded that open rivalry with the Communists was not enough. A conspiratorial organization had to be eliminated from the labour movement.

In 1945, the task seemed insuperable. The Soviet Union was a powerful and admired ally. Its Canadian agents had the ear of governments. In British Columbia, where the CCF was in offical opposition, a Liberal government worked with the Communist-run British Columbia Federation of Labour to win labour votes. Even CCFers deplored the vigorous anti-Communism of leaders like David Lewis and Angus MacInnis.

Still, the Communists could overplay their hand. In British Columbia, the government-labour committee handed the CCF an easy victory when it endorsed the meagre standard of a forty-four-hour week and a single week's paid vacation. During the Ford strike, Communist leaders undercut their negotiators and infuriated the CCL by demanding a struggle to the death, and then by

Top

Shipowners in 1946 found much to complain about in their dealings with the Canadian Seamen's Union. However, reciting the provisions of the Canada Shipping Act was a tactical mistake for it reminded other Canadians that merchant seamen were bound by laws that might have made Captain Bligh blush. In the circumstances, a little lawlessness was no sin. The real issue, unknown to either the owners or the seamen, was whether J.A. Sullivan, the union leader, had called the strike to benefit his members or on orders from Moscow. (Toronto Daily Star, May 28, 1946)

Though Pat Sullivan's defection armed shipowners with some powerful arguments for not negotiating with the CSU, fresh leaders were found and the struggle continued. (Public Archives Canada PA 93867)

Top

Members of the Canadian Seamen's Union, arrested by officers of the Ontario Provincial Police, worked in a tough, ill-paid trade whose members were probably more important in Canada's war effort than any of the armed forces. Initial public sympathy evaporated when the union regularly tied up lake shipping. The government, sensing the public mood, did nothing to prevent deep-sea shipping owners from selling their vessels to foreign companies and wiping out Canada's merchant fleet. (*Public Archives Canada PA 93868*)

RCMP and pickets from the Canadian Seamen's Union do battle near Welland during the 1946 strike. Canadian seamen worked in a tough, ill-paid trade. Merchant seamen had probably been more important to Canada's war effort than any of the armed forces. But public sympathy evaporated during a series of postwar strikes, particularly along the Great Lakes. Sensing the public mood, the government intervened and remained complacent as Canada's once-dominant merchant marine passed to foreign owners and flags. (*York University Collection*) inviting other CCF affiliates to join an illegal one-day general strike. Conroy, who had used the Communists as a counterweight to his arch-rival, Millard, was outraged. A trade unionist above all, Conroy was indignant that anyone, CCF or Communist, would put political interests ahead of union principles.

While the Communist-CCF battle raged most fiercly in the CCL, turning its annual conventions into debating brawls between the opposing forces, the first major explosion occurred in a TLC affiliate, the Canadian Seamen's Union. In 1944, the American Federation of Labor had calmly handed jurisdiction over all seamen in the United States and Canada to its affiliate, the Seafarers' International Union. At once the SIU had set out to do bloody battle with the CIO's Communist-dominated affiliate, the National Maritime Union. While that fight raged, the TLC defended its affiliate. So did public opinion and Canada's new labour legislation. By early 1947, the CSU dominated Canadian lake shipping and had won most of Canada's deep-sea merchant fleet.

Suddenly, in the spring of 1947, the CSU's president and the TLC's secretary-treasurer, Pat Sullivan, resigned both jobs, summoned the press, and told all. For the first time, a prominent Communist union leader explained how strikes and disruptions had been ordered by party strategists, how the 1946 strike was aimed at disrupting European recovery shipments, how the union payroll was used to support Communist officials and organizers.

However sincere and accurate Sullivan's revelations were, they did nothing to save his union. Employers had fresh arguments to refuse to negotiate with a Communist conspiracy. Bengough and other TLC associates repudiated their former colleague and, for a time at least, rallied to the CSU. As Sullivan had predicted, the union began the first of a series of hopeless battles with deep-sea ship owners in 1948. Part of their strategy involved coaxing members of the Brotherhood of Railroad and Steamship Clerks into a sympathy strike. For Frank Hall, brotherhood vice-president, ardent anti-Communist, and veteran leader of the non-operating railway unions in Canada, this was provocation enough. When the TLC called an emergency meeting to support the Seamen, Hall and his fellow Canadian vice-presidents of international unions picketed the gathering. In turn, when the TLC met in convention in 1948, Hall's old enemy, Percy Bengough, demanded and obtained suspension of the brotherhood. Summoned to meet with the AFL in Washington, Bengough and John Buckley emerged proudly to proclaim, "Co-operation yes, Domination no!"

It was rhetoric but no more. By now the SIU had devoured the National Maritime Union, and it was ready for Canada. The CSU, under Communist orders to give British dockers a pretext to strike, was in the throes of a hopeless strike against East Coast ship owners. Even TLC allies were outraged when union leaders deliberately misrepresented a unanimous arbitration report so that their members rejected it. By the spring of 1949, the SIU had swallowed Sullivan's small breakaway Canadian Lake Seamen's Union. Now the ship owners cheerfully signed agreements with the big American union. CSU members, often fervently loyal to their own organization, went down fighting. Frank Hall and his vice-presidents waited out the year and watched with relish as the 1949 TLC convention expelled the remnants of the CSU and insisted that all affiliates in future pledge allegiance to democratic principles and to His Majesty the King. A year later, the Canada Labour Relations Board revoked the CSU's certification on the grounds that it was a Communist organization.

Within the CCL, the struggle against Communist influence was longer but a little more straightforward. The war also had more fronts.

Communist influence in the United Auto Workers, one of the CCL's more powerful affiliates, was decorously hidden behind the affable personality of George Burt. Elected with Communist backing to displace Charles Millard in 1940, Burt had been responsive enough to Communist pressure to run as a Liberal in 1945, but he could also sensibly argue that his balancing act was necessary in a deeply divided union. His conversion followed dutifully when the international union changed hands. Walter Reuther, one of the socialists who switched to Roosevelt's New Deal when Communists destroyed the old Socialist party in the United States, finally won his long struggle for the UAW leadership in 1947. For Reuther, a labour-backed CCF was the kind of party his own country should have had. Reuther's pressure gradually brought Burt's Canadian district to the same position, although Burt took his time about it, cautiously balancing and backing and filling to the frustration of Mosher and Millard.

The fight in the UAW showed patience and the value of an American ally. The British Columbia struggle had to be waged against seemingly hopeless odds. Communists controlled every major union in the province — Mine-Mill, the Shipyard and General Workers, and, above all, the International Woodworkers of America. Nigel Morgan, the Labour Progressive leader, was as much an eminence in British Columbia as Millard was in Ontario. So was Harold Pritchett, president of the B.C. district of the IWA and once its international president. Against skilled tacticians, organizational muscle, and massed union funds, what enemy could prevail? Certainly it would not be the local CCF, predominantly middle class, permeated by Communist sympathizers, and suspicious of even sympathetic union leaders. Help would have to come from outside.

Early in 1947, the CCL dispatched Millard's lieutenant, William Mahoney, to lead the counter-attack. He found a counter-attack in progress, even within the IWA. It needed leadership and a little ruthlessness. Communists used small, tightly-disciplined cells to control unions; Mahoney followed suit. Communists used the votes from moribund locals; Mahoney prodded little locals to re-affiliate to the central labour bodies they had abandoned in disgust or as an economy. Within weeks, Mahoney could report that anti-Communists controlled the Vancouver Labour Council. The postwar disappearance of Canada's shipping and shipyard industries, with their Communist-run unions, was a bonus for the right. A drunken, slanderous speech by Harvey Murphy of Mine-Mill to delegates at the B.C. Federation convention in 1948 gave Mahoney another chance. Having lost a crucial vote 65 to 66, Mahoney instantly knew which of his delegates had switched. With the errant member suitably supervised, the next two votes were won by a single vote. By the end of a long, tense session, exhausted delegates had handed the B.C. Federation to CCL (and CCF) leadership.

Such victories would still be insignificant as long as the British Columbia district of the International Woodworkers remained firmly under the leadership of Harold Pritchett and a solidly Communist team. This time Mahoney turned to the only large non-Communist local, No. 1-357 at New Westminster. By odd coincidence, two of its members now demanded to know where an unaccounted $9,000 had gone from the union books. Indignant union officials handed their books over for a comprehensive audit. The results, showing unauthorized payments of $150,633, were so damning that union leaders concealed the report. The union's international headquarters, with CCL support, insisted on an investigation. Somewhere between panic and outrage, the IWA leaders ignored Pritchett's advice and set about severing relations with the international. On October 3, a carefully packed convention proclaimed the Woodworkers Industrial Union of Canada. Funds, property, and records were hurriedly transferred, hidden, or passed to the sympathetic Mine-Mill union.

The switch fooled no one. Mahoney, Stewart Alsbury of Local No. 1-357, and IWA officials from the United States soon reconstituted the union. Court orders sought, largely in vain, to recover the funds. Despite picket-line violence and a savage beating of Alsbury, the Communist breakaway soon succumbed. Pritchett had been right. In the crisis, members had stayed with their union, not with their leaders.

Nowhere was the CCL campaign against the Communists as ingenious or as successful as it had been in British Columbia. In Ontario, the 1948 suspension of the Mine, Mill and Smelter Workers allowed the United Steelworkers to win over workers at the International Nickel smelter at Port Colborne and to launch a series of successful raids on Mine-Mill locals across northern Ontario. When Mine-Mill refused to allow the CCL to reorganize its mining jurisdiction, it was expelled. The last Communist stronghold, the United Electrical Workers, played

CCF members elected in 1945 assembled outside the Parliament Buildings in far smaller numbers than they expected. Communist candidates had cost the CCF at least eight seats directly and Communist support for the Liberals had blocked effective union support. Long before the cold war became fashionable, some CCFers had begun a battle to curb Communist influence in the labour movement. (CCF News—National Film Board Photograph)

a more cunning game. Its leaders, Clarence Jackson and George Harris, apologized when accused of slandering their CCL rivals and promptly repeated their language in other words. In the United States, their union was expelled from the CIO in 1949 and the jurisdiction handed to a new International Union of Electrical Workers. In Canada, the CCL found itself in the embarrassing position of helping the new union organize against one of its oldest affiliates. Since the UE gave no clear grounds for expulsion, Mosher and his colleagues looked forward to an open, brutal struggle.

Suddenly they were saved. Norman Dowd, the CCL's elderly executive secretary, discovered that the UE's per capita payment was long overdue. Ten days later, when the cheque had not arrived, Mosher joyfully seized on the pretext to suspend the troublesome union. His decision, protested by a number of scrupulous or sympathetic union leaders, nonetheless carried. By the inadvertence of its own international office, the United Electrical Workers was out of the Canadian Congress of Labour.

By 1950, little remained of the once-imposing Communist presence in the Canadian trade union movement. Expulsion of the Fur and Leather Workers from the CCL in 1950 and the United Fishermen from the TLC in 1954 removed the last Communist-controlled unions from major labour central bodies. Communists in the labour movement did not, of course, vanish. Unions expelled from the congresses survived if, like the UE, Mine-Mill, and the Fishermen, they could hold the allegiance of their members. They did so primarily by shunning politics, veiling their Communist allegiance, and per-

Communist-controlled unions like Mine-Mill survived the cold war by working very hard for their members, burying any reference to political connections as red-baiting, and becoming enthusiastic nationalists. Leaders like Ken Smith, at the microphone, and Harvey Murphy, far left, held on to support in Sudbury and the interior of British Columbia after their union had vanished elsewhere in Canada and the United States. (Canadian Paperworkers)

suading employers that they could be responsible and possibly less militant than better-connected unions.

Although CCFers had triumphed within the labour movement and party support gradually grew in the CCL and even in the TLC, it was really too late. In 1948 the CCF had struggled back to official opposition in Ontario, but in 1951 it was almost annihilated. In the federal election of 1949, CCF candidates fought off the latest Communist weapon — this time an affectionate and wholly unwelcome embrace. They emerged with a mere thirteen seats, 13.6 percent of the popular vote. As a party or a movement, the CCF was in retreat.

The labour war had begun between the CCF and the Communists long before the world had been awakened by Czechoslovakia and the Berlin Blockade to the reality of a cold war. However, CCFers could not have prevailed without a growing climate of resentment among Canadians in and out of the labour movement at a political organization which owed its primary allegiance to the Soviet Union. CCFers were forever bewildered and indignant at the speed with which Communists could manipulate organizations and issues like peace and profiteering. Many of them would not have had the stomach for the tough, remorseless organizing which drove Communist influences from a major role in the unions. They and their heirs have romanticized and exaggerated the Communist contribution to union growth in the 1940s, while disparaging the contribution of anti-Communists like Charles Millard and Freddy Dowling, who not only built stronger unions but helped to make them foundations for a social democratic movement in Canada.

The struggle for political allegiance could not have been avoided. It is impossible to see how either the TLC or the CCL could have survived into the fifties with the kind of strong Communist influence they experienced in 1945. The sad part of the struggle was that it was fought almost exclusively among union leaders. Union members remained a mute chorus in the struggle, cheering neither the Communists nor the CCF, their support always claimed but rarely demonstrated. The political militants, CCF and Communist, might agree only in despising the quietism of Sam Gompers; their members lived out his doctrines to the letter.

CHAPTER 20

The Merger Movement

As soon as the struggle for the political allegiance of the Canadian labour movement began to fade, it hardly seemed to matter anymore. Canadians did not appear to need radical reforms; everyone seemed to be on the way to personal fulfilment without them. If the Communists were being discredited, the CCF had entered a steady, irreversible decline.

Some observers have compared the fifties to the twenties. There was a similar rapid economic growth, a corresponding Americanization of both ownership and life-style, and an expansion of material well-being. Prosperity stumbled briefly, recovered with the Korean War in the summer of 1950, and continued with barely a hesitation. While the rest of the industrial world struggled to repair war damage, North Americans enjoyed enormous economic advantages. Like their neighbours, Canadians began to assume that pre-eminence was a natural right.

For people whose lives had been scarred by the depression, times seemed very good indeed. It was a decade without protest movements because, as in the twenties, failure seemed proof only of personal maladjustment and, unlike the twenties, there was a structure of social benefits to cushion misfortune. Within a few years, Canadians came to count on regular wage and salary increases. Such expectations made the purchase of homes, cars, appliances, and the new television sets seem possible for Canadians who had never before been able to afford them. It was an age of acquisition.

For the most part, women had accepted their reduced role in the work force after 1945. Among the young, prosperity expressed itself in early marriages and a soaring birthrate. The sudden postwar baby bulge created a demand for new

The Noranda strike of 1953 was part of a campaign that established the Steelworkers in the mining industry of Quebec and northern Ontario. Though governments on both sides of the border were unsympathetic, legislation discouraged some of the tactics mining companies had used in earlier decades. The Steelworkers was also able to finance a prolonged series of strikes across the north, although it was a hard struggle. (National Photography Collection PA 120511)

homes, hospitals, schools. It combined with the birthrate contraction of the thirties to create an aging work force. The 1951 census found that the population had grown 50 percent since 1931, but the number in the ten to twenty age range had actually fallen. That meant that young people entering the labour market in the fifties could almost name their price, particularly if they had taken advantage of expanded opportunities for education. Immigration became vital to sustain growth. The flood of newcomers matched the pre-1914 period, and once again Canada looked to other countries to prepare skilled workers. The demand so far exceeded the supply that organized labour almost forgot its traditional hostility to immigration.

Because both workers and their union leaders were relatively older, fresh concerns joined the traditional demands for higher wages and more leisure. Older workers worried about occupational health and pension plans, job security and seniority. In turn, union negotiators faced management teams willing to change the image of an authoritarian boss with new techniques of manipulation and "human relations." The goal was co-operation, and the lubricant was a prosperity in which all could make gains. Strikes occurred, but only rarely were they the merciless, violent struggles of the past. The threats and indignation on both sides had a ritual look to them, and settlements usually came soon.

By no means did all Canadians gain from the fifties. In a decade when most Canadians acquired television, the plough-horse and stooked wheat vanished. So did most small farms. Traditionally prosperous agricultural regions of Canada were undermined by commercial agriculture and depopulated by big city attractions. Canadians celebrated a fivefold growth in their oil and gas industry and hardly noticed as coal mining died. Only in Cape Breton did it survive, almost as a government-subsidized make-work project. On the railways, diesel engines replaced the traditional steam locomotive, ending or transforming traditional trades. However, cheap oil and massive highway construction also undermined Canada's huge railway system just at the moment when it could have paid for itself. Some of the most dramatic chapters in Canadian labour history had been written by miners and railway workers; now they seemed destined to join coopers, cordwainers, and cigar makers.

Few industries escaped change. Across the country the trend was consistent: more people in professional, clerical, and sales occupations; fewer blue-collar manual workers. Forced by law and prosperity to come to terms with the workers on the plant floor, employers sought to reduce their dependence on those workers. White-collar workers, unorganized but disdainful of unions, posed no such threat.

Union members might notice the trend, but unemployment insurance now existed to tide them over to the next job, and in the growing industrial regions of southern Ontario and Quebec, this was never too far away. For their leaders, the answer was to break the white-collar barrier just as, only a decade before, they had cracked the factory gate. During the war years, unions had even won a few locals among the chartered banks in Montreal, Toronto, and Vancouver, but the postwar drive was different.

The centrepiece was a campaign to organize the fifteen thousand employees of the T. Eaton Company in Toronto. As Local No. 1000 of the Retail, Wholesale and Department Store Union, they would have been the biggest single union in Canada and a big key to open the retail sector. Financed by Millard's Steelworkers and headed by his best white-collar organizer, Eileen Tallman, the union began signing up members in 1948. Three years and a quarter of a million dollars later, the Eaton drive had become the closest thing to a crusade in the English-speaking union movement. It attracted bright new organizers like Lynn Williams, a future Steelworkers international secretary-treasurer. It also failed. The big department store had counter-attacked with wage increases, a pension plan, an enormous staff turnover, and the clear message that "nice" people did not belong to unions.

For at least the foreseeable future, the Eaton verdict was final. If unions wanted to grow in the fifties, it would not be through white-collar organizing or in the even tougher area of small, marginal plants. The fringe of ill-paid workers

The drive to organize the T. Eaton Company became the CCL's major bid to break through the barriers that kept unions out of white-collar and largely female occupations. The campaign drew on the best organizing talent the congress could muster and a healthy share of its funds. The steering committee included Charles Millard, Eileen Tallman, Jim MacLachlan of the Retail-Wholesale Union, Fred Dowling, David Lewis, George Burt of the UAW, and Pat Conroy, secretary-treasurer of the CCL. (Public Archives Canada PA 120535)

in the service industries grew rapidly during the decade, but they remained as immune to organization as the big factories once had been. If unions wanted to grow, it would increasingly be at each other's expense. *Raiding* meant winning over the support of members of another union, usually on the free-enterprise argument that the raiding union could deliver better service and more bargaining muscle. Sometimes, like the free-enterprise system itself, it went hand in hand with false claims and under-the-table-payments to employers or union officers. At stake were the dues dollars now guaranteed by automatic payroll deduction.

Most unionists deplored raiding in principle. It had all the disadvantages of other forms of competition. It was costly, unpredictable, and wasteful. It spawned bitter enmities. It affected bargaining effectiveness and realism when rival unions tried to outbid each other. Increasingly, labour's central organizations had assumed the responsibility for policing their affiliates' jurisdictions. However, the splitting of the AFL and CIO in 1936 and the TLC and CCL after 1939 created a potential open season for the contending bodies. Expulsion of Communist unions made raiding their locals virtually a patriotic duty. In Quebec, the growth of the Catholic syndicates added a further complication.

Originally, the differences between the AFL and TLC and their brash new opponents could be described by the competing principles of craft and industrial unionism. That distinction rapidly vanished during the Second World War.

Faced with huge new war plants and the Wagner Act to help them, many of the AFL's most traditional craft unions forgot their principles in a drive for members. The Carpenters organized anyone who worked with wood. The Boilermakers made a dive for the shipyards. The International Association of Machinists battled with the UAW for jurisdiction in the aircraft factories. More experienced and more solidly financed, both AFL and TLC unions kept well ahead of their industrial rivals' memberships — but at the expense of the cherished craft principle.

Expulsion of the Communist unions made them doubly vulnerable. Except in Sudbury and a regained beachhead at Port Colborne, the Steelworkers drove Mine-Mill from Ontario; but it suffered a setback in British Columbia. The United Electrical Workers also held most of its jurisdiction, and when the TLC expelled the United Fishermen in 1954, there was hardly even an attempt to raid. In the fifties, Communist unions learned to hide their politics, work hard for their members, and remind employers that they would be a little more reasonable than their tougher, better-financed rivals. The benefit, for the Communists, was a steady income and a chance to employ their apparatus of organizers.

While most of Vickers's workers were French Canadian, the picket sign was one of the rare examples of French in the big Montreal shipyard. In 1952, language issues were rarely raised because most union officials and negotiators were themselves English-speaking. (Public Archives Canada The Gazette, *September 9, 1952)*

Top

In the early 1950s, Quebec's Catholic syndicates and the industrial unions of the CCL made common cause against the government of Maurice Duplessis. Romeo Mathieu, secretary of the Quebec Federation of Labour, and Gerard Picard, bespectacled head of the CCCL, lean on adjoining seats amidst their followers. (Fred Dowling)

When the Catholic syndicates took on Dupuis Frères, the Montreal department store that symbolized French Canada's challenge to the English-speaking economic élite, other unions believed that the CCCL had finally become a labour organization like the others. A final reunion of all Canadian organized workers seemed to be on the cards. (Public Archives Canada PA 93888)

As the Communists became tranquillized, the Catholic unions grew steadily more aggressive and more like their materialistic rivals. The Asbestos strike of 1949 had only been a beginning. Antagonism to the Duplessis government kept expanding. Employers, who had once cheerfully signed with their Catholic syndicate, confident that matters could always be arranged with a little contribution to local parish funds, learned their lesson. So did the church. In 1950, the chaplains who had once virtually controlled the syndicates were directed to perform a more modest sacerdotal function. The Abbé Camirand, who had provided some of the spirit behind the Asbestos strike, was transferred.

In the early fifties, the Canadian and Catholic Confederation of Labour found itself engaged in a number of nasty strikes. At Louiseville, its textile workers battled with provincial police. Politically, it found itself in a steadily closer alliance with the Canadian Congress of Labour unions, partly because jurisdictional lines were clearer, chiefly because of a shared militancy. In revenge, the Duplessis government bestowed its favours increasingly on the TLC unions in Quebec.

Among several dramatic and violent CCCL strikes of the early fifties, the most significant was against Dupuis Frères. The Montreal department store had become almost a national institution in Quebec as it struggled to prove that French Canadians could compete with Morgan's, Ogilvy's, and the Toronto interlopers, Eaton's and Simpson's. The price was paid largely by the employees. The company prided itself on hiring widows, the disabled, and the elderly, but it paid accordingly. A deferential Catholic syndicate barred the store to non-confessional unions. The company precipitated problems by bringing in a "new broom" manager, determined to reform staff and methods. The syndicate, suddenly on the defensive, turned to Gerard Picard.

The result was a long, bitter conflict. It demonstrated the new willingness of the CCCL to take on a revered Quebec institution much as it would an international corporation. After certification on January 24, 1951, more than fifteen months passed without a contract. Employees earned an average of $30.00 a week, while the Montreal average was $46.60. Finally, when an arbitrator's report had supported the union and the company refused to budge, a strike began on May 1, 1952. From the first it was a struggle. The store opened its doors and proclaimed itself "self-service" at a 20 percent discount. Immediately, city police were on hand. Strikers answered with insults, threats, and attacks on strike-breakers. Strikers and stink-bombs; police responded with arrests and armies of reinforcements. Mayor Camillien Houde denounced the strikers as Communists and was pelted with eggs in the St. Jean Baptiste procession. Yet in the end it was the company that backed down. The new manager was fired. A richer wage settlement, a forty-hour week, paid holidays, and union security were all guaranteed. On July 26, the Dupuis Frères strike ended.

The strike cost the CCCL some nationalist friends who found nothing to criticize when its targets were English-speaking employers. The confederation, according to one of its radical leaders, Michel Chartrand, had broken with those who defended the French language by starving those who spoke it. For the rest of Canada's divided labour movement, the Catholic confederation had become more of an equal, and perhaps more of a rival.

Raiding and rivalry were poor excuses for growth. Experts and prophets in the United States and Canada agreed that, whatever the advances of organized workers in the previous decade, the future would be difficult. In the United States, the freedoms of the Wagner Act had been sharply curbed by the Taft-Hartley Act. In a growing number of states, "right to work" laws cancelled union security clauses and enforced the open shop. While Ottawa and the provinces did not follow the example (never having conceded as much earlier), pressure for restrictive legislation grew.

One of the few significant increases in union strength had come when Canada herself expanded to include a new province. Newfoundland's entry in 1949 pushed the total union membership in Canada to just over a million. It was not a very militant addition. Work for wages had always been scarce in Newfoundland, and neither of the two major industries, fishing and logging, had much of a history of unions. The Fishermen's Protective Union, founded by William Coaker in 1909 and moribund by 1949, had been a marketing co-operative with significant political influence during its heyday just before the First World War. It had virtually collapsed, like fish prices, in the 1920s.

Newfoundland had already contributed its share of union leaders to Canada, including the shrewd and agile Silby Barrett of the Cape Breton coal miners, but islanders were known as docile, cautious folk. The chance to earn wages was such a privilege that overtime was paid at half the normal rate, not at a premium. As elsewhere, unions developed only where skills were scarce or strategically located. A sealskinners' union developed because the skill was rare and desperately needed when the annual hunt was landed. Printers, masons, moulders, and ship carpenters had founded early unions, and, as elsewhere, the printers formed a wider connection with the International Typographical Union. Miners at the rich Wabana iron deposits on Bell Island formed their own union. However, such organizations still had their reality as well as their roots in their mutual benefit provisions.

While Newfoundlanders contemplated confederation, mainland unions seized their opportunity. The CCL despatched Donald MacDonald, a Cape Breton steelworker, who promptly signed up the Wabana miners for his union. The Newfoundland Federation of Labour, a weak and conservative body, sought help first from the TLC and then, when it failed to act, from the AFL in Washington. When the American body began chartering locals, the Canadian congress responded vigorously and a sharp rivalry began. Union with Canada brought a construction boom to Newfoundland. Mainlanders, brought to the island for their skills, also brought demands and expectations, which Newfoundland workers quickly absorbed. The era of labour peace and docility was coming to an end.

The rivalry in claiming Newfoundland's small and divided union movement illustrated the absurdity of the rivalry between the two main Canadian central organizations. By 1951, the TLC had 522,000 members; the CCL, 350,000. The gap seemed unlikely to narrow. Separately, each congress lacked the resources to tackle serious white-collar organizing or the slow, costly work of bringing unions to small plants. Leaders recalled that the original split had not come on Canadian initiative, but at the insistence of the AFL and its affiliates. Almost as a ritual,

Years before, as the youthful Canadian head of the Brotherhood of Railroad and Steamship Clerks, Frank Hall had read A.R. Mosher's union out of the TLC. Thirty years later, still running their respective unions, Hall and Mosher helped reunite Canadian labour in a new congress. (Public Archives Canada The Gazette, Montreal)

CCL conventions called on the leaders to bring the congresses together; in 1944, the TLC had called for "serious study" of reunification. In 1948, both congresses denounced Prince Edward Island legislation ordering its locals to sever international affiliations. Later that year they joined with the CCCL to condemn labour legislation brought forward by the Duplessis government in Quebec. In 1950, both the TLC and the CCL supported the government on the Korean War and condemned it in a joint statement for ending the railway strike by compulsory arbitration. In December, the congresses, joined by the CCCL and the railway running trades, launched a National Consultative and Co-operative Committee to campaign for rent and price controls.

Yet each apparent step towards a genuine reunion was fated to be followed by another step backward. In 1945, the CCL had given official support to the CCF; the TLC urged its members to re-elect King. In Quebec, the TLC deserted the common front to improve its position with the Duplessis government. Within a year of helping to form the National Consultative Committee, the TLC had walked out. Its president, Percy Bengough, snorted indignantly that there was nothing to be gained when one of the partners was affiliated to a political party.

Differing political strategies had become, in fact, one of the few clear distinctions between the CCL and the older congress. The TLC's non-partisanship was enforced by an executive that included active Liberals and Conservatives, a growing number of CCFers, and some fervent non-partisans. However, as important as principle was personality. Years of bad-tempered competition had become embodied in the two old men who presided over the congresses — Bengough and the CCL's A.R. Mosher.

The younger congress had suffered its own painful personality battles soon after its Communist affiliates departed. As though free at last to express his anger, Pat Conroy chose the 1951 convention to resign in a final fiery demonstration against his enemy, Charles Millard. Shaken and embarrassed by the departure of one of its leading officials, the CCL next was compelled to watch as its president's own union, the Canadian Brotherhood of Railway Employees, presented its dirty linen at a trial in which Mosher set out to expel his chief lieutenant, J.E. McGuire. The scandal, complete with charges and insults, climaxed at the CBRE convention in May, 1952. For three days, McGuire defended himself and attacked the elderly Mosher. The union upheld its president, but only by a margin of 190 to 162. From such scandals, merger talk came as a relief.

The Canadian congresses could talk about merger; it could only be possible if the American central organizations went first. For many of the same reasons, but more suddenly, the AFL and the CIO began to patch up their differences. A

The merger convention that created the Canadian Labour Congress reached its climax with the election of the former TLC president, Claude Jodoin, to head the new organization. A.R. Mosher of the CCL shared the gavel after years of imposing "Mosher's Rules" on unruly delegates. Ontario's Premier Leslie Frost and David Archer, president of the Ontario Federation of Labour, shared the podium with varying degrees of solemnity. (Marcel Ray)

significant factor was the death, in 1952, of both William Green of the AFL and Philip Murray, president of the CIO. Both had been coal miners and protégés of John L. Lewis, the big, eloquent autocrat of the United Mine Workers. Both had symbolized the split. Their successors, a former New York plumber and AFL official, George Meaney, and the UAW president, Walter Reuther, could make a fresh start. On April 7, 1953, both of the big American organizations had agreed to a no-raiding pact. The Canadian congresses followed suit within a year, appointing a Montreal labour lawyer, H. Carl Goldenberg, to act as permanent arbitrator in any dispute. A Unity Committee, four members from each Canadian congress, began work.

Personalities changed in Canada, too. In the wake of the McGuire trial, in which his own flouting of retirement rules had been an issue, Mosher at seventy-three announced his forthcoming resignation. An old and ailing Percy Bengough resigned. His successor was Claude Jodoin, a Montrealer whose parents had lost their fortune in the depression. Jodoin had gone to work as an organizer for the International Ladies' Garment Workers' Union. He was a contrast to the aging craft unionists who had preceded him.

By 1955 the process in both countries had become a tide. On February 9, 1955, an AFL-CIO unity committee announced agreement; the TLC-CCL committee made its announcement on March 9. Later that year, without visible dissent, both congress conventions ratified the arrangement. Frank Hall, who

David McDonald, international president of the United Steelworkers, and Charles Millard, Canadian director of the union, differed on a great deal, especially politics. Millard stood his ground and usually won his arguments. (United Steelworkers)

had forced the expulsion of Mosher's CBRE a third of a century before, was still available to speak passionately for the merger. On April 23, 1956, the first merger convention opened on the grounds of the Canadian National Exhibition in Toronto. The 1,620 delegates represented just over a million affiliated members.

Promoters of the new organization emphasized that they had done more than produce a respectful imitation of an American development. Even by name, the new Canadian Labour Congress was more united than an American organization that persisted as the AFL-CIO. In its financial structure, the CLC had compromised between the four cents per member per month collected by the TLC and ten cents for the CCL. The new tax, seven cents, was intended to provide an organizing potential. Mosher's retirement eased the problems of finding a new executive. Jodoin became president; the CCL's secretary-treasurer, Donald MacDonald, took on the same post in the new organization.

The most real obstacle to the new congress had been the CCL's persistent identification with the CCF. Paradoxically, as the party's national strength faded, its support in the TLC had grown. John Porter, conducting research for his book on Canada's elites, found in 1955 that 45 percent of TLC leaders and 93 percent of the CCL's backed the CCF. Only 12 percent of the TLC group backed the Liberals; 20 percent called themselves non-partisan. At the same time, the decline of the party made it absurd, even to the CCF's national president, David Lewis, that it should stand as an obstacle to the merger. The result was an elaborate compromise, acceptable to both the CCF and to the new CLC leaders. The new congress would have a political education department. It would also initiate talks with free trade unions, farm organizations, co-operatives, and the CCF, leading to a new political party.

In the euphoria of the merger convention, nothing seemed impossible to the new labour organization. The energy wasted in bickering and raiding could be poured into organizing the unorganized. Other labour organizations, dwarfed by the new congress, would join its ranks. Within months, the tiny remnant of the One Big Union and two venerable railway unions, the Locomotive Firemen and the Railway Trainmen, had joined. The Canadian and Catholic Confederation of Labour would surely not be far behind. Even among some CCFers there was elation. A new name, a new program, and a new structure might be the electric shock that would save Canadian socialism from oblivion.

If anything was needed to confirm the unionists' optimism it was a dyspeptic outburst from the Canadian Manufacturers' Association. The new congress, complained the CMA, was a dangerous monopoly.

CHAPTER 21

Times of Frustration

When Henry Ford announced that he would raise his workers' wages to the then-stupendous level of a dollar an hour, he had a very simple explanation. Unless workers like his could afford the seven hundred dollars for a mass-produced Model-T, he was unlikely to move the ugly-looking rattletraps off his lot.

Ford's rivals imitated his anti-union attitude but not his wage policy. The result contributed to both the Great Depression and to an industrial unionism tough enough to force even manufacturing giants to the bargaining table. The union power backed by law in the United States and Canada allowed working people to own not only a car but also a home and the growing variety of consumer goods produced for them.

In 1956, few Canadian workers shared the worries that had led their leaders into the merger movement. Nor could they quote the official statistics which showed that the average industrial wage — $62.40 a week — had doubled since 1945 and almost tripled since 1939. While inflation had taken its toll, worker purchasing power in Canada's favoured industrial regions had doubled since the grim depression days. Families could plan for one of the new flickering black and white television sets, confident that payments could always be made on the instalment plan. The future stretched ahead with the same comforting certainty that Canada would always be governed by the Liberal party.

Of course, there were exceptions to Canada's complacent blessedness. In Cape Breton, the coal and steel industry were in tragic decline. Newfoundland fishermen who heeded their premier's advice to haul up their dories and move to town were more likely to earn government welfare than an industrial wage. Most Canadians knew of families crushed by huge medical and hospital bills.

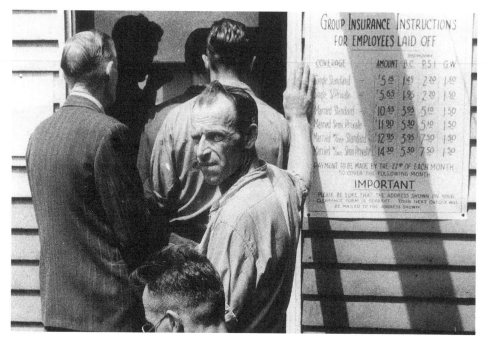

Even before the Diefenbaker victory in 1957, Canada began feeling the pinch of recession. Faltering wheat sales in the West hurt the farm implement industry in the East. Workers, accustomed to layoffs as a short break for retooling, suddenly began to wonder whether they would ever get their jobs back. (Public Archives Canada PA 93792)

Nevertheless, most workers with a union contract, and many without, now counted on two weeks of paid vacations every year. The forty-hour week had become almost commonplace in mills and factories. Premium pay for overtime was no longer a rare privilege.

However, Canada's postwar prosperity had been a reward for good luck, not good work. With the rest of the industrialized world in ruins by 1945, the United States and Canada could sell virtually anything they produced. Perhaps, by ingenuity and hard work, Canada might have built herself a permanent lead. Instead, she built on the large short-term benefits of her "special relationship" with the United States. One by one, the technological gains Canadians had built for themselves in wartime industries vanished. Shipbuilding was gone by 1950. The aircraft industry, electronics, and communications followed. Only the Jeremiahs spoke of it then, but Canada was returning to her old dependence on the raw materials her people pulled from the ground. Once again, Canada's fortune would depend on the uncertainties of world prices and world markets.

The impact was felt in the old-fashioned ways — layoffs, bankruptcies, plant closings. Industrialists, accustomed to selling whatever they made at a profit, blamed everyone but themselves. The prime scapegoat was unionism. What easier explanation could there be for the triumph of high-quality German and

Japanese imports than the high wages and low productivity of Canadian workers?

By most standards, unionism in the fifties looked complacent and a little conservative, much like the rest of society. Union leaders claimed that their movement had "matured" from the aggressiveness of the late forties. Contract demands focused on pensions, health and accident insurance, job security, and longer vacations. Members wanted job escape more than cash. Company strategies also switched. For years it was unions that presented demands; management responded. In 1945, Lemuel Boulware, General Electric's chief negotiator, adopted a bold new strategy. Instead of waiting for the union demand, he prepared the company's final and only offer, mailed it to the workers, told the press, and dared the United Electrical Workers to take it or leave it. They took it then and later. *Boulwarism*, with its rigid defiance of union negotiators, won more admirers than imitators on the management side, but in the late fifties, with inventories high and orders slow, many companies could afford strikes. Workers, suddenly aware of long lists of unemployed, could not. Tied into a continental economy by their international links and because so many members worked in branch plants, Canadian unions rapidly felt the impact of the hostility.

In 1957, the Liberal government sailed confidently into yet another federal general election. Long experience, tight money, and a budget surplus confirmed its right to re-election. Instead, the Liberals emerged humiliated and narrowly defeated by a Progressive Conservative party transformed in the populist image of John Diefenbaker. After a single session marked by generous social policies, the Tories called a second round. On March 31, 1958, John Diefenbaker commanded the biggest majority a Canadian parliament had ever seen — 208 to 49 Liberals and a pathetic handful of only 8 CCFers.

Unionized workers were almost as captivated by the Diefenbaker vision as other Canadians; their leaders were far more apprehensive. Most of them had been bred in the era of "Iron Heel" Bennett. When he studied the political affiliations of Canadian labour leaders, John Porter had found that only a tiny handful admitted to being Tory. It was not surprising. A Tory judge might be the real author of P.C. 1003, but almost the entire machinery of collective bargaining had developed under a Liberal government. Backed by its huge majority, answerable to powerful business and financial interests, would the Diefenbaker government dismantle a system which, however imperfect, had made unionism possible for a million Canadians?

In fact, the fears proved groundless. Diefenbaker's minister of labour, Michael Starr, confessed that he had considered opening the 1948 legislation for amendment. Faced with a furious babble of conflicting demands, he rapidly forgot his intentions and busied himself elsewhere. If Canadian unions found bitter enemies in the fifties, they were in the provincial capitals, not in Ottawa.

On paper, some of the most hostile developments occurred in British Columbia. In 1952, a conservative, business-based Social Credit party had collected Liberal and Tory votes to edge out the CCF and win power under W.A.C. Bennett. Early in his career, Bennett declared war on the militant local union movement. Amendments to labour law promised loss of checkoff and decertification for unions engaged in illegal strikes. In fact, the penalties remained threats to be defied by angry and embattled unions. Far more shocking for a union movement which believed that it had finally won a secure legitimacy was the fate of a Steelworkers' local union at Murdochville, Quebec.

As far back as 1952, the Steelworkers had mustered support from four-fifths of the Gaspé Copper Mines employees, but the company successfully stalled certification, favouring a feeble mining affiliate of the Trades and Labour Congress. That union vanished with the TLC-CCL merger, and the Steelworkers returned at once, collected cards, and won certification from the Quebec Labour Relations Board. Within a month, the company, a subsidiary of Noranda mining interests, had a court order barring certification. Legally, the union was in limbo. The miners, with years of pay claims and grievances outstanding, voted for a strike. Somehow, Steelworkers officials persuaded them to wait a little longer. Six months passed. On March 3, amidst rumours of mass layoffs, the company fired the union president and several union organizers. Patience ended.

That night there was a picket line around the property. In two days the strike was effective. The company had no trouble collecting a court injunction or in launching suits against union officers. The strike was plainly illegal. On April 25, fifty provincial police arrived to protect non-strikers. Violence flared. More police came. The company announced that it was firing disloyal employees. Some strikers responded with dynamite. One of them died. Gradually, Canadian labour leaders began to heed both the tragedy and the significance of Murdochville. If a union that had obeyed the law could be destroyed, what happened next? On August 18, Claude Jodoin, president of the CLC, and the diminutive leader of the Catholic confederation, Gerard Picard, led a joint protest march to the company gates. As provincial police watched, strike-breakers stoned the procession from the slopes along the road. Back at the little company town, a gang of thugs pillaged the union office and overturned twelve cars.

Processions and protests made no difference. On October 5, the remaining three hundred strikers voted to go back to work. Only a hundred were accepted. The company took the Steelworkers to court. After appeals had gone all the way to the Supreme Court of Canada, the bill for damages, interest, and legal costs had become $2,660,749.

Murdochville could be put down to the notorious anti-unionism of Maurice Duplessis and his Union Nationale. What would happen in a province whose premier had once been a socialist organizer as well as the biographer and admirer of one of its few radical figures? Surely Joey Smallwood would welcome an organization which would try to do for Newfoundland's loggers what Sir William Coaker had attempted to do for the outport fishermen?

Long before Newfoundland entered Confederation, loggers had been organized into at least three rival associations, often headed by a dominant individual who earned his living from the dues and who bargained feebly with the two powerful companies, Bowater and Anglo-Newfoundland. The predictable result was fifteen years of labour peace, meagre wages, and miserable conditions in the camps. A Woods Labour Board helped to ease some of the problems of jealous organizations and their respective chieftains.

At the Murdochville strike, Claude Jodoin discovered that presidency of an organization of a million trade unionists did not entitle him to police protection from rock-throwing strike-breakers. The Murdochville defeat was a first setback for the CLC and a warning that the postwar period of labour tranquillity was over. (United Steelworkers)

After Confederation, the Newfoundland loggers were an obvious organizing target. The International Woodworkers of America had been highly effective in British Columbia, but by the time it had emerged from the bitter battle against the Communists, the aggressive Brotherhood of Carpenters and Joiners had entered the Newfoundland field. J.J. Thompson, elderly leader of the biggest logger organization on the island, was reported ready to give his members to whichever union guaranteed him the best old age security. The Carpenters won that competition, but the IWA chose to appeal directly to the loggers themselves.

Almost at once the mainland union ran into trouble, not so much from loggers who could hardly believe the pay and conditions of West Coast loggers, but from the companies and the government. A first certification bid was rejected because the union "had not acquired status" in the province. Bowater suddenly discovered that its loggers were independent contractors. It took two years before the IWA was in a position to negotiate with Anglo-Newfoundland. A conciliation board recommendation, backed by the labour minister, was accepted by the union but rejected by the company. With obvious reluctance, the IWA began a strike on January 1, 1959.

Like the Noranda subsidiary at Murdochville, Anglo-Newfoundland plainly decided to defeat the IWA union. When the IWA advised its members to stay in the camps because it was expecting an early settlement, the company expelled them and then blamed the union. At first the strike was quiet, but company

Even before a Newfoundland policeman was killed in a picket-line scuffle, some observers wondered whether police were under orders to provoke striking loggers into violence. Once the tragedy occurred, RCMP and constabulary members knew that they would have public support for suppressing the strike. CLC leaders might denounce the killing of a legal union but they were powerless. (Ed Seymour)

efforts to recruit strike-breakers from Newfoundland's hard-pressed fishermen led to inevitable clashes on the trails and logging roads. The IWA, only a middle-sized union, looked to the rest of the Canadian labour movement for help. With the Newfoundland strike taking on crusading dimensions, the CLC obliged with a fund of $856,000. As the IWA struggled to distribute relief and keep up morale, the toll of arrests from picket-line clashes rose to a hundred.

On February 12, with almost no warning, Joey Smallwood waded into the conflict. In a masterpiece of emotional oratory, the provincial premier announced that he was setting out for Gander to "free the loggers of Newfoundland from the tyranny of a foreign union." To the outrage of the province's weak labour federation and to the protests of a few brave journalists, Smallwood created his own union, the Newfoundland Brotherhood of Wood Workers. Then he hurried back to St. John's and, in a special session of the legislature, simply decertified the IWA and, for good measure, the Teamsters' brotherhood.

That did not end the strike. On March 10, a contingent of RCMP, reinforced by Newfoundland constabulary from St. John's, set out for Badger. The sixty-six policemen formed a phalanx and marched back and forth through a growing crowd of loggers. For an hour they clubbed their way through the crowd. Then, as tempers flared, some loggers fought back. William Moss of the constabulary crumpled under a blow from a two-foot stick of birchwood. He was dead.

So was the strike. Smallwood had found a martyred victim of the "foreign union." At Grand Falls, vigilantes smashed the IWA headquarters. The death ended the wave of sympathetic editorials. Within days both of the big employers had signed with Smallwood's union. Once again, a legal strike with legitimate grounds had been utterly defeated, this time with a crudeness of government interference which even Maurice Duplessis would not have dared.

Even then, the humiliation of the Canadian labour movement was not complete. Throughout the IWA drive, the Carpenters' union had bided its time. In 1958, the island loggers had favoured the IWA over the Carpenters by 86.4 percent. Still the Carpenters waited. Finally, on June 27, 1961, Smallwood's union, now by law and bargaining rights dominant in the industry, was handed over, lock, stock, and contracts, to the Carpenters.

If there had been one goal of the 1956 merger, it had been to end that kind of squalid rivalry. Whatever its errors of haste and inexperience, the IWA in Newfoundland had won legitimacy among the loggers and throughout most of Canadian unionism. It was the first great test of the young Canadian Labour Congress to discipline its affiliates. It failed. The unrepentant Carpenters made it clear that they could well save the million dollars a year it cost to belong to the congress. Under no circumstances would it accept a CLC-supervised ballot on the allegiance of Newfoundland loggers. For two years, from 1962 to 1964, the Carpenters stayed out of the congress. When they returned, they paid their dues and made not a single concession.

The Murdochville and Badger strikes were deeply disturbing because they showed that apparently long-established practices of union recognition and bargaining could easily be destroyed by governments without significant public outrage. This was all the more alarming because of brand new threats to Canadian unionism.

In a sense, the threat of technological change was one of the oldest fears of skilled workers. Labour's own history in Canada illustrated the point. Of the trades which had long ago launched a union movement, the coopers, the cigar makers, and the moulders had either vanished or approached extinction. Only the typographers remained, and already their trade was threatened. The Brotherhood of Locomotive Firemen and Enginemen had come to Canada in the 1880s, but the coming of diesel power ended the role of men who had once fed the fire-boxes of steam locomotives. Railways, as conservative as their employees, hesitated to make a change. Shrinking revenue from the recession hardened their resolve. Earlier in the decade, the packinghouse industry, with forceful pressure from its union, had shown one way to share the benefits of improved methods with its workers. A new device, which literally blew the hides off carcasses, threatened to eliminate one of the most skilled and well-paid trades on the killing floor. Canada Packers established a fund based on added profits

Locomotive firemen and enginemen were victims of a new technology—diesel locomotives that eliminated all but a tiny part of their role. As skilled workers in an old and honoured craft, they followed an historic path of resistance. (Public Archives Canada PA 93724)

from the new machinery. It retrained affected employees, safeguarded their wage rates and seniority, and softened any resentment by a general raise. Locomotive firemen were not destined to be so lucky.

The CPR proposal was by no means brutal. Firemen on diesel engines used for freight and yard service would be phased out by attrition. The brotherhood would not hear of it. If the Canadian railway could eliminate firemen, other North American lines would follow suit. The union was in a fight for its existence, and Canadian firemen found themselves in the front line. So did other Canadian railwaymen. On January 2, 1957, more than sixty-five thousand CPR employees walked out to support 2,850 firemen. Faced with a nation-wide rail shutdown for the first time since 1950, Parliament ordered the men back on January 11 and appointed Mr. Justice R.L. Kellock to investigate. Kellock's report gave no comfort at all to the brotherhood when it appeared a year later. By claiming that firemen were indispensable for safety reasons, the brotherhood had backed itself into an indefensible position. Once again the brotherhood launched strike action. This time there was no support from the other railway

The penalty for driving a cement truck through a Teamsters' picket line could be a savage beating. Unfortunately for the picketers, no one noticed that a press photographer was on hand, seeking a little sensation for the front page. Violence in Toronto's construction industry provoked a Royal Commission and a number of ineffectual resolutions. (York University)

unions. By the time the firemen gave up, they had only confirmed the company case that they were superfluous.

The firemen's brotherhood had been one of the first of the old railway unions to foresake independence by joining the CLC. The move had not gained its members more than a year's reprieve. No more than the nineteenth-century English Luddites, with their machine-breaking response to new machinery, had the congress been able to stop a job-robbing change in its tracks. Instead, it had provided fresh evidence to its enemies that unions were agencies for feather-bedding and make-work for their members. The tragic plight of aging men whose only capital was an obsolete skill was again obscured.

During the fifties, the most effective weapon against unionism in the United States had been appalling evidence of racketeering and corruption in major labour organizations. Dave Beck, head of the Teamsters and an AFL-CIO vice-president, was shown to have sordid connections with West Coast gangsters. The investigations of a committee headed by Senator John B. McClellan, conducted under the harsh light of television, exposed not only the Teamsters but lesser unions like the United Textile Workers, the bakers' union, laundry workers, and distillery workers' organizations. When Dave Beck was reluctantly retired (and went to prison), the Senate committee had no trouble finding even more damning evidence about his successor, James Hoffa. Other unions — those of the operating engineers, hotel and restaurant employees, meat cutters, and carpenters — all fell under investigation too.

Corruption was no novelty in American unionism. Critics had always claimed that labour racketeers could use the threat of strikes and slowdowns to extort payoffs for themselves. The trucking industry, with a host of small employers occasionally operating on the wrong side of a complex network of laws, was particularly vulnerable to a powerful, unscrupulous union. Investigators made it easy for crooked leaders to win sympathy from their members when they exposed the union side of corrupt deals and forgot about employers. The philosophy that unions were a business dispensing services to their members, not ideological crusaders for a better world, provided its own subtle invitation to corruption by leaders and acceptance by the rank and file.

In Canada, there had been no such history. The stakes were smaller, and so were most unions. Canadians might cheerfully attribute their relative immunity to labour corruption to their own virtue, and perhaps to the fact that the Gompers "business union" philosophy had never been quite so pervasive. However, at the heart of the labour movement lay a painful embarrassment, Hal C. Banks.

The price of ridding Canada of a Communist seamen's union had been the importation of a corrupt union. A Liberal government, shipping companies, and the TLC were all complicit. When Banks sought Canadian citizenship, Claude Jodoin was one of the guarantors of his good character. The muscular tactics and the Do Not Ship list which Banks had used against the Canadian Seamen's Union remained to secure his hold over lake seamen. To finance his own lavish life-style, as well as meeting union costs, Banks raised dues. To add members, he dealt directly with companies, promising complete legal protection if their existing unions brought suit for breach of contract. If that failed, strong-arm tactics were available. The Norris inquiry into the Seafarers' International Union in Canada eventually found seventy-five incidents of beatings and violence, mostly against other unions.

By 1959, pressed by other affiliates, including the biggest Canadian national union, the Canadian Brotherhood of Railway, Transport and General Workers, the CLC executive bit the bullet, suspended the SIU, and, a year later, persuaded the biennial convention to expel it. That only brought trouble to the surface. Ships manned by men from a CBRT-sponsored successor union faced boycotts, picket lines, and violence when they put into American ports. Paul Hall, president of the SIU and no great improvement on his Canadian lieutenant, supported Banks and easily won the backing of the AFL-CIO. In desperation, when quiet diplomacy and even humble appeals failed to move the American union leadership, Claude Jodoin reluctantly turned to his own government.

The outcome did much to confirm the prejudice that governments should not meddle in union affairs. Canadian government pressure in Washington utterly

Top

Although ministers of the new *Progressive Conservative* government had no particular reason to be fond of Canada's union leaders, they carried on most of the policies of their Liberal predecessors, including dutiful attendance when UAW leader George Burt drew attention to the ailing state of Canada's auto industry in the late 1950s. (*Archives of Labor and Urban Affairs, Wayne State University*)

Canadian labour had been proud to claim that it was free of the corruption that congressional investigation found in American unionism. It could not hide Hal Banks, the ex-convict summoned to Canada by shipowners, the government, and the TLC to get rid of the Communist-run Canadian Seamen's Union. Banks could not have survived without tacit support from his own union members and most of the rest of the Canadian movement. (*Information Canada*)

failed. President John F. Kennedy took his labour advice from the AFL-CIO. In a hopeless situation, the CLC persuaded affiliates to boycott SIU-manned ships. This forced the government to launch an official inquiry with a private promise from the minister of labour, Michael Starr, that it would not lead to the kind of investigation Senator McClellan and Robert Kennedy had run in the United States. The promise could not be kept. Under Mr. Justice T.G. Norris, an investigation of the SIU could not help becoming a recital of violence and corruption in which the CLC was daubed with flying tar. "The labour movement bears, and is conscious of bearing, a heavy burden of guilt in allowing so intolerable a situation to develop and to continue," confessed the CLC brief.

Contrition did not bring absolution. The Norris inquiry recommended a trusteeship for not just the SIU but for all five maritime unions. The congress, which had denounced government control of Newfoundland in 1959, found itself compelled into limp, reluctant acquiescence only five years later. In the end, the SIU lost nothing by its conduct except its president, for Banks skipped $25,000 bail and found safe sanctuary with Paul Hall in the United States.

Critics of unionism during the fifties had revived the old and familiar image of labour as a powerful monolith. It was a portrait for which union leaders had their own sneaking affection. The oratory of the merger convention of 1956 had promised new worlds to conquer. A sad series of defeats and humiliations had exposed the divisions and the fundamental vulnerability of organized labour in Canada.

At the same time, the humiliations had come as part of an adverse economic climate. If governments in Quebec and Newfoundland backed companies against their workers, it was because ailing economies could not afford disruptions or the impression of an unruly labour force. If an organization like the CLC could not get tough with an insolent affiliate like the carpenters' union, it was because it desperately needed the million dollars a year in affiliation dues. Times were tougher than anyone could have expected in 1956. By 1960, unemployment in Canada was about as bad as it had been in 1939, and no one who could help it was going on strike.

No one called it a depression. That once-familiar word was now reserved for the thirties. Almost superstitiously, it seemed more prudent to call it a recession. And no more than R.B. Bennett had caused the disaster of the thirties was John Diefenbaker responsible for the recession which coincided with his years in power. More than his Liberal predecessors, he was eager to approve spending on the poor and the old. His ministers launched a host of schemes, contradictory, confused, and sometimes excellent. However, ordinary Canadians now expected their government to rescue them from bad times. They remembered the prosperity of the Liberal years and from Ottawa they now learned only of indecision. Promised surpluses turned invariably into substantial deficits.

In 1956, thanks to a cautious prior compromise with the CCF, the political policy of the new Canadian Labour Congress had been carefully muffled and deferred. In the Diefenbaker victories of 1957 and 1958, labour had played little role, although unionists claimed credit for three new seats the CCF won and held in northern Ontario. However, the crushing defeat of the CCF elsewhere forced action. Either democratic leftist politics would die in Canada or the congress

The commitment of the CLC and the CCF to found a new political party for the democratic Left, labour, and "the liberally minded" was confirmed at Montreal in 1958. The agreement was appropriately symbolized by Stanley Knowles, about to become a CLC vice-president, Claude Jodoin, Thérèse Casgrain, David Lewis, and M.J. Coldwell, with a portrait of J.S. Woodsworth looking on for good luck. The Parti Social-Démocrate was the CCF's latest and unavailing effort to win friends in Quebec. (Public Archives Canada C 567)

must help to revive them. A reshuffled CLC executive allowed a Liberal-leaning vice-president, Gordon Cushing, to be replaced by two active CCFers, Stanley Knowles, a defeated M.P., and William Dodge. The 1958 CLC convention voted almost unanimously to launch discussions with the CCF, farm organizations, and like-minded groups and individuals to launch "a fundamental re-alignment of political forces in Canada." A new party must be born.

The decision was far from painless. Veteran CCFers were heartbroken at the disappearance of a name and symbols that had held their loyalty for a generation. Government employees withdrew from the congress despite every assurance that their political neutrality would be respected. The conservative craft unions stayed with the congress but did nothing to involve their members in the procession of meetings, conferences, seminars, and rallies which laid the foundations for the "New Party." In Ottawa, CLC relations with the new Diefenbaker government would never have been easy, but they were made harsher by the New Party organizing campaign. Positions on government boards and commissions, hitherto almost guaranteed to CLC nominees, were handed instead to loyal Tories. The reason was obvious. True to the principles of patronage, suspicious Conservatives were determined to allow no plums to pass to CLC-nominated socialists.

Despite the resistance, both the congress and the CCF leadership persisted. The founding convention of the New Party, at Ottawa from July 31 to August 4, was a smooth triumph for union organizing efficiency. The CCF sent 710 delegates; 613 came from union organizations; another 318 represented the

The NDP's founding convention in Ottawa in 1961 was a demonstration of union organizing and administrative skill. However, once the new party was launched, most unions withdrew to the sidelines to see how it would fare. (Steel Labor)

"New Party Clubs," organized to attract a new "liberally-minded" following. Across the country, a campaign to persuade local unions to affiliate with the New Party meant that almost 200,000 thousand unionists had been persuaded to contribute five cents a month.

By adjournment on August 4, the New Democratic party had been born. Its program was a complete agenda of social democratic aims, from full employment to nuclear disarmament, from universal health insurance and portable pensions to co-operative federalism, bilingualism, and multiculturalism. Its leader, Tommy Douglas, the diminutive premier of Saskatchewan, had been backed by almost all the union votes in the hall. It was easy for jounalists to claim, as the hot, stuffy, Ottawa arena grew silent, that labour's new party, backed by a million members and their families, could have any prize it wanted. After five years of humiliation and defeat, Canadian labour had a winner.

CHAPTER 22
Prosperity and Discontent

Canadians got few rewards for their massive support of John Diefenbaker in 1958. By 1960, unemployment reached near-depression levels. Hardest hit were hinterland industrial regions of the Maritimes, Quebec, and British Columbia, but wealthy southern Ontario was not immune. "Black Friday" — February 20, 1959 — was the day the federal government cancelled the Avro Arrow and devastated one of Canada's few high-technology industries.

The years were not totally barren. Prairie farmers rejoiced at a government ready to sell their wheat to a Communist China. Federal support for technical education began to channel thousands of young Canadians away from the job market, returning them later better qualified. As in all other depressions, a majority of Canadians knew of unemployment at second hand. They could enjoy stable prices, bemoan welfare spending, and repeat well-worn rumours about the abuse of unemployment insurance. Others could believe that a blustering, indecisive Diefenbaker government was no more than a second coming of R.B. Bennett.

Faced with recession, unions proved no more effective than the government. Membership stagnated and, after 1960, began to fall. In 1958, 34.2 percent of the non-agricultural work force had belonged to unions; by 1964, the share had slumped to 29.4 percent. Major corporations and their unions survived bad times as well as good; it was at the fringes that organized labour was defeated. After an eight-week strike, Kaufman Rubber employees in Kitchener were obliged to beg for their old jobs. An eight-month strike at Brandon Packers in 1960, scarred by violence and intimidation, ended only when the United Packinghouse Workers officials met with absentee owners in Toronto and

239

extracted a settlement. That did not prevent a Royal Commission. It found enough evidence of theft and fraud to send the owners to jail, but the union came in for savage criticism. There was no glamour and little progress in organizing on the edges of an industrial ghetto of ill-paid, vulnerable workers.

During the fifties, that ghetto grew with the flood of New Canadians. Most of the traditional techniques of exploiting immigrant workers returned, from the contract labour boss with his threats of instant deportation, to the reluctance of the craft unions to get involved. In Toronto, where a construction boom absorbed a ninth of the entire nation's building investment during the decade, Italian immigrants provided the labour force in home and apartment construction. Disciplined by a web of violence and intimidation, kept in ignorance of even their few legal safeguards, building labourers were obliged to work from dawn to dusk for as little as fifty cents an hour. Most of the craft unions, securely in control of major construction projects, concluded that home building was simply impossible to organize. Five local unions in the building trades banded together as the Brandon Hall group, found sympathizers from the Italian community, and took on the challenge. The outcome was a set of brutal, violent strikes in 1960 and 1961 — inevitably illegal because the legal routes were impossibly slow — and a Royal Commission under H. Carl Goldenberg that exposed the industry to any who cared to know. His recommendations, carefully balanced between employers and unions, offered little help to the unorganized.

The fifties had transformed Toronto into a cosmopolitan metropolis. Much of the price for the stylish new architecture, the subway and expressways, and the glittering night-life was paid by immigrants who rarely shared the benefits of unionized workers. A rare exception was the staff of the Royal York Hotel. Nonetheless, when the CPR hotel employees struck in May of 1961, they were promptly dismissed. More than a year later, when the strike collapsed, over half of the 1,350 strikers had permanently lost their jobs.

Defeat did not come exclusively to unions of badly paid immigrants; it could also happen to the aristocrats of labour. Local No. 91 of the International Typographical Union was the proud ancestor of Toronto's labour movement. However, new technologies threatened the jobs of every printer in North America. The Toronto printers might have compromised when the city's three dailies modernized their plants in the early sixties, but their union headquarters far away in Colorado gave them no choice. Toronto would be the battle line in the defence of historic work rules. It was also a rout. When the strike started in the summer of 1964, advance preparations and a corps of professional strike-breakers kept the papers publishing with barely a flutter. The conservative printers, who had scorned the violence and radicalism of lesser unions, were reduced to picket-line scuffles in a struggle for their jobs. They lost. By 1965, humbled and desperate, the union voted to go back. The publishers refused to take them. By 1972, when the ITU officially conceded that the strike was lost, Toronto printers had lost their jobs, their savings, and many of them their craft.

In the fifties violence had been rare. In the sixties bloodshed in labour disputes grew more common. In January, 1963, frustration at delays goaded members of the Lumber and Sawmill Workers Union into an illegal strike against Spruce Falls Pulp and Paper Company at Kapuskasing. The company

Top

*Immigration to Canada during the 1950s brought new armies of workers to traditional ill-paid occupations. Unions, which had fought and won battles for earlier ethnic groups, often found it hard to relate to newcomers from Italy, Portugal, The Philippines, and the Caribbean. (*Labour Gazette)

The Toronto printers' strike of 1964 was a defeat for the city's oldest union. The confidence of the Labour Day parade faded gradually as the city's three newspapers proved that they could stay in business with new, automated equipment and carefully recruited crews of strike-breakers. Toronto, as the ITU had foreseen, was the precursor of developments across North America. (York University)

Quebec provincial police with drawn pistols hold back pickets as a striker throws a brick at a truck.
The 1960 teamsters' strike ushered in a decade in which labour practices accepted since the 1940s
once again came under attack from both management and unions. (York University)

ignored the strike. Independent contractors, or "settlers," kept up the supply of
pulpwood. Strikers retaliated. Abuse led to scattered acts of sabotage. On
February 10, after strong warnings against violence from union leaders, four
hundred strikers piled into cars and set off for Reesor's Siding. There, in a
clearing, settlers had piled their logs. Brushing aside a handful of provincial
police, the men broke a chain and rushed to dismantle the piles. Suddenly, the
door of a nearby shack flew open and twenty armed settlers poured out. A
fusillade rang out. Before the police could stop the shooting, three strikers lay
dead; twelve more were wounded. In the aftermath, murder charges were laid
and dropped. Company and union, horrified by the tragedy, agreed to compulsory arbitration.

It was easy to believe that such tragedies, like those of the thirties, were the
bitter price of bad times and that recovery was on its way. The American
economy had begun to strengthen in 1961. Canada, buoyed up by its wheat sales
and by the sudden, panicky devaluation of the dollar in 1962, followed suit. It
came too late to help John Diefenbaker. On June 18, his battered party clung to
power only because Quebec voters had turned from the old parties to support a
right-wing spellbinder named Real Caouette and twenty-five spokesmen for his
version of social credit. A year later, torpedoed by its own leader's vacillations,
the Tory government broke up and the Liberals were back in power, though
only by a minority.

T.C. Douglas addresses an NDP convention. The former Saskatchewan premier was the new party's most valuable asset during its first decade. A witty idealist, Douglas shone on the platform and clothed the NDP with the moral principles most of its members yearned for. He could not, however, conquer a strong prejudice against unions in politics, which extended even to union members themselves. (Murray Mosher)

For all its condemnation of the Diefenbaker regime and its publicized efforts to create a new party, the CLC could claim little credit for the outcome. The New Democratic party, once the lights were turned off and the convention delegates had left, was a foundling. Tories, Liberals, businessmen, and editors had poured scorn and indignation on the new party. Employers threatened to cancel checkoff arrangements if any money went to the NDP. Sceptics in labour ranks, silent until then, now cautiously expressed their doubts. The congress research director, Eugene Forsey, disassociated himself publicly from the party for its policy on Quebec. On the other extreme, Hazen Argue, the last national leader of the CCF and a left-wing candidate for the NDP leadership, denounced "union domination" and deserted the party for the Liberals.

From the first, CLC leaders had explained that, once launched, the new party would be independent of labour, much as Britain's Labour party owed no allegiance to the Trades Union Congress. Affiliation would come by democratic votes in local unions, with dissenters free to opt out of any contribution. However, the "hands off" strategy did not save the party from charges of labour domination — fatal for potential farm and middle-class backers — while it did deny it effective organizational and financial backing. The former CCFers, exhausted and a little disillusioned with their "New Party," were left to take up the struggle. The new party, in consequence, looked steadily more like the old one. In its first two elections, it could attract only about one union member in five and a total vote of 12−13 percent. That was better than the CCF but a long way from the dreams of the 1961 founding convention.

It was the Liberals who benefited from the Diefenbaker downfall and from labour disaffection in Quebec, Ontario, and much of British Columbia. In 1960, a year after the death of Maurice Duplessis, Jean Lesage had led the Liberals to power in Quebec. A few weeks later, Louis Robichaud gave the Liberals a second victory in New Brunswick. Both of the new regimes ushered in an activist style that would characterize the decade. Much of the outrage that greeted the NDP in 1961 came from a fear that many of its policies, like those of the CCF in the 1940s, were ideas whose time had come. A Royal Commission, appointed by the Diefenbaker government and headed by Chief Justice Emmett Hall, was proving that Canada wanted and needed universal health insurance. Canada's only CCF government, under T.C. Douglas and Woodrow Lloyd in Saskatchewan, proved after a difficult, exhausting struggle that such a plan could be made a reality. The Diefenbaker recession had also persuaded many Canadians that their economy could no longer be left to chance; even business tycoons admitted a need for planning.

The Liberal government that took office after the April, 1963, election faced a country that expected change. Canadians now demanded the legislative response to the remarkable demographic and economic changes of the fifties. In Quebec, traditional institutions and values crumbled. To replace the church, the family, and the rural myth, the Lesage government had to create, almost overnight, an elaborate bureaucracy, a comprehensive set of educational and social institutions, and a control of economic power that could only come through nationalization. In a few years, the new Quebec government would prove to the Québécois that the state could be the most powerful instrument of survival ever conceived. At the same time, many steps of that development brought Quebec into almost deliberate confrontation with Ottawa.

The confrontation was more unpleasant because Ottawa's agenda was also long. The changes demanded by Canadians in the sixties, from highways to portable pensions, were in the provincial domain; the financial resources, which alone gave Ottawa the muscle to manage the national economy, were federally controlled. And economic management was critical. By 1964, unemployment in Canada had dropped almost to 4 percent, but it could still be found in tough, concentrated pockets. Thanks to an articulate American socialist named Michael Harrington, poverty was back on the public agenda in the mid-sixties, and it grew, like a cancer, in the Atlantic provinces, in the north, and in crowded inner-city slums. People expected government to act, and, as usual, they found American examples in John F. Kennedy and Lyndon Johnson.

Change was not only demanded; it seemed affordable. Canadian wages and prices habitually had lagged behind those of the United States. The reward was an export sales boom. Buoyant government revenues gave Ottawa and the provinces enough and to spare. A population living on consumer credit found no crime in government deficits. Public policy also felt a new generational pressure. For most Canadians over thirty, the depression had been a more formative experience than even a world war. It had taught them to cherish security and to buffer it with material safeguards — a home, a car, a steady job.

Public hostility to unions increased when strikers carried their conflict to the homes of other workers. Taking along a daughter could dispel the suspicion that the picketer was "watching and besetting" for the purpose of intimidation. (York University)

Miners at Thompson, Manitoba, burn a conciliation board report in 1964 as a preliminary to launching a strike. The Thompson revolt was a warning that workers, who had never experienced the depression, would make very different demands on both unions and management than their more cautious parents had. (Public Archives of Canada PA 120633)

Younger people, raised in that security, took it for granted and even felt suffocated by it. The institutions their parents had helped create, including unions, meant little to them. If they belonged, it was more often because of a union security clause than by choice.

In the early sixties, Canadian unions had suffered in more than numbers. Most of the romantic sympathy they had once attracted had worn off. Until 1960, their reputation for integrity had stood in contrast to the parade of sordid corruption dredged up by American investigations; the Norris inquiry ravaged that reputation. The Landrum-Griffin Act, which imposed legislative checks on the internal democracy and financial integrity of American unions, had seemed needless in Canada until the revelations of how the Seafarers' International Union had operated. If Hal Banks had rounded up members with help from the shipping companies, the more virtuous Canadian Maritime Union had followed an almost identical route in getting jurisdiction over employees of Upper Lakes Shipping. Union members disciplined by their organization might have no appeal against decisions that could cost them their livelihood — except costly procedures within the union itself, with their own leaders sometimes acting as prosecutor and judge. The United Auto Workers was almost alone among major unions in having an independent appeal tribunal.

Yet the legislative environment, which had shaped the Canadian labour movement by the 1960s, was as complacent and as closed-minded as the most entrenched union leader. If unions were now accepted and legally integrated, the philosophy of many politicians and the interests they represented was unaltered: unions were a necessary evil. "In the field of Labour-Management relations," an Ontario legislature committee stated in 1958, "the dominant public interest lies in the preservation of public peace and the protection of the individual worker against oppression." To fulfil that philosophy, Ontario imitated most other Canadian provinces by making certification even more difficult to achieve; henceforth, every non-voter in a certification election constituted an effective no. Unions, regularly denounced for failing to organize the unorganized, found that the odds were stacked against them. Leisurely certification proceedings, easily delayed by management or rival unions, could make it next to impossible to organize waitresses, construction workers, or employees in a small fabricating plant. When the vote was held, a year or more later, employees had quit or been fired, the construction job was complete, or the company had folded.

Once organized and certified, a union had little leverage in forcing an employer to the bargaining table. Mackenzie King's faith in the endless processes of conciliation and mediation had been based, in part, on a conviction that time cooled off anger and impatience. Union leaders argued that it could also bring it to a boiling-point. A generation of working the system had taught bargainers on both sides that it was dangerous to make concessions at an early stage, that mediators simply produced majority and minority reports that sometimes merely cost bargaining points. Experience had also taught that playing by the rules could be as fatal as it had been for the IWA in Newfoundland. Labour had learned that illegal strikes and even picket-line violence would be forgiven as part of the settlement terms if a union fought hard and successfully enough.

In short, twenty years after P.C. 1003 there was a lot wrong with Canada's industrial relations system. Ordinary union members needed safeguards against their own organizations. Union organizers faced impossible legal barriers to extending unionism to people who needed it most — but politicians and the public preferred to protect individuals from unions. The delays and the succession of stages which were the unique Canadian contribution to industrial relations had never been much of a solution to labour conflict; now they were part of a growing problem. In railway negotiations, the breakdown was so acute that, since 1950, virtually every set of negotiations had been brought to a grumbling, dissatisfied conclusion by the threat of yet another settlement legislated by Parliament. That threat, in turn, made earlier negotiation almost meaningless. The courts had also come to play a role in Canadian labour conflict they had largely lost in the United States. Employers could seek *ex parte* injunctions against picketing and other strike action without even representation from the other side, and many judges were notoriously willing to grant them.

At the same time, fresh demands were about to be put on the system. The growing demand to negotiate technological change during the life of a contract was one. At the heart of the industrial relations system was the principle that a contract was inviolate during its life. Even arguments about its language could only be submitted to arbitration. However, an employer could introduce changes during the contract which might effectively undermine key elements. Early in 1965, for example, the Canadian National Railway took advantage of its new, more powerful diesel engines to eliminate its traditional divisional points at Nakina, Ontario, and Wainwright, Alberta. More than twenty-eight hundred union members of the running trades — conservative, cautious, and craft-conscious — responded to this threat to fellow workers by booking off sick and paralyzing the line. It was, in effect, an illegal strike, imperilling the jobs and pension rights of several thousand workers. It ended only with the promise of a Royal Commission. In his report, Mr. Justice Samuel Freedman of Manitoba castigated the union for breaking the law, but for the first time he articulated a demand that would be repeated for a decade: management must take labour into its confidence when changes were due. The cost of protecting the victims of change is part of the total cost of change. It must be borne by those who benefit, not by those who lose.

The mood that led conservative railwaymen to risk their jobs and pension rights to protest a company policy began to permeate Canadian labour in 1965. There were many reasons. Prosperity had now begun to breed the first stages of inflation. Prices were perceptibly rising; wages, held down by two- and three-year contracts, must follow. Union strength began to increase again. The automobile industry, hard hit by a recession that sent its American owners to pulling production and capital back to the United States, was at least temporarily transformed by an Auto Trade Pact that promised a continental rationalization and guaranteed a spurt of quick investment. UAW membership rose by thirty-three thousand in two years. The Steelworkers gained eighteen thousand. It was time for union members to catch up, and any leaders too slow to think out the message got it loud and clear from the ranks.

An early target, almost incidentally selected, was the *ex parte* injunction. Employees of the Thomson-owned Oshawa *Times* had been shivering on the picket line since January 27, 1966. In a union town, their low wages were a challenge. Mass picketing led in hours to an injunction. The injunction, in a town where even policemen were members of the labour council, produced even more massive defiance. Hurriedly, before a judicial response could be handed down, the Ontario premier, John Robarts, helped patch up a settlement. Sensing victory, Claude Jodoin staged a highly publicized CLC meeting in Oshawa on February 11 to plot an anti-injunction campaign. Within weeks he had his next battle. At Peterborough, a handful of women employees had held out against Tilco Plastics. The employer, already condemned for bargaining in bad faith, had no trouble in securing an injunction against picketing. Flushed with the Oshawa triumph, local and Oshawa unionists gathered on February 23 to defy the court order and offer their chivalrous support. This time police and courts had a different response. Chief Justice William Gale sent five of the pickets to jail for two months and twenty-one others for fifteen days. To soothe labour's fury, Premier Robarts immediately appointed a Royal Commission under a venerable figure from labour's past, Mr. Justice Ivan Rand. Meanwhile, in British Columbia, a similar defiance led to prison terms for Paddy Neale of the Vancouver and District Labour Council and Tom Clark of the International Woodworkers of

The obvious grievances of strikers at the Oshawa Times *led to mass picketing of the Thomson-owned newspaper, defiance of a court injunction, and an early settlement. However, what might be done in a strong union town could not be safely repeated in nearby Peterborough. (Arthur Heyworth)*

America. The CLC discreetly cooled its campaign but its efforts had not been in vain. *Ex parte* injunctions in labour disputes had become, if not obsolete, more rare.

It was a small victory, easily overlooked in a time of turmoil. During the early winter, wildcat strikes preceded walkouts at a number of auto plants. Toronto construction was halted for two months. Ontario's tomato crop was imperilled by a seventeen-day strike at the Heinz Company in Leamington. Through the autumn, Teamsters locals in Ontario and Quebec joined in a bewildering flurry of walkouts, directed as much against their own cautious leaders as against the trucking companies. Union members voted down a proposed settlement and led a three-month strike in the winter of 1966 that won them the guarantee of a forty-hour week.

Strikers at Tilco Plastics in 1966 were mostly women, opposing an employer who made no secret of his determination to drive out the union. However, when local unionists tried to repeat the experience at the Oshawa Times *and defy an* ex parte *injunction against mass picketing, they were swiftly jailed and sentenced to prison terms. The law might be unfair; it was also enforced. Both Peterborough and Oshawa voted NDP in 1967. (Textile Workers' of America—Ed Seymour)*

By 1965, the Steelworkers was as secure representing International Nickel Company workers as its Mine-Mill rival was at the adjoining Falconbridge property. The victory gave it little comfort. Negotiations in the summer of 1966 began with a sixteen-thousand-member wildcat strike, which union officials took almost three weeks to get under control. A settlement was signed and then rejected by angry members. When a settlement was finally achieved on September 16, after three days of a legal strike, it gave the Sudbury miners the highest rates of any Steelworkers on the continent. Even at that, only 57 percent of the local approved the contract. The rebellious mood spread to Hamilton on August 5, when a violent wildcat strike broke out at the Steel Company of Canada. Strikers smashed cars, assaulted police and their own union officials, and voted down a settlement recommended by their leaders. Their impatience was rewarded by a contract that made the Hamilton men the best-paid steelworkers in the world.

Not since the postwar years had there been such a succession of major strikes. In 1965, Canadians experienced their first national postal strike. In 1966, the International Woodworkers of America closed the British Columbia forests for two weeks. Part of its settlement was a guarantee of six months' notice of technological change and a promise to retrain displaced workers. The Packing-house Workers struck Canada Packers for ten weeks. Vancouver and Toronto municipal workers struck in the autumn of 1966. However, the storm centre was Montreal. The mood of change reflected in the "Quiet Revolution" may have begun at the top of the Quebec hierarchy, but by the mid-sixties it reached into the heart of French-Canadian society. In Montreal the catalyst was Expo 67, the grandiose scheme to celebrate Canada's centennial year with a huge world's fair. Working to an impossible schedule, millions of dollars in construction contracts spewed out for expressways, hotels, a subway system, and the artificial islands in the St. Lawrence River where the fair would be held. In the desperate rush, construction workers could name their price or hold the entire project to ransom. Wage rates soared. Prices followed. Other workers struggled to catch up.

Thanks to Canada's divided labour jurisdiction, Ottawa was soon involved. The Pearson government manoeuvred from weakness, not only in the atmosphere of an increasingly alienated Quebec but also in a Parliament where Liberals were still a minority. In the autumn of 1965, confident that prosperity and their legislative program would give them an easy victory, the Liberal government had called an election. On November 8, voters gave them a stunning rebuff. Lester Pearson had to face a new parliament with his strength virtually unaltered. Only the New Democrats had made real gains, winning 18 percent of the votes though few additional seats. Its gains were highest in industrial areas where the mid-decade impatience was fermenting.

For the Pearson government, 1966 brought a series of crises in labour conflict. The Montreal longshoremen came first. Despite their lively nineteenth-century reputation, the Montreal dockers had given their port a reputation for labour peace, efficiency, and remarkable freedom from pilferage. They had accepted low wages as the price of security in their seasonal jobs. Now the stevedoring companies demanded drastic cuts in gang size because of new cargo-handling machinery. Expo wage levels added to the men's anger, and, if that was not enough, harbour police began ticketing their cars for illegal parking. On April 19, 1966, the port of Montreal was closed by its first illegal strike in memory. On May 9, the dockers came out again. Conciliation and mediation both failed. The shutdown of Montreal and the other St. Lawrence ports was a crippling economic blow, and there was the added frantic pressure of the Expo 67

Hamilton police remove a prisoner during the short but violent wildcat strike at Stelco in the summer of 1966. The outbreak was a warning that workers were as angry at their unions as at the company and that a new generation of workers could no longer live patiently with their frustrations. (York University)

projects, forever behind schedule. A settlement demanded non-stop negotiations by federal cabinet ministers and a final session in the prime minister's office before the strike ended on June 14.

Meanwhile, upstream, the 1,260 employees of the St. Lawrence Seaway Authority promised to shut down the system on June 17 if they were not granted wage parity with their American fellow workers. The union demanded a 35 percent increase over two years; a conciliation board proposed 14 percent. Within hours of the deadline, Senator Norman Mackenzie, the government's chosen mediator, announced that the strike had been averted. The price was a 30 percent increase. Mackenzie preened himself that he had not given in to parity. The press and the Conservative opposition trumpeted that the 30 percent settlement — dubbed the "Pearson Formula" — had given official government approval to a wildly inflationary level of expectations. Pearson, himself, belatedly recognized that the price of averting a strike might be too high.

The seaway settlement undoubtedly helped spread inflationary wage pressures west from Montreal. It immediately affected the extraordinarily complex negotiations with railway employees. Although Canada's dependence on railways had steadily decreased with the growth of road haulage and air travel, railway contract negotiations had become a recurrent national crisis since the postwar period, almost always involving ministers, the prime minister, and the threat of emergency legislation. Not since 1950 had the crisis gone full term, but the pressure was building. Ottawa had become doubly involved because the railway companies insisted that federal coffers share in any added wage bill through fresh subsidies. Negotiations were also complicated by the rivalries of operating and non-operating, national and international unions in the industry, and by the retirement of Frank Hall, as tough in disciplining his own ragged ranks as in facing the companies and government.

Railway contracts expired at the end of 1965. However, no strike was legal until the long ritual was played out. When the mediation boards finally reported, their recommendation of an 18 percent increase might once have been considered generous, but not in the wake of the Montreal and seaway settlements. The government faced a dilemma. The press, business, and the Tory opposition demanded that Parliament be called to prevent a strike. Nervous union leaders quietly warned the prime minister that their men were so incensed and out of control that they would almost certainly defy Parliament if there was not at least a short strike to settle their emotions. As Pearson nervously weighed the alternatives, the railwaymen settled the issue. Wildcat strikes in Toronto and Montreal in August convinced the union leaders to hurry the strike call. Parliament, summoned for the first time since 1950 to end a strike, met only after the strike had begun. Even then the government fumbled, proposing that the men be ordered back for even less than the conciliators had proposed. As the nation watched impatiently, the NDP finally convinced the government that it would have to do better. After grudgingly guaranteeing the men at least their 18 percent increase, Parliament ordered the strike to end. By September 6, service was restored.

To Liberals since Mackenzie King, and perhaps to most Canadians, the primary purpose of industrial relations was to achieve not economic justice or

Richard Grange of Canadian Driver Pool displays the resources a modern strike-breaking firm could offer its customers in the late 1960s, from guard dogs to a telephoto camera to record the faces of militant unionists. Not on display was a friendly relationship with a few zealous police officers. (Marc Zwelling)

industrial democracy but peace. By that standard the system in 1966 was not working. Even the effectiveness of unions in disciplining and restraining their members appeared to be crumbling. As he watched the elaborate, pointless, and self-defeating ritual of the railway negotiations drag into the inevitable political crisis, Lester Pearson looked in desperation for better ideas. The problem was too urgent for a Royal Commission. A task force sounded more efficient. Dean H.D. Woods of McGill University was, he was told, the man for the job. Together with the University of Toronto's John Crispo, Abbé Dion of Laval, and Dean A.W. Carrothers of the University of Western Ontario, surely Woods would find the new answers the system needed.

CHAPTER 23

Public Interest, Public Service

In the first half of the twentieth century, Parliament and provincial legislatures had grudgingly established machinery for collective bargaining between private employers and their workers. The public sector was different. Unlike other employees, the public's servants performed work too vital to be left to the vagaries of the free market in either prices or wages. Moreover, a constitutional principle was at stake. In 1885, Manitoba's first Civil Service Act had made it clear that any request for a raise "shall be considered as a tendering of the resignation of such member." Little changed. "The Queen does not negotiate with her subjects," proclaimed Quebec's premier, Jean Lesage, in 1964. A more democratic argument was that, since Parliament was supreme, elected members could not be compelled to ratify spending decisions reached at some remote bargaining table. Consultation and discussion might be contemplated, and even welcomed, but to strike against a government was tantamount to civil war. Police strikes in Quebec, Toronto and other cities in 1919–20 had been followed by wholesale dismissals. Postal workers who joined Winnipeg's general strike in 1919 or who walked out in Toronto in 1922 were sternly disciplined. When Joe Davidson went to work as a sorter in Toronto in 1957, some of the older workers who went over to greet him were accompanied by soft calls of "Cuckoo, cuckoo." They were still shunned as the "scabs" of 1922.

In principle, civil servants in Canada traded the benefits of unionization for blessings few working people enjoyed: the prospect of superannuation at the end of a working life and, provided they did not fall victim of a partisan purge after a change of government, relatively secure employment. The proposition that governments should, somehow, be model employers was much slower to

Top

With the era of public service strikes, Canadians began to revise some assumptions about what was indispensable. Plastic garbage bags stacked in a nearby park could make a strike of sanitation workers barely tolerable even during the summer. Most people even adjusted to postal strikes although some businesses were driven to bankruptcy by unfilled orders and uncollected bills. (Labour Gazette)

One of the major transformations of the 1960s was the emergence of federal and provincial employees as militant members of the union movement. Civil servants, once the victims of political patronage and later strictly aloof from politics, returned in the seventies as a force in their own right, fighting cutbacks and pay restraint policies. (Public Service Alliance of Canada) emerge. The "fair wages" resolution of 1900 established that federal government contracts would be performed for the "prevailing rate" of wages in a locality. No government wished to annoy local employers by overpaying their workers.

The Post Office had the longest experience of employee organization. The Railway Mail Clerks Association was born in 1889 under the wing of the railway brotherhoods. The Federal Association of Letter Carriers followed in 1891, and the Canadian Postal Employees' Association (for inside workers) in 1911. The Winnipeg militants of 1919 were part of a breakaway Western Federation of Postal Employees. To broaden its appeal, the western group evolved into the Amalgamated Postal Workers and, still later, the Amalgamated Civil Servants of Canada.

In 1909, members of other federal government departments in Ottawa linked their associations in a Civil Service Federation, insisting that they intended no more than to serve social and benevolent functions and to make occasional polite representations to their employer. They were as good as their word. Several provincial and municipal employee associations formed in the same period shared the same spirit. They reminded their members of the dignity of public service and their obligations to the taxpayers. In 1911 two hundred Ontario civil servants met at Queen's Park to consider "the necessity of a Civil Service Association, pointing out its possibilities in the way of improving the Service, promoting social togetherness, urging healthy athletics and co-operating with one another in the purchasing of supplies." Members agreed that they needed the government's permission to proceed. It was cheerfully granted. It was in much the same spirit that many historic and effective unions had been formed in the previous century. Indeed, by 1919, the new CSAO had opened discussions with the government on pensions and, since wartime inflation cost salaries half their value, on wages too. Never forgotten was the realization that, even after civil service reforms in the 1920s, political patronage played a major part in appointments, promotions, salaries and dismissals. Incorporated in 1920 as a charitable organization, Manitoba's Civil Service Association, organized months after Winnipeg's 1919 general strike, promised that its goal was "the largest possible measure of joint action between the government and its employees." Most early MCSA leaders were senior government officials; five of the first 24 officers were women.

Across Canada, public services remained modest in size, income and competence. In 1941, even with a war on, 342,934 men and women worked in education, health or government service, barely 8 percent of the Canadian workforce. The Second World War brought changes. The example of industrial unionization was contagious. By 1944, Montreal city employees, including police and firefighters, not only had organized unions but had struck successfully. Unhampered by tradition, the new CCF government in Saskatchewan extended its new Trade Union Act to cover provincial employees and offered them the right to strike. Most of them formed a union and affiliated with the TLC. Ottawa and other provinces were unpersuaded. Mackenzie King had another model, Britain's "Whitley Councils," a post-1919 development for unorganized industries and civil servants. In 1944, Ottawa authorized a Whitley-style Joint National

Council, so that an "official" side of deputy ministers and personnel experts could discuss hours, overtime, leave entitlements and kindred matters with a "staff side" chosen from the civil service associations. The cabinet could accept, alter or ignore Joint Council advice as it preferred.

Postwar prosperity initially undermined civil service bargaining power. Anyone who complained of a low salary or poor prospects could easily find a better job. Inflation and the growing size and complexity of government gradually rebuilt the pressure for better salaries and benefits. By 1951, salaried public employment absorbed 12 percent of the workforce. The share grew as hospitals, schools and suburbs exploded with population growth and affluence. By the 1960s, two in ten Canadian workers depended on public funds for all or part of their income. Years of full employment and rising wealth for most Canadians, and the advent of younger, less grateful employees, brought a mood of militancy that fed on the frustration of more obsequious elders. Governments felt the heat.

In 1957, with an election approaching, the Liberal government appointed a veteran diplomat, Arnold Heeney, to head the Civil Service Commission and to report on wages, working conditions and job classifications. Heeney recommended pay raises and a Pay Research Bureau to establish rates comparable with private sector wages, but his report was delivered to a Conservative government deeply suspicious of an overgrown and Liberal-infected civil service. The new finance minister, Donald Fleming, simply announced that pay raises would be frozen until further study. He needed the money for his unavailing efforts to balance the federal budget. The Tories' new Civil Service Act in 1961 agreed that the Pay Research Bureau would share its data with civil service organizations.

By then, federal civil servants and their provincial counterparts had a lot to discuss. Frustration levels varied with rank, but professionals and trades alike shared a bitter sense of betrayal. Generous pay increases to federal employees on the eve of the 1962 election did not make them grateful. By the 1963 election, leaders of three of the major parties had pledged their support for the once-revolutionary notion of collective bargaining for government employees. Narrowly victorious, the Liberals asked Heeney to serve as chairman of a Preparatory Committee on Collective Bargaining. A Bureau of Classification appeared in the fall of 1964 to unravel the baffling tangle of salary scales. Heeney's final report in 1965 recommended what the Civil Service Federation and its rivals had wanted since 1958: a process of negotiation that led to compulsory arbitration. Governments would be free to reject an award – but only by a vote of Parliament.

By the time Heeney reported, events had again bypassed him. As early as 1960, British Columbia civil servants had gone on strike against their Social Credit government. Like Saskatchewan's public employees, they affiliated with the TLC and then with the CLC.

A powerful impetus for change came from Quebec. In 1960, the Catholic unions had reversed their drift to the CLC, shed the last vestiges of clerical control, and emerged as the Confederation of National Trade Unions (*Confédération des syndicats nationaux*). One motive was political. While Catholic unions

Public sector unions gradually came to dominate the Canadian labour movement in the 1970s and, in return, union involvement politicized public employees. Demonstrations of political concern did not prevent governments from creating recessions, wiping out jobs, and wrecking the economy, if not Canada. (Ontario Federation of Labour)

and the CCL's industrial unions had fought Duplessis, much of the former TLC in Quebec had backed him in return for favours. A Liberal victory in 1960 changed the players. Gérard Picard, the last president of the Catholic confederation, had backed the New Party movement and became the NDP's first associate leader. His successor, Jean Marchand, had backed the Liberals in opposition. He would share the fruits of victory.

In 1963, Quebec Liberals finally delivered a promised Labour Code, complete with a requirement for union check-off and a sharp reduction in government meddling with collective bargaining decisions. However, there was no mention of unions for civil servants. Marchand exploded. The province, he warned, would be set on fire. The rival Quebec Federation of Labour called a special convention and talked of a general strike. Underpaid hospital workers staged illegal walkouts. In August, 1963, the once conservative teachers' federation insisted that any right of association would be meaningless without the right to strike. The Lesage government finally listened. In 1964, a revised Code emerged, covering all workers, with the exception of police, firefighters and a few narrowly-defined categories of essential workers.

There was a small wrinkle in the Code; civil servants could affiliate with any labour organization that did not openly back a political party. By no coincidence, only Marchand's CNTU qualified. The arrangement seemed an enormous bonus to an ambitious organization. It seemed unlikely that civil servants, hospital workers or liquor store employees would be very militant or need much service. Instead, their dues would cover the CNTU's mounting costs. In practice, like the industrial workers of the 1940s, Quebec's public employees had abysmal wages and a huge backlog of grievances. Almost as soon as the new law was proclaimed, Quebec Liquor Commission workers tested it with a prolonged strike. Highway workers and hospital employees soon followed.

In the 1940s, Quebec's French-speaking Catholic teachers had defied the Duplessis government and lost. In 1959, they reappeared in the guise of a dutiful professional association, but a few years of the Quiet Revolution restored the old militancy. Illegal walkouts in 1963 and 1964 persuaded the Lesage government to add teachers to the growing list of Quebeckers who could legally strike. In 1966, under the leadership of Raymond Laliberté, teachers dropped the word "Catholic" from their title. Three years later, they dropped an old commitment to "social Christianity" and pledged instead to uphold the "Rights of Man." By 1970, when Yvon Charbonneau was elected president, the *Corporation des enseignants du Quebec* (CEQ) was a union by any standard, and Quebec workers, public- and private-sector, had moved from the back row to the front rank in labour militancy.

If Jean Lesage's government struggled to stay ahead, Ottawa seemed to have lost control. Fed up with low pay and a host of mean little injustices that stemmed from political patronage and low-level supervisors, postal workers were the angriest federal workers. Post Office officials ignored warnings that only a big wage increase would keep employees on the job during the summer of 1965. Negotiations dragged on, month after month. Finally, on July 23, the government announced that it had handed the problem to Judge J.C. Anderson for a solution. That day, Montreal postal workers walked out. Next day the strike spread to Vancouver, Toronto and other cities. Union officials were helpless. On July 27, they announced a settlement only to have it decisively rejected by the Montreal local. Only on August 7, under the threat of sending troops and students to do their work, did Montreal workers return. Instead of a government offer of $300, the strikers settled for $550 and Judge Anderson's strong advice that the Post Office become a crown corporation, subject to the IRDIA.

The 1965 postal strike was as decisive as the Algoma strike of 1943. Canadians discovered that they could live without postal service, but at a high price. Postal workers discovered that public sympathy ended the moment they struck for their rights – but only by striking could they budge the government. Bitter and resentful, they sought leaders like Toronto's Joe Davidson and Montreal's Jean-Claude Parrot, tough and uncompromising enough to fight Ottawa and the Post Office. Meanwhile Post Office managers planned vengeance, not adjustment. New technology and soaring volumes of mail offered a solution. Instead of being a low-wage, labour-intensive industry, the Post Office would become the most automated in the world. If corporations wanted a lesson in how to combine radical technological change with a maximum of rancour, disruption and delay, Canada Post would be the model.

Despite the turbulent, strike-ridden atmosphere of 1966, Liberals, Conservatives and New Democrats worked in surprising harmony to create a public service bargaining structure which offered the hitherto unthinkable option of the strike. With the Post Office strike and Quebec as cautionary tales, experts and politicians agreed that federal employees would have the right to choose between compulsory arbitration, mediation or a strike. Both the experts and the Civil Service Federation president, Claude Edwards, agreed: the vast majority of public employees would never even think of walking out. On February 20, 1967, the Public Service Staff Relations Act (PSSRA) and two companion bills became law.

Designed by the veteran Ontario labour lawyer Jacob Finkelman, the PSSRA gave the government more rights than the IRDIA allowed private employers. The armed forces, the RCMP and senior officials were excluded, and bargaining rights were extended to only 260,000 of Ottawa's 400,000 employees. The Treasury Board, the department that monitored government spending, became the employer, though effective authority was so widely dispersed among departments and levels of supervisors that union negotiators soon complained that they bargained chiefly with phantoms. A host of issues, from working conditions to staffing levels, were excluded from negotiation. For groups that chose them, strikes were possible only after conciliation and a waiting period – a near-guarantee that serious bargaining would occur only in the final days before a walkout. A Public Service Staff Relations Board would serve as a labour relations commission, defining bargaining units, settling incidental disputes, and operating with as much independence as it could manage when the employer paid the bills.

In its way, the PSSRA was as significant as the Trade Unions Act of 1872 and P.C. 1003. Canada's labour movement had organized virtually all it could of a predominantly male, blue-collar and shrinking industrial workforce, and, like its U.S. counterpart, which had begun to decline in the 1950s, it was losing its share of the labour market. With the public sector – now a fifth of the Canadian workforce – open to be organized, Canadian unionism began to grow, from a quarter of the non-agricultural labour force at the beginning of the decade to well over a third by 1970. Other jurisdictions followed the lead of Quebec and Ottawa. In Ontario, a tradition of charter flights, a Christmas singsong and intimate chats between the premier and the manager of the Civil

Frequent postal strikes during the 1970s sometimes left employees themselves deeply divided. Though the Letter Carriers' Union was far less militant than the inside workers of the Canadian Union of Postal Workers, they bore the brunt of public indignation. (Canadian Press)

Service Association of Ontario dissolved in bitter internal battles between conservatives and young militants. The turning point came after sweeping recommendations from a Committee on Government Productivity, eagerly embraced by a new premier, William Davis. Designed to end ad hoc, politically motivated decision-making, the COGP supplanted paternalism with the bureaucratic rule of experts.

With some reluctance on both sides, government workers and their association found that they needed each other. Productivity demands, downsizing and privatization turned the CSAO into a union. The process included some bitter fights, including the firing of some key CSAO staff by general manager Harold Bowen, and his ouster a year later by his opponents. The battle coincided with debate on the notorious Crown Employees' Collective Bargaining Act, a law that guaranteed the CSAO full bargaining rights for Ontario government employees and then barred the right to strike and to negotiate on twenty-one different issues, from training to pensions. Judge William Little, advisor to Ontario's Conservative government, dismissed public service strikes as a form of incipient insurrection: "I cannot accept the proposition that anyone who joins the public service would have the right, in conjunction with others, to withdraw his services with the sole object of compelling a duly-elected government to meet his demands." Ontario left its employees to the mercy of three-member arbitration commissions.

The struggle to repair hostile legislation turned the CSAO into a union. Flamboyant tactics by Bowen's public relations-conscious successor, Jake Norman, helped. Norman let his staff bargain outrageously, raising expectations which no government could have matched, but which left unhappy workers feeling robbed. Without the right to strike, the CSAO was as free as the government to be unreasonable. Jim "Foghorn" Fuller, a meat inspector, delighted delegates to the last CSAO convention by roaring, "I am seldom civil and I am a servant to no man." In 1974, the old CSAO became the new Ontario Public Service Employee Union.

In Manitoba, the combination of militant new civil servants in the 1960s and election of Ed Schreyer's NDP government in 1969 produced a catalytic reaction. By opposing Schreyer's offer of the right to strike and to political action, the old-guard leaders made themselves vulnerable to a harsh arbitration award. The MGEA's counterpart to "Foghorn" Fuller was John Pullen, a labour department inspector, who brought down the house at the critical 1973 convention by railing: "We got the bloody crumbs off the table, that's all we got, we got the crumbs off the table." By the end of 1974, the MGEA had affiliated to the Canadian Labour Congress.

By the early 1970s, every province had accepted some form of collective bargaining with its employees, though Alberta and Ontario had refused to concede the right to strike. As legal barriers crumbled, so did obstacles of tradition, status and suspicion. Hospital and social workers, teachers, librarians, university employees, municipal workers, even professional engineers with Ontario Hydro and other big public utilities, demanded the right to bargain collectively. While some groups, such as teachers, preferred to work through erstwhile professional associations and federations, many welcomed the expertise

The decision by Montreal firemen and police to conduct a "study session" to press for early settlement of contract demands led in 1969 to wild riots, looting, and a violent assault on the Murray-Hill Bus Lines garage. For the first time since 1933, troops were called out to help restore order in a strike situation. The experience was a prelude to the October crisis of 1970. (Canadian Press)

and resources that only unions could give them. The Canadian Union of Public Employees was the product of a 1963 merger between 53,000 members of the National Union of Public Employees and the 30,000-member National Union of Public Service Employees, its former CCL rival. In a decade, CUPE doubled its membership, surpassing the United Steelworkers as Canada's biggest union organization. Low dues, an openness to modern public relations style, and a host of eager young organizers gave CUPE an inside track on municipal and hospital workers, but legislation and the public mood helped clear the way. Under pressure to adapt to the new environment, the major federal employee organizations, the Civil Service Association and the Civil Service Federation, cautiously accepted a merger, though old departmental components, such as the National Defence Employees and the Customs and Excise Officers were carefully preserved. In November, 1966, the 120,000-member Public Service Alliance of Canada became the country's third largest union, with Claude Edwards as president. The CLC eagerly embraced it as an affiliate.

Unionization of Canada's public employees changed more than membership statistics. Labour in Canada had always been a predominantly male and blue-collar institution. Public sector unions added hundreds of thousands of members who were women, middle-class or both. People from a wide gamut of trades and occupations, many with no private-sector counterparts, such as lighthouse keepers and air traffic controllers, became part of the labour movement. The newcomers threatened a number of traditions. As members of Canadian-based organizations, they threatened the traditional dominance of international unions in the Canadian labour movement. One potential issue, the CLC's commitment to its own political party, caused problems in some provinces, particularly British Columbia and Ontario, where government employees were banned from affiliating with a political party. In practice, CLC affiliates were free to decide their own political stance, and there were many that cheerfully ignored Congress policies. The leaders who emerged in the new public-sector unions tended to have NDP sympathies and even an imprudent yearning to mobilize their members for the cause. NDPers could boast that the CCF had made Saskatchewan a pioneer in unionizing public employees without significant friction. Hidden in the future were the strains that would develop when NDP governments faced tough bargaining and even strike-ridden relations with their employees.

The biggest change for unions was barely perceived in the sixties: the advent of large numbers of women, ranging from professionals to unskilled workers, in a male-dominated labour market. During the decade the female share of the workforce grew from 27 to 34 percent, and to 43 percent by the end of the 1970s. Few noticed at first, because women initially crowded into the ill-paid, non-union jobs they had always dominated. Memories of the Eaton Drive and other failures had convinced organizers that women in sales, secretarial and service work would never be unionized. In industries like clothing and textiles, where women had been organized, union leadership was routinely dominated by men.

By illuminating coincidence, Canada's centennial, the PSSRA, and the appointment of the Royal Commission on the Status of Women all happened in 1967. Judy LaMarsh, the Pearson government's sole female cabinet minister, pressured her colleagues to launch an investigation into every aspect of the lives and prospects of Canadian women. Unions and how they served women were part of the mandate. Summoned to testify, most unions had nothing to say. Women unionists, insisted the Quebec Federation of Labour, enjoyed equality with men in most but not all respects: "It has unfortunately been impossible, we must admit, to secure real implementation of the principle of equal pay for equal work in certain sectors." Since equal pay for equal work was enshrined in law, a union movement which cared profoundly about the issue might have made more impact. Of course, unionists guarded their hard-earned differentials, and employers sheltered behind narrow definitions of

One consequence of rank-and-file rejection of settlements was a more sophisticated attempt by union leaders to explain to their membership what had been accomplished during bargaining. (United Steelworkers)

"equal work," and laws which banned women from working on night shifts, lifting heavy weights or labouring underground in a mine. In the absence of better evidence, the Royal Commission accepted the cautious judgement of Sylvia Ostry at Statistics Canada that, other things being equal, a Canadian woman earned 75–85 percent of a man's wage. Better evidence soon proved that the estimate was far too generous.

The male leadership of most unions had regarded women's concerns with some sympathy, little understanding and low priority at bargaining time. Maternity leave and equal pay for equal work seemed a reasonable agenda. Expectations began to change with surprising rapidity. In the 1960s, as more women went to work, even more expected to stay for a career. By the 1970s, as inflation drained family purchasing power, economic motives were as pressing as changing social values: supporting a family on a single income became a fair prescription for poverty. Women not only insisted on escaping from traditional low-wage job ghettos, they demanded new respect and income levels for nurses, office staff and homemakers. Equal pay must be for work of equal value, as defined by complex formulas. Like politicians and business executives, union leaders could no longer judge these needs from the comfort of a nearly all-male club. In the labour movement, the advent of public service unions meant that women would have a new and growing constituency of sympathetic voters. In 1970, a woman named Shirley Carr persuaded fellow office employees at the Niagara Falls city hall to form a local of CUPE. They made her their president. Fourteen years later, she was president of the Canadian Labour Congress.

Public-sector unionization and the 1960s revival of French-English tensions embittered relations between the CLC and its far smaller Quebec rival, the CNTU. In 1960, about a quarter of the CNTU's members worked in the public sector; by 1971, barely 40 percent of its 206,000 members worked for private companies. With its enlarged membership and financial base, its political connection and its appeal to Quebec pride, the CNTU carried new weight in Ottawa as well as Quebec City. In 1965, it demanded the right to represent workers in the CPR's Angus Shops in Montreal. The Canada Labour Relations Board said no: with seventeen unions already involved in railway bargaining, there was no room for another. The CNTU was indignant; the CLC, with a majority of labour nominees on the Board, was smug. But in 1965, the CNTU's Jean Marchand became a federal cabinet minister. By 1968, the government had framed legislation to reshape the CLRB to suit the CNTU. Now the CLC was outraged at "one of the most blatant expressions of political partisanship which we have observed." The bill died with the premature dissolution of Parliament and the Woods Task Force inherited another issue.

It was easier to agree that public employees had the right to organize, bargain and even to strike than to foresee the practical consequences that soon followed. In urging a national health insurance system, for example, the Hall Royal Commission had estimated the costs on the unspoken assumption that nurses, orderlies and other health employees would continue to accept modest wages. Many other public services, from operating grain elevators to snow removal, tended to be low-wage, labour-intensive activities. The public could sympathize with low-paid workers without realizing that either the remedy had to come from its own pockets or it would suffer the consequences in unshipped grain or blocked highways. Unless an employer dominated a community, few citizens were affected by private-sector labour disputes. They had no such immunity when hospitals, schools or government liquor stores were surrounded by pickets or when wage settlements increased taxes.

By the late 1960s, there were many issues in the once-tranquil labour relations scene, and several governments sought academic or judicial wisdom. In Ontario, where picket-line violence and defiance of *ex parte* injunctions had invaded the 1967 election, Mr. Justice Ivan Rand was summoned from retirement. Those who remembered his ingenious formula for union check-off would be disappointed. The price of banning injunctions, Rand insisted, was that unions must become legal entities, able to sue and be sued. Mass pickets, boycotts and sympathetic walkouts were intolerable. Above all, Rand urged an

Australian-style labour court, with power to end strikes and lockouts. The Ontario government thanked Rand, listened to the uproar from the labour movement, and buried the report. British Columbia's Social Credit government sent Mr. Justice Nathan Nemetz to Europe to find solutions for the province's labour turbulence. Nemetz came home with arguments for labour-management committees, better-trained mediators and a permanent industrial inquiry commission. The government created a Mediation Commission, with power to impose its own settlements on disputes referred by the government. Within months, the Commission was suspect among employers and detested by unions. By 1972, anger at the Commission helped defeat the Social Credit regime.

The Woods Report, presented in March, 1969, was different. To those who had dreamed of clever solutions to labour strife, Woods and his colleagues offered little comfort. Conflict had no mysterious cause. Inflation, fuelled by prosperity and by Washington's decision to finance the Vietnam War by borrowing, sent prices climbing. Armed with the right to strike, employees would use it to pressure their bosses. Once both sides had measured their strength, relations would settle down. Whatever its problems, the adversarial system fitted "our heritage of western values," and there were no better alternatives. The rights of workers were integral to the values of liberal democracy.

As befitting a group of academics, Woods and his colleagues had ideas. Employer associations should be encouraged as a counter to labour organizations. The government must do more to protect individual union members. The CLC-CNTU battle over the CLRB might be solved by replacing it with an appointed, independent board. A three-member public interest disputes commission could tackle strikes in essential services, with power to help work out solutions and, if necessary, to recommend "seizure, trusteeship, partial operation, statutory strikes and compulsory arbitration ..."

The work of the Woods Task Force, modified by labour and management critics, was embodied in the Canada Labour Code of 1972, the first real revision of federal bargaining legislation since 1948. For the first time a Canadian statute declared that "the common well being" was promoted "through the encouragement of free collective bargaining and the constructive settlement of disputes." Woods's pleas for a new non-partisan labour relations board was respected; so was his concern for the democratic rights of individual union members. The right to collective bargaining was extended to professionals, to owner-operators of trucks and to fishermen in "share of catch" operations.

The sharpest debate over shaping the new Code was how far workers would be consulted about technological change. For the first time, a narrow, carefully-guarded breach was opened in the inviolability of a valid collective agreement. Accepting more from Mr. Justice Freedman than from Woods, the new Code demanded ninety days' notice of "any technological change likely to affect the conditions or security of employment of a significant number of employees" and allowed negotiations and even the possibility of a legal strike. Management decisions would be exempt if they were shared before a contract was signed. Predictably, employers and editors worried that Canada would lose a valued tradition of secure labour contracts. The Canadian Chamber of Commerce raged that the government was "legalizing Luddite-like conduct, aimed at arbitrarily stopping progress and promoting feather bedding."

Missing from the new Code was Woods's proposed "public interest disputes commission." Quiet lobbying by both unions and employers had buried the idea. Politicians and their official advisors would be left to their common sense. That may have been a mistake. Adding almost a million workers to the labour movement and fuelling their militancy with a huge surge of inflation guaranteed that the 1970s would see even more labour turmoil than the 1960s, and in areas where Canadians had little experience of, or tolerance for, labour's traditional tactics.

The true public interest needed a sensible interpretation. Common sense is always scarce.

CHAPTER 24

Justice and Nationalism

On April 4, 1968, Liberals gathered in Ottawa and with what, in retrospect, seemed surprising reluctance, chose Pierre Elliott Trudeau as Canada's new prime minister. Not since Mackenzie King had Canadians had a national leader with even remote links to the labour movement. Trudeau had been close to Jean Marchand during the 1949 Asbestos strike and afterwards he had introduced a book on the events and their meaning. As editor of *Cité Libre*, Trudeau had attacked the Duplessis regime. Outraged at Pearson's reversal on nuclear arms, in 1963 Trudeau had backed the NDP. Yet two years later, he had been the junior member of the "Three Wise Men" from Quebec who had entered the Liberal caucus. Far more had been expected of the CNTU's Jean Marchand and Gérard Pelletier, editor of *La Presse*, but it was Trudeau who shone on television and in Parliament. As justice minister, he legalized homosexuality and made divorce easier. "The state," he declared, "has no business in the bedrooms of the nation."

Those who knew Trudeau well realized his complexity. Collectivist values fundamental to unionism as to Quebec nationalism had no place in Trudeau's philosophy. Like many intellectuals, he viewed the union movement as a tool to be used or set aside. Constitutions, world politics, the relations between French and English in Canada could arouse his passions; economic issues fundamental to the welfare of most Canadians frankly bored him. On the other hand, he had a style that suited a newly-affluent Canada. What did he offer? "New guys with new ideas," he told a TV interviewer; "Stuff," he told another. No one asked him what he meant. Trudeau seemed to fit his time. With easy intellectual brilliance and unconventional style, he personified liberation. His campaign slogan, "A Just Society," and his occasional reminders that there would be "no more free stuff" seemed to combine idealism and candour. French Canadians saw one of their own in power; English Canadians rejoiced that Trudeau talked back to Quebec nationalists and braved their stones and bottles at an election-eve St-Jean-Baptiste Day parade. Before events could give him a record, Trudeau won the Liberals a majority on June 25, 1968.

Many Canadians in 1968 were in an impatient mood. The standard cliche of the early Trudeau years was youthful revolt in schools and universities. Few, except for union leaders, saw that the same phenomenon occurred in the workforce. Pressures were usually felt in material demands that Samuel Gompers would have recognized: "more, more, more." The baby boomers who had overcrowded maternity wards and schools were now positioned to set fashions, and they expected both the freedoms their parents had sacrificed to security, and the financial means to enjoy them. Music, clothing, and, for a minority, drugs and sexual freedom required leisure and money. Television not only gave demonstrators, eccentrics and publicity-seekers the chance to see themselves on the evening news, it also encouraged a sense of entitlement to prompt gratification. Like university presidents, labour leaders faced the "non-negotiable demands" of younger members.

Youthful radicalism had a political dimension. In 1969, New Democrats found themselves wrestling with a revolt – essentially academic, middle-class and young – from those who insisted that they would "waffle to the left instead of waffling to the right." The so-called "Waffle Movement" demanded a return to the old-fashioned socialism of the thirties, whatever voters might think. While "The Waffle" was defeated with plenty of union help at the NDP's 1969 convention, the times spawned a new generation of radical leaders and revived the youthful dreams of some of their elders. Even Communists and Trotskyites wrestled publicly with radical youth factions. One of them, the Revolutionary Marxist Group, found jobs at Toronto's main post office and added to its turmoil.

In the mood of the late 1960s, labour's commitment to its political party began to pay off. In 1967, Ontario voters gave the NDP 27 percent of their ballots, more than in any election since 1943. In 1969, Manitoba New Democrats paused in an election campaign against a Tory government to pick Selkirk M.P. Ed Schreyer as provincial leader. A few weeks later, on June 25, half a century after the General Strike collapsed, Manitobans elected their first-ever NDP government. Two years later, on June 23, 1971, Allan Blakeney won 45 of Saskatchewan's 60 seats for the NDP. On August 30, 1972, seventy years after British Columbia had elected its first socialists, Dave Barrett moved the NDP from 12 to 38 seats and beat the unbeatable W.A.C. Bennett.

In all three provinces, union leaders fought hard for the NDP, anti-labour policies had stirred voters, and union members had much to expect. In Saskatchewan, the Liberals had believed that forcing strikers back to work guaranteed them re-election. They were wrong. Fed up with Bennett's blustering failure to bring peace between workers and their bosses, B.C. voters were willing to give Barrett a turn, particularly when the B.C. Federation of Labour made it clear that he was not their favourite. Union members gained a lot in

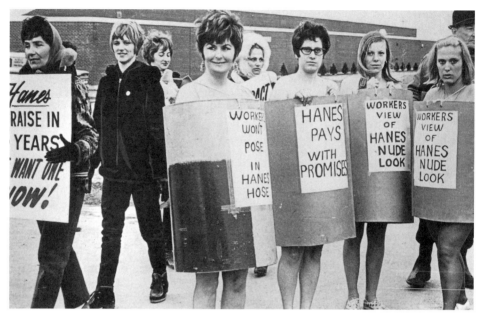

Unions trying to organize women found that labour legislation made it hard to organize small, anti-union plants. Strikers at Hanes Hosiery in Toronto did their best to attract public attention, but their American employers kept their reputation as a non-union company and most of the women lost their jobs. (Retail, Wholesale Department Store Union–Bill Haines)

what the NDP promptly dubbed "The Three Happy Provinces." Minimum wages rose sharply. Housing, day-care, social services and support for the elderly were priorities for all three governments. Rent controls and effective machinery to protect tenants helped low-income people in Winnipeg and Vancouver. The Blakeney government removed the Liberals' deterrent fee from Medicare; Schreyer led other provinces in wiping out the premiums. All three governments re-wrote provincial labour laws to remove a pro-management bias. In 1972, Manitoba allowed secondary boycotts of allies of strikebound firms. Strikes or lockouts were legal the day after a contract expired, and every possible process or delay was eliminated so that employers and unions could bargain without recourse to the courts or government. Saskatchewan's NDP government pioneered health and safety legislation that allowed workers to shut down unsafe workplaces without loss of pay.

British Columbia was the NDP's biggest challenge. Labour minister Bill King summoned Paul Weiler, a Toronto law professor with the uncommon opinion that lawyers seldom help get settlements. Bennett's Mediation Commission was scrapped and British Columbia got a Labour Relations Board of lay members. To make strikes possible in hospitals and other vital services, Weiler gave both sides a voice in determining who the essential workers were. B.C.'s new labour law angered business by banning strike-breaking and allowing secondary pickets. Union leaders condemned a legislated "open season" for dissatisfied workers to switch unions, and a provision for unionists with religious scruples to divert their dues to charity. An increasing source of bitter disputes was bargaining a first contract between anti-union employers and workers with appetites bigger than their bargaining strength. Weiler had a solution: the new Board would impose a bare-bones first contract and let both sides get used to living with it. Despite grumbles from both sides – or perhaps because of them – Weiler's reforms began to cool the hottest, nastiest labour climate in Canada.

Trudeau's commitment to a "Just Society" was shrewdly ambiguous but, for many Canadians, it was an incitement to remedy the many injustices that had always been pushed down the reform agenda. The government found time to consider persistent poverty, and the plight of Native and Métis peoples. Feminism, remembered in history books as a struggle for the vote and mothers' allowances, was reborn with fifty years of unfinished business to transact. Many new expectations revolved around the workplace. Armed with evidence from the report of the Bird Royal Commission and the experience of working together to make it effective, women insisted that they would settle for nothing less than equal partnerships in the affairs of the world. Society must accommodate itself to the change, whether in the public provision of child care or the readjustment of masculine values. Women's issues would provide the major social dynamic of the next quarter-century.

Trudeau came to power at the end of five years of remarkable social reforms, amongst them Medicare, the Canada Pension Plan, Canada Student Loans, and home-owner grants. Yet Canada had not become a social democracy. Some benefits, complained critics, helped the rich more than the poor. In 1969, a Senate committee headed by David Croll reported that one Canadian in five had no share of postwar affluence. If such Canadians were to be helped, at a cost business would tolerate, some experts had an answer: end programs like Family Allowance or Old Age Security which covered all Canadians, when most did not really need them. Reserve benefits for the deserving. Return to a more elegantly managed means test. Cap old age security at $80 a month. Invent a Family Income Security Programme to replace universal family allowances.

Most Canadians were outraged. This was no way to the Just Society. Like its successor fifteen years later, the Trudeau government fled the sudden storm. Instead, the government expanded Unemployment Insurance into a pallid version of a "guaranteed annual income." Legislation in 1971 removed a $7,800 income ceiling for subscribers to the plan and promptly added 1.3 million new contributors. Maximum benefits rose to $2.50 an hour and the eligibility period for entitlement fell. If national or regional unemployment exceeded 4 percent, benefit periods would grow. Sickness or pregnancy entitled subscribers to up to fifteen weeks of entitlement. The changes provoked a predictable furore. Opponents complained that higher benefits would destroy the work ethic. Suddenly compelled to be contributors, the better-off complained that teachers or business executives would never face the indignity of unemployment. The more perceptive noted the problems of mixing insurance and welfare. Benefit rates too meagre to support a household might be pin-money to an unemployed member of an otherwise affluent and fully-employed family.

Louis Laberge of the Quebec Federation of Labour played a flamboyant role in the complex union politics of the 1970s, winning a massive transfer of power and resources from the CLC. He developed his own autonomy from national and international unions on the claim that he was in a life-and-death struggle with the CNTU. (Canadian Paperworkers)

For their part, union leaders had few complaints, beyond concerns that government now regarded a 4 percent jobless rate as the equivalent of full employment. Like 5 percent mortgages, such numbers would soon seem like the good old days. Another 1971 chunk of the "Just Society" was a Canada Labour Standards Act, imposing a minimum wage of $1.75 an hour, significant notice for layoffs, severance pay after five years' service, statutory holidays and guaranteed annual holidays or a 5 percent wage supplement in lieu. Thanks to the Bird Commission, the act required the government, not the victims, to make the case against employers who refused equal pay for equal work. Cynical unionists called the act a charter for the unorganized, but Trudeau's first term record was more progressive than most labour critics would ever admit.

One reason was that most unionists were preoccupied by the tougher, angrier side to the new prime minister's relations with labour. When postal workers struck in 1968 for a 29 percent increase, Trudeau let the Post Office shut down for three weeks and forced the union to settle for 15.1 percent. With Expo 67 a success, the government allowed the St. Lawrence Seaway to stay closed until its workers settled for two-thirds of their demands. If unions wanted the right to strike, they – and the public – could live with the consequences.

Trudeau's links with Marchand and the CNTU had worried the CLC. On the eve of nationalization in 1963, CUPE had lost its local at Shawinigan Light & Power to the CNTU. Montreal's transit workers switched to the CNTU from the Canadian Brotherhood of Railway, Transport and General Workers. Over three years, the CNTU added 9,356 members from CLC affiliates. In 1964, Louis Laberge, a former machinist, emerged as the tough, wily leader of the

CLC-affiliated Quebec Federation of Labour. From 1964 to 1967, the CNTU and Laberge's QFL waged a rough, no-holds-barred struggle for members. In a brilliant counter-attack, CUPE took 7,500 Hydro-Quebec employees from the CNTU. The industry that symbolized Quebec's Quiet Revolution had chosen a Canada-wide union.

Laberge caught Quebec's effervescent political moods, matched the CNTU in nationalist rhetoric, and bodychecked in the corners. When he took on the QFL presidency, Laberge demanded and got what no other provincial federation then possessed, his own organizing staff, shock troops in the fight with the CNTU. When Congress affiliates denounced him in 1967 for arranging a secret no-raiding pact with the CNTU, a furious Laberge resigned as a CLC vice-president and threatened more trouble to come. As acting president of the Congress after Claude Jodoin was felled by a stroke, Donald MacDonald was compelled to patch up a face-saving compromise on the eve of the 1968 convention. Whether or not Canada would concede special status to Quebec, Laberge won it for the Quebec Federation of Labour within the CLC. Within a few years, the QFL had formally backed Quebec's sovereignty.

Like Canadians generally, the labour movement had to deal with a resurgent and radical-tinged Quebec nationalism. It was less predictable that international unions would become a prime target for English-Canadian nationalists. The debate itself was old, but traditionally the internationals had infuriated employers and conservatives rather than the Canadian left. The merger of the All-Canadian Congress of Labour with the CIO unions in Canada in 1940 had silenced the most strident union critic of American-based unions. Only the tiny National Council of Canadian Labour, founded at Hamilton in 1948, promoted hostility to American union connections, but its influence was limited by a cosy relationship with employers and a tiny membership. The CNTU's nationalism hardly discriminated between U.S. or Canadian linkages. Nor did the sole surviving confessional labour organization, the Christian Labour Association of Canada (CLAC). Created in 1952 by supporters of the Dutch Reformed Church, CLAC's religious requirements kept it from winning certifications until Mr. Justice J.C. McRuer ruled in 1963 that he could not grant rights to a union that read from Karl Marx and deny them to one that used the Bible and psalms. While CLAC was mainly limited to small towns in southern Ontario, its efforts on behalf of members who refused to pay dues because of religious scruples embarrassed large unions with membership security clauses such as the Steelworkers or CUPE.

The attack on the internationals grew out of an older debate sharpened by Walter Gordon's Royal Commission report on Canada's economic prospects, published in 1958. Like other thoughtful Canadians, union leaders worried about U.S. dominance of some of the key economic sectors in Canada. By backing the NDP, whose 1961 platform had clear measures to promote Canadian ownership, research and jobs, labour concerns were clear. However unionists had some bitter memories of economic nationalism. Canadian employers had often demanded wage sacrifices from their employees and then sold out for the best American offer. "Nationalism never put a penny in a worker's pocket," warned Larry Sefton of the United Steelworkers, "and it never will." "Boundaries," declared an old labour slogan, "were made by the bosses."

Canadian nationalism after 1967 owed much to the positive pride generated by Expo 67 and the celebrations of the centennial of Confederation, but it was better defined by negatives. U.S. racial strife, decaying cities, the Vietnam war and the advent of Richard Nixon helped make Canadians a little happier with their side of the border. For a few years at the turn of the decade, Canadians enjoyed a higher standard of living than their neighbours and a stronger dollar. American unions, defending their jobs from foreign imports, often forgot to ask for exemption for Canadian members from protectionist bills before Congress or from "Nixonomics," President Nixon's ingenious attempt to pass the costs of the Vietnam war to American trading partners. When the 1965 Auto Trade Pact moved briefly in Canada's favour, U.S. politicians demanded its repeal. Eager for U.S. markets and a chance to sell their companies to richer bidders, Canadian business abandoned its old protectionism. Historically a Tory preserve, economic nationalism moved left, with a new rhetoric of "U.S. imperialism," "colonialism" and "enforced dependency."

Diefenbaker Tories had given critics a powerful weapon against international unions. The Corporations and Labour Unions Returns Act (CALURA), proclaimed in 1963, demanded specific categories of financial information and then presented the statistics in ways that suggested that U.S.-based unions took twice as many dues-dollars from Canadian members as they ever returned to Canada. For nationalists, this was better ammunition than reminders of Hal Banks or denouncing the UAW for seeking U.S.-Canadian wage parity. What Canadian unionist wanted to pay a dollar for fifty cents' worth of benefit? The truth was complex. By excluding union spending on rents, travel, education, research, telephones, legal expenses and affiliation dues, CALURA reports made national unions look like huge profiteers too. In 1974, for example, international unions collected $52.7 million in Canada and paid back $25.2 million. National unions collected $28.2 million but paid out only $13.7 million. From 1970 to 1974, CALURA figures suggested that the International Association of Machinists had made a $1 million profit from its Canadian members. In fact, its Canadian members cost almost half a million dollars more than they paid. For most internationals, the cost of servicing a vast, bilingual country far exceeded Canadian dues and assessments.

Of course, it was always easy to collect grievances against internationals. Highly centralized, business-minded and burdened by an aged leadership and an increasingly hostile legislative environment south of the border, American unions could be as insensitive to Canadian concerns as any corporation. Intervention from Washington, Detroit or Cincinnati might be justified, but local resentment at trusteeship or the dismissal of a Canadian official was sharpened when the ruling came from a foreign city. Local 91 of the International Typographical Union blamed orders from Colorado Springs for its disastrous 1964 strike against the Toronto newspapers. Many international unions made no bones about their disapproval of the "socialist" NDP. In the Steelworkers, Charles Millard and Bill Mahoney told their international president, David McDonald, to mind his own business. Some Canadian districts of anti-political internationals took a wicked pleasure in inviting Tommy Douglas, David Lewis and other eloquent NDPers to fill the "Canadian speaker" slot at international conventions. Other Canadian affiliates respected the "no politics" clause of their international constitution and politely avoided involvement in CLC-sponsored NDP campaigns. Some of their members grumbled.

The pioneers in left-wing union nationalism were often Communists, defeated in the cold war struggles of the 1940s and 50s. In the unions they still controlled, such as the United Electrical Workers and the United Fishermen and Allied Workers in B.C., Communists expounded a fervent, if tactical, Canadian nationalism. In fact, some left-wing nationalists had deserted the Communist Party because of its subservience to Moscow. Kent Rowley and his wife, Madeleine Parent, both of them Communists, had led some of Quebec's biggest textile strikes. In 1952, they had been fired from the United Textile Workers in favour of what their international president gracefully called "safe, clean staff." Rowley and Parent emerged from the fifties at the head of a 1,300-member Canadian Textile and Chemical Union. Their radical, nationalist principles were intact, but they had abandoned their Communist memberships. The 1960s would be their moment.

As part of the AFL-CIO merger, a number of unions in the pulp and paper industry got together as the United Paperworkers International Union. British Columbia paperworkers had been comfortable in their old union, headed as it was by an octogenarian U.S. socialist, but they were less satisfied with the new arrangement. In 1963 several thousand members left to form the Pulp and Paper Workers of Canada. In 1969, when Rowley and Parent created a Council of Canadian Unions, the PPWC was an early affiliate. So was the remnant of the once-powerful Mine Mill and Smelter Workers at Falconbridge. The Machinists lost a dozen small western plants to CAIMAW, the Canadian Association of Industrial Mechanical and Allied Workers, though nationalism was less an argument than bad servicing and poor contracts.

Nationalists who denounced U.S.-style "business unionism" were most successful when they could promise unhappy workers a better deal and bigger incomes. Rowley's most dramatic achievement came in October, 1972, when two thousand Kitimat smelter workers voted to leave the United Steelworkers to become the core of yet another CCU affiliate. Meanwhile, Rowley's own union attracted youthful, idealistic radicals by waging violent strikes at Texpack in Brantford and Artistic Woodworking, a picture frame factory in the Toronto suburbs. In 1975 the Council renamed itself the Confederation of Canadian Unions and claimed 20,000 members, almost all of them defectors from internationals.

CLC unions had to respond. From its inception, they denounced CALURA. The more powerful affiliates fought off the CCU with better service and tougher bargaining. The Steelworkers beat back raids at Salmo, Kimberley and Trail and took quiet pleasure when the nationalistic CUPE also had to fight off CCU challenges. Some changes were cosmetic. A 1968 CLC committee, appointed to study the CLC's constitution and structure, devoted most of its efforts to defending international unions. The report dismissed most nationalist criticisms while urging more authority for the Congress and more mergers

Henri Lorrain of the Canadian Paperworkers Union led his fifty thousand members through a high degree of autonomy in an international union into full independence in 1974. (Canadian Paperworkers)

for its affiliates. Such decisions, the committee obviously understood, would be made in the U.S. That year, when the militant United Packinghouse Workers merged with the Amalgamated Meatcutters, the Canadian districts were granted the title "Canadian Food and Allied Workers." In 1970, the new union absorbed an unexpectedly successful drive, led by Father Desmond McGrath and a former Liberal M.P., Richard Cashin, to organize Newfoundland fishermen and fish-plant workers. Recollecting the tragic history of the IWA in the 1950s, leaders of the new union shrewdly adopted the title of Newfoundland Food, Fishermen and Allied Workers to reassure local workers that they had not been captured by "come from away's."

Canadian workers might not want the CCU but they shared the nationalist mood. In 1969, members of the oldest important national union, the Canadian Brotherhood of Railway, Transport and General Workers, rejected their officers' advice to merge with an old rival, the Brotherhood of Railway and Airline Clerks (BRAC). Six years later, Canadians in BRAC had persuaded the international to create a highly autonomous Canadian district, with its own officers, funds and constitution. When the United Brewery Workers merged with the International Brotherhood of Teamsters in 1972, most Canadian locals demanded independence. By 1975, with help from the new Canada Labour Relations Board, they had succeeded. The Teamsters absorbed the lesson and established a Canadian Conference. Appointed to the Senate by the Liberals, Teamsters' vice-president Ed Lawson moved from Vancouver to a new head-quarters in Ottawa. Canadian rank and file were not consulted.

Far from robbing Canadian unionists, some internationals discovered that, as their own organizational and financial strength dwindled, a Canadian district was a luxury they could no longer afford. After years of futile spending in Canada, the Communications Workers of America reached an amicable separation with its four thousand Canadian members in 1971. Within five years, the new Communications Workers of Canada had done the impossible and organized 14,000 Bell Canada technicians and then 2,500 operators. Financial considerations also persuaded the United Paperworkers to allow its Canadian district to vote on independence. In 1974, a big majority led to the new Canadian Paperworkers Union (CPU). As in many separations, relations turned sour on the property settlement. The new union found itself cut off without its expected share of the international's treasury.

Shoved by nationalist criticism and transformed by the vast influx of delegates from nationally-based public-sector unions, the CLC rapidly abandoned its defensive 1968 response. That year it rescinded its prohibition against Communists, paving the way for the return of the Electrical Workers and the United Fishermen. At least they would not add their strength to Rowley's CCU. In 1970, delegates solemnly voted for a code of standards which all affiliates must follow, including the right of Canadian members to vote for their own officers and councils, and the right of Canadian-elected leaders to speak for their union in Canada. (Checking on the response in 1973, Congress officials found that among 90 internationals, 43 boasted full compliance, 28 had achieved partial compliance but 19 had done nothing. Chief among them were the major construction unions and one of the earliest founding partners of Canadian unionism, the Typographers. The hold-outs represented almost two hundred thousand Canadian unionists.)

None of this appeased nationalists or a generation that regarded compromise as a dirty word. When CLC delegates headed to Vancouver for their 1974 biennial convention, they were warned to expect as stormy a showdown for union nationalism as the Berlin convention of 1902. Public-sector unions demanded their share of CLC executive posts. Louis Laberge announced that the QFL must have full control of organization, education, public relations and most other Congress functions, plus the necessary funds. The Canadian Union of Public Employees mobilized delegates from every tiny local to back its demand that provincial government associations be compelled to affiliate to CUPE before they could join the Congress. Convention organizers had expected 1,500–1,700 delegates at Vancouver; thanks to CUPE, they had to find space for 2,500. As usual with CLC showdowns, the hard issues disappeared into the back room. Laberge got his way. Shirley Carr, head of CUPE's Ontario division, and Julien Major of the newly national Paperworkers were guaranteed election as executive vice-presidents. In return, CUPE conceded that the provincial government employees could enter the CLC if they formed a separate national union of their own. A little disappointed at the lack of a fight, delegates added a few more conditions to the code of self-government.

As Ontario vice-president of the Canadian Union of Public Employees, Shirley Carr led the 1972 "Catch Up" campaign for Toronto's hospital workers. On the steps of the Ontario legislature, she challenged a government that allowed people to be poorly paid but denied them any right to strike because they were essential workers. (Canadian Union of Public Employees)

Lynn Williams, a graduate of the Eaton Drive of the early 1950s, showed that a Canadian could win top office in the largest international, the United Steelworkers. In 1976, he became the union's secretary-treasurer and, in 1983, the president. (Julien Lebourdais)

Unions affiliated to international trade secretariats such as the Metalworkers Federation must allow Canadian branches to affiliate separately, and they must remove constitutional and policy barriers to "the full enjoyment of political, cultural and social rights" by their Canadian members.

The aftermath was an uncomfortable test of the CLC's authority. Advised that nationalist extremists had taken over the Canadian organization, the AFL-CIO's building trades withheld their affiliation cheques. Though the convention had granted a 25 percent increase in dues, the lost income forced the Congress into a large and growing deficit. However, the building trades also received a hot torrent of indignation from some of their Canadian locals. Joe Morris, the CLC president and a veteran of the International Woodworkers, made a respectful pilgrimage to Washington and the flow of funds resumed. The $750,000 deficit was easily covered by a belated cheque for $850,000.

Morris had only stalled the defection of the traditional international craft unions: within eight years they would leave the CLC for their own central body. A national union, CUPE, had become the largest single labour organization in Canada, displacing the United Steelworkers. By 1975, for the first time, national union membership in Canada matched the strength of the internationals. By the 1980s, membership in national unions far exceeded international unionists. The uniquely Canadian phenomenon of the U.S.-controlled international union went into sharp decline.

Canadianization of the CLC was linked to another, even more fundamental phenomenon: the nature of work. Automation, the spectre of the sixties, had seemingly threatened every job. Real change comes more slowly. Faced with a vast flood of job-seekers as the baby boomers hit the job market, Canada set world records in job creation, but very few of them were in the traditional areas of natural resources and manufacturing. One reason was life-style. The children of a more affluent Canada had accepted at least one piece of advice from their parents: few wanted a lifetime of industrial labour. More to the point, investors in the 1970s had found other sources of cheap labour. The "de-industrialization" of Canada had begun. Employment growth came in information-handling and services to people. By the 1980s, the major areas of job creation would be among sales clerks, waiters and financial services.

The 1960s had seen the unionization of the public sector and continued exclusion of unions from large areas of private sector employment. The effects on the Canadian labour movement were enormous, and evident when the CLC met at Vancouver in 1974. Public-sector employees would steadily outnumber blue-collar industrial workers as they, in turn, had outnumbered workers in trades and crafts. Barely apparent but growing were workers who spent their lives handling information.

How Canadians would accept the trend, time would very soon tell.

CHAPTER 25

Quebec and the Common Front

Much had happened in Quebec since Jean Marchand left for Ottawa in 1965. Under his successor, Marcel Pépin, the alliance with the Liberal party began to fray. After years of supporting a conservative, corporatist nationalism, Quebec's intellectuals joyously embraced the revolutionary Marxism they read about in a radicalized *Cité Libre* and its successor, *Parti pris*. Ideas that Michel Chartrand had espoused through long, lonely years were now at the height of fashion. Since Catholic unionism had never accepted economic liberalism, it was even easier for the CNTU to attack capitalism than it was for Laberge's Federation. And in a Quebec where an English-speaking minority had almost monopolized wealth and economic power, there was much to attack.

In 1966, the Union Nationale was back in government. The costs and uncertainties of change had become too burdensome to many Quebeckers. Quebec's "Quiet Revolution" had kept most of its material rewards for the province's middle class. Ordinary Quebeckers had gained a sense of pride and a corresponding sense of frustration that their incomes and status had lagged behind their English-speaking neighbours. The new government struggled ineffectively to get the province's finances in order, a task made more difficult now that teachers and public employees had the right to strike. Lacking the shrewd ruthlessness of a Duplessis, and working in very different times, Daniel Johnson and his successor, Jean-Jacques Bertrand, merely added to the frustrations of urban workers. Their rhetorical nationalism worried investors without giving Quebeckers any added sense of power.

Having condemned Expo 67 with its artificial islands and its huge cost overruns as a classic extravagance, most Canadians then took pride in its success. It was not often that Canadians could boast of their style and imagination. Quebeckers had another view: Expo was their national achievement and proof of their evolution as a nation. General de Gaulle's ringing *"Vive le Québec libre!"* was not foreign mischief-making but a simple acknowledgement of what should have been normal. In the wake of Expo 67, Quebec, and Montreal in particular, was left with half-empty hotels, unused taxis, an army of unemployed, a huge debt and all its old problems of slums, pollution and crime. Canadians offered no help with that burden.

By the end of 1967, Quebeckers had their first powerful independence movement, headed by René Lévesque, a former Liberal cabinet minister who had entered politics after a long, bitter strike of Radio-Canada producers in 1959 and who had nationalized Quebec's English-owned private power companies. When Canadians asked their ritual question, "What does Quebec want?", René Lévesque now had an answer: sovereignty plus an association with Canada.

Quebec's labour organizations reflected the resentments and frustrations of wage- and salary-earners. Extreme nationalism had not been a Quebec union tradition. Before the 1960s, French-Canadian nationalism had had a right-wing, clerical, even an occasionally fascist tinge. Through most of the 1960s, the CNTU, QFL and the Catholic teachers' union went no farther than urging bilingualism, biculturalism, and a special status for Quebec within Confederation. In 1964, the CNTU even opened a Toronto office. Not until 1965 did the QFL even enter a float in Montreal's St-Jean-Baptiste Day parade, a traditional outpouring of Quebec patriotism. Until 1967, both Quebec labour organizations ritually denounced talk of separatism. Increasingly, a Marxist-tinged post-colonial nationalism offered a satisfying emotional outlet.

Even before Lévesque's new movement, Quebec looked ready for a noisier revolution. Since 1964 a series of mailbox explosions, thefts of arms and store robberies had been associated with a vaguely-structured *Front de libération du Québec.* Romantic intellectuals fancied themselves as revolutionaries, and egged on younger militants to fresh exploits. The perpetrators – mostly unemployed youth and occasional soldiers of fortune – usually ended up in jail.

Just how explosive Montreal could be was suddenly made apparent. On October 6, 1969, 3,000 police officers, denied wage parity with their Toronto counterparts by an arbitrator's award, defied the law and gathered *en masse* for a "study session" at the Paul Sauvé Arena, led by union leader Guy Marcil. They were soon joined by 2,400 fire fighters. Within a few hours there were six bank holdups and fifty stores were robbed. Provincial police who tried to keep order were seized by flying squads of Montreal police and escorted to the Arena.

Meanwhile, two hundred members of the radical *Mouvement de libération du taxi* mustered their cabs at the Arena and rode off to attack Murray-Hill Bus Lines, a company that monopolized airport service. While a crowd watched and unidentified snipers exchanged rifle shots, angry cabbies burned buses and the Murray-Hill garage. In the fusillade, a provincial police corporal was fatally shot. Through the night, mobs roved the commercial district, looting shops, smashing windows and pillaging Mayor Jean Drapeau's restaurant, *le*

Les gars de Lapalme *had established their own co-operatively owned company to collect Montreal mail when the government decided to switch the contract to four separate firms. The drivers lost both their company and their union rights. Their struggle to change the government's mind focussed Quebec working-class resentment against Ottawa. (Murray MacGowan)*

Vaisseau D'Or. By midnight, troops from Valcartier joined provincial police to patrol Montreal streets. A tearful Marcil pleaded with his Montreal colleagues to obey the law and go back to work. Their reward was a pay settlement far closer to their demands than the original arbitrator's award. Drapeau blamed the trouble on militant members of the federally-funded Company of Young Canadians.

Pierre Elliott Trudeau despised the weakness that allowed disorder and chaos in Montreal, as he had detested Pearson's feeble compromises. Far from yielding to Quebec demands for special status in Canada, French and English must be equally at home across the country, and both must share real power in Ottawa. Government, he insisted, must be ruled by rationality. A fellow reformer, Eric Kierans, former president of the Montreal Stock Exchange, took on Post Office reform. He swiftly endorsed the expert solution for coping with growing mountains of mail: exciting new technologies, modernized facilities, and a ruthless assault on the easygoing, corrupt muddling that had come to characterise the organization. An obvious target was the system of collecting mail in major cities. Ill-paid drivers in worn-out vehicles worked for private contractors who were well fortified with political influence. The obvious answer was to break up the deals, start some competition and reap the benefits.

Supporters crowd around Michel Chartrand, stormy petrel of Quebec's labour movement and president of the CNTU's Montreal Central Council. The "patience" urged by a flourished picket sign was not the quality most people would have associated with Chartrand. (Canadian Paperworkers)

Simple answers may be wrong. In Toronto, Kierans found himself in a battle with the Teamsters, but the Montreal situation was far worse. A company called Rod Services had collected mail for years until its drivers, organized by the CNTU, had formed a co-operative called Lapalme Inc. and won the contract. Thanks to Kierans, four new companies were given the work, and the 450 Lapalme drivers lost their jobs and their company. By April 1, 1970, half of them had been absorbed in the Post Office; the rest became *"les gars de Lapalme,"* a few hundred embittered men whose war on Ottawa ranged from demonstrations to sabotage. Only when *"Les gars"* turned on their own union, the CNTU, did their star fade. A particularly abusive sally by one of the luckless drivers provoked Trudeau to answer *"Mange de la merde."*

Telling a worker to "eat shit" was a measure of how far the prime minister and Quebec unionism had diverged. Montreal union leader Michel Chartrand had shared his upper-class education with Trudeau, and their paths had often crossed. A born agitator and a former leader of the Quebec CCF, Chartrand was head of the CNTU's Montreal Central Council, a powerful base for someone intent on prodding the CNTU leadership in a socialist and nationalist direction. In 1968 the Confederation endorsed a manifesto proclaiming the need to protect workers on a second front – as consumers. In 1970 the annual manifesto proclaimed "There is No Place for Quebec in the Current Economic System." After Montreal's 1969 language riots, QFL resolutions demanded the right to work in French. In 1970, the CNTU demanded that French become the sole official and working language of Quebec. The English language might be a fact, but its use was not a right. At the ritual "cap in hand" between Ottawa ministers and trade unionists, Trudeau and Chartrand tangled verbally. When the two men threatened to square off, aides intervened.

In April, 1970, a youthful Robert Bourassa led the Liberals back to power with the promise of 100,000 new jobs. Confederation, he insisted, could be made profitable to Quebec. Lévesque's new party won a fifth of the votes, but only six seats. Six months later, on October 5, 1970, a tiny handful of unemployed youth added to the FLQ tradition by seizing the British trade commissioner. Bourassa's government wavered. A week later, another group seized Bourassa's labour minister, Pierre Laporte. Nationalist intellectuals appeared to be cheering on the terrorists. Trudeau saw a democratically-elected government disintegrating. To save the lives of the FLQ captives, Quebec ordered the FLQ's manifesto read on radio and television: among the demands was reinstatement for "*Les gars de Lapalme.*" In Montreal, Claude Ryan of *Le Devoir* talked with René Lévesque and prominent labour leaders, Laberge and Chartrand among them, about the need for a provisional government.

On October 14, with Quebec police exhausted and baffled, Bourassa finally asked Ottawa for troops. The law gave Ottawa no choice, but Trudeau went farther. Before dawn on October 16, he proclaimed the War Measures Act, declared a state of apprehended insurrection, and authorized police to arrest anyone who might remotely be suspected of FLQ connections. On October 18, Laporte's strangled body was found in the trunk of a car. The romantic age of liberation died as the news spread, and a wave of revulsion swept across the country. Support for repression soared everywhere. In all, 419 people were arrested, including Michel Chartrand and more than a score of prominent radical union leaders. By the end of October, the crisis was over; by December, the kidnappers were in Cuba or in jail.

At the time, Quebeckers were as enthusiastic about Trudeau's tough response as other Canadians. For a few days they had experienced fear and uncertainty, and they had not enjoyed it. In time, the mood changed. Like some other Canadians, Quebeckers concluded that Ottawa had over-reacted. Those seized in police raids and those who sympathized with them wanted vengeance for their humiliation and for the defeat of the popular reform movement, which had expected to defeat Mayor Jean Drapeau in Montreal elections. To union leaders, burning to avenge their humiliation, Quebec's labour movement became a ready-made revolutionary instrument. A series of regional meetings had been designed to lead to the founding convention of a radical labour party in the fall. The October crisis had intervened. Why bother to campaign for votes? Unions themselves would seek power. The ideas of radical syndicalism, buried at Winnipeg in 1919, re-surfaced in Quebec. In

Montreal's riot squad lines up against demonstrators during the La Presse *strike of 1971. Like other Quebec strikes, collective bargaining issues were overshadowed by politics, particularly resentment at the newspaper's ownership by Paul Desmarais's Power Corporation. (Labour Canada)*

1971, the CNTU's militant staff armed members with a study guide entitled *"Ne comptons que sur nos propres moyens"* – "Let us count only on our own resources" – as uncompromising in its text as in its title.

Quebec unionists were not transformed from conservatives to radicals by a few months or years of Marxist slogans. Their manifestos, as historian Jacques Rouillard noted, were much clearer about ending capitalism than about how to replace it. However the new rhetoric helped them interpret an economic system run largely by Americans or English-speaking Canadians in a new and nastier light. By 1972, the manifestos of the CNTU, the QFL, and even the CEQ were committed to achieving a socialist Quebec, however vaguely defined. To underline the point, on October 29, 1971, Chartrand's council mobilized 14,000 Montrealers and launched them at police barricades to support a strike at the Montreal daily, *La Presse*. The real target was the newspaper's owner, Paul Desmarais's Power Corporation, and its ally, the Bourassa government.

The Bourassa regime bore little resemblance to the Lesage team of 1960. The years of bold new programmes, to be financed somehow in the future, were over. Nor, as the Union Nationale had discovered, could Quebec always be distracted by pointless wars with Ottawa. The young premier had pledged that he could rebuild Quebec prosperity and deliver a promised 100,000 new jobs. His technocratic competence was his guarantee. His strategy depended on huge capital projects, like the development of hydro electricity potential on the rivers that fed James Bay. In turn, that depended on an investor confidence that had to be built on internal tranquillity, a dependable labour force, and tax restraint. All of these, Bourassa's enemies would do their best to deny him. As allies, they could count on workers who no longer believed the old message that *la survivance* depended on low wages, docility and religious faith. Indeed, in a few short years, Quebeckers had become the most secular of Canadians.

The first challenge came almost by accident. In 1972 the new government faced seventy-five different sets of negotiations, with 200,000 public-sector employees ranging from hospital workers to high school teachers. With an unexpected ease, Quebec's three major labour bodies, the CNTU, the QFL and the CEQ, decided to pool their efforts in a Common Front. All three shared a deep frustration with the government and all three had adopted similar militant manifestos. It was not hard to find common demands: a minimum wage of $100 a week for any public sector worker and annual increases of 8.3 percent for three years. After all, both the Canadian Senate and Quebec's Castonguay Commission on social services had agreed that $100 was a minimum income for a family of four, and 70 percent of Quebec's public employees in 1971 earned less.

The Bourassa government was unmoved. Minimum wages were a matter for the Department of Social Affairs, not all public employees had families, and the union demands would add an $875 million load on provincial taxpayers. Its best offer was 4.8 percent, ultimately raised to 5.3. Separately and together, negotiations reached an impasse. The government could not imperil its economic strategy; the Common Front was in no mood for compromise.

Generations earlier, syndicalists had argued that political action was a waste of time: through the general strike the workers could bring the state to its knees. Consciously or not, the Common Front had come close to mounting the syndicalist challenge. After a short delay, so that workers could clear up a sudden snowfall, the Common Front staged a one-day walkout on March 28, 1972. Both sides were pleased. Union leaders rejoiced that workers had almost universally obeyed the strike call. The government claimed that business had survived the disruption unscathed. Court injunctions had kept hospital workers and half the employees of Hydro-Quebec on the job. Neither side felt any new pressure to compromise.

On April 5, Common Front negotiators closed their briefcases, and talks ended. On April 10, a full walkout began. A day later, it had become the biggest strike in Canadian history. Hydro workers defied the injunctions, though only until their union, CUPE, reminded them of the dire penalties in store. Hospital employees, less carefully led, also walked out, forcing their institutions to empty three-quarters of their beds. Most of the sick, elderly and infirm went home: the rest depended on harried supervisors. A government minister denounced English-language newspapers for alarmism over the plight of the sick; the news was accurate, he explained, but not in the public interest. Teachers were part of the strike: a million and a half students enjoyed an impromptu holiday. The Bourassa government claimed to be calm and talked of negotiated settlements.

Finally, it had had enough. On April 22, despite a twenty-four hour filibuster by the tiny Parti Québécois contingent, the National Assembly approved tough legislation to stop the walkout and to suspend public servants' right to strike for two years. As a sop, the government offered arbitration, and no less than the government's final 5.3 percent offer.

In the defiant mood of the Common Front, that could not be the end. Louis Laberge and CEQ leader Yvon Charbonneau breathed defiance. For six hours, Marcel Pépin pleaded with his members to defy the law "if they can find the courage." To his dismay, three members of his own executive insisted that the CNTU – and Pépin – had gone too far. After urging defiance, Pépin and his fellow union leaders went on television to advise a general return to work. The aftermath was painful. Even during the strike, hospital union leaders had been jailed and heavily fined for contempt of court. Three officers of a small hospital union at Rivière du Loup were condemned to three months in prison and fines of $2,500, while their union was fined $10,000. Officers of the union at the Jewish Hospital of Hope got a month each. In all, 49 local union leaders were jailed, fined or both. On April 26, Pépin, Charbonneau and Laberge were charged for speeches urging workers to defy injunctions. In court, they looked at the array of riot police, waited a few minutes for the judge to appear, and walked out. The judge sentenced them in absentia to a year in jail. On May 9 a cheering throng escorted them to the Quebec Court House to begin their sentence. "There is no justice in Quebec," explained Laberge.

In the aftermath of the strike, there was other violent talk. Junior college teachers demanded a general strike. Chartrand's Central Council set a date – May 1 – and demanded dismissal of the three CNTU executives who had insisted that the law be obeyed. On May 10, the day after Pépin, Laberge and Charbonneau were jailed, angry workers at Sept-Iles blockaded the town and took over its radio station. Men with baseball bats and iron bars clashed with provincial police. On May 11 a man was killed when a car crashed into a picket line. At Mont-Joli, Thetford Mines and St. Jerome, workers seized radio stations to communicate their frustration. Paradoxically it was in Montreal that the protest fell flat. On May 12, when unionists fanned out across the city and neighbouring communities to enforce a general strike, they met a frustrating indifference. Passions were spent. The fundamental caution of working people emerged. Among private sector unionists, as conscious as their neighbours that they would pay higher taxes for higher wages, there was a limit to sympathy for public sector workers.

National and international labour organizations scolded Quebec for jailing the three Common Front leaders. The federal NDP leader, David Lewis, claimed that "any judge who has the stupidity to impose a savage sentence of one year in jail on the three union leaders has no right to be on the bench in any court of the land." Despite their initial refusal to appeal, an intermediary from the Parti Québécois persuaded the three leaders to try their luck. Besides, they were needed at the bargaining table. Ultimately the Supreme Court ruled that the three leaders must complete their sentences. Lesser officials were let off with a week in jail and smaller fines, on the argument that they had merely obeyed orders and that they had no money. By the autumn, most of the Common Front unions had settled: in return for an additional year on the contract, the government met the $100 minimum wage demand and improved the wages of the lowest-paid.

As in Winnipeg in 1919, syndicalism turned out to be more dangerous to unions than to management. Hardest hit was the CNTU: in a few months it lost a third of its members. The federation representing Quebec's civil servants had dropped out as the Common Front struggle was getting under way, arguing that it could do better on its own. Bus drivers for the Montreal Transit Commission and ALCAN workers followed soon after; revolutions were not to their taste. When the CNTU's annual convention dissolved in uproar, the three leaders who had dissented from Pépin, Paul-Emile Dalpé, Jacques Dion and Amédée Daigle, collected a caucus of other, more conservative members to debate strategy. The CSN council upheld Pépin, suspended "the Three 'D's" and waited scornfully while they created a breakaway *Centrale des syndicats démocratiques* (CSD). Officially launched at Quebec City on June 9, the CSD claimed the allegiance of 40,000 Quebec workers including most of the former Catholic syndicates in textiles, manufacturing and mining, among them the union that had waged the Asbestos strike of 1949. Conservative, private-sector members of the CNTU had had enough of their public sector brethren.

Put to the test, the Common Front claimed a labour unity that was more apparent than real. Bourassa's James Bay project revived an old battle between the QFL and the CNTU for control of construction labour. Elsewhere in Canada, strong craft unions dominated the building trades by the 1970s, with hiring halls as the sole source of approved labour. Quebec employers had to choose between the QFL's international affiliates, the CNTU and, from 1972, the CSD. Since rates and working conditions were first bargained and then imposed by Quebec's system of "decrees," union rivalries were supposed to make little difference to employers but they could not escape the struggle as too many construction workers and their unions battled for scarce jobs.

In Quebec, international craft unions had traditionally dominated the building trades in Montreal, while the CNTU's strength was chiefly among construction workers in the hinterland. That changed with the huge building projects of the 1960s and 1970s. Montreal construction workers, unemployed after Expo, clamoured for their share of work in the huge new Hydro-Québec developments on James Bay – the chief fruit of Bourassa's pledge of 100,000 new jobs. Legislation in 1968 and, after a violent jurisdictional fight at a Sept-Iles construction site, again in 1972, attempted to keep the peace. By common consent, it failed. Between 1970 and 1974, provincial police investigated 540 episodes of conflict on construction sites, some of them very bloody.

In 1973 a re-elected Bourassa government announced that, for the sake of peace (and an undisclosed election commitment to the QFL's construction unions), representation on James Bay construction sites would be limited to only one of the rival labour bodies. Though ostensibly it controlled 80 percent of construction workers, QFL unions won a surprisingly narrow vote. Then, on March 20, 1974, the deal turned to ashes. After a contractor refused to fire two CNTU members, QFL construction unions shut down the LG-2 dam site. Fed up with both employers and union officials, the workers went on a

Judge Robert Cliche, flanked by Brian Mulroney on his right and teacher unionist Guy Chevrette on his left, delivers a characteristically blunt opinion. While the Cliche Commission revealed how far gangsterism had profited from Quebec's labour rivalries, it also gave its employer representative a springboard to a national audience. (Labour Canada)

rampage, smashing equipment, burning buildings and causing $35 million in damages from damage and delay.

A shaken labour minister, Jean Cournoyer, promised a thorough inquiry, headed by former Quebec NDP leader, Judge Robert Cliche, and aided by Tory labour lawyer Brian Mulroney and Guy Chevrette of the *Corporation des enseignants du Québec*. The resulting investigation far surpassed the Norris Inquiry as an embarrassment to organized labour in Canada, and particularly in Quebec. It was not hard for the Commission to figure out who was chiefly responsible for the trouble. Under Andre "Dédé" Desjardins, head of the QFL's Building Trades Council, a sordid collection of goons, recruited from the Montreal underworld, had served as union officials, stewards and enforcers. René Mantha, co-ordinator of a heavy equipment operators' union, swore on his mother's head that he had never committed violence and then listened to taped conversations of himself ordering the beating of a rival union officer. Other testimony revealed a network of loan-sharking, extortion from unionists and employers, illegal lotteries, blackmail and political patronage, not least the deal made to get the QFL its James Bay monopoly.

In their report, Cliche and his colleagues blamed the government and industry as well as unions. Bribe-givers needed bribe-takers. Cliche wanted trusteeship for the worst unions, government-run hiring halls, tight certification for construction workers to eliminate the over-supply, secret ballots to adopt collective agreements and a ban on criminals holding union office. At least initially, Laberge and his colleagues were not particularly penitent. As testimony poured forth, they had set up their own trusteeship of the worst organizations – though the trustee depended on the co-operation of his charges. Labour would "fight like dogs," warned Laberge, against any attempt to implement the Cliche proposals. Montreal's Olympic facilities, badly behind schedule for its 1976 deadline, were a useful hostage for a week's strike by construction workers. Perhaps, Laberge suggested, the games would have to wait for 1977.

On the majority side of public opinion for once, the Bourassa government held its ground. Four union locals were put under three-year government trusteeship, and a Quebec Construction Bureau was created to oversee wages, working conditions and labour supply. Encouraging or supporting an illegal strike became a crime – with the burden of proof on the striker. This, in itself, should have been grounds for a bitter fight but, after consultation with other affiliates, Laberge concluded that his dog would run away. Study sessions, called to defend the construction unions, were neatly diverted into a show of support for a long, violent strike against United Aircraft at Longueuil. After a little quiet bargaining, the QFL accepted the trusteeship and even the law on illegal strikes but preserved the union hiring halls – to be run henceforth on strictly ethical principles.

Far more than the James Bay affair, the United Aircraft strike aligned unions with nationalist opinion, particularly at a time when the Bourassa government was denounced by its critics as needlessly subservient to foreign capital. United Aircraft (later Pratt & Whitney) was a tough employer which had beaten its UAW local in a 1967 strike, and was not ashamed to keep its 2,000 workers below industry rates. Negotiations began in 1973 and dragged through 1974 as the union sought cost-of-living adjustments (COLA), a levelling-up of the lowest wages, and limits on overtime. At the end of 1974, 85 percent of workers voted to strike, the company had collected strike-breakers and fired union militants. When picket lines formed on January 9, 1975, violence followed at once. After months of fights, bombings, attacks on company executives' homes, smashed cars and a bargaining impasse, about half the strikers had gone back to work, and UAW officials complained that local union officers had misused some of the $2 million the strike had cost. Even when the union accepted a meagre contract, there were further months of negotiation before the final 500 strikers had a hope of getting their jobs back. When 34 of them occupied part of the plant, provincial police drove them out, injuring 16 workers.

The United Aircraft strike was a savage throwback to a bitter past – or a warning of the future. The immediate benefit was a commitment from the Parti Québécois that they would legislate against scabs. Propelled by another long, violent CNTU strike at Robin Hood Mills in Montreal, where armed thugs shot eight strikers, the Lévesque government kept the PQ's promise on July 26, 1977. Bill 45 not only forbade employment of strikebreakers during a legal strike but also legislated compulsory check-off of union dues, made certification much easier and guaranteed workers their jobs after a labour dispute.

The James Bay rampage and its painful aftermath left scars that ultimately affected the entire Canadian labour movement and cost the CLC thousands of members. The trouble began in 1972, when the International Brotherhood of Electrical Workers decided to make a voluntary union pension plan mandatory. Its 13,000 Quebec members deserted in protest to form their own Interprovincial Brotherhood. For the time being, the AFL-CIO accepted the situation and, in 1973, the QFL agreed that locals that broke with their international could still stay with the Federation. In the wake of the Cliche report, the QFL demanded and then exercised its right to investigate its affiliates and to pass judgement on their morality and efficiency. Leaders of the construction unions, still angry that they had had so little backing from the QFL in the face of the Cliche findings, seethed. Meeting at San Diego in 1979, the AFL-CIO's Building Trades Department finally expelled the errant Quebec electrical workers and commanded that the Quebec Federation do so as well.

As any Canadian could have predicted, Laberge and his federation defied the challenge and, with help from a sympathetic government, won official recognition for "FTQ-Construction," a grouping that within months won 70 percent of Quebec's construction unionists. All that remained to the AFL-CIO chartered *Conseil provincial des métiers de construction* was 21,757 members. Outraged by such defiance north of the border, Building Trades officials in Washington responded by denouncing the QFL and, more seriously, by suspending dues payments to the Canadian Labour Congress. As in 1974, American union leaders assumed that the Canadians would submit. They found that attitudes in Ottawa had changed in the intervening five years. A defiant Congress suspended its ten construction affiliates with their 229,783 members, a loss of an eighth of the CLC's income. In time it would produce a lasting schism.

The CLC was cautious about its Quebec affiliate; it had good reason. By the end of 1976, Quebec had a government committed to sovereignty and Quebec unionists had played a major role in the change. In 1970, when Lévesque's Parti Québécois fielded its first candidates, QFL officials claimed that half its members had voted for them, something no one ever claimed for the QFL's federal protegé, the NDP. In 1973, 76.1 percent of QFL members backed Levesque's candidates. In 1976, the PQ leader could count on the QFL's "tactical support." Thanks to its constitution and because the PQ did not promise "fundamental change in social organization," the CNTU withheld endorsement but its sympathies were no secret. The pay-off was the most sympathetic labour legislation in the country within a year of the victory. The PQ sought membership in the Socialist International (against the effective opposition of the NDP) and, on the basis of early performance, had earned it. On the other hand, for those who took stock of such things, in no Canadian province did opinion polls suggest such a widespread and deep distaste for unionism and its public manifestations as in Quebec. In time, that would matter. Unionism was built on the instinctive solidarity of Quebeckers against outside threats, but memories of the Common Front, of devastation at LG-2 and of the violent riots in Montreal troubled a profoundly peaceful people.

CHAPTER 26

Scapegoat for Inflation

By the 1970s, some of the oldest surviving sections of Canada's labour movement could mark their centennials. From a time when a few thousand members gathered in a few dozen semi-legal organizations, unionism in Canada mustered 2,173,000 members in 1970, contributing almost $100 million a year in dues. From a dollar a day for a six-day week, the mythical average worker earned $3.01 an hour for a 39.7-hour week. Even in the quarter-century since 1945, wages had quadrupled and, despite inflation, their purchasing power had doubled. In 1870, sickness, injury, unemployment and old age had been economic catastrophes: by 1970, most Canadians could depend on Medicare, Unemployment Insurance, workers' compensation plans and a web of government-backed pension and security plans. Almost every significant advance had been foreseen and fought for by the labour movement and, by the same token, denounced as ruinous to the economy by business leaders and their powerful allies.

Labour's gains in the postwar years had fuelled the consumer boom which, in turn, had sustained North American prosperity. Half a century earlier Henry Ford had reached the sensible conclusion that if his workers could never afford to buy his shiny, black Model T's, he would not sell many. Though Ford hated unions, he raised wages. Economists might debate the influence of unions on workers' incomes, but unions themselves, and the employers who fought them, had no doubt of their influence. Organization gave working people money to spend on a new home in a suburb, on a family car, vacations, higher education for children, and on the procession of gadgets, from postwar pressure cookers to colour television, which had inserted themselves in the average way of life.

In the early 1970s, labour could boast of its share in electing three NDP governments headed by Premiers Ed Schreyer of Manitoba, Allan Blakeney of Saskatchewan, and Dave Barrett of British Columbia. The experience was traumatic enough to convince Liberals, Conservatives, and Social Crediters that nothing but personal rivalry kept them apart. A united opposition defeated Barrett in 1975 and Schreyer in 1977. (Canadian Paperworkers)

Like his Liberal predecessor, Sir Wilfrid Laurier, Pierre Elliott Trudeau had no real interest in economics and only the most conventional understanding of its processes. However, far more than world affairs or the constitution, economic issues would dominate his long tenure of power. Wealthy by inheritance, Trudeau easily grasped the effect of inflation on savings and accepted the advice of bankers, business and his own advisors that inflation was an enemy he must, in his own phrase, "wrestle to the ground." In 1969, the Trudeau government ignored warnings of imminent recession and endorsed the Bank of Canada's decision to squeeze the money supply. Dean John Young of the University of British Columbia was invited to head a new Prices and Incomes Commission as a way of bringing moral suasion to bear on inflation-causers. Described as "an optimist loose in a world of pessimists," Young tested his good cheer by proposing guidelines of 5 percent for 1969 wage increases and 2.5 percent for prices. Business was politely non-committal; labour spokesmen were downright indignant. In 1970, Young provoked still more union outrage by urging a 6 percent guideline.

In the inflation debate, union leaders found themselves in a difficult position. In a free market, others could hike prices, fees, rents or other charges more or less as they chose; under collective bargaining, workers could only hope to catch up with inflation when their contracts came due and negotiations started. Prices could be raised discreetly and often; wage negotiations happened every two or three years. The resulting gains were often exaggerated by bargainers eager to sell members on a new contract. Union leaders might claim that they were only trying to catch up with price rises caused by business greed and government mismanagement, but too often pay raises were the only inflation factor in the public spotlight. Price hikes happened in the shadows. When labour organizations spoke out, as they did against the Young guidelines, editorial writers and politicians portrayed them as selfish. When the CLC and the CNTU joined late in 1969 to demand a prices review board and a temporary price freeze, they looked self-serving when they insisted that wages be excluded.

Whatever their public image, union leaders could never forget that they were elected by their own members, not by the public. Being a "sweetheart" was not flattery in union jargon. Wage controls and even bargaining restraint was out of the question until members were freed from two- and three-year contracts and could catch up. Bargaining strategies called for COLA clauses and contracts as short as a year, despite the added costs and fatigue of more frequent negotiation. Inflation, some argued, should be as good a reason as technological change for opening a contract in mid-term. Meanwhile, no union anxious to keep its members could possibly accept constraints on its bargaining.

By 1970, Canada had tipped into a serious recession. Experts, secure in their university or government offices, could insist that it was the normal working-out of the business cycle or an overflow of the slump that also hit the United States. Others, directly hit by unemployment or bankruptcy, blamed Trudeau and his government. Certainly a nation trained to believe in the Liberals, whatever their faults, as flawless economic managers, was sharply disillusioned. Meanwhile, unions and their members paid the price. Despite inflation, bargainers had to settle for moderate increases and long-term contracts. Canadian steelworkers rejected the no-strike Experimental National Agreement adopted by their union in the United States, but then did their best to keep labour peace until a more propitious time. The United Auto Workers' international president, Leonard Woodcock, came to Mississauga in person to wind up a long, bitter strike at McDonnell-Douglas Aircraft. A long strike against General Motors had left the union broke. In 1971, strikes cost only 2,867,000 working days, the lowest total since 1964.

The recession also made it seem futile to go on organizing. Workers at a score of low-paying enterprises – Procter-Silex, Hanes Hosiery, Alpine Meats, Pure Spring Canada among them – lost their strikes and often their jobs. When the respected Peterborough *Examiner* fell to the Thomson Newspaper chain, its unions were broken in a bitter struggle. Even strong unions in big plants were not exempt. A thousand UAW members at Acme Screw and Gear in Toronto tried to save their jobs by an eighteen-month wage freeze. Hailed by editorial writers as the dawn of a new day, the union's gesture was betrayed when the company declared itself bankrupt and promptly re-opened under a new name and with no union. At another Toronto plant, Dunlop Rubber, six hundred aging workers lost their jobs, pensions and prospects when the company closed the plant. The resulting outcry forced the Ontario government to require early notice of future large plant closures. For the Dunlop workers, it was too late.

In the autumn of 1972, the Trudeau government sought re-election. Though Ottawa tried hard to cut unemployment in the pre-election months and boasted that "The Land is Strong," the Liberal campaign faltered. A year earlier, after a tough struggle with the Waffle's candidate Jim Laxer, David Lewis, architect of the NDP, had won the party leadership. Lewis's campaign focussed on corporations that gobbled up government grants while deferring billions of dollars in federal taxes. Lewis's slogan, "corporate welfare bums," caught fire with the media, only to be grabbed by the Conservatives and twisted into an assault on beneficiaries of the enlarged Unemployment Insurance system. Allegations of people "ripping off" the system and spending holidays in Hawaii served the Tories well. On election night, the Liberals barely clung to power; the Tories were poised for an early kill. Having won the NDP 31 seats, Lewis was left to make what deals he could with Trudeau. (A costly post-election hunt for "welfare bums" living well on Unemployment Insurance found few offenders.)

The pre-election boom helped push inflation to 4.9 percent; food prices rose 8.6 percent in 1972. Union members, coming off two- and three-year contracts, needed a lot to catch up. Time lost from strikes tripled that year – 7,753,000 days. The following year was a little easier but, thereafter, strike days soared. The inflation rate doubled and, in 1975, tripled. The bitterest strikes were really against governments, either as ultimate arbiter or as ultimate paymaster, or both. In 1973, railway union leaders warned that they could not control their members if Parliament, as usual, ordered them back to work. To raise pressure and defer the inevitable intervention, they tried rotating strikes. The public was not appeased. Travellers stranded at Port aux Basques, auto plants shut down for lack of parts or prairie grain stalled at elevators were problems enough for politicians. On August 30, Parliament was summoned to end the dispute. Outside, eighteen hundred furious railwaymen demonstrated. Having opposed the law, the NDP's David Lewis was summoned to the front steps to persuade the workers to obey it. They shouted him down. A hundred and fifty of the angriest demonstrators burst into the Parliament Buildings, smashed windows and fought security guards. The back-to-work act passed on September 1; not until September 11 were the railways functioning again. The government charged six unionists for defying the law and, when the railway unions threatened to strike again, accepted "extenuating circumstances."

The railway strike was only the hottest of a series of disputes. In the spring of 1974, Ontario hospital employees made it clear that, on May 1, they would defy the ban on strikes if their hopelessly inadequate wages were not raised. Technically they bargained with hospital boards: in fact the money came from the provincial government. Backed by a well-managed publicity campaign, the workers persuaded most people that they were as ill-paid as they were essential. Just before May 1, Ontario's government found the cash. Nurses also made it clear that they would follow the same militant route if their professional training could not earn them more than ambulance drivers. In April, 1975, Ontario granted increases of 45 and 50 percent.

During the brief period when his party held the balance of power in Parliament, from 1972 to 1974, David Lewis found that he had more responsibility than power. One unpleasant task was trying to persuade angry railway workers to obey a back-to-work order passed by Liberals and Conservatives over NDP objections. (New Democratic Party)

Outside Quebec, scarcity and a resulting increase in salaries had done as much as professional status to keep teachers away from open confrontation. "Grey-listing" unfriendly school boards and threats of mass resignation gave teachers' federations influence. As the impact of a collapsing birth-rate in the 1960s hit schools in the 1970s, the prospect of shrinking enrolments and funding cutbacks threatened teachers' gains. So did Bill 274, legislation based on a report that condemned mass resignation and working to rule as "degrading techniques of the past." In future, said a Tory government, compulsory arbitration would suffice. On December 18, 1973, 108,000 Ontario teachers left their classrooms in protest. In 1974 and 1975, teacher strikes in York County, Windsor, Thunder Bay, Timiskaming and Ottawa won cost-of-living clauses and pay increases of 15–29 percent and showed that laws could not stop strikes. Ontario's Conservatives, dependent after a 1975 election on NDP votes, grudgingly passed legislation that allowed walkouts, though only after elaborate procedures governed by an Education Relations Commission.

One of the reasonable certainties of labour organizing was that teachers would remain professional. In the 1970s, the certainties were overthrown. In Ontario, government legislation banning teachers from the right to strike provoked a massive demonstration. The government hurriedly changed its mind. (Julien Lebourdais)

Across Canada, teachers, nurses, hospital workers and even police turned militant. After a series of illegal walkouts, New Brunswick hospital workers finally convinced the provincial government to offer a bonus of $125 and to open the contract five months early. In both Nova Scotia and New Brunswick, police won the right to strike. They promptly used it, leaving a number of Maritime communities to experience a few days of vandalism before the RCMP – or a hurried settlement – intervened. Editors, politicians and millions of ordinary people insisted that an innocent public had been held to ransom. Unionists disagreed. Far from being helpless, innocent victims of public-sector strikes, taxpayers elected the governments that did the negotiating. "We're sorry we're essential," chanted railway workers in 1973.

So long as Trudeau led a minority government, inflation ceased to be an issue for him. Instead of wrestling inflation to the ground, he now insisted that the problem was imported. He had a case. Huge Russian wheat purchases in 1972 explained soaring food prices. Arab discovery of the Organization of Petroleum-Exporting Countries or OPEC led to huge increases in energy costs in 1973–74. Another explanation came from J.K. Galbraith, the renowned Canadian-born Harvard economist. Giant corporations and big unions, he claimed, could set prices and wages to suit themselves, at whatever cost to the rest of the world. As a self-confessed "socialist," Galbraith's answer was government controls. The U.S. president, Richard M. Nixon, was an unlikely convert. In August, 1971, Nixon imposed a ninety-day wage and price freeze, followed by government-enforced restraint on wages, prices, rents and profits. While the measures provoked a storm of controversy, politicians noted that Nixon had no trouble winning re-election in 1972. No one noticed the dirty tricks.

Nixon's success helped convert Canada's Conservatives. Their leader, Robert Stanfield, began talking of a ninety-day freeze as a device to break inflationary expectations. So did John Young, when his much-abused Prices and Incomes Commission finally reported. Support for controls was not uniquely Conservative. Galbraith espoused them as a "socialist." So did all three of the NDP premiers, led by Manitoba's Ed Schreyer. The Toronto *Star* embraced the idea of a ninety-day freeze with its usual single-minded enthusiasm. The Liberals, however, claimed to be dead opposed. The minister of finance, John Turner, declared controls unnecessary; André Raynauld, chairman of the Economic Council, called them "an expression of despair." Far from succeeding, critics insisted, the U.S. had abandoned controls as unworkable. So had the British.

Organized labour was as adamant as the Liberals: nothing could interfere with free collective bargaining. When David Lewis, as NDP leader and a veteran labour lawyer, offered the CLC's 1972 convention some avuncular advice about moderating demands and concentrating on the gap between the poorest workers and the better off, he was heard in stony silence. As a minority government, the Liberals had good reason to cultivate trade unionists. To put his humiliating 1972 near-defeat behind him, Trudeau decided to give the people what they wanted, from a little glamour at Sussex Drive to lower taxes. With NDP support, the government introduced bread and milk subsidies and held down domestic oil prices. Too late to make a decisive difference, the Liberals finally promised a full-scale, publicly-owned oil company.

Whatever bankers, Tories and civic moralists might argue, the Trudeau minority made Canadians happier than the Trudeau majority. Sensing a trap by the summer of 1973, David Lewis began seeking a pretext for an election. Forgetting that the Liberals got credit for NDP policies, other party leaders and M.P.s resisted. When dissolution finally came in the spring of 1974, the Liberals controlled the timing. In his 1974 budget, John Turner mixed popular tax cuts, the 1972 Tory promise to index tax exemptions, and a rich helping of the "corporate welfare" Lewis had denounced. Trapped by their principles, the NDP had to vote out the government. Then, unable to explain precisely why they had knocked out so popular a government, Lewis's campaign was effectively sidelined, while the Liberals attacked Stanfield's proposal for a

Nixon-style ninety-day freeze. Despite ritual endorsement by the CLC's 1974 convention, delegates gave the Lewis a cool reception. On July 8, he and half the NDP caucus lost their seats and Trudeau had a new majority.

Victory for Trudeau was more than a vindication of shrewd tactics; it was also an opportunity for the Liberals to rebuild the bridges to the labour movement that had collapsed half a century before. In his history of the NDP-Labour relationship, Gad Horowitz had warned that the new party would have about fifteen years to prove itself. Union leaders were success-oriented; if the NDP experiment did not pay off, they would look elsewhere. The 1974 election was such a moment. Unionists poured public and private criticism on the NDP. John Munro, the Liberal labour minister, made discreet overtures. A new Canada Labour Relations Council offered union leaders a forum, with business and government, to explore such problems as strife in the Post Office or the perennial trouble in Canada's grain export system. Federal funds would support union education efforts. Elderly union officials could retire to dignified positions in the federal government.

While Munro discreetly set out to corral union votes and more of his colleagues caught their breath, prices started to soar. In 1974, inflation rose to 12.3 percent; experts warned that double-digit inflation could be a fixture. Union demands and the strikes to back them up increased dramatically. Governments tried to set an example of restraint by holding back public-sector wages. Alberta's 18,000 civil servants defied the law in a two-day walkout. Ontario government workers won major concessions two days before the deadline for an illegal strike. Faced with a new Common Front in 1975, this time limited to hospital workers, the Quebec government surrendered after a few days of strikes. Federal grain handlers refused concessions until Munro flew to Vancouver to give the union what it wanted.

By 1975, even NDP governments were in trouble with their employees. To gain concessions, Saskatchewan civil servants staged two days of "study sessions." In British Columbia, staggering under a cyclical decline in demand for its forest products, unemployment soared. The Woodworkers had prudently avoided a strike by settling for an extra $1 an hour. Eager to prove their militancy, the rival Pulp and Paper Workers and the Canadian Paperworkers struck for $1.50. The result was a crippling summer-long strike. On October 7, Dave Barrett's NDP government did what it had condemned predecessors for doing: it summoned the legislature and ended not only that strike but also two others that had closed supermarkets and threatened propane supplies. Union officials and the B.C. Federation of Labour professed outrage; privately many union members were grateful. The Woodworkers union, in particular, was fed up with being victimised by the ambitions of rival unions in the woods.

Until 1974, Pierre Elliott Trudeau had occasionally included controls among his inflation-fighting options. In the campaign, however, he had mocked Stanfield's control program as "a proven disaster looking for a place to happen." "They won't freeze prices and profits," he warned audiences, "So what are they going to freeze? Your wages." Crowds cheered. With a clear majority, Trudeau's options were again open. Suddenly, Canada's inflation problem was no longer imported or due to a shortage of supply; increasingly the cause was "cost-push" or, more specifically, inflationary wage demands. Using the links Munro had developed, Turner urged CLC leaders to accept voluntary guidelines – 8 percent for wage demands in 1976. The Congress was embarrassed. It remembered the hostility provoked in 1969 when it had bluntly rejected restraint. Instead the CLC offered support, on terms Turner was not likely to accept: higher pensions, rent controls, regulation of gas and oil prices, full employment and a guarantee that real wages would rise.

Turner's budget on June 23, 1975, was the government's answer: while he criticized controls, Turner attacked wage demands as the inflation villain. Other ministers echoed the message. "Today's wages can kill our competitiveness and, with it, our prosperity," Alastair Gillespie, the energy minister, told directors of the Canadian National Exhibition in August. If union leaders failed to show courage and statesmanship, he added, "they must know that their failure to show this kind of leadership is a monumental sellout of the Canadian future." An affluent audience applauded uproariously.

To help make its point, the government got some useful public relations help from an honest but outspoken unionist. That summer, the 20,000 members of the Canadian Union of Postal Workers again paralysed the postal service to fight for a 30-hour week and a 71-percent pay increase. Pestered by a reporter, CUPW leader Joe Davidson insisted that the public understood the workers' demands. "But what if they don't?" demanded the reporter. "Then to hell with the public," answered an exasperated Davidson.

On September 10, John Turner quit. Perhaps he felt frustrated in his career; ostensibly his views on how to combat inflation had been rejected. On October 14, at the end of a Thanksgiving weekend, Canadians were warned to stand by for a message from the prime minister. On newsstands, the current *Maclean's* carried an interview in which Trudeau repeated his old arguments against controls. The television message was different. Inflation had become intolerable. The answer, after all, was controls. For 2.3 million workers in large private firms and as many as 2 million in the public sector, no one would be allowed wage increases over 8 percent for inflation plus 2 percent for productivity, with an upper maximum of $2,400, plus concessions to the lower-paid. Price rises must be justified by increased costs. A new Anti-Inflation Board would identify offenders and a special administrator would roll back excessive wages and prices and enforce rulings with stiff fines. In the ensuing weeks, clouds of announcements, appointments, clarifications, regulations and exemptions poured out of Ottawa. A former Liberal minister, Jean-Luc Pépin, would chair the board; Donald Tansley, a tough official who had learned his trade in Saskatchewan's CCF government, would be the administrator.

Canadians responded to the Trudeau programme with shock, anxiety and relief. As in October, 1970, people wanted action. To be sure, commentators recalled Trudeau's warnings that controls would affect wages more than prices. As if to confirm the warning, business responded with cautious approval. With the exception of Quebec, which insisted on creating its own structure as a gesture of autonomy, and with nervous reservations from NDP premiers, nine provincial governments invited the new AIB to apply the programme to their employees.

As minister of labour, John Munro could intimidate the CLC with threats to act on the misleading but impressive-looking statistics on money sent out of Canada by international unions. However, his influence vanished when the Trudeau government decided to introduce comprehensive wage and price controls in the autumn of 1975. (Jacob Martin)

The loudest exception to the approving chorus was organized labour. For once, the CLC was pushed by its affiliates. If voluntary restraints had been unacceptable, mandatory controls were an abomination. The one unquestionable service North American unions provided their members was collective bargaining. Whatever the talk of solidarity or a "movement," most union members paid dues to get benefits. Even promoters of "social unionism" understood that reality. Yet, in a single unheralded blow, Ottawa had virtually abolished unionism's central role. What else could there be but outrage?

Some of it was directed at the NDP. Though Ed Broadbent, the acting federal leader, and Stephen Lewis, NDP leader of the opposition in Ontario, greeted the Trudeau announcement with appropriate indignation, where the NDP held power, it had approved. "With all [their] warts and imperfections," Ed Schreyer had stated during the 1974 campaign, "… guidelines are better than no guidelines at all." In Regina, the NDP government created a Public Sector Price and Compensation Board and ran it more flexibly than the AIB, but Allan Blakeney made no concession to indignant unionists: "As a socialist, I believe in planning our economy. I know of no democratic socialist who does not favour economic planning. This includes incomes policy." In British Columbia, where Barrett had called an election in the wake of his back-to-work legislation, union anger at his support of the AIB was discreetly muted. Other causes – notably a government that had tried too much too fast, and the disappearance of competing right-wing parties – ensured a Social Credit victory under W.A.C. Bennett's son, Bill. Labour militants insisted, without much evidence, that a more pro-union NDP would have won.

Alienated from its own political party, CLC leaders found themselves with strange allies. Right-wing economists, inspired by Milton Friedman of the University of Chicago, had their own explanation of uncontrolled inflation. Instead of big corporations and unions, as Galbraith claimed, the villain was government itself. Public spending, financed by an expanded money supply, forced prices up. Struggling for arguments in its first official response to the AIB legislation, the Canadian Labour Congress adapted the monetarist critique to Canada. As part of a constitutional challenge to federal wage controls, the CLC mustered an array of academic economists, headed by Grant L. Reuber, a future Tory deputy minister of finance and bank vice-president.

Trudeau himself helped forge an alliance of labour leaders and business when, in an end-of-year interview, he talked about a post-controls Canada in which massive government intervention might still be needed. Perhaps, he mused, a kind of "social corporatism" might evolve, with business, labour and government working as co-operative entities. As bankers and business leaders responded in horror at the prime minister's questioning of the free market, the CLC president, Joe Morris, reminded them that unions had seen the threat first: "no other institution or group in Canada society recognized the danger to democracy that was implicit in the anti-inflation programme." Morris's instinctive response was understandable in a man who associated "corporatism" with Mussolini's Fascism.

More visionary members of the CLC staff had another view. Pulling the CLC's representatives out of the Economic Council of Canada and from Munro's new Canada Labour Relations Council had been a mistake. Maybe "social corporatism" was an opportunity for the Congress to share real power. If the government was determined to set the nation's wages, the CLC must be at the table to represent Canadian workers. By seizing the initiative, the Congress might play the same powerful role enjoyed by central labour bodies in Sweden or West Germany. Within the labour movement, embracing "social corporatism" would not only allow the CLC to put the CNTU and other lesser rivals in their place, it would be able to dictate to its union affiliates instead of doing their bidding. This was the basis for "Labour's Manifesto for Canada," adopted by the 1976 CLC convention at Quebec City with barely a dissenting vote, after Morris heeded delegates' shouts and changed the words "social corporatism" to "social democracy." The fact that a convention dedicated to battling any form of wages policy would vote for an "incomes policy" buried in the document was quite understandable. Neither delegates nor their leaders had read or understood the document and, two years later, it was discreetly buried. As for the prime minister, he had long since reaffirmed his devotion to free enterprise. Labour was left to its lonely protest.

Critics of controls had warned that, whether they were right or wrong, they would be unworkable. The evidence began to accumulate. A few unions rushed settlements under the deadline; others were left waiting. One group of Quebec asbestos workers got a $2.87 raise; others were allowed $1.09. Pépin had promised "rough justice," but rigid enforcement of controls amidst all the complex realities of wage determination proved impossible. Workers at two large garages in Newfoundland had their wages rolled back by 98 cents an hour while employees at smaller garages kept their gains. At Thompson, Manitoba, hard bargaining earned INCO workers an 18 percent raise. The AIB demanded a rollback to 12.9 percent. There was uproar. The union, company, and Premier Ed Schreyer all intervened to insist that the increase maintained an historic relationship with wages of other INCO workers at Sudbury. Moreover, it was also the pattern settlement with other mining operations in northern Manitoba. The rollback threatened an entire industry with crippling labour turnover. The administrator reluctantly gave ground, but he was not dissuaded from fining the Manitoba Liquor Commission $300,000 for overpaying its employees. Such justice was too rough for Schreyer. By 1977, his government had ended its acceptance of the AIB.

For organized labour in Canada, 1976 was a year of shadow-boxing with employers, and futile confrontation with government. Strike time exceeded even the 1975 total, reaching 11.6 million days. Close to a million of them were lost in a national Day of Protest on October 15. Most others were sacrificed to win wage gains which were just as promptly rolled back by the AIB, often with added penalties from the administrator. The CLC's constitutional challenge, claiming that wage and price controls were beyond the powers of a peacetime government, failed miserably before the Supreme Court of Canada.

The Day of Protest, initiated by convention delegates at Quebec City on May 17, became a desperate test of the CLC's prestige. B.C.'s labour board announced that protest action was legal; in Ontario and elsewhere, such strikes were illegal. After a nervous day, Congress officials announced that 1,054,744 workers had joined the protest, and breathed easier when the media accepted the statistic. Unions like the Steelworkers and the Auto Workers, whose leaders had been most sceptical about a general strike, loyally did their share and paid the price in fines and dismissals for illegal walkouts. Others, like CUPE, whose delegates had spearheaded the militant resolutions at the CLC's May convention, were less visible in October. One thing was certain: the experiment would not soon be repeated. In 1977, labour disruptions in Canada cost less time than in any year since 1961.

Only in Quebec did the anti-controls struggle achieve any success and the message was buried in all the forces that led René Lévesque and his Parti Québécois to power on November 22, 1976. With or without controls, most of organized labour was committed to the PQ, though only the Quebec Federation of Labour offered an official endorsement. Louis Laberge coyly avoided committing himself to separation: "I am a Québécois and I am in favour of

Faced with the Trudeau government controls program, Canadian workers were torn between their concern for rising inflation and warnings from their union leaders that the Anti-Inflation Board would affect wages more than prices. The Canadian Labour Congress organized a succession of events during 1976, culminating in a Day of Protest on October 14, when almost a million Canadian workers left their jobs for a day. (Canadian Union of Public Employees)

telling the federal government to mind its own business, and leave Quebec's concerns alone." Early in 1977, on the claim of following an independent economic policy, the new government cancelled the enforcement provisions of the Quebec version of the AIB.

By then, Ottawa was also looking for a way out. By the end of 1976, the federal government boasted that the annual cost-of-living increase had fallen to 7.5 percent, well within the goal of 8 percent inflation. Critics answered that the main reason was that food prices had risen only 2.7 percent and that, for the most part, they had been exempt from the controls programme. Meanwhile business analysts complained that uncertainty about government policy had seriously slowed investment in Canada. Unemployment pushed upward to reach 7.5 percent by the end of the year and 8.5 percent by the end of 1977. By March, 1978, more than a million Canadians were hunting for work. In the second year of controls, far from falling to the planned 6 percent, inflation climbed to 9 percent. The world passed judgement on Canada's economy and ruled that the Canadian dollar was worth only 90 cents U.S. and falling.

However badly Canada's business and political leaders had failed in their struggle with inflation, they had one success: a hostile, resentful labour movement had been pinned as the national scapegoat for inflation, and now it would be blamed for the recession that followed. The public's own employees bore the brunt. Huge ads financed by the right-wing National Citizens' Coalition spread the notion that bargaining and strikes had earned civil servants huge salaries and inflation-indexed pensions. In fact federal employees paid hard cash for secure pensions and their salaries, except for the lowest-paid and mainly female job classifications, had fallen behind the private sector. In politics, facts made little difference. The Trudeau government responded by announcing that future salary settlements would be governed by ACTC – "Average Comparability of Total Compensation." Among the by-products was a long, bitter strike by government clerks in the winter of 1980. The private sector's preference for underpaying women, just as much as "rug-ranking" and fetching the coffee, prolonged a needless strike.

It was a sad warning of times to come.

CHAPTER 27

Recession and Hard Times

In launching its anti-inflation programme in 1975, the Trudeau government made a shrewd political calculation: protests from furious labour leaders could be safely ignored. Isolated from public opinion and even from its own rank and file, the CLC's campaign had little impact. Pollsters offered the citizenry a mischievous but revealing question: what did they most fear – big government, big business or big labour? By the mid-70s, the usual answer was labour, with government second.

The reasons were sadly clear. In Canada's peaceable kingdom, labour was no sweetheart. After reflection, business had become almost as alarmed at the Trudeau government's anti-inflation techniques as the CLC, but new lobbying organizations, such as the Business Council on National Issues (BCNI), and even the more strident Canadian Federation of Independent Business, applied their pressure discreetly. Meanwhile unionists marched, waved placards, shouted slogans and revelled in headlines and photo opportunities. Organized labour had squarely opposed the only solution Ottawa had offered to inflation but the reason – defending the principle of free collective bargaining – was not particularly convincing to a public that believed, on the whole, that there was too much striking and too much struggle. The messy, unpredictable phenomenon called freedom had never entirely appealed to Canadians.

There certainly were a lot of strikes in the mid-1970s. In 1966, a record of 6,178,000 days lost to strikes had been sufficient to launch the Woods Task Force. In six of the ten years of the 1970s, the strike record was worse, reaching 11.6 million days in 1976. Critics complained that only Italy had a worse record. Union sympathizers answered that Australia, where most strikes were illegal,

In an era of growing social conservatism, Canadian labour leaders showed little sign in the eighties of turning their backs on radical courses, even at some cost to the allegiance of their members. Bob White, Canadian UAW director, was a strong supporter of the peace movement although many of his members believed that defence contracts would create jobs. UAW loyalty to White was cemented, however, by his shrewd bargaining tactics and his union's idealistic heritage. (United Automobile Workers)

was third in strike-days, and that Canada lost a lot more time because of industrial illness and injury. Bargaining in inflationary times was tough. Normally, nineteen out of twenty collective agreements were settled without a strike or other disruption. In 1973, it took a strike to settle 18.3 percent of major settlements. That was not because unions were jumping the gun. In the 1969–73 period, only 14 percent of negotiations dragged on for over ten months; in 1973, 28 percent took longer than that.

Most veteran negotiators had welcomed the cool caution of Dean Woods and his task force; now even veterans began talking of the need for fundamental changes. Increasingly, union members refused to ratify agreements and sent negotiators back for more. "Employers can hardly be expected to make a serious final offer," warned Shirley Goldenberg, McGill University's expert in labour relations, "if this offer is likely to become a floor for future bargaining." William Kelly, the former railway unionist who had emerged as Labour Canada's best mediator, argued that the adversarial system might not be suited for the public service. Faced with uncompromising militants in union ranks, he and others began to argue that union bargaining committees should be able to reach settlements without reference to the union membership. A fresh panacea was "final offer selection," with an arbitrator free only to pick one side's last proposal. Another formula, "Med-arb," led from mediation not to a strike but to compulsory arbitration.

A seemingly more radical notion emerged in the late sixties, dragging old roots behind it. Assorted forms of "industrial democracy" surfaced in both radical pamphlets and business magazines. A phrase that simultaneously included Mackenzie King's "employee representation plans," Yugoslav workers' control, German "co-determination," American profit-sharing and British guild socialism was easier to debate than apply. Advocates ranged from anarchists, promoting tiny co-operative workshops, to the uranium millionaire, Stephen Roman, whose version included abandoning unions. Government officials, professors, and occasional union leaders and business executives toured Europe to ascertain the secret of labour peace and productivity. In their baggage they brought home schemes for worker-directors, job enrichment, shop floor consultation and an all-enveloping term, "Quality of Working Life" or QWL.

American innovators repackaged an old idea of letting workers buy into capitalism: ESOP or Employee Stock Option Plans. Surely if workers had even a tiny share of ownership they would have a commitment to the common welfare. While some unions were captivated, others warned members that no management would allow them to gain control or even a respectable influence. Common sense reminded workers that, if their enterprise went broke, employees would lose their savings as well as their job.

Like most prophets, enthusiasts discovered that their way was hard. Employers feared a whittling away of their prerogatives, unions suspected a trick to undermine their influence, and both sides felt more comfortable with their traditional adversarial culture. Moreover, reformers seldom recognized that unions in Canada had secured "industrial democracy" through grievance procedures and contract bargaining. The enthusiasm of some CLC staffers for "social corporatism" survived as little more than an embarrassing footnote. The most significant union response to the notion of industrial democracy was the Solidarity Fund (*Fonds de solidarité*) created by Louis Laberge's Quebec Federation of Labour in 1982–83 with enthusiastic backing of the Parti Québécois government as a device to save or create jobs for union members.

The real problems of the Canadian economy in the 1970s could not be solved either by scapegoating labour or devising manifestos. American insistence on borrowing to finance the war in Vietnam, two oil price shocks in 1973 and 1979, desperate borrowing at extortionate rates by poorer nations, among them members of the Communist bloc, and the rise of the Pacific rim as an industrial power changed the terms of world trade. In the seventies, multinational corporations used their global strategies to move mass production from North America to countries with cheap labour, nearby natural resources, and minimal environmental constraints. By focussing on engineering as well as entrepreneurialism, Japan surpassed European and North American competitors in their own market while shrewdly protecting their own home base. Japanese theories of management, earnestly if inadequately studied, seemed to suggest that workers could be made loyal, productive and happy despite a level of unionization only slightly higher than in the United States.

While the economic problems of the decade had a global dimension, Canada had some special features of its own. One was a traditional dependence on natural resources, the most price-sensitive component of world trade. Another was an acute lack of indigenous research and development, a by-product of branch-plant forms of industrialization. More important than most people could ever recognize at the time was demography: after the huge natural growth in the 1950s, Canadian birth-rates had collapsed, nowhere more so than in Quebec. Birth control and smaller families encouraged women to stay at work; easy divorce, inadequate support payments, and the impact of inflation on family incomes forced them to stay there. In a single decade, women's share of the Canadian workforce grew from 29 to 40 percent. In 1957, the Gordon Commission had predicted ten million Canadians in the labour force by 1980; when the year arrived, there were twelve million.

To a degree that few contemporaries appreciated, Canada's economy achieved miracles in job-creation in the 1970s. Although employment in the resource and manufacturing sectors had shrunk or stabilized, paid employment rose from 6,839,000 in 1970 to 9,648,000 in 1977, a net growth of 2.8 million jobs, the great majority of them in services and information-handling. Women, in particular, were absorbed in offices and in human services to the young, the sick and the elderly. If productivity failed to keep pace with the investment, this was not due to the laziness of affluent youth but to their excessive availability.

Even unions felt the impact of new information technology, as their resources were diverted to acquire computers and people to operate them. Union researchers found themselves armed with a powerful new tool. Media relations and public information were transformed. Ambitious unions used the new technologies of desktop publishing to replace mimeographed newsletters and grimy newsprint with glossy four-colour magazines to meet the expectations of their members. Labour hired more staff to provide members with expertise in a host of new areas, from workplace health and safety to pay equity and sexual harassment.

Denouncing society's preoccupation with materialism and growth was a perennial occupation for radicals and intellectuals. A sudden preoccupation with threats to the "ecology," best symbolized by the Club of Rome's 1972 bestseller *The Limits of Growth*, not only prepared rich countries for manipulations by the world oil cartel, but also popularised the hitherto unfashionable view that sensible human beings should be content with less. Such views were most popular among those who had already achieved wealth and comfort, but they also undermined the faith among less favoured folk that they were entitled to seek more for themselves and their children. Sam Gompers's slogan of "more" became a little uncomfortable in a labour movement accustomed to find itself close to the vanguard of intellectual trends. Linked to the no-growth ideology was an even more pervasive condemnation of the side-effects of technology and science. Asbestos, once valued as a saviour from the scourge of fire, turned out to be a prime cause of cancer. Nuclear power, once a seeming salvation for regions without coal, oil or hydro potential, joined mercury, DDT, poly-chlorinated biphenyls (PCBs) and a host of other products and processes that threatened the natural environment and human health.

The anti-growth and anti-technology movements offered both benefits and problems for working Canadians. The environmental movement made it easier to press for industrial health and safety legislation in Ottawa and the provinces. Consumer legislation improved the quality and safety of cars, home appliances and the artifacts of a consumer society, as well as adding to their cost. Legislation led to complex regulations, and officials (often unionized) to enforce them. Rising incomes buffered the effects of inflation, but they also drew working people into higher tax brackets and added more of them to the traditional critics of public spending. Personal income taxes bore a rising share of the costs of government while the corporate share dwindled.

More than their American neighbours, Canadians had always expected strong government initiatives, from the rescue of bankrupt railways in 1919 to the creation of Petro-Canada in 1975. Canada's universal Medicare programme, completed in 1967, soon offered a proud contrast to the greed-ridden anarchy of the American health-delivery system. Yet inflation, rising deficits and a pervasive sense of disillusionment began to sour public faith in government. The postwar consensus about full employment and social justice began to fragment in the 1970s. "One of the problems of being a social democratic government," Manitoba's Ed Schreyer confessed, "is the tremendous expectations as opposed to what can be accomplished." In the autumn of 1977, Manitoba voters united behind a hard-line Conservative assault on taxes and social-welfare spending to end Schreyer's eight-year term in power. Angry that Schreyer had not intervened to help them win a couple of hard-fought strikes, unionists took credit for a 4 percent drop in NDP support.

Across Canada, governments faced a similar mood of resentment at rising taxes, frustration that demands were not met, and exasperation that even such traditional public services as the Post Office worked so badly. In contrast with the ebullient sixties, governments cut services and raised taxes in a seemingly futile struggle with inflation. Disillusioned by the failures of Keynesianism and ideologically drawn to free-market arguments, economists began to identify the state, not unions or corporations, as the prime source of inflation and economic failure. Regulations, public enterprise and costly social programmes had diverted resources which, neo-conservatives insisted, the market could use more wisely. Less than two centuries after his death in 1790, Adam Smith's ideas seemed reborn.

As usual, Canadian opinion moved more cautiously than the emotional groundswells that swept Margaret Thatcher's ultra-Conservatism to power in Great Britain in 1979 and Ronald Reagan to the White House in 1980. However, Canadian politicians felt the trend and moved to follow it. In 1976, Ottawa made Unemployment Insurance harder to get. A year later, full federal support for the costs of Medicare and post-secondary education was curtailed; at the same time, provinces won the freedom to divert the money to roads, tax cuts or whatever their own priorities dictated. Rich provinces and poor cut university spending, closed hospital wards and forgot about promises to create new day-care centres. Physicians practising under Medicare began to forestall a threatened fall in their incomes by "balance billing" – charging patients the difference between Medicare payments and their own fee schedule. Some scarce specialists began opting out of provincial health insurance, leaving patients to claim their costs.

When politicians and the public attacked government, their target was often the millions of beneficiaries of the public payroll. By 1976 more than a third of working Canadians were employed by a government or a crown corporation; the great majority enjoyed union protection. A decade of public-sector strikes had shown people that they could survive without hitherto vital services. A garbage collectors' strike meant mounds of plastic bags in a public park. Private courier services circumvented postal disruptions; transit strikes inspired car pools. School boards, municipal councils and even higher levels of government learned that being tough sometimes paid political and financial benefits. Ottawa waited out a seven-week postal strike in 1975. That winter, Toronto high school teachers trudged picket lines for two frigid months, while tax revenues accumulated in school board coffers. Increasingly, strikers were more likely than politicians to be blamed for disruption and costs of a work stoppage.

The public mood encouraged governments to squeeze rights they had granted a decade before. In 1977, the Ontario legislature ended a transit strike after only three days. Employees who had angrily defied a similar law in 1975 for five days sensed the public mood and dutifully returned to work. In 1978, the Canadian Union of Postal Workers started a legal strike which Parliament immediately ended. When Jean-Claude Parrot, Joe Davidson's successor as head of CUPW, breathed angry defiance, he and other leaders were jailed. When the postal union demanded that the CLC call a general strike, the request was politely ignored. Congress leaders seethed at a government bargaining position as rigid as CUPW's, but they, too, could read the public mood.

The Anti-Inflation Board and its agencies died in 1978, months before its due term, and without reference to Trudeau's 1976 promises that all elements of society, including labour, would be consulted. The reason was simple: another of the dramatic reversals that marked the Trudeau style. A midsummer visit to Bonn, when Canada became the newest and junior member of the annual economic summit of major powers, had exposed Trudeau to the new orthodoxy: controls were unnecessary because a free economy was self-regulating.

Market-driven self-regulation functioned in a series of tides, rising and receding. By 1977, recession was in progress. From 1976, as the stock markets that gauged the western industrialized world began to slide, jobs began to vanish. Investors looked elsewhere for places to put their money. By the winter of 1977, 944,000 Canadians were officially out of work, the highest rate of unemployment since 1940. A year later, the total broke through a million, 9.7 percent of the workforce. In Newfoundland, where one in four was out of work, and in other hard-hit regions, thousands gave up the search for a job and accordingly vanished from the unemployment statistics into an unmeasured category of "discouraged workers."

Mass unemployment was an enemy modern unionism could not fight. Collective bargaining depended on law and the labour market. Neither was helpful. In an age-old strategy, governments began bribing employers to stay in business and create jobs. They had no patience with union organizers, seeking exploited workers. Strong unions with healthy finances, luck and skill, could sometimes prevail. Feminist organizations helped the Auto Workers win bargaining rights for employees of the tiny Fleck Manufacturing plant at Clinton, Ontario. Employees at Fotomat, Radio Shack and a scattering of small fabricating plants joined the Steelworkers after managers ignored their legal rights. Once organized, of course, nothing could prevent firms from going out of business and leaving workers and the public to blame the union.

Except in Quebec where the Péquiste government banned strike-breaking by "replacement workers" after the particularly violent strike at Robin Hood Mills, and in the few provinces where NDP governments had made certification easier, Canadian unions seemed close to the limit, with a membership of 40 percent of non-agricultural workers.

Unions could, of course, make a greater effort to attract the huge new female share of the labour force. On the basis of its record in the government-owned telephone systems in western Canada, the Communications Workers finally replaced an employees' association as representative for Bell Canada's operators in Ontario and Quebec – but only as new technology threatened drastic shrinkage of their occupation.

In 1977, the Canada Labour Relations Board ruled that unions could organize each of 7,500 individual bank branches rather than entire systems. Hopes that 150,000 new members might soon be added to labour's ranks faded when the banks turned out to be rich and stubborn adversaries, with automated banking machines as a technological fall-back. Furious threats from the CLC that unions would shift $100 million in deposits made little difference. An independent, strongly feminist Service, Office and Retail Workers' Union of Canada (SORWUC) and the CLC-sponsored Canadian Union of Bank Employees (CUBE) encountered equal frustration and ended their days in bitter wrangling.

Growing unemployment made organizing more difficult. Employees were reminded that loyalty to the company paid bigger dividends than devotion to the union. Employers mobilized workers, and sometimes even their unions, against consumer and environmental legislation that threatened their jobs. Workers for Reed Paper, at Dryden, Ontario, defended the company and their livelihoods when they denounced claims that mercury pollution had devastated a nearby Indian reserve. Unionized glassworkers defended throw-away bottles. Asbestos workers in Quebec and fluoride miners in Newfoundland paid a terrible price in health because of their work, but their homes as well as their jobs were forfeit when crusading environmentalists closed up their industries. In the 1980s there were few other jobs to be had for workers with little formal education and no computer skills.

As always, there were pockets of defiance. In the wake of massive layoffs, low world prices and a growing inventory, International Nickel demanded sweeping concessions in work rules in return for a meagre ten cents an hour. Aware that a strike would be long and possibly futile, Steelworker officials recommended acceptance. Members at Port Colborne agreed; INCO's Sudbury workers voted 61 percent to strike and stayed out for eight and a half months. At the cost of life savings, heavy debt for their union and a dismal year for local businesses, Sudbury's miners had a few gains to show for their defiance. Other members cheered and elected the Sudbury leader, Dave Patterson, as the Steelworkers' district director for Ontario, but few were eager to follow the Sudbury example. Across Canada, strike activity fell back to levels reminiscent of the early 1960s.

In tough times, of course, labour could switch from industrial to political action. It had done so in the 1940s, and again in the Diefenbaker recession, when it helped create the NDP. It could do so again. Normally, ambition might have persuaded Dennis McDermott, the UAW's 56-year-old Canadian director, to seek higher office in his international union. The presidency of the CLC had become little more than a retirement job, but that was the prize McDermott sought and won in 1978.

Ambitious, abrasive and publicity-conscious, McDermott's manner and language often reinforced public stereotypes of the typical labour leader, but paradoxically he was determined to cure fellow-unionists of their "damn the public" attitude. He was not soft-spoken. To help solve unemployment, CLC delegates had voted for a thirty-two-hour work week. McDermott drowned the notion in scorn. For Canadians to work four days when their competitors worked six was economic folly. The INCO strike was simply "stupid." Having endured abuse from CUPW members, McDermott gave his own opinion of "ideological ego-trips and permanent, perpetual obstruction."

Unless labour won public support, McDermott recognized, it could not regain what union members had forfeited in 1974, a strong voice in Parliament. The NDP's decline in 1974 had given the Trudeau government an argument for ignoring unions and such left-wing causes as health insurance, education and the special problems women faced in the workforce. The Liberals had forgotten John Munro's brief gambit towards labour while the Conservatives had become increasingly embarrassed by the "progressive" part of their title. When Joe Clark became leader in 1976, even symbolic gestures to placate labour were forgotten. Clark's innumerable enemies within his party made it clear that he was already suspect as a "red." Canadian conservatism in the 1970s finally became a clone of the American Republican party.

In the circumstances, most of the old arguments for the CLC's political tactics needed to be dusted off. Mobilizing labour's political strength had always been easier said than done. For twenty years, the CLC and most of its affiliates had paid no more and sometimes a lot less than lip-service to the NDP. In Quebec, Laberge's QFL had tied its fortunes to the Parti Québécois. Among the construction unions, some of whose American heads had backed Ronald Reagan, the NDP was one more factor in helping to edge them out of the Congress. The few unions that found the courage and the cash to survey their own members' attitudes soon discovered that few of them had any allegiance to the labour movement's political or social goals nor even to their own elected leaders. Unions were strictly for benefits. Nor had dwindling purchasing power or rising unemployment pushed Canadian workers and their families to the NDP. On the contrary, bad times made them frightened,

Ed Broadbent gets some advice from Tommy Douglas as he prepares to speak to the NDP's 1975 convention. The son of an Oshawa General Motors employee, Broadbent was the first NDP leader to have no direct links to the CCF. (Ed Boyer)

conservative and more responsive to messages from the past than about the future.

When a federal election was called for May 22, 1979, the CLC's political effort was still on the drafting table, but union financial support enabled the NDP's Ed Broadbent to wage a federal campaign that came close in professionalism and scale to those of his richer rivals. Broadbent's message – the need for a publicly-controlled industrial strategy – was strong enough to recover the ground lost in 1974 and, by the accidents of the electoral system, to move the 26 New Democrats to a key position in a Parliament of minorities. Most workers and their families voted Liberal but others, with their richer neighbours, helped make Joe Clark prime minister.

Within eight months, the Clark government was a might-have-been. Undermined by long months of making plans and the Alberta government's refusal to compromise on energy policy, even with its friends, the Conservatives made few friends and too many enemies. From September, opinion polls guaranteed a Liberal victory and they continued unswerving through a bungled vote of confidence, a dissolution and a winter election. New Democrats suffered from an empty treasury and benefited from a stronger union "Parallel Campaign" that endeavoured to canvass workers where they worked. The impact was modest but helpful: the NDP emerged with 31 seats and 21 percent of the vote, although Pierre Elliott Trudeau had emerged from retirement to win his third and final absolute majority.

The circumstances of 1980 were special. A leader who had sworn to unite Canadians across the barriers of linguistic and cultural division found Quebec on the verge of a referendum that would allow René Lévesque to negotiate his province out of Confederation. Virtually without voice in the new Liberal government, western Canada heard its own separatist voices. Instead of the bridgeable differences of class and economic interest, Canada was torn by great gulfs of cultural and regional hostility. Trudeau's solution was characteristically personal: he would unite Canadians around his own goal of constitutional reform. He would enshrine his passion for individualism in a Charter of Rights and Freedoms that would forever undermine the collectivism that he had never accepted either in the "wigwam" of Quebec nationalism or on the picket lines of Canadian unionism.

The stage was set by the May 20 Quebec referendum. The province's unions officially and massively supported the "oui" demanded by the Parti Québécois; their members, surveyed as closely as any electorate in Canadian history, seem to have narrowly voted "non." No more than other Canadians in 1980 were Quebec workers eager to run new risks. For the next two years, Ottawa seemed transfixed by constitution-making. It was a preoccupation that organized labour, like most Canadians, stubbornly refused to share. This was an understandable mistake. Entrenching the right to strike, or even tidying the jurisdictional tangle of labour laws, meant participating in a game dominated by lawyers, professors and politicians. Nor was the NDP much help. Having endorsed principles – patriation, an entrenched bill of rights, and a strong central government – that the CCF had urged as long ago as 1933 and which Trudeau included in his proposals, Ed Broadbent and his caucus found themselves sidelined, as women, Native people and NDP provincial governments campaigned for more. Apart from a bland assurance from Bryce Mackasey (now a Liberal backbencher) that labour's rights were fully covered by the "right of association," any threats from an individualistic Charter to union collectivism were scarcely mentioned.

There was another reason labour ignored constitution-making: the economy. Canada could not escape the worst of the deepening economic depression that had struck the United States and most of Europe by the early 1980s. Even before the victories of Thatcher and Reagan, the new monetarist orthodoxy had taken hold, with high interest rates as its most visible sign. Joe Clark's downfall had coincided with interest rates that soared to an unprecedented 21 percent for house mortgages. Small businesses, home-buyers, and almost anyone who depended on credit faced disaster. Working people, with twenty-five years of rising real incomes, suffered a double disaster. From 1975 to 1982, their real purchasing power fell $33.00 a week – dropping Canadian wage-earners from second to fourteenth place among the industrialized nations. Now they faced a recession that went deeper than any since 1938.

Monetarists had not set out to punish home-buyers or even workers; they simply insisted that credit had to be squeezed to bring inflation down. By the same token, breaking a horse's leg keeps it from running away but it is not much use at ploughing time. After reaching 13 percent in 1981, inflation slowly fell but the economy fell with it. Thanks to policies set largely in Washington, reinforced by the scramble of banks to recover debts from dubious creditors, business and labour began to hurt. In March, 1982, 1.2 million Canadians hunted for work; a year later there were 1,658,000 unemployed – and 335,000 more had given up a hopeless search. Interest rates, foreign competition and the 1979 oil price surge hit the auto industry. Chrysler Corporation skidded into bankruptcy only to be rescued by governments on both side of the border, at the expense of drastic concessions by its unionized employees. The presence of the UAW president, Douglas Fraser, on the Chrysler board was a reminder that industrial democracy could be part of a corporate strategy – when the corporation was sinking for the third time. Once it had recovered, Chrysler no longer had room for a unionist on its board.

Concessions to Chrysler encouraged other employers to demand their share. In basic steel, mining, manufacturing and even in the service industries, U.S. unions bartered contract concessions to save jobs. Paid holidays began to slip away. Seniority rules were bent. Overtime restrictions – paradoxically at a time of soaring unemployment – were eased. Two-tier wage structures allowed companies to hire new workers at far cheaper rates than older employees. Canadians locals were urged to copy. Resistance was hard. At INCO, miners struck again in 1981 and then returned to work only to be laid off and collect Unemployment Insurance until vast stockpiles of nickel found buyers. Stelco workers faced a strike both sides clearly expected. It took months and millions of dollars from the Steelworkers' strike fund before Stelco felt enough pain to settle – and only as a prelude to mass layoffs. For the workers, it was a victory of the spirit, not the flesh. Of 8.8 million days lost from strikes in 1981, the Stelco strike represented 1.5 million.

Union leaders put as bold a face as they could on the bargaining crisis. CLC delegates in 1982 pledged to oppose pay cuts or concessions. "We're going to be bloodied," warned McDermott, "but we cannot afford to have a crack in the dam." Affiliates were commanded to bargain for shorter hours and affirmative action for women, while the CLC would support Unemployment Action Centres and organize a "March for Jobs." "Members join unions to make gains," insisted Bob White, McDermott's successor as head of the Canadian UAW, "they don't need a union to make concessions." Reality was a little less militant. In fact, most contracts settled that year lost their COLA clauses and fell far behind inflation. Plant closings and mass layoffs cut into union ranks. In 1982, for the first time in twenty years, Canadian union membership fell – from 3.62 million to 3.56 million members. Between 1980 and 1983, the United Steelworkers lost a quarter of their Canadian members; the UAW fell by a fifth. Falling income forced cuts in union staff and services. In 1983, 98 percent of major collective agreements were settled without a strike.

The debilitating divisions that had helped cripple Canadian unions in the 1930s reappeared. The long, festering conflict between the CLC and its construction affiliates ended with the formation on May 1, 1982, of a new Canadian Federation of Labour (CFL) with 213,000 members. James McCambly, a veteran British Columbia union leader, became president. Another hundred thousand members, including the Carpenters, left the CLC but remained independent. Officially, the schism was due to the failure of the Congress to discipline the QFL, but there were other grievances, from the CLC's commitment to the NDP to Congress insistence that convention delegates be chosen by union locals and not by union headquarters, as was the AFL-CIO custom. In turn, that reflected an underlying grievance among conservative craft unionists: a congress in the hands of nationalists, militants and assorted troublemakers who had nothing in common with the venerable, dignified and generally affluent crafts. The new Federation's founding convention, in May, 1982, was blessed not only by a galaxy of U.S. union leaders but also by Pierre Elliott Trudeau, rejoicing in a rare ovation from a union audience. The CFL's constitution solemnly proclaimed political neutrality and a "pro-active, responsive unionism." "There are a lot of people," claimed McCambly, "saying we were on the right track."

Divided, falling in strength, and seemingly unable to protect itself or its members, organized labour had become a scapegoat for an economic disaster it had not caused and could not prevent.

CHAPTER 28
Levelling the Playing Field

For a century, a Canadian labour movement dominated by its international unions had frequently been identified with the Americanization of Canada. Corporate executives had raged at Yankee agitators filling honest Canadian heads with thoughts of eight-hour days and paid holidays. Intellectual nationalists had lumped U.S. union bosses with Wall Street capitalists and Hollywood moguls as threats to the Canadian way of life. In the eighties, much of that changed. American culture, capital and politics invaded Canada as never before, but Canada's labour movement – or most of it – found itself a major institutional core of resistance. At stake for the labour movement were not just the jobs that a separate Canadian economy had preserved, but the social programmes, labour legislation and the collectivist values that had made Canada a distinct and valid alternative to the American way.

Embattled and enfeebled, the U.S. labour movement entered the 1980s with barely 18 percent of its work force organized, half the "union density" in Canada, and shrinking annually. The unionized mines, mills and factories of the north-eastern states evolved into a crumbling rust belt as investors sought faster profits in "Sunbelt" states where "right to work" laws guaranteed cheap non-union labour. Unlike Canada, U.S. courts insisted that anything employers said to denounce unions was part of the right of free speech. Certification votes occurred only when the employer was good and ready. Unions had no political voice: Democrats, once labour's party, found union support an embarrassment; nor did backing Ronald Reagan in 1980 save PATCO, the American air controllers' union. When the air traffic controllers staged an illegal strike, Reagan fired them all and crushed the union. The AFL-CIO was helpless.

Unions were different in Canada. While the AFL-CIO was dominated by a self-indulgent gerontocracy, CLC affiliates boasted new leaders. Bob White was still in his early forties when he replaced McDermott as head of the UAW in Canada. In 1983, after Grace Hartman retired, Jeff Rose, a student radical of the 1960s, was chosen to head CUPE. John Fryer of the National Union of Provincial Government Employees, was only a little older. In 1983, at the depth of the recession, Canadian unions signed up 56,000 new members; in 1986, they organized 99,845. By 1987, the Steelworkers, hardest hit of the big industrial unions, had restored its Canadian strength, largely by accepting almost any groups of workers who wanted to affiliate with a strong union.

Canadians lagged on the road to the right. Pierre Elliott Trudeau wound up his 1980 campaign with such a fervent appeal to social justice and economic independence that Liberals captured votes from the NDP. Back in power, the Liberals delighted nationalists and enraged the oil industry with the National Energy program, a bold blueprint for energy self-sufficiency. They even attempted sweeping tax reforms. In 1981, after a few years' hard experience of a right-wing Tory government, Manitobans restored the NDP. Faced with recession and falling revenue, Howard Pawley's government scrapped plans for massive cutbacks and persuaded provincial employees to contribute to a job-creation fund. Once again, social services regained their priority. So did job-creation for Native people in the province's North. In 1985 even the Yukon, last frontier for individualists, unions and Native people, formed a successful coalition and handed power in the territorial legislature to Tony Pennikett and the NDP.

Trends are easier to postpone than divert. By 1981, the symptoms of a right-wing shift were apparent. The business and financial community successfully trashed the Liberals' tax reform and Trudeau fired the finance minister, Allan McEachen. Few Liberals stayed for the fight. Re-elected in 1981, René Lévesque abandoned his social-democratic agenda and began to serve the new French-Canadian business elite his language laws had helped create. By 1982, Conservatives and Social Credit controlled seven of the ten provinces. On April 26, they added an eighth, when Allan Blakeney's NDP suffered a devastating defeat. Faced with strikes by hospital and power workers in the middle of a Saskatchewan winter, Blakeney had legislated a settlement. An outraged labour movement did nothing to save its former friends. It was not only union defectors, of course, who cut the NDP from 44 to 8 seats. Grant Devine, the new Tory premier, made no bones that hard times were coming for socialists and their labour allies.

Fresh from constitution-making, Pierre Elliott Trudeau finally confronted the nationwide recession. Faced with shrinking revenues, mass layoffs, and a rising federal deficit, Trudeau chose to tackle inflation. On June 28, 1982, the government announced that it had abolished federal public-sector bargaining for two years. Workers would have to be satisfied with raises of 6 percent in the first year and 5 percent in the second. Provinces and private employers were urged to follow the "6&5" guidelines, extending them to prices, rents and fees. To underline its policy, Ottawa invited non-union contractors to bid on federal construction projects when local union contract settlements exceeded the guidelines. Most provinces went along. Ontario promptly imposed a limit of 5 percent limit on its wage settlements, and a one-year ban on public-sector strike. British Columbia immediately overrode its collective agreement with government employees. Saskatchewan's Grant Devine ordered that raises be held below inflation to "set a good example." Quebec's PQ government went farther. Blaming the recession and shrinking cash flow, the Péquistes repudiated the generous pay settlements approved in the pre-referendum period of 1980. On January 1, 1983, provincial employees, from professors to ambulance drivers, found themselves with a three-month pay cut of 19 percent.

Reactions were predictable. Business offered grudging approval and complained that the guidelines were too generous to workers; unions cried foul. Dennis McDermott urged the CLC's own economic recipes on the prime minister and, by September, was preaching a "holy war" on the government. Quebec unions dropped their support, public and private, for the Parti Québécois. A new "Common Front" was proclaimed by the CNTU, CEQ and QFL. Thousands of militant unionists tore up their PQ membership cards. The government was dismayed but unmoved. More significantly, members of the militant Social Affairs Federation first announced and then abandoned plans for a general strike. Lévesque, union leaders explained, must not be given the pleasure of standing up for the sick. The wage cuts remained. Realistically, as the recession deepened and layoffs spread, "6&5" began to look like a pretty good raise.

The recession, like the Great Depression, hit the hinterland regions hardest. Resources, the glamour industries of the seventies, faded as world markets collapsed. One thing was different: the answer to the depression had been an activist New Deal and, for Canada, wartime socialism. Now the official remedy for the recession seemed to be a drastic dose of free enterprise, deregulation and a deliberate shift of income to the rich.

Political change in Canada, like the winds, often comes from the West. On June 1, 1983, a new Alberta law subjected hospital workers to compulsory arbitration. Later that year, pleading the impact of recession on the building trades, Alberta's Tory government allowed "double-breasting": companies could spin off non-union subsidiaries to undercut the parent with cheaper wages. Saskatchewan's Tory government came up with a new Trade Union Act that made it harder for unions to strike, imposed heavy fines if they did so illegally, and made it easier for members to undermine union solidarity. Newspaper editors proclaimed that Premier Devine was a better friend of workers than his NDP predecessor.

In British Columbia, Social Credit had regularly talked of axing civil servants and cutting costs but it held power by moderation. Bill Bennett's third victory over the NDP on May 4, 1983, was no exception. No one expected a real change. They were wrong. In July, Bennett summoned the MLAs and presented a legislative menu that could only have been dreamed up by the business-funded Fraser Institute. Bennett's majority proceeded to boost taxes, privatize services, and abolish rent controls and the Human Rights code and the agencies that enforced them. School boards and local councils were stripped of their powers. Civil service unions would no longer be permitted to bargain over transfers, classification, or work hours. A quarter of B.C.'s employees would be fired without regard to seniority. To set an example, the Ministry of Human Resources promptly fired 599 full-time staff, almost all of them child-care workers. Economy was not the sole motive. Much as Duff Pattullo had once wanted to imitate FDR's New Deal, Bill Bennett wanted to show that he could give B.C. a Reagan Revolution. People fought back. A summer-long organizing campaign borrowed the name and the graphics of Lech Walesa's anti-Communist Polish workers' organization. B.C. Solidarity united the elderly, teachers, social workers, human rights defenders and, above all, B.C.'s labour movement. Its protests summoned tens of thousands of marchers to spill over neatly trimmed lawns in front of the Legislature. The climax was an escalating general strike that closed government offices, then schools and threatened, by mid-November, to close down the province. Hours away from a confrontation reminiscent of Quebec in 1972 or Winnipeg in 1919, union leaders met with Bennett at Kelowna. On November 13, they figured they had won all they could: as it made its cuts, the government solemnly agreed to respect seniority.

The Kelowna agreement, accepted by Art Kube, president of the B.C. Federation of Labour, and by Jack Munro of the International Woodworkers, outraged Solidarity's militants. A People's Commission on Alternatives for B.C. had been waiting to take over power. Instead, it insisted, labour leaders had sold out the revolution. Yet, to Kube, Munro and their colleagues, revolution had never been on the agenda. The alternative to compromise was a hopeless battle with an elected government. Solidarity dissolved in bitter recriminations. In 1984, Social Credit attacked unions directly, restricting the right to strike, adding to the rights of union dissenters and forcing open job sites such as Vancouver's Expo 86 to non-union labour. This time, British Columbia unions made their protests alone.

At a time when the recession and its solution both turned on global, if not continental, economics, Canadian unionists seemed the last powerful repository of nationalism. Sometimes nationalism created a team spirit within international unions: Canadian steelworkers took legitimate pride that one of their own, Lynn Williams, had become secretary-treasurer of the international in 1978, and in 1984 Canadian votes made the difference with their overwhelming support when he defeated an American for the presidency. For a Canadian to win the top job in what, until recently, had been the biggest affiliate of the AFL-CIO, was a national achievement, though few Canadians outside the USWA even noticed.

Among international unions, none had seemed more logical than the UAW. A single union fitted an industry dominated by three giant corporations and internationally integrated by the Canada-U.S. Auto Pact. Yet, in the 1980s, the border split the industry and the union. Big cars had been relegated to Canadian auto plants, critics claimed, because the energy crisis had cut sales. Then, when the OPEC cartel cracked and oil prices tumbled, Canadian-made gas-guzzlers were suddenly back in style. Chrysler's van-wagon, also built in Canada, unexpectedly became the success of the decade. In Canada's auto industry, there was no recession in the early 1980s; for Canadians in the UAW, this was

Bob White, flanked by Phil Bennett, ponders the issues during the 1983 negotiations with General Motors that led Canadian members out of the United Auto Workers and into their own union. By coincidence, a National Film Board crew found itself recording an historic moment in Canadian labour history. (Canadian Autoworkers Union)

the time for hard bargaining. UAW leaders in Detroit were appalled. Times were tough for U.S. factories, and locals had no desire to take on the big companies for the sake of their Canadian district. UAW leaders soon learned that Bob White was stubborn, shrewd and lucky. It took White's members a five-week strike in 1982, but Chrysler's Lee Iacocca yielded up to Canadians most of the concessions he had grabbed two years earlier to avoid bankruptcy.

U.S. autoworkers were not pleased. Some 4,500 UAW members had suffered layoffs to help Canadians make their gains. Two years later, as the UAW faced off with General Motors, a similar scenario unrolled. Owen Bieber, the UAW president, settled with GM for profit-sharing and a bonus; White called it a mug's game, since the company, not the union, determined profit levels. Besides, White's members were determined to make gains. And they did, after a two-week strike that forced layoffs of 40,000 U.S. auto workers and left Bieber even angrier than General Motors management. White was angry too. In mid-strike, Bieber had threatened to withdraw his mandate. "I'm an internationalist," White told his Canadian council, "but true internationalism requires us to be in control of our own destiny." UAW leaders were in no mood to make special conditions for what one of them termed "spoiled children from Canada." Though it took months of painful wrangling to settle the property and financial details, the new Canadian Auto Workers was born in 1985 with a strike fund of $35 million – about half their per capita share of the old UAW fund.

The shattering of the UAW as an international left the United Steelworkers as the major international within the Canadian Labour Congress, and the Teamsters and the Carpenters as major unions outside it. Bob White's bold gamble had succeeded because his bargaining strategy had delivered the goods. There were deeper reasons, too. Canadian members were less comfortable than Americans with profit-sharing, they had been less impressed when the UAW president joined the Chrysler board, and they were far less willing than Americans to regard Chrysler president Lee Iacocca as a folk-hero. The noisy, flag-waving patriotism of U.S. labour conventions grated on Canadians, and not simply because it celebrated the Stars and Stripes. There certainly were Canadian unionists who consciously opted for American labour institutions and values but, after 1983, they were more happily identified with the Canadian Federation of Labour.

Canada's Catholic bishops began 1983 by urging the prime minister to embrace job creation as a moral response to the sickness of 1.5 million unemployed. Surely, they urged, the needs of the poor should take priority over the desires of the rich. Trudeau was as scornful of the Catholic hierarchy as were most business leaders. Bishops, he explained, are not very good economists. Instead, he handed Canada's economic troubles to a Royal Commission on the Economic Union, to be headed by his friend and former architect of the AIB, Donald S. MacDonald. Even MacDonald, once a moderate nationalist, may have been surprised that he was propelled so forcefully towards an old but recurrent Canadian nostrum: free trade. Yet, in the new orthodoxy, it was not surprising. Scores of academic economists, recruited by the Commission, communed with the late Adam Smith and emerged clothed in his ancient wisdom. Business lobbyists, better organized and more self-confident than at any time since the twenties, now shared the free-trade faith. The Business Council on National Issues, like its lesser competitors, insisted that, in a world of protectionist trade blocs, it was time for Canada to pocket its pride and make whatever accommodation was needed by the United States. The era of protection, regulation and public enterprise was over.

In the 1980s, this was news that most Canadians were not yet eager to hear. If they had a remedy for Canada's ills, it was simply to get rid of Trudeau, and the polls showed a formidable rise in Conservative support, even at the expense of the NDP. In May, 1983, Tories chose Brian Mulroney to replace Joe Clark as Tory leader. Among delegates, Mulroney's message had been sufficiently clear to attract right-wing Tory leadership aspirants – Peter Pocklington, Michael Wilson, Sinclair Stevens – for the final ballot. Yet Mulroney was no ideologue. His goal was to make the Conservatives as dominant a party as the Liberals had been throughout his lifetime. To do so, he would need a lot of middle-of-the-road votes. To get them, he was ready to support bilingualism in Manitoba, to proclaim Canada's universal social programmes a "sacred trust," and to condemn Bill Bennett's assault on public services, unions, and the poor as extremism.

Brian Mulroney had specialized in industrial relations, and he was a skilled negotiator. In 1983, he was also the man who had just closed down the Iron Ore Company of Canada at the behest of its American owners. Yet he had managed the deed without enraging the workers. It was a feat made easier because Mulroney had grown up the son of an electrician at the *Chicago Tribune*'s paper mill in Baie Comeau. Like other workers' sons in the postwar affluence, he had gone to university and collected professional credentials. Mulroney entered law with a dense network of friends in Quebec's English and French elite. He had dreamed of power and he had admired the Union Nationale because in his boyhood, they had it. That made him a hostile spectator to much of the Quiet Revolution. As a youngster who depended on U.S. investment for his prospects, he had no share of the concern other Canadians felt about American economic power. It had always been good to Brian Mulroney. Mulroney knew, of course, that many Canadians felt differently. In his leadership campaign, he rejected the free-trade nostrums offered by John Crosbie, his Newfoundland rival and Joe Clark's former finance minister. That issue, Mulroney insisted, had been settled in 1911. Such attitudes made it easier for unionists to accept the increasing inevitability of a Tory victory.

The CLC routinely reaffirmed its quarter-century of backing for the NDP, but Ed Broadbent's party had slumped to a mere 11–12 percent in the polls, low enough to jeopardize its official party status. For a lot of Canadians, beating Trudeau was too important to waste a vote on a friendly loser. When Trudeau resigned at the end of February, 1984, Liberal managers looked for a successor who could take Tory votes. Fresh from a Bay Street law office, former finance minister John Turner was the choice. Flushed by a sudden lead in the polls, Turner launched his party into a September 10 election, and promptly presided over a disaster that exceeded even Lester Pearson's 1958 fiasco. Liberals emerged with a mere 40 seats, while the Conservatives swept 211 constituencies and every province. The only other winner, in light of its pre-election gloom, was the NDP, with 18 percent of the vote and 31 seats. Ed Broadbent's residual popularity, and a reminder that "ordinary Canadians" would need friends in the face of a Tory sweep, postponed oblivion for the NDP.

"Ordinary Canadians" could believe that they had little to fear from a Mulroney government. Like the Liberals in 1935 and 1963, the new government soon took credit for post-recession recovery. By May, 1985, unemployment had fallen below 11 percent for the first time since 1982. Dropping the Canadian dollar to an historic low of US$0.70 in the winter of 1986 made it easier to do business in the United States and easier to create jobs in Canada. By April of that year, unemployment was down to 9.6 percent. And, for Tories too, the pleasures of being in power were more important than any ideological agenda of deregulation, privatization and "downsizing" government. Indeed, as a succession of scandals soon revealed, the pleasures of power were too great for some ministers and M.P.s.

For the prime minister, a particular goal was winning something that had eluded every Conservative party leader in the century: a second majority. To

CLC president Shirley Carr was a leader against the Mulroney government's free trade deal with the United States. Union leaders saw that there was no protection in the deal for jobs, collective bargaining, or Canada's network of social programs. (Ontario Federation of Labour)

achieve it, he would be governed by public opinion. When Michael Wilson, the new finance minister, tampered with a "sacred trust" by de-indexing old age security, it took only a few days of uproar from the elderly to reverse the policy. A round of spending cuts was followed by public generosity to any group with a grievance, from drought-ridden farmers to depositors in two bankrupt Alberta banks. Unions found Mulroney a pleasant surprise. The fact that Mulroney's first labour minister, Bill McKnight, was a Saskatchewan farmer created no apparent ideological friction. Indeed the new regime hurried to settle outstanding negotiations with the Public Service Alliance, and even with the abrasive Jean-Claude Parrot of the Postal Workers.

Union leaders were prominent when the new government summoned a National Economic Conference. Funding for a Canadian Labour Market and Productivity Centre, created by the Liberals as a pre-election gesture, was confirmed by Tories, possibly because it was as much a dream of Tom D'Aquino, super-smooth president of the BCNI, as of the CLC's secretary-treasurer, Shirley Carr. When a government task force headed by Claude Forget proposed sweeping cuts to Unemployment Insurance, labour prepared for battle behind a minority report from Nancy Riche of the National Union of Provincial Government Employees. Forget's report was shelved. For all its talk of free enterprise and downsizing, the government proved as susceptible to job-saving investments as its predecessor, provided they were in politically-sensitive regions. While most government jobs went to deserving Tories, CLC president Dennis McDermott was appointed Canada's ambassador to Ireland. His successor, Shirley Carr, was appointed in 1985 and confirmed in 1986: the first woman to head the Canadian Labour Congress. Nancy Riche joined her as an executive vice-president.

Mulroney could not, of course, be blamed for provincial labour laws. Desperate to keep tire plants built by the French-owned, anti-union firm of Michelin, Nova Scotia's Tory government changed its labour law to compel any union seeking certification to win a majority at each of a company's plant. The rule frustrated Bob White's Canadian Autoworkers after two long, costly campaigns to win Michelin workers; with the company threatening to pack up if it got a union, it was surprising that the CAW even came close.

Another employer tactic was to stall a first contract. Even if employers had to recognize a union, nothing obliged them to hurry into a first agreement. The few provinces that imposed a first contract never went beyond a bare-bones agreement. Recruits to the union movement increasingly found that they had little to show for a year of union dues and possibly a six- to twelve-month strike. The Retail, Wholesale and Department Store Union, loser in the Eaton Drive in the 1940s, declared in 1984 that history would be remade after it organized six Eaton's branches in southern Ontario. More than a year later, after a bitter six-month strike, the union suffered the double humiliation of having to accept the employer's first offer (and imposing it without a vote to save members' jobs) and then enduring decertification. When Manitoba's Labour Relations Board imposed a first contract on an Eaton's branch in Brandon, the store promptly fired half its employees and forced the union to make fresh concessions. Within a year, most of the Eaton retailing empire was again union-free.

Even Alberta's Conservative government was embarrassed when Peter Pocklington took advantage of the mid-eighties decline in meat consumption to smash the union at Gainers, his Edmonton meat-packing plant. Among other concessions, the flamboyant millionaire and hockey promoter demanded a five-year pay freeze and $6.99 an hour for new hires, and prepared to bus in strike-breakers. Most of Edmonton's police force spent the summer of 1986 protecting busloads of scabs from angry packing house workers. When Pocklington boasted that the strikers were gone, the struggle changed from a battle against pay cuts into a fight to save jobs. After six months and pressure from the provincial premier, Don Getty, Pocklington took back 900 strikers – but on his terms, and with the company pension surplus in his pocket.

In Quebec, where the newly pro-business PQ had been beaten by an even more pro-business Robert Bourassa in 1986, workers shared a comparably bitter experience when a newly-minted millionaire, Raymond Malepart, bought out the Manoir Richelieu, a resort hotel at Pointe-au-Pic, and rid himself of its unionized staff. The CNTU found itself in a battle with scabs, the provincial police, and citizens who wanted business, whatever the working conditions. An even more brutal demonstration of the new corporate style in labour relations was the decision by Quebec-based Dominion Textile in 1985 to lock out its

Supporters of the Eaton strikers outside Toronto's posh Eaton Centre also found themselves defending the right to picket on property controlled by mall owners. The legal battle had major consequences in the struggle to organize the growing numbers of retail workers. (Canadian Labour Congress)

notably ill-paid workers and their highly-conservative CSD union, after negotiators refused major wage cuts and a shift system that eliminated overtime rates for weekend work. Most of the textile plants accepted the company's terms. The two exceptions, at St-Timothée and St-Jean, were shut down, the machinery removed, and 900 jobs vanished. Union members were suitably traumatised. The company, which had pleaded foreign competition and imminent bankruptcy as justification for its practices, reported 18 percent profits in 1986 and 32 percent in 1987.

Between them, new provincial legislation and the struggles at Eaton's, Dominion Textile, Gainers and elsewhere seemed to unionists to import something of the raw, brutal atmosphere of American labour struggles. Indeed American consultants advertised high-priced seminars for Canadian businesses wishing to operate in a "union-free environment." Business periodicals reminded their readers that, if they had no taste for Japanese-style human resources management, there was a far more old-fashioned version closer at hand, in the southern U.S. states or in the so-called "Maquiladora" industries across the Rio Grande in Mexico, where an hour of Canada's lowest minimum wage bought a hard day's work. Among the earliest departures was Fleck Manufacturing, a small, rural Ontario auto parts manufacturer, whose women workers had become a symbol of the possibility of organizing low-pay, small-town factories. Fleck re-opened in Mexico as a "Maquiladora" industry.

Long before business gurus had urged their colleagues to "think globally," Canadian union leaders had gone beyond their borders. After AFL-CIO leaders abandoned the International Confederation of Free Trade Unions, the CLC had persisted. Some Canadians like Dan Benedict played a leading role in co-ordinating truly international co-operation against exploitative multinational companies. No country had more experience of international unionism – and of the destructive protectionism which split them apart. Vancouver transit workers left their international union soon after its convention voted for a "Buy America" policy for U.S. transit systems. Canadian union members built buses too. Some unionists recognized that Canada would be safe for union and social-democratic values only when they were shared worldwide. In 1985 the Steelworkers responded to the famine in Africa by offering members a Humanity Fund as a voluntary check-off for members and locals, with the proceeds directed to the human and environmental crises of the world. By 1989, more than 34,000 members in 170 bargaining units had collected $700,000 a year, almost all of it committed to hunger projects in Africa and Latin America. Canadian steelworkers had given unionists everywhere a working model for practical idealism.

Like corporations, unions in the eighties sought mergers as a means of survival in hard times. In 1986, the Amalgamated Meatcutters and the Retail Clerks had become the United Food and Commercial Workers, the biggest AFL-CIO affiliate. Its 156,000 Canadian members made it fourth in the CLC. The UFCW let Canadians elect their own director, meet in their own Canadian Council and establish a supplemental Canadian strike fund. Not everyone was happy. In March, 1987, the CFAW's Newfoundland fishermen and their ambitious leader, Richard Cashin, negotiated better terms with Bob White's Canadian Auto Workers. Why would fishermen would belong to a union of central Canadian factory workers? "They drive cars, don't they?" answered White. The UFCW was not amused but, fearful of losing the CAW and its national union allies, the CLC found elaborate reasons not to intervene. Because the UFCW had taken its claims against Cashin and other officials to the courts, explained Congress mediator Carl Goldenberg, the CLC was unable to intervene. Nova Scotia, New Brunswick and Newfoundland fishery workers split between UFCW and CAW affiliates. Canada's Atlantic fishery faced its imminent disaster of vanished cod stocks with the added problem of bitter union rivalry. Merger attempts often drew bad blood: at the last moment, members of the Canadian Paperworkers Union balked at a merger with the Alberta-based Energy and Chemical Workers Union when they realized that French-speaking members would fall from 40 to 20 percent of the membership.

If fishermen could ally themselves with Autoworkers, jurisdictions became meaningless in the eighties. Unions in the shrinking blue-collar occupations had to diversify or die. The Steelworkers recruited women organizers and accepted the notion of composite locals, grouping a variety of workers. By the end of the decade, the USWA had added such non-traditional metalworkers as taxi drivers in Montreal and Quebec, hotel employees in Quebec and Toronto, and supermarket clerks in western Ontario. The CAW organized Rio Tinto miners in Nova Scotia. Facing government downsizing and privatization, public sector unions reached beyond government. By 1988, 32 percent of the members affiliated to the National Union of Provincial Government Employees worked for colleges, hospitals, liquor commissions and educational institutions, some of them in the private sector. Teachers' federations remembered that teachers also worked in private schools. Organizing, of course, was never easy. A year-long strike at Alma College at St. Thomas, Ontario, sponsored by the Ontario Secondary School Teachers Federation, ended when the girls' private school simply closed its doors.

Throughout the 1980s, international unions faded steadily as a share of Canadian organized labour: by 1986 they were less than 40 percent of Canadian union strength. Vanished jobs killed more unions than raiding. The International Woodworkers of America fell from 63,000 members in 1982 to 48,000 in 1986. Though most internationals in Canada lost strength, the decline in the U.S. was steeper. By 1986, Canadian members formed a larger share of the AFL-CIO than they had been twenty years earlier.

Even in a conservative decade, unions found new ways of fighting for their members. Like other Canadians, unionists had discovered the environment in the 1970s but it took until the 1980s to collect knowledge about workplace heath and safety and develop awareness among workers. One result was a growing mountain of claims on provincial workers' compensation systems. Former McGill University student activist Stan Gray helped give Hamilton workers their own independent clinic for recognizing and treating occupational sickness and injury. Unions elsewhere took heart from his example. The pension needs of an aging workforce put unions into bitter confrontation with employers. Were pension fund surpluses corporate property, available for whatever shareholders desired, or were they a windfall for workers, an opportunity to improve existing pensions or to finance inflation protection? They found that the law favoured employers like Conrad Black, who enriched his huge holding company from pension surpluses at Massey-Ferguson and from Dominion Stores. Both companies (and their workers) promptly fell into corporate ruin.

In 1986, Donald S. MacDonald's Royal Commission reported. It urged Ottawa to negotiate a continental free trade arrangement, with necessary safeguards for Canadian institutions, values and autonomy. A massive stack of supporting reports spelled out the arguments. Labour's lone voice on the Commission, Steelworkers' national director Gérard Docquier, dissented. Louder voices drowned his protest. In a maudlin ceremony in Quebec City a year earlier, Brian Mulroney and President Reagan had joined in crooning "When Irish Eyes are Smiling." More privately, they had pledged to work for free trade across the U.S.-Canada border. What about Mulroney's old views? Circumstances, officials explained, had changed. As a great trading nation, Canada would be isolated as the world formed its blocs. A wave of protectionism in the U.S. Congress could slam the door on the market for eighty percent of Canada's exports. Ten years of the Trudeau government's Third Option had simply demonstrated that Europe and the Pacific Rim were not alternatives.

A labour movement that routinely challenged the wisdom of economists was not as easily converted. Nor would it be co-opted. Even before he left for Ireland, Dennis McDermott rejected the government's invitation to join an advisory council on the free trade negotiations. As former Auto Pact negotiator Simon Reisman was prodded toward a deal by Mulroney ministers, Shirley Carr committed the CLC to a $1.5 million campaign against free trade, privatization and deregulation. Canadians, she warned, were threatened with "not only mass unemployment but mass disruption in their way of life." A free trade deal was not simply a tariff cut – most tariffs had long since vanished – it was an assault on a host of so-called "non-tariff barriers" to trade, most of them visible chiefly to the eye of the beholder. Supporters boasted that free trade would turn both countries into "a level playing field"; but no one had doubts about which side the border had to be flattened. One of the biggest bumps on the Canadian side was a labour movement more than twice as powerful as its American counterpart, but other distinctions included Medicare, Unemployment Insurance, Canadian-content regulations, regional development assistance, and anything else Americans might label as "unfair competitive advantages" for Canadians. Glib comparisons with the European Economic Community had little relevance to the marriage of one country to another ten times as large. Opponents warned that U.S.-owned branch plants and their millions of jobs could vanish once huge U.S. producers could merely add a Sunday shift to supply the Canadian market. Quebec separatists, passionately in favour of the deal, expressed their own inverted warning: free trade would benefit Quebec because it could well mean the death of Canada.

The free trade negotiations progressed in an atmosphere of secrecy and mild unreality. There had been too many such negotiations in the past to believe fulfilment possible, particularly within the tight timetable Reagan and Mulroney had accepted. What outsiders did not know was that, by 1987, Mulroney had convinced himself that free trade was the issue that could rescue his government from a mid-term morass of scandals and frustrations, and demonstrate to business backers that their substantial campaign contributions had been well spent. When negotiations reached an impasse in September, 1987, an angry Simon Reisman flew back to Ottawa. Mulroney telephoned Reagan, and sent his negotiator back with an escort of cabinet ministers and orders to sign any deal he could get. On October 3, the deed was done. Three months later, Mulroney and his cabinet assembled in full formality to ratify the new

Canada's new ambassador to Ireland, Dennis McDermott, passes the gavel to his successor as president of the Canadian Labour Congress. Fourteen years earlier, Shirley Carr had been an office worker at Niagara Falls City Hall. Her rise symbolized the dramatic growth of women's place in both the Canadian workforce and its union movement. (Canadian Labour Congress)

Free Trade Agreement or FTA; meanwhile, Reagan paused at his California ranch to scratch his signature. The last word would belong to Canadian voters.

The free trade debate confused Canadians. More were strongly opposed than fervently in favour, but most voters shifted awkwardly. Though Tories had once been the party of protection, four-fifths of them now claimed to favour the Mulroney deal. Liberals, the party of Reciprocity under Laurier and the younger Mackenzie King, were officially opposed. New Democrats were adamantly opposed, but almost half their voters liked the idea. In Quebec, organized labour stated its formal opposition, but their members listened to their elites, business and political, federalist and sovereignist, found them enthusiastically in favour, and wondered. Hadn't Quebec discovered that it had a late-blooming *"goût des affaires"* – a taste for business? Everywhere, workers feared for their jobs if free trade went through – or if it didn't, and export sales of lumber, steel or auto parts faced impossible U.S. trade barriers. Seven of ten provincial premiers had welcomed the news on October 3, 1987. Manitoba's Howard Pawley was not one of them, but on April 26, 1988, resentment at his sympathy for French minority language rights and an ill-timed boost in auto insurance rates overwhelmed his NDP government. A Tory, Gary Filmon, won narrowly, with the Liberals an unexpected second. Manitoba's government was now on Mulroney's side. Ontario Liberals, elected in 1985, opposed the deal, but Premier David Peterson felt the heat from his business backers.

The free trade dispute ended the truce between the CLC and the government. So did the delayed emergence of a Conservative agenda of downsizing and privatizing government services. In 1987, managers at Canada Post announced a drastic plan to cut deliveries and privatize local post offices. A crown corporation at last, the Post Office took on the normally subdued Letter Carriers and, for the first time since the 1920s, attempted to defeat them with strike-breakers. When the high-cost strategy failed, the Post Office was forced to settle. Then the attempt was repeated in the fall, with only slightly more success. In the wake of the dispute, both sides claimed victory but the union had protected its members' seniority rights. In 1988, when the Canada Labour Relations Board forced both major postal unions into a merger, Parrot's more militant and slightly larger CUPW narrowly prevailed over the Letter Carriers, though the struggle languished in the courts until 1991. Pre-election politics made $15 million available to the Canadian Federation of Labour's new Working Ventures fund, a counterpart to the QFL's Solidarity Fund. The CFL had limited its concerns about free trade to a few concerns about job security. Mulroney's political preoccupations and personal resentments burst out after his wife, Mila, was brushed by a picket sign as the two pushed past Moncton demonstrators protesting the closing of CN repair shops. It was, Mulroney stormed, entirely the fault of the NDP.

Federal hardball was an echo of what was happening in the provinces. In 1986, Fraser March, leader of Newfoundland's public employees, went to jail and his union lost thousands of dollars in fines and legal costs after an illegal strike to raise his members' incomes to the poverty line. In 1987, Saskatchewan's Grant Devine slapped a one-year pay freeze on the province's public-sector workers. When University of Saskatchewan professors struck for ten days in 1988, they were legislated back to work without even provision for finding a settlement. In British Columbia, voters were denied the chance to defeat Bill Bennett when Social Credit picked Bill Vander Zalm to replace him. A former Liberal and Socred welfare minister who had once talked of putting the poor to work with picks and shovels, Vander Zalm relied on short memories and a generous settlement for B.C. government employees to beat the NDP in 1986. A year later, B.C. unions had second thoughts, as a government that privatized everything from highway signs to textbook delivery created its own Industrial Relations Council, gave sweeping power to the courts in labour disputes, made decertification easier and allowed employers to use the courts to seek damages from an illegal strike or picket. As in Alberta, B.C. Social Crediters also allowed "double breasting" on building sites.

During 1986, support for Mulroney had plummeted to such depths that his re-election seemed impossible. Then, while Liberals plotted, conspired and undermined their leader, support for the NDP began to grow, nowhere as dramatically as in Quebec. By mid-1987, polls showed the NDP with 40 percent of popular support, and more than half the votes in Quebec. Cynics looked for hard evidence; backers were satisfied with growing membership, the promise of star candidates, and hope of the long-sought NDP breakthrough in Quebec. Laberge's Quebec Federation of Labour politely announced that it would again take the NDP seriously. Michel Agnaieff of the CEQ emerged as the NDP's latest Quebec leader. Across Canada, union leaders could hope that the long investment in the NDP would pay off.

Yet strong backing, particularly in Quebec, brought problems. If Quebec wanted both the NDP and free trade, what should Ed Broadbent be saying? Mulroney's pre-dawn constitutional deal at Meech Lake in 1987 seemed easy to support: special status for Quebec and more power for the provinces had been NDP policy since the 1960s, but not all NDPers agreed – least of all in the Yukon, which had given the NDP a slim majority in 1984 and an M.P., Audrey McLaughlin, in 1986. Polls revealed another, more disturbing weakness: voters liked the NDP's humanity but had absolutely no faith that it could manage the economy, partly because it was seen to be union-dominated. The tactical answer, of course, was that elections have many issues and the NDP would campaign on all of them, from national day-care to an equitable tax system. Free trade, an economic issue, would not necessarily be put front and centre.

Perhaps that made sense when NDP campaign plans were made late in 1987, but by 1988, as the free-trade issue polarized Canada, NDP support began to collapse, the Liberals stalled, and the Tories regained a lead. The Pro-Canada Network, including the CLC, demanded an election before the Mulroney government ratified the FTA. No other issue, in union eyes, mattered as much. When the Liberals used their Senate majority to force a free-trade election, they elbowed the NDP into an also-ran. For Broadbent and his backers, that was a double disaster because, at 25 percent in the polls, they were neck-and-neck with Turner. There was no flexibility. Broadbent's game plan was set. Union muscle and money gave New Democrats as good a campaign as they had ever had, but there was nothing to spare for second thoughts. The national television debate helped give John Turner a renewed lead in opposing free trade. Exhausted from a three-hour French-language debate the previous night, Broadbent was in no shape to wrestle it back. The Tories had left themselves time to recover; corporate millions gave them the means to do so. On November 21, 1988, Brian Mulroney won his second parliamentary majority. Forty-three percent of Canadians had given a belated mandate for free trade. Opponents had split their votes. Labour's party had 43 seats and 20 percent of the vote, more than it had before but, to the unconcealed fury of union leaders, it was still a third-place loser.

The Free Trade Agreement would prevail. The playing field would be levelled and Canadian working people would have to live with the consequences.

CHAPTER 29

Struggling to the Millennium

For a lot of Canadians, 1989 was about as good as it got in the Mulroney years. Average weekly earnings rose 8 percent, well ahead of inflation, a contrast to most years since 1978. Only about one worker in fourteen was looking for a job. Business insisted that the biggest labour issue in Canada was the lack of skilled workers. 1989 was the year the Berlin Wall fell, Europe's Communist regimes began to collapse and the cold war had to be cancelled for lack of an enemy. In Ottawa, senators briefly stalled the Mulroney government's new 7 percent Goods and Services Tax. Business rejoiced too. With the Free Trade Agreement, North America was set to become a "level playing field" for those who wanted to get rich. Those who didn't or wouldn't could fall into Canada's social safety net of minimum wage laws, Unemployment Insurance and social assistance. Of course, with Ottawa and most provinces running huge deficits and spending up to half their revenue just to pay interest on their debts, how much longer would the safety net last?

In 1990, Statistics Canada found that of 13 million Canadians in the non-agricultural paid workforce, 3.84 million belonged to unions. Unions were strong in British Columbia, Quebec and strongest of all in Newfoundland, where public sector unions and newly-created fishery organizations had recruited half the workforce. As in 1980, Canada's "union density" was more than double the United States rate. Indeed, Canada was one of the few industrialized countries where union membership had grown in the eighties. And, Diane Galarneau reported for Statistics Canada, belonging to a union had, on average, brought members higher wages, shorter hours and, if they were part-timers, more hours of work.

The fight over free trade put Canadian labour solidly on one side, defending systems of social justice the union movement had fought for generations to achieve. Among the bumps on the "level playing field" the Mulroney-Reagan deal would flatten was Canada's strong and militant labour movement. (United Steelworkers)

To employers and their political allies, of course, that was only an argument for imitating Ronald Reagan, who had crushed U.S. air controllers for daring to strike, or for Margaret Thatcher, who had destroyed Britain's miners' union and cut the TUC's affiliates by a third. Would the nineties do the same to Canadian unions? Polls showed that unions were as unpopular ever. Business propaganda was only part of the explanation; except as nay-sayers, what did labour have to say to workers without work and no place on a seniority list?

Forecasters predicted a militant 1990. Tough strikes in construction and the steel industry ended with modest gains and long layoffs. The CAW won a short, sharp battle with the Big Three for better compensation after plant closures. It was a wise priority. By the spring of 1990, companies began reporting empty order books and quarterly losses. Factory shutdowns and layoffs made headlines as managers closed old or inefficient plants and switched production from country to country. By the summer of 1990, 1.1 million Canadians were officially unemployed.

Red ink meant layoffs. Corporate managers boasted of "right-sizing" their workforce: INCO, which had 52,000 employees worldwide in 1970, was down to 16,000 by 1994. Privatization and mergers also cost jobs. Sold off, Canadian National Railways cut a third of its workforce. Trading losses cost the jobs of thousands of Canadian Airlines and Air Canada workers. The rest absorbed drastic pay cuts. Dylex blamed cross-border shopping and the GST when it released 11,300 employees. In business in St. John's since 1859, Ayers closed 60 stores across Canada in a day. A foolish investment in Texas wiped out jobs at People's Credit Jewellers. Algoma Steel survived only because a worker-government rescue package included drastic wage cuts and the sacrifice of over half the company's payroll. After generations of keeping unions out by generous labour policies, DOFASCO dropped a third of its workers. A merger of Molson and O'Keefe closed seven breweries. IBM's boast that "Big Blue" never fired anyone faded after thousands of jobs vanished in the Toronto area alone. Even the Bank of Canada cut a hundred jobs; private banks wiped out thousands, as automatic tellers replaced people.

Was job-loss due to the recession, free trade or new technology? Economists blamed debt-burdened, nervous consumers. When the 7 percent GST took effect in 1991, replacing a 12 percent manufacturers' sales tax, no one saw any prices fall. Shoppers went over the U.S. border if they could, pushing Canadian retailers into losses and layoffs. By the winter of 1992, 600,000 people had given up their search for non-existent jobs. Another 1.56 million went on looking; by February, 1993, 1.7 million hunted for work. For the first time in generations, the proportion of women with jobs declined. The work, wages and taxes of under 12 million supported 28 million Canadians. And those wages were shrinking. Apart from managers, whose salaries stayed well above inflation, average Canadian real incomes fell steadily from 1990 to 1995. Unlike in the eighties, union members fared no better and sometimes worse than unorganized workers. After M.P.s and senior government managers got a raise, federal salaries were frozen at 1990 levels, and stayed there until 1998. Millions of workers on provincial or municipal payrolls took pay cuts or buy-outs. In 1991, Labour Canada admitted that average family earnings, $42,612, were lower than the 1980 average of $44,521. After the 1995 census, Statistics Canada found that average total income had fallen even lower: between 1980 and 1995, men's incomes had dropped an average of 7.6 percent to $31,117 in 1995, while women's earnings had risen 15 percent to $19,208. Average family incomes were 6.7 percent lower than in 1989. A million and a half children lived in poverty, double the number in 1989.

Other issues aggravated the problem. In the summer of 1990, a two-month Mohawk stand-off over land claims near Montreal led to a Royal Commission to explore aboriginal rights and land claims. This fitted Canadian labour's social justice agenda, but non-aboriginal workers in heavily unionized resource industries worried about their jobs in fishing, logging and mining. That June, the Meech Lake Accord, with its promise of constitutional reconciliation between Quebec and the rest of Canada, collapsed, and Quebec sovereignty revived as a movement and an issue. A fresh accord was concocted by the Mulroney government and provincial premiers at Charlottetown in August,

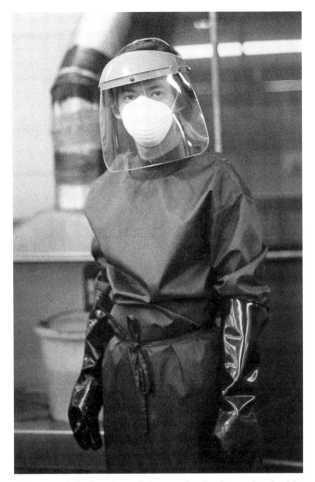

Environmental consciousness helped unions fight new battles for worker health and safety. Unions needed allies and expertise to battle employers and their political allies. Mass unemployment made workers nervous about losing jobs if companies shifted work to countries where enforcement was lax or non-existent.

1992. In the face of denunciations by Quebec separatists, former prime minister Pierre Elliott Trudeau, and Preston Manning of the new Reform Party, Canadians rejected it in a 1992 national referendum, setting the stage for a return of the Parti Québécois and a squeaker of a federalist referendum victory in Quebec in 1995. Investment and jobs avoided the province and Canada. With Quebec's labour movement formally committed to Quebec independence, the CLC had nothing much to say.

Faced with the worst economic conditions since the thirties, what could unions do? In 1990, Shirley Carr beat back a radical challenge to her CLC presidency and joined a council that advised the Mulroney government on free trade issues. It was better to be inside than shouting from across the street.

Unions have structures. Ken Signoretti, executive vice-president of the Ontario Federation of Labour, Mayor Hazel McCallion of Mississauga, Leo Gerard, director of District 6 of the United Steelworkers, his international president, Lynn Williams, and his Canadian director, Gerard Docquier, all congratulate Josephine Urh, first president of a new Peel-Halton Steelworkers Area Council.

Would she be heard anywhere? In 1956, the new CLC had represented over two-thirds of Canadian unionists; by the end of the 1980s, it mustered 57 percent. The CNTU, the CFL, the CSD and the CCU had collected a bare 14 percent among them. The second largest block of Canadian unionists, ranging from the Brotherhood of Teamsters to hospital nurses, had no link with any Canadian central labour body. Through the nineties, the CLC did its best to find affiliates. Ontario's English Catholic Teachers Association and Secondary School Teachers' Federation joined in 1995. The CFL schism faded in 1997 when the International Brotherhood of Electrical Workers returned, leaving Jim McCambly with nothing much but his Labour Venture Capital Fund. A quarrel with the sovereignist-minded Quebec Federation of Labour, started when convention delegates chose fiery post office union leader Jean-Claude Parrot over the QFL nominee, ended that year with a "sovereignty-association" agreement that left the Quebeckers with their dues and their own policies.

Sometimes there was good news. Long before it was expelled from the AFL-CIO and the CLC in 1960, the Teamsters had been a byword for corruption and fraud on both sides of the border. Like the SIU, a scattered membership plus goon tactics helped Teamster leaders like Dave Beck, Jimmy Hoffa and Jackie Presser stay in power. Rebels were threatened, beaten, and, with collusive employers, fired. In 1981, at a Teamsters' convention, a B.C. truck driver named Diana Kilmury demanded an ethical practices committee. Later, Kilmury claimed to believe that if she told the union that racketeering was bad, it would put a stop to it. And so it did, though it took another brutal decade, a union reform movement, and a 200-item U.S. indictment that included Liberal senator Ed Lawson, the Teamsters' Canadian vice-president. In 1991, reformer Ron Carey became international president, with Diana Kilmury as one of his vice-presidents. Montrealer Louis Lacroix replaced Lawson, and the Teamsters began to clean up. In 1992, the union returned to the CLC.

Union merger-mania was a mixed blessing. Having spurned the Oil, Chemical and Atomic Workers, the 70,000-strong Canadian Paperworkers joined 40,000 Communications and Electrical Workers and 30,000 Energy and Chemical Workers in 1992 to form the Communications, Energy and Paperworkers Union (CEP). Then the CEP acquired NABET's 8,000 members and 3,200 members of the Southern Ontario Newspaper Guild in 1994. Two veteran unions, the Amalgamated Clothing Workers and the International Ladies Garment Workers united on both sides of the border in 1995 as the Union of Needletrades, Industrial and Textile Employees (UNITE). By mid-decade, most of Canada's CPR and CNR shopcraft unions had joined the CAW; so did the United Electrical, Radio and Machine Workers, the United Fishermen and Allied Workers, the predominantly western and nationalist CAIMAW, and, despite Steelworker protests, Mine-Mill's last local, No. 598 at Falconbridge. The United Steelworkers gained another veteran industrial union, the United Rubberworkers. Like corporate mergers, not every marriage worked. When 20,000 Canadian members of the RWDSU rebelled at the U.S. union's decision to join the United Food and Commercial Workers, the Steelworkers were the successful suitor. Some marriages were imposed. In 1989, the Canada Labour Relations Board had forced the Letter Carriers Union to merge with CUPW, the inside workers' union. When CUPW prevailed, angry LCUC members fought the issue through the courts – and lost.

Whatever the promised synergies, union mergers are rarely a sign of strength. With mass unemployment, militancy faded. A strike could not reopen a factory or store, or prevent privatization; it merely cut off unemployment and severance benefits. A resolution by the Communication Workers to punish runaway industries brought fervent applause but little action. Concession bargaining, denounced in the eighties, was no sin in the nineties if it saved or even delayed mass layoffs. Strike activity in the early nineties fell to levels unknown since the 1920s. When Montreal's Nationair locked out 450 flight attendants in 1991 for demanding more than $15,600 a year, it got by comfortably with replacement workers and contracts from Ottawa to fly peacekeepers to Bosnia. A 1994 strike at the Irving Refinery at Saint John ended after 27 months. Only the law saved a third of the jobs. After cutting 243 pilots, Air Canada forced the rest to swallow a 10 percent pay cut. When pilots from the company's regional lines tried to join their seniority list, Air Canada's pilots quit their union, CALPA, in disgust. Meanwhile, workers at the struggling Canadian Airlines made even deeper concessions, some of them compensated by a worker role in management.

Increasingly union leaders wear a female face. Flanked by NDP MPs Lorne Nystrom and Svend Robinson, Linda Torney, president of the Metro Toronto Labour Council, Julie Davis, secretary-treasurer of the Ontario Federation of Labour, and Frances Lankin, NDP member of the Ontario legislature and former OPSEU leader, head Toronto's 1995 Labour Day parade.

During the 1980s, more and more professionals, from nurses to university professors, had converted their associations into collective bargaining agencies, usually in search of leverage when their employers responded to government cutbacks with layoffs and salary caps. The 1988 strike at the University of Saskatchewan was a foretaste of experience in the nineties, when a number of university faculty associations, including Manitoba and York, formed picket lines. Professors could stop classes and create emotional turmoil, but their cash-strapped institutions could seldom give them any satisfaction. After almost two months, York professors settled for 1 percent over three years, lost a rich early retirement package and any right to continue teaching after age 65.

The nastiest Canadian strike of the decade pitted Peggy Witte and her Giant gold mine in Yellowknife against the Canadian Association of Smelter and Allied Workers, a small, nationalist union. When Witte refused to budge, miners struck on May 23, 1993. Witte summoned strike-breakers, and the RCMP flew in reinforcements to protect them. Tensions rose and the territorial government pleaded for federal intervention. Instead, on September 18, an underground blast killed nine of Witte's miners. The strike collapsed. Months later, a striker, Roger Warren, confessed, withdrew his confession, was convicted and sentenced to twenty years. Peggy Witte became a business hero.

Women delegates cheer a decision by the NDP's twelfth biennial convention to guarantee women equality with men in the party's executive and council. The NDP was the first federal party to elect a woman leader – just before its disastrous showing in 1993. (Canadian Association of Labour Media)

In previous hard times, unions turned to political action. With more parliamentary seats than ever in 1988 and Yukon M.P. Audrey McLaughlin as leader, the NDP should have been an effective ally. Yet neither McLaughlin nor the party could deal with a public that had lost faith in the NDP's economic competence. Public ownership, centralized planning, and taxing the rich sounded like empty old slogans. So did the NDP's apparent indifference to deficits. Even union members criticized the NDP's dependence on organized labour.

Yet where were the alternatives? Political elites blamed job losses on Canada's post-Meech instability as a country. Unions and nationalists found the villain in free trade – enlarged in 1992 to include Mexico in a North American Free Trade Alliance (NAFTA). Business gurus praised the up-and-down business cycle as the market's way of expelling waste and inefficiency and restoring "shareholder value," and denounced "payroll taxes" like Unemployment Insurance and workers' compensation premiums. Influenced by union-controlled mutual funds like the CFL's Working Ventures fund or the QFL's Solidarity Fund, even some workers now echoed business ideology. Financiers and economists denounced government deficits and the borrowing that ate up scarce capital.

While various forces contributed to the recession, many economists fingered Canada's uncontrolled deficit as prime villain. Ever since John Turner's election-winning budget of 1974, Ottawa had annually spent a lot more than it brought in – $30 billion more by 1980. Despite Tory cuts and controls, huge job losses sent Unemployment Insurance costs soaring. By 1992, the deficit approached $40 billion. Then, after years of over-fishing, Canada's Atlantic fishery suddenly collapsed. Tens of thousands of Canada's workers in Canada's poorest provinces faced destitution. To help them would cost more billions.

Though Ottawa slashed its own programs, freezing salaries and selling crown corporations, most of its spending took the form of transfers to individuals and provinces. Deficit control hurt. Unemployment Insurance was an example. Just when a million workers needed the benefits they had paid for, the Tories imposed tougher regulations to make it harder to collect. With benefits exhausted or denied, hundreds of thousands lined up for provincially-funded welfare. Reduced federal payments to provinces, or "downloading," forced the provinces to borrow or raise taxes to finance health care, welfare and post-secondary education, or to cut them back. Meanwhile, as businesses closed, jobs vanished, and incomes fell, tax revenues dwindled.

It was a tough time to be in politics, and even tougher to be in the public service. After the rapid unionization of the 1960s and 1970s, and major improvements in income, benefits and working conditions, the 1990s were pay-back time for public employers. Job security was no longer a trade-off for low pay and drudgery. In the 1990s, governments concluded that very little could not be downsized or privatized, even police, prison guards, and fire services. PSAC and its provincial counterparts could protest and even strike, but the public was suffering too much to sympathize, and governments increasingly legislated an end to strike. Far from splitting the difference between final offers, governments more often imposed their own terms. If public employees were unhappy, they could quit. With massive cuts and layoffs making civil service job security an ancient memory, chances were good that unhappy workers would be leaving anyway.

By 1990, the NDP held power only in the Yukon. That year, Ontario premier David Peterson called a snap election for September 10. Confident of victory, he lost. An astonished Bob Rae won 38 percent of Ontario's votes and 74 seats, an eighteen-seat NDP majority in Canada's biggest, richest province. It was the dream, or the nightmare, of a century. Faced with a deepening recession, Rae postponed costly campaign promises, accepted Peterson's spending estimates, and added $10 billion to Ontario's debt. Friends and enemies raged that he had not done enough. On second thought, business denounced him for over-spending.

Rae focussed on low-cost reforms, giving 90,000 crown employees the right to strike, amending labour laws to ban replacement workers and preparing employment equity legislation to force employers to hire disabled, female,

Ontario's first NDP premier is congratulated by radical lawyer Clayton Ruby. Bob Rae had expected to retire after the 1990 election. Instead, he headed an utterly inexperienced government faced with a massive recession, a chronic deficit, and the need to adapt Canada's most exposed province to the impact of the 1988 Free Trade Agreement. Rae learned fast. His followers, and the province, took a lot longer. (Julien Lebourdais)

Native, and visible-minority workers. Business hated the new regime. The NDP made other enemies. Rae bowed to public opinion and the courts, ignored retail unions, and allowed Sunday shopping. When the NDP tried to implement public car insurance, it discovered that the FTA required huge compensation to private insurers. Union and party supporters felt betrayed. On October 28, 1992, thousands of Ontario police officers gathered at Queen's Park to denounce the NDP for reviewing their use of firearms and for imposing civilian review.

Rae's spending did not lift the recession. By 1992, Ontario was losing 500 full-time jobs and 11 businesses a day. One in nine people shared $6.1 billion in social assistance and another 600,000 made do with Unemployment Insurance. As the government struggled with retraining and job-creation and provincial revenue sagged, the deficit ballooned to $17 billion. For 1993–94, it would be $19 billion. Ontario's creditors intervened: cut the deficit or interest

Ontario premier Bob Rae struggles to explain his Social Contract to a labour movement that had supported his NDP government but never felt much ownership. Surrounding him from his right are education minister Dave Cooke, labour minister Bob Mackenzie, municipal affairs minister Mike Breaugh, and health minister Ruth Grier. (Julien Lebourdais)

rates would skyrocket. Other provinces with similar problems would soon learn the right-wing solution: cut public spending, fire droves of civil servants, teachers and nurses, slash welfare cheques. Rae tried a different tack. To find $9 billion, his government slapped a surtax on the better off, sold its share of Toronto's Skydome, and cut $4 billion in spending. He needed $2 billion more. If each of 902,000 tax-supported workers, from professor to snow-plough operator, accepted a small three-year cut, Rae promised, as his part of the bargain, more workplace influence and a greater union voice in government. Indeed, unions were invited to see the government's books and offer advice.

Rae's Social Contract was idealistic and, to union leaders, utterly unacceptable. Endless consultations went nowhere. Contract inviolability was a rooted principle of Canadian industrial relations and here was a pro-labour government trying to rip up a signed agreement. Layoffs were preferable. The NDP government refused to budge and party councils upheld Rae. By June, ultimatums from both sides expired. On July 7, Ontario's legislature voted 66–59 for

Ontario teachers had been among the angry critics of Bob Rae's NDP government but they soon found themselves at war with his successors. The Harris government took over education funding, cut staffing, extended teaching hours, enlarged classes, and wiped out programs. When 126,000 teachers walked off the job for two weeks in the fall of 1997, they got more support than they expected.

a three-year pay freeze and 12 unpaid holidays for public-sector workers earning over $30,000. OPSEU, CUPE and other public sector unions were furious. OPSEU promised war at the next election. CUPE ordered its locals to break with the Ontario NDP. Eager to build an alliance with the big public-sector unions, the CAW cut off political funding. In November, the Ontario Federation of Labour formally withdrew support. When federal New Democrats faced Canadian voters in the 1993 federal election, explaining Bob Rae's government was their biggest problem, among friends and critics alike. On October 25, the NDP kept only 7 percent of the vote and nine seats, too few for official party status. Audrey McLaughlin was reduced to pleading with the CLC for continued backing: the best she could get was a two-year review.

Not all unions blasted Rae. Few welcomed the Social Contract but, like Rae and his colleagues, private-sector unions had learned to live in a harsh world. In 1992, when the NDP's labour reforms were in peril, few union leaders had bothered to show support. Finally, the Steelworkers mobilized a powerfully supportive campaign. During the Social Contract uproar, they and other unions hunted for a compromise. The old schism between national and international unions was again apparent, particularly when the CAW lined up with CUPE, OPSEU and other public sector unions, and began organizing campaigns in areas the Steelworkers traditionally dominated.

When the Ontario NDP went down to defeat in June, 1995, the outcome was another surprise. Instead of electing the seemingly popular Liberals, Ontario voters lurched to the other side of the political road. Conservatives took 80 seats and 45 percent of the vote. Mike Harris's "Common Sense Revolution" promptly banned photo-radar, restored Medicare coverage to elderly "snow-birds" in Florida and cut welfare payments by 22 percent. The NDP's labour law reforms soon vanished, followed by even older rights. So did the NDP's employment equity program, and thousands of the jobs Rae had tried to protect. When the Legislature opened, police drove back 5,000 demonstrators with batons and pepper spray. Harris cut taxes, imposed workfare, closed hospitals and used provincial police to smash student demonstrators at Queen's Park and Native demonstrators at Ipperwash.

Labour did what it could. The OFL organized Days of Protest, starting cautiously in London on December 11, 1995, in Hamilton the following February, where 100,000 mobilized, and other one-day shut-downs of Kitchener, Sudbury, North Bay and, in May, a two-day demonstration in Toronto. On February 25, OPSEU used its last chance to strike by calling out the 59,000 provincial workers allowed to do so. By April, 90 percent of the 35,000 who voted were willing to call it off in return for better pensions and seniority rights for those laid off. OPSEU leader Leah Casselman could do little more than congratulate her members on their solidarity. The Tories, unmoved by the disruptions, boasted of their indifference to mere "pressure groups." On March 18, a provincial police riot squad attacked protesters with a brutality that shocked even the Toronto city police in attendance. Pollsters reported that Ontarians did not like the turbulence, but they liked Harris's agenda. Faced with widespread public acceptance and a return of prosperity, Ontario unions were divided. The OFL's fortieth convention in 1997 divided bitterly on an increasingly deep divide between pro-NDP internationals and post-NDP national unions. By a narrow margin, delegates chose former Rubberworker Wayne Samuelson over a CAW nominee.

If Mike Harris had a model, it was Alberta's Ralph Klein. Chosen leader of a failing Tory government in December, 1992, the former Calgary mayor introduced a beer-bellied populism that fed on the same red-necked, right-wing image Preston Manning was using to build his Reform Party. Klein won his own majority in June, 1993, annihilating a fifteen-seat NDP caucus. He promptly privatized Alberta liquor stores, ignoring their unionized employees, and launched a personal assault on health, education and welfare costs. Faced with the threat of huge layoffs, Alberta's Union of Public Employees took a 2.3 percent cut, seven unpaid holidays and a two-year wage freeze. Apart from those who were hurt, most Albertans professed to love the results. By 1997, Klein could campaign on his record of reducing the provincial deficit to zero, make no promises, and win an even bigger margin. The province's unionists laid low and, as usual, prayed for better times. In Manitoba, the Conservatives' Garry Filmon was less flamboyant but, even after two terms in office, no less ideological. In 1996, workers in government-run agencies, including AUTO-PAC agents, home care workers, even employees at the provincially-run casino, struck against 2–3 percent wage cuts, giving Manitoba the most days lost since the Winnipeg General Strike, but to no avail.

Saskatchewan was different. By the early 1990s, Grant Devine's Tory government had brought the province to the edge of financial ruin. In a two-party system, an NDP victory under Roy Romanow became certain and, given the province's near bankruptcy, painful. Like Tommy Douglas in 1944, Romanow had to steer Saskatchewan back from a fiscal precipice without a slasher's instincts. He was helped by realism, experience, and a well-informed public, assets Ontario's NDP government had lacked. Romanow raised taxes, cut small rural hospitals that served mainly as community job-creators, and won solid re-election in 1995. Provincial labour reforms protected part-time workers and made it easier to certify unions and reach settlements, but cautiously avoided a ban on replacement workers.

An NDP victory also became inevitable in British Columbia. Bill Vander Zalm's career ended in conflict-of-interest scandals, and Social Credit imploded. On October 17, 1991, Mike Harcourt found himself with 41 percent of the vote and 51 seats, an easy majority. The new government promptly implemented recall and initiative rules and guaranteed that British Columbians would vote on future constitutional amendments. Less hurt than other regions by the 1990s recession, the province presented the NDP with other huge problems: reconciling the irreconcilable claims of business, labour, environmentalists and First Nations in managing forests and fishing. Meanwhile, opposing media tarred Harcourt with an old fundraising scandal at the Nanaimo Commonwealth Holding Society that had little nothing to do with him or his government.

Whatever else was laid-back on the West Coast, it was certainly not politics or economics. In November, 1995, with the NDP lagging in the polls, an exasperated Harcourt quit. His successor, Glen Clark, minister of employment and investment, was actually the first active trade unionist to become a provincial premier. In short order Clark fired senior officials of B.C. Hydro for alleged conflict of interest, forestalled strikes in health and education and called an election to celebrate his balanced budget. Clark's campaign against Harris-style conservatism won him a shaky victory – 39 seats to 36 for the combined opposition, and fewer votes than the Liberals. It was barely enough when B.C. voters discovered that the balanced budget had depended on fiscal juggling. Trade disputes, a failing salmon fishery and an Asian debt crisis began to unravel B.C. prosperity. Campaigning against Ottawa and U.S. fishing interests could carry Clark only so far.

Quebec, as usual, was not like the other provinces – but not very different. In September, 1994, the Parti Québécois returned to power with informal but enthusiastic union backing. A Keynesian and single-minded sovereignist, Jacques Parizeau bent every effort to winning his 1995 referendum on sovereignty and, with backing from Quebec's union leaders, came within a percentage point of a majority. Frustrated and discredited by his angry attack on "money and the ethnic vote," Parizeau quit. His successor, Lucien Bouchard, was the man who had imposed brutal wage cuts in 1981, after the earlier referendum, and he had been a Mulroney minister. In 1990, furious at compromises on the Meech Lake Accord, he quit to form the sovereignist Bloc Québécois. In 1994, a struggle with necrotizing fasciitis cost Bouchard a leg and almost his life, and sent his prestige soaring. To win, he insisted, the PQ must balance its budget. The medicine was identical with every other province – hospital shutdowns, wage cuts, buy-outs and public sector job loss. The means were different. Buoyed by his personal popularity, Bouchard could summon all the leaders of a Quebec nation – business, labour, intellectuals and social groups – to impose a consensus even militant unionists could not defy. QFL, CEQ and CNTU leaders might resent the pressure but, apart from a few compromises and postponements and much private grumbling, they went along.

In Ottawa, economic recovery began officially in early 1993. Tories prayed that good news and a new leader might save them. That summer, the economy slumped again, and Mulroney's successor, Kim Campbell, predicted that high unemployment would continue for years. Jean Chrétien's pledge of "Jobs, jobs, jobs," and a Red Book of appealing and often expensive promises gave the Liberals 177 seats and 42 percent of the vote. Once elected, the Liberals decided within months that the GST, FTA, NAFTA and the civil-service pay freeze were all right after all. The main difference with Liberals was their largely unexpected determination to cut the federal deficit, whatever the cost in jobs, health, education, welfare, regional benefits and federal jurisdiction. The first phase began in 1994, with drastic defence cuts, eliminating a score of bases, 15,000 military positions and more than twice as many civilian jobs, most of them unionized.

The full strategy was revealed on February 27, 1995, with finance minister Paul Martin's second budget. In a few minutes, he ended $2.3 billion in business subsidies, cut Canada Pension Plan payments, and promised to priva- tize Petro-Canada, the CNR and Transport Canada's air navigation system. Payments to provinces for health, education and welfare were combined in a Canadian Health and Social Transfer, and then cut by $2.5 billion immediately and another $4.5 billion in 1997–98. Later that year, prairie farmers lost their $560 million grain transportation subsidy. Martin's biggest savings would come from wiping out 45,000 civil service jobs over three years, with either a buy- out or an unpaid year of leave for those who hoped for a vacancy. In three years, Trudeau's deficit had been wiped out, at a devastating cost of health services, doubled and even tripled fees for most Canadian college and univer- sity students, and big cuts in social assistance. Across Canada, public sector workers could protest and even strike, but to little effect. In the wake of the catastrophic failure of Atlantic cod stocks, Newfoundland premier Clyde Wells imposed a $70-million cut in the provincial payroll. When teachers and civil servants grumbled and threatened, Wells called an election for May 3, 1993, on whether unions or voters ruled the province. He won easily. A year later, strikes won few concessions. Nova Scotia teachers were militant until other government employees refused to back them; they then yielded to demands from John Savage's Liberal government for a 3 percent, three-year salary roll back, an end to study leave and early retirement of 2,400 teachers.

Despite Chrétien's election promises, Kim Campbell had been right. Unem- ployment barely declined under the Liberals. Canada, experts professed, expe- rienced a "jobless recovery." Business blamed low job creation strictly on payroll taxes. Unemployment Insurance premiums had reached a maximum of $1,245 a year in 1994, double the cap in 1986. After years of studies and reports, notably the Forget Commission which had reported to a Conservative

Jeff Rose was typical of the highly educated, articulate workers swept up by the wave of public sector unionization. With graduate degrees from the University of Toronto and the London School of Economics, Rose was a city planner before he joined CUPE Local 79. From 1983 to 1993, he was president of Canada's largest union. (Canadian Association of Labour Media)

government, the Liberals' Lloyd Axworthy was determined to act. The complaints were familiar. Half the beneficiaries lived in Quebec or the Atlantic region, and 40 percent of the benefits went to those who had claimed UI at least three times in five years. As a subsidy to regions and resource industries, UI cost employers and workers in Ontario and the West $2.9 billion a year. While the 1994 budget cut $5.5 billion from UI over three years, the real reforms came at the end of 1995.

Under the renamed Employment Insurance (EI), claimants could get no more than $418 a week, for no more than 45 weeks. By measuring work by hours, part-time workers could now qualify though the large number of hours needed to be eligible made the gain illusory. Repeated users – usually seasonal workers – would get less each time. While some of the savings allowed lower premiums and more money for wage subsidies, job-creation and retraining, extra billions would be used to cut the federal deficit. Meanwhile, critics noted, one in three unemployed workers would be ineligible for benefits. Bitter protests in New Brunswick, Nova Scotia and Quebec's Gaspé were unavailing,

*Canadian Labour Congress president Bob White welcomes child rights crusader Craig Kielburger and
Asmita, a ten-year-old from India, at the CLC's 1996 convention. Child labour in under-developed
countries provides North Americans with brand-name consumer goods. (Canadian Labour Congress)*

though many Liberal M.P.s from Atlantic constituencies would pay with their
seats in the 1997 general election.

Of course, jobs were created as the economy revived, though fewer and
worse-paid than politicians and economists had anticipated. Statistics Canada
warned that "moonlighting" at a second job and high rates of overtime denied
work to the unemployed. Many new jobs were part-time, low-skilled, ill-paid
and temporary. Technology and cost-cutting made "McDonaldization" a labour-
market reality. While governments cut spending on education, young people
discovered that even a degree and technical training offered none of the hopes

of a job or higher incomes that their parents had enjoyed. Low incomes and insecurity might well be their permanent fate.

Employers were unrepentant. Competing in a global economy meant squeezing costs. Consultants advised corporations to collapse job classifications, regain unfettered control over the office or the factory floor and forget about old-fashioned loyalty to long-term employees. Only shareholders and lenders mattered. Quality of Working Life and other genial experiments of the eighties vanished. The nineties were proving to be a grim decade for most working people and their unions. While the prospect of a new century and a new millennium brought some of the optimism of a century earlier, there were wounds to lick and some old alliances to rebuild. In Britain and France, social democracy revived, though with few of the ideas and values that had distinguished an earlier generation of socialists from the more humane conservatives. Would that happen in Canada? Should it? Could the growing schism between national and international unions, and between public- and private-sector unionists be bridged? Would Canadians choose to share a single country, capable of accommodating different allegiances and identities, or would the challenge of diversity be too much to bear? A new era brought many questions. It also offered one guarantee and one assurance: there would certainly be many more battles, but the labour movement gave Canadian workers a tough, flexible defender, with more imagination and dedication than its detractors. The nineties might be tough, but so were Canadian unions and their members.

CHAPTER 30

Millennial Thoughts on Working People

On the verge of a new millennium, Canada and its working people face acute problems. An aging population will depend for support on the progeny resulting from the shrunken birth-rates of the post-1960 generation. Meanwhile, those same young people face a lifetime of lower incomes and little of the social security their elders enjoyed for much of their lives. Whatever opportunities free trade may create for wealthy investors, the rules of comparative advantage will restore much of Canada to its traditional role as a resource provider, at a time when Canadians have belatedly become aware of the limits of their resources of water, wood, land and fish. Barring an equalization of incomes among countries, which is neither impossible nor likely, Canadian manufacturers and service-providers will have to seize on niche products and markets, a strategy demanding an entrepreneurial nimbleness with few local precedents.

Futures are not inevitable; they are chosen. In the future, as in the past, the labour movement will have a voice in the kind of country Canada will become. Unionists underestimate their political influence, chiefly because they spend more time making threats than carefully applying pressure. The Canadian labour movement has been healthy for the same reason American unionism is sick: the political climate. Most governments, most of the time, have accepted that workers have a democratic right to collective bargaining, whatever they (or Canadians) may feel about strikes.

Not even Mike Harris or Ralph Klein have promoted "right to work" legislation, though they have ideologues in their entourages who, like the National Citizen's Coalition, would cheerfully do so. In the eighties, the political climate turned conservative even before Brian Mulroney arrived. The brutal nineties

354

have put business to a test it has not passed very well. Canadians are poorer now, and they know it. If they lack any alternative beyond profound cynicism, labour and its intellectual allies bear some responsibility for offering little more than some old, worn-out slogans.

An unconscious ally of the assault on Canadian unionism has been the Charter of Rights and Freedoms. In the eighties, unions and central labour bodies found themselves entangled in a series of disputes, ranging from the right to use dues for political purposes to protecting Workers' Compensation from being subverted by private litigation. A number of courts passed judgement on the Rand Formula and the assumption that the Charter right of association had to include a corresponding right of "disassociation." In 1987, the Supreme Court of Canada ruled that, whatever Bryce Mackasey may have promised in 1981, the right of association did not guarantee collective bargaining or the right to organize. In 1992, Mr. Justice Gilles Letourneau, later of Somalia Commission fame, insisted that the Charter was no guarantee of the right to strike. If Canadian courts followed American examples, unions might someday lose control of how their dues were spent.

American influences already shaped industrial relations and their weight would grow. Canadian capital had invaded the United States, primarily for access to urban property development and the entertainment industry; U.S. capital was directed at resources and industries. New owners seldom found that a unionized workforce was one of an acquisition's assets. A more brutal, U.S.-bred style of union-busting spread north to infect companies, regardless of national ownership. The bombing of the Giant mine in Yellowknife in 1992, with its nine victims, may have been the work of a desperate union member, but it was an act virtually without Canadian precedents. American experience taught that delay in certification and negotiation was a wonderful way to undermine a young union. Proving "bargaining in bad faith" was notoriously difficult. After all, it was the union that was making the demands. For unions, free trade was more than a threat to branch-plant jobs; it was a weapon against unionism itself. If there was to be a "level playing field" for trade between Canada and the United States, union bargaining power was one of the bigger lumps to be bulldozed. It would be done, as it had been in the United States, by deserting regions where labour was intractable and returning, if at all, when poverty and humility had been sufficiently ingrained.

A third threat to Canadian unionism was the prospect of a long-term conservative dominance in Ottawa and the provinces. Changing parties in Ottawa in 1993 changed almost nothing. Like the Mulroney government in 1984, the Chrétien cabinet had no union-busting agenda, but neither had it any commitment to the people who worked for the government. By its second mandate, tens of thousands no longer did so. Some took buy-out packages, others found their work privatized and were left to sell their skills to an employer bent an recouping a substantial investment, preferably through lower wages and more exacting working conditions. Not until 1998 did the 1990 wage freeze melt – with a 2 percent increase. Lower-paid civil servants and members of the armed forces depended on food-banks and part-time jobs – if they could find them – to support their families.

In the 1990s, Canadian unions followed their employers' lead by merging and amalgamating in a struggle to match resources with mega-corporations. The United Needletrades, Industrial and Textile Employees, or UNITE, could trace its roots to almost a dozen once-powerful unions in the garment, textile, and related industries. (Ontario Federation of Labour)

The labour movement did not sit quiescently, waiting for its doom. As they always have, unions responded to their members and the issues of the times. The dramatic increase in women's share of employment, the growth since the 1970s of a multicultural, multi-ethnic workforce, the developing crisis of an aging population, the overdue awareness of environmental threats to workers, and our collective future: all of these realities have changed unions and challenged them.

In the late 1990s, few of the stereotypes of Canadian unionism fit. Anyone who depicts Labour as a middle-aged male labourer in a plastic safety helmet should remember that almost half of all unionists are women. Thanks to teachers and public employee unions, Canadian unionists are more likely than the general population to have a post-secondary education and university degrees. Only the middle-age characteristic fits, but the evidence is growing that younger workers want what unions give their members – a chance for dignity, economic security and a chance to serve a broader community than oneself.

In the face of a tightening business-government alliance, labour added to its reforming agenda. The eighties had broadened old and new gender issues, from maternity benefits to sexual harassment. Unions were persuaded that

Longer, fuller lives are one of the blessings unions have helped bring to working Canadians, but will the elderly lose out with cuts to Medicare and threats of user pay? Unions must organize retirees, to protect their right to a decent life and a fair share of the wealth they helped create. (Ontario Federation of Labour)

paternity leave was as necessary as maternity leave. Negotiators had to develop language to cope with sexual harassment, recognizing that fellow unionists might be the accused as well as the accuser. Members were divided over AIDS testing and restrictions on smoking in the workplace. It had been easier for them to accept affirmative action on hiring women, disabled and visible minorities when their own children could aspire to a better future than work in the plant. In the nineties, inheriting the old man's job, with a decent hourly wage, paid holidays and fringe benefits looked a lot better than flipping hamburgers – or no job at all. When it came to sharing, tough times could be mean times. Yet it was its generous, humane agenda that had allowed a union movement to survive in an economic ideology fuelled by selfishness and greed; idealism, as much as pragmatism, is a labour recipe for longevity.

Unions survive in our society because, although they are heirs to all the faults of humanity, they also embody humanity's highest virtues of faith, hope and love. Men and women who have nothing to sell but their skill and their strength cannot afford to be divided. Like all their ancestors, they will find that human organizations are imperfect. Unions will be condemned as petty, short-sighted and sometimes casual about the rights of their members. Unions will protect their shortcomings with a solidarity bred in insecurity. They will also find men and women with the vision and courage to remedy their faults and to realize new dreams. Through organization, working people will go on trying to realize the hopes that drew them or their ancestors to this country. They will build on success and try to learn from setbacks.

And if workers in their millions cannot build a better Canada, it can never be built.

Canada's Largest Unions

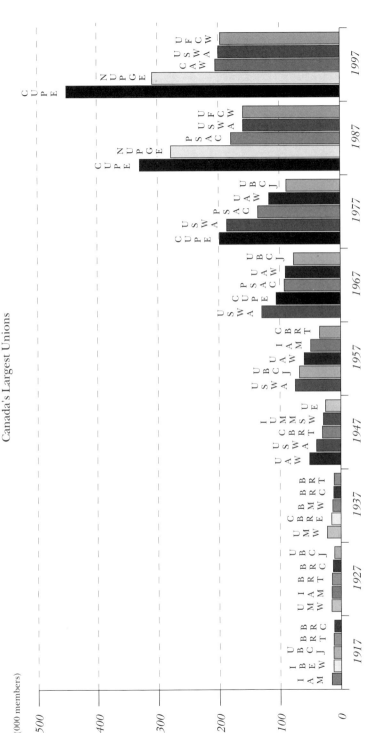

(000 members)

The changing nature of the organized workforce is evident in the unions that mustered the largest membership. In 1917, for example, Machinists, Electrical Workers and Carpenters benefited from wartime munitions contracts. Militant coal miners and well-entrenched railway unions survived the difficult interwar years but new industrial unions like the the Autoworkers and Steelworkers dominated the affluent years after 1945. In the 1960s, unionization of public-sector workers was apparent in the rise of CUPE. In the eighties, unions of municipal, provincial, and federal employees outweighed all others. By abandoning rigid jurisdictional boundaries and amalgamating smaller unions, Autoworkers, Steelworkers, and Food and Commercial Workers regained strength while public-sector workers suffered harsh cuts. (Source: *Labour Organizations in Canada, 1921–1997*)

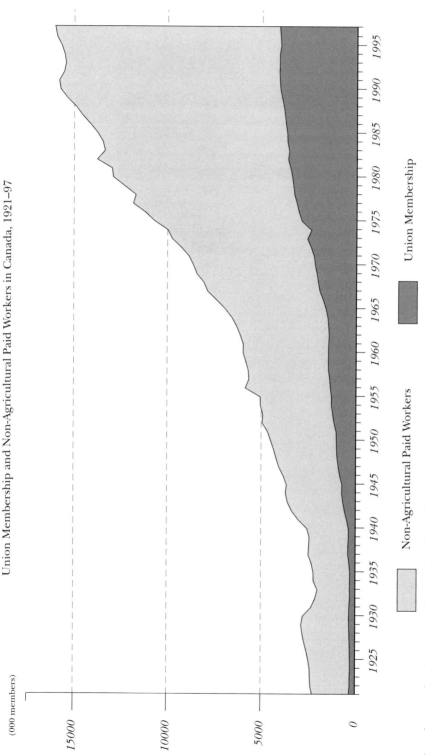

Union Membership and Non-Agricultural Paid Workers in Canada, 1921–97

(000 members)

Non-Agricultural Paid Workers   Union Membership

Since farm workers have generally been denied the right to organize, and unpaid workers have yet to attract union attention, the only workers available for unions to organize are described by a mouth-filling phrase. Their numbers have grown rapidly, particularly as women surged into the workforce in the 1960s. The unionized share grew too, with some exceptions, at least until the 1990s when hard times and a hostile political climate have led to stagnation and a slow decline. (Source: *Labour Organizations in Canada, 1921–1997*)

Membership in Labour Central Organizations

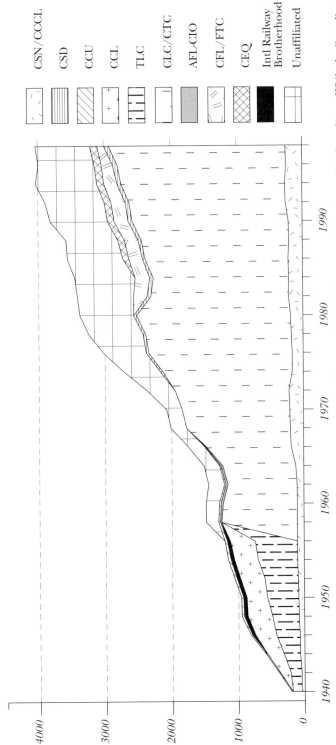

(000 members)

CSN/CCCL	
CSD	
CCU	
CCL	
TLC	
CLC/CTC	
AFL-CIO	
CFL/FTC	
CEQ	
Intl Railway Brotherhood	
Unaffiliated	

Canadian unionists sometimes sing an old labour song, Solidarity Forever, but they guard their differences as jealously as other Canadians. While the Canadian Labour Congress is the biggest organization, even in Quebec the CNTU/CSN has grown proportionately in a sympathetic climate. In contrast, the conservative building trades in the Canadian Federation of Labour were particularly vulnerable to anti-union legislation and folded. Little remains of the tiny but ambitious left-nationalist organization, the Confederation of Canadian Unions. Many Canadian unionists, particularly in the professions, are not affiliated to any central organization. (Source: Labour Organizations in Canada, 1946–1997)

Further Reading

ABBREVIATIONS

CHR – *Canadian Historical Review*
L/LT – *Labour/le Travail*
MQUP – McGill-Queen's University Press
M&S – McClelland & Stewart
QU/IRC – Queen's University Industrial Relations Centre (or Department)
RHAF – *Revue d'Histoire de l'Amérique Française*
UTP – University of Toronto Press

Early labour history in Canada was often a by-product of the work of labour economists, seeking to explain how unions and labour legislation came into existence. Robert Coats, later the Dominion Statistician, was the first of a long line of scholars from the political economy tradition. Harold Logan, Clare Pentland and Eugene Forsey were others. Some, like Charles Lipton, viewed labour history as the fulfilment of a radical political vision for Canada – or its frustration. Others – all too few in Canada – have contributed as participants and observers from within. Morden Lazarus, Alfred Charpentier and Tom McEwan and latterly, with the help of professional writers, Bob White, Jack Munro, and Grace Hartman have presented their own perspective as labour leaders.

In the 1960s, interest in labour and trade union history grew dramatically, as part of a larger explosion in the study and writing of Canadian history. New themes have joined the old preoccupation with organizations, strikes and politics. The examples of E.P. Thompson in Britain and the *Annales* School in France encouraged historians to integrate family life, culture, religion, fraternal associations and every other aspect of social existence to create a much more textured understanding of our past. In Canada this awareness is best represented by *Labour/le Travail* (*L/LT*), a journal of labour history launched in Halifax in 1976 and sustained in St. John's by Greg Kealey, but the reflections can be found in every part of the country.

GENERAL READING

A number of authors have attempted to give Canadians a comprehensive view of their labour movement. None – including the author of this volume – has satisfied every need. Harold A. Logan's *Trade Unions in Canada: Their Development and Functioning* (Toronto: Macmillan, 1948) presented Canadian labour to generations of industrial relations students but it is now obsolete. Stuart Jamieson's *Industrial Relations in Canada* (Toronto: Macmillan, 2nd ed., 1973) provided a brief overview, but historians were even more grateful for *Times of Trouble: Labour Unrest and Industrial Conflict in Canada, 1900–1966* (Ottawa: Privy Council Office, 1968), prepared for the Woods Task Force and a valuable reference, though limited by its terms of reference. Charles Lipton, *The Trade Union Movement of Canada, 1827–1959* (Toronto: NC Press, 1973) was a pioneering effort marred by too many errors and too much preaching.

The influence of the radical British historian, E.P. Thompson, in Canada is illustrated by Bryan D. Palmer's *Working Class Experience: Rethinking the History of Canadian Labour, 1800–1991* (Toronto: M&S, 2nd ed., 1993). A briefer product of the same school is Craig Heron's *The Canadian Labour Movement: A Brief History* (Toronto: James Lorimer, 2nd ed., 1996). Two books of essays reflect the evolution of the dominant school in the field: Gregory S. Kealey and Peter Warrian (eds.) *Essays in Canadian Working Class History* (Toronto: M&S, 1976) and Bryan D. Palmer (ed.) *The Character of Class Struggle: Essays in Canadian Working-Class History, 1850–1985* (Toronto: M&S, 1986).

Canadian provinces have their own distinct union cultures and histories. The pioneering provincial labour history was Paul Phillips' *No Power Greater: A Century of Labour in B.C.* (Vancouver: Broadway Printers, 1967). An able scholar, Jacques Rouillard, tackled Quebec's union experience in *l'Histoire du Syndicalisme Québécoise* (Montreal: Boréal Express, 1988). Provincial labour federations recruited journalists to tackle their respective provinces: Warren Caragata, *Alberta Labour: A Heritage Untold* (Toronto: James Lorimer, 1979); Doug Smith, *Let Us Rise: A History of the Manitoba Labour Movement* (Vancouver: New Star Books, 1985), and Bill Gillespie, *A Class Act: An Illustrated History of the Labour Movement in Newfoundland and Labrador* (St. John's: Federation of Labour, 1986).

Much important material on labour's story is contained in government documents and official publications. The monthly *Labour Gazette*, published by the Canadian Department of Labour from 1900 to 1978, was a mine of statistics and summaries of countless reports on conflicts and conciliation, labour market conditions, cost of living data and much, much more. *Labour Organizations in Canada* and *Labour Legislation in Canada* are valuable annual publications. The *Canada Year Book* includes a slightly dated chapter of labour statistics. Many union newspapers are readily available on microfilm through the excellent library of Labour Canada in Hull. A catalogue of holdings is available.

The demise of the *Labour Gazette* made it difficult to find a general source of news on Canadian labour developments. Industrial relations professionals have been well served by *The Current Industrial Relations Scene in Canada* (Kingston: QU/IRC), launched in 1974 by Donald Wood and continued by Pradeep Kumar. Statistics Canada's *Perspectives on Labour and Income* is frequently helpful.

HISTORIOGRAPHY

The writing of Canadian labour history has been characterised by strong opinions, strongly held. Michael Cross provided a cheerful introduction in "To the Dartmouth Station: A Worker's Eye View of Labour History," *L/LT* 1 (1976). The dominant figure in working-class history since the 1960s has been Greg Kealey, whose perspectives are summed up in the essays in his *Workers and Canadian History* (Montreal and Kingston: MQUP, 1995). Ken Osborne offered a perceptive overview in *Hard-working, Temperate and Peaceable: The Portrayal of Workers in Canadian History Textbooks* (Winnipeg: Manitoba Monographs in Education, 1980). Guided by the devoted work of Douglas Vaisey and Jim Thwaites, *Labour/Le Travail* became the indispensable guide to the bibliography of Canadian labour and working-class history.

CHAPTERS

1. Working People   A landmark in understanding Canadian workers in the nineteenth century is Paul Craven's collection in the Ontario Historical Studies Series: *Labouring Lives: Work and Working in Nineteenth Century Ontario* (Toronto: UTP, 1995). The chapters and their authors give some measure of its scope: Terry Crowley, "Rural Labour"; Jeremy Webber, "Labour and the Law"; Ian Radforth, "The Shantymen"; Lynne Marks, "Religion, Leisure and Working Class Identity"; Paul Craven, "Labour and Management on the Great Western Railway"; Bettina Bradbury, "The Home as Workplace"; Craig Heron, "Factory Workers." Less limited in time and place is Michael S. Cross (ed.) *The Workingman in the Nineteenth Century* (Toronto: Oxford, 1974). Two academic studies based on early social research in the two largest Canadian cities are Michael J. Piva, *The Conditions of the Working Class in Toronto, 1900–1921* (Ottawa: University of Ottawa Press, 1979) and J.T. Copp, *The Anatomy of Poverty: The Conditions of the Working Class in Montreal, 1897–1929* (Toronto: M&S, 1974). A fascinating alternative is Jean de Bonville, *Jean-Baptiste Gagnepetit: les travailleurs montréalais à la fin du XIXe siècle* (Montreal: l'Aurore, 1975). A more ambitious treatment of a much narrower field is Bryan Palmer, *A Culture in Conflict: Skilled Workers and Industrial Capitalism in Hamilton, Ontario, (1860–1914)* (Montreal and Kingston: MQUP, 1979), esp. chaps. 2–4. The Royal Commission on the Relations of Labor and Capital looked at working conditions and problems in Ontario, Quebec, New Brunswick and Nova Scotia between 1887 and 1889, and its report was condensed by Greg Kealey, *Canada Investigates Industrialism* (Toronto: UTP, 1973, reprint).

A remarkable article on the hardships of working-class life in Canada is Judith Fingard's "The Winter Tale: Contours of Pre-Industrial Poverty in British America, 1815–1860," *Historical Papers* (1974). Another illustration of her skill as a social historian is *Jack in Port: Sailortowns of Eastern Canada* (Toronto: UTP, 1982). On the same theme, see Eric Sager, *Seafaring Labor: The Merchant Marine of Atlantic Canada, 1820–1914* (Montreal and Kingston: MQUP, 1989). Workers have homes and families. Bettina Bradbury, "Pigs, Cows and Boarders: Non-Wage Forms of Survival Among Montreal Families, 1861–91," *L/LT* 14 (1984); John Bullen, "Hidden Works: Child Labour and the Family Economy in Late Nineteenth Century Urban Ontario," *ibid.* 18 (1986), and Peter de Lottinville, "Joe Beef of Montreal: Working Class Culture and the Tavern, 1869–1889," *ibid.* 8–9 (1981–82), all illuminate other themes of working-class history. Janet Guildford and Suzanne Morton edited *Separate Spheres: Women's Worlds in the 19th Century Maritimes* (Fredericton: Acadiensis Press, 1994). On the ethnic dimensions of labour mobility, see Bruno Ramirez, *On the Move: French Canadian and Italian Migrants in the North American Economy, 1860–1914* (Toronto: M&S, 1991).

2. Getting Organized   E.A. Forsey's *Trade Unions in Canada, 1812–1902* (Toronto: UTP, 1982) opened up the origins and early development of Canadian unionism in all its diversity. Angela E. Davis, *Art and Work: A Social History of Labour in the Canadian Graphic Arts Industry to the 1840s* (Montreal and Kingston: MQUP, 1995) reveals a more complex scene than earlier accounts of "the Art preservative." Conflict does not, of course, always depend on structures, as Clare Pentland demonstrated in "The Lachine Strike of 1843," *CHR* 29 (1948), and Ruth Bleasdale in "Class Conflict on the Canals of Upper Canada in the 1840's," *L/LT* 7 (1981). Nor do all structures resemble unions. See M.S. Cross, "The Shiners' War: Social Violence in the Ottawa Valley in the 1830's," *CHR* 54 (1973). Pentland's *Labour and Capital in Canada, 1650–1860* (Toronto: James Lorimer, 1981) made a strong but imperfect case for a "pre-industrial" capitalism, answered (for those who enjoy academic disputation) by Alan Greer, "Wage Labor and the Transition to Capitalism: A Critique of Pentland," *L/LT* 15 (1985). Still valuable as a perspective on early unions are articles by J.I. Cooper, "The Quebec Ship-Labourers' Benevolent Society," *CHR* 30 (1949); Margaret Heap, "La grève des charretiers à Montréal, 1864," *RHAF* 31 (1977); and G.S. Kealey, "Artisans Respond to Industrialism: Shoemakers, Shoe Factories and the Knights of St. Crispin in Toronto," *Historical Papers* (1973).

3. International Ideas   Daniel O'Donoghue, sometimes labelled the father of Canadian labour, found a sympathetic biographer in Doris French, *Faith, Sweat and Politics* (Toronto: M&S, 1962). The origins of organized labour in Quebec are covered swiftly by Rouillard, *Histoire du syndicalisme*, by Paul Desrosiers and Denis Heroux, *Le travailleur Québécois et le syndicalisme* (Montreal: Presses de l'Université du Québec, 1973), and most recently and thoroughly by a team of scholars in James D. Thwaites (ed.) *Travail et syndicalisme: naissance et évolution d'une action sociale* (Québec: Presses de l'Université Laval, 1996).

Contrasting views of the Nine-Hour movement and its political consequences are presented by Donald G. Creighton, "George Brown, Sir John A. Macdonald and the Working Man," *CHR* 24 (1943) and, in a more analytical way, by John Battye, "The Nine Hour Pioneers: The Genesis of the Canadian Labour Movement," *L/LT* 4 (1979). On the roots of three "internationals" in Canada see Peter Bischoff, "La formation des traditions de solidarité ouvrière chez les mouleurs Montréalais: la longue marche vers le syndicalisme, 1859–1891," *ibid.* 21 (1988); Ian McKay, *The Craft Transformed: An Essay on the Carpenters of Halifax* (Halifax: Holdfast Press, 1985) (esp. chap. 1), a history of Local 83 of the UBCJA; and Sally Zerker, *The Rise and Fall of the Toronto Typographical Union, 1832–1972: A Case Study of Foreign Domination* (Toronto: UTP, 1982), esp. chaps. 4–5.

4. Political Movement   French's *Faith, Sweat and Politics* described O'Donoghue's venture into politics as the first labour candidate to win a significant election in Canada. A more important source is Bernard Ostry's "Conservatives, Liberals and Labour in the 1870s," *CHR* 41 (1960). Another view is offered by Martin Robin in "The Working Class and the Transition to Capitalist Democracy in Canada," *Dalhousie Review* 47 (1967) which, in turn, is the introductory chapter in Robin's *Radical Politics and Canadian Labour, 1880–1930* (Kingston: QU/IRC, 1969). On the wider significance of the Grand Trunk strike, see Desmond Morton, "Taking on the Grand Trunk: The Locomotive Engineers' Strike of 1876–77," *L/LT* 2 (1977). Reports of CLU conventions were published by Leslie Wismer (ed.) *Proceedings of the Canadian Labour Union Congress* (Ottawa: Trades and Labour Congress, 1951). A report on the vigorous labour press in the 1870s and revived in the 1880s is found in Frank Watt, "The National Policy, the Workingman and the Proletarian Idea in Victorian Canada," *CHR* 40 (1959). See Palmer, *Culture in Conflict*, chap. 4 for the impact of labour politics in Hamilton.

5. Labour Reformers   The Knights of Labor, as befits their pioneering significance, have attracted considerable attention in Canada. Palmer's *Working Class Experience*, chaps. 3–5 summarises much of a longer case he and G.S. Kealey offer in *"Dreaming of What Might Be": The Knights of Labor in Ontario, 1880–1890* (Cambridge: University of Cambridge Press, 1982 and Toronto: New Hogtown Press, 1987). In his own book, *Toronto Workers Respond to Industrial Capitalism, 1867–92* (Toronto: UTP, 1980), Kealey did even more to illuminate the old themes of labour and politics than to illustrate his own concern with class and culture. Palmer, *A Culture in Conflict*, chap. 6 deals with the order in Hamilton. A major statement of the Knights' case for "labour reform" was written for Americans by a Canadian, T. Phillips Thompson, *The Politics of Labor* (Toronto: UTP, 1975, reprint). On Thompson and his times, see Ramsay Cook, *The Regenerators: Social Criticism in Late Victorian English Canada* (Toronto: UTP, 1985), esp. chap. 9.

On the Knights and politics, see Robin, *Radical Politics*, chap. 2; Bernard Ostry, "Conservatives, Liberals and Labour in the 1880s," *Canadian Journal of Economics and Political Science* 18 (1961); and Desmond Morton, *"The Globe* and the Labour Question: Ontario Liberalism in the 'Great Upheaval,' May 1886,"

Ontario History 73 (1981). See also Russell Hann, "Brainworkers and the Knights of Labor: E.E. Sheppard, Phillips Thompson and the Toronto News (1883–1887)," in Kealey and Warrian, *Canadian Working Class History*. On fiction relating to the Knights, see Mary Vipond, "Blessed are the Peacemakers: The Labour Question in Canadian Social Gospel Fiction," *Journal of Canadian Studies* 10 (1975). Lynne Marks looks at an aspect of Knights' ideology in "The Knights of Labour and the Salvation Army: Religion and Working-Class Culture in Ontario, 1882–1890," *L/LT* 28 (1991). Eric Tucker has contributed a number of insights into this period, among them (with Judy Fudge), "Forging Responsible Unions: Metal Workers and the Rise of the Labour Injunction in Canada," *L/LT* 37 (1996).

6. Hinterland Labour   The most comprehensive treatment of the Nova Scotia labour movement is still Paul MacEwan's *Miners and Steelworkers: Labour in Cape Breton* (Toronto: Samuel, Stevens and Hakkert). But see also Judith Hoegg Ryan, *Coal in Our Blood: 200 Years of Coalmining in Nova Scotia's Pictou County* (Halifax: Formac, 1992). On the PWA, see Ian McKay, "'By Wisdom, Wile or War': The Provincial Workmen's Association and the Struggle for Working Class Independence in Nova Scotia, 1879–1896," *L/LT* 18 (1986). See also McKay on the social history of coal miners in "The Realm of Uncertainty: The Experience of Work in the Cumberland Coal Miners, 1873–1927," *Acadiensis* 16 (1986). An interesting sidelight on miners' unionism can be found in Donald MacLeod's "Colliers, Collier Safety and Workplace Control: The Nova Scotia Experience, 1873 to 1910," *Historical Papers* (1983). A Newfoundland dimension to labour's struggle can be found in Briton Cooper Bush, "The Newfoundland Sealers' Strike of 1902," *L/LT* 14 (1984). The dominant figure in Newfoundland's early working-class history was William Coaker: see Ian D.H. McDonald, *To Each His Own: William Coaker and the Fishermen's Protective Union in Newfoundland Politics, 1908–1925* (St. John's: MUN, ISER, 1987).

Edmund Bradwin, *The Bunkhouse Man* (Toronto: UTP, 1972, reprint) described conditions in frontier work camps at the turn of the century. Ian Radforth begins at that point in his impressive *Bushworkers and Bosses: Logging in Northern Ontario, 1900–1980* (Toronto: UTP, 1987) esp. chaps. 1–2. See also Edward McKenna, "Unorganized Labour versus Management: The Strike at the Chaudière Lumber Mills, 1891," *Histoire Sociale/Social History* 4 (1972), deals with unfamiliar problems of the hinterland worker. See also Douglas Baldwin, "The Life of the Silver Miner in Northern Ontario," *L/LT* 3 (1977). On working conditions in the West, Donald Avery, *Dangerous Foreigners: European Immigrant Workers and Labour Radicalism in Canada, 1896–1932* (Toronto: M&S, 1979), and Lynne Bowen, *Boss Whistle: The Coal Miners of Vancouver Island Remember* (Lantzville: Oolichan Books, 1982), a model of its kind. On British Columbia, see Phillips, *No Power Greater*, chaps. 2 and 3; Tina Loo, *Making Law, Order and Authority in British Columbia, 1821–1871* (Toronto: UTP, 1994); Robin, *Radical Politics*, chaps. 2 and 3; Mark Leier, *Red Flags and Red Tape: The Making of a Labour Bureaucracy* (Toronto: UTP, 1995), on the Vancouver Trades and Labour Council; and Jeremy Mouat, "The Genesis of Western Exceptionalism: British Columbia's Hard Rock Miners, 1895–1903," *CHR* 71 (1990).

7. Trades and Labour   The decade of the 1890s is dealt with in part by Palmer, *Culture in Conflict*; essays by Harvey J. Graff and Wayne Roberts in Kealey and Warrian, *Essays in Canadian Working Class History*; and Ian McKay, "Capital and Labour in the Halifax Baking and Confectionery Industry during the Last Half of the Nineteenth Century," *L/LT* 3 (1978). The transformation of labour radicalism in the decade is illuminated by Gene Homel, "Fading Beams of the Nineteenth Century: Radicalism and Early Socialism in Canada's 1890's," *L/LT* 5 (1980) and Mark Leier's *Red Flags and Red Tape*. One feature of the period was the fleeting possibility of an agrarian alliance. See Ramsay Cook, "Tillers and Toilers: The Rise and Fall of Populism in Canada in the 1890s," *Historical Papers* (1984).

8. Gompers's Shadow   Robert Babcock, *Gompers in Canada: A Study of American Continentalism Before the First World War* (Toronto: UTP, 1975) is appropriately disparaging of Canadian capacity to judge our own self-interest. The impact on Quebec is reviewed by Jacques Rouillard, "Le Québec et le congrès de Berlin (1902)," *L/LT* 1 (1976) and by Babcock, "Samuel Gompers and the French-Canadian Workers," *American Review of Canadian Studies* 3 (1973). For a view of labour in the post-1900 period, see also Jacques Rouillard's *Les travailleurs du coton au Québec (1900–1915)* (Montreal: Presses de l'Université du Québec, 1974). The militancy of the era is explored by Craig Heron and Bryan D. Palmer, "Through the Prism of the Strike: Industrial Conflict in Southern Ontario, 1902–14," *CHR* 58 (1977), and by Ian McKay, "Strikes in the Maritimes, 1901–1914," *Acadiensis* 15 (1986). Further illustrations are Craig Heron's "The Crisis of the Craftsman: Hamilton's Metal Workers in the Early Twentieth Century," *L/LT* 6 (1982) [chapter 1 in *Working in Steel: The Early Years in Canada, 1883–1935* (Toronto: M&S, 1988)]; and Michael J. Piva, "The Toronto District Labour Council and Independent Political Action: Factionalism and Frustration, 1900–1921," *L/LT* 4 (1979).

For a view of an important, often overlooked sector, see Wayne Roberts, "Artisans, Aristocrats and Handymen: Politics and Unionism among Toronto's Skilled Building Trades Workers, 1896–1914," *ibid.* 1 (1976). See also Yvon Fortier, *Menuisier charpentier: un artisan du bois à l'ère industrielle* (Montreal: Boréal Express, 1980). Telephone workers have been a logical focus of interest in gender-based studies. See Michele Martin, *"Hello Central?" Gender, Technology and Culture in the Formation of Telephone Systems* (Montreal and Kingston: MQUP, 1991); Joan Sangster, "The 1907 Bell Telephone Strike: Organizing Women Workers," *L/LT* 3 (1977); and Shirley Tillotson, "We May All Soon Be 'First Class Men': Gender and Skill in Canada's Early Twentieth Century Telegraph Industry," *ibid.* 28 (1991).

9. Business, Labour and Governments   The best description of Canadian business attitudes to labour remains Michael Bliss, *A Living Profit: Studies in the Social History of Canadian Business, 1883–1911* (Toronto: M&S, 1974), pp. 74–94, amplified in *Northern Enterprise: Five Centuries of Canadian Business* (Toronto: M&S, 1987). Michael Piva, *The Condition of the Working Class in Toronto*, chap. 6, describes the business counter-attack. H.S. Ferns and Bernard Ostry, *The Age* *of Mackenzie King: The Rise of the Leader* (Toronto: James Lorimer, 2nd ed., 1975) had a low view of Canada's best-known industrial relations practitioner; Paul Craven, *"An Impartial Umpire": Industrial Relations and the Canadian State, 1900–1911* (Toronto: UTP, 1980) is more knowledgeable and sympathetic. See also Jeremy Webber, "Compelling Compromise: Canada Chooses Conciliation over Arbitration, 1900–1907," *L/LT* 28 (1991). On the use of force against strikers, Desmond Morton, "Aid to the Civil Power: The Canadian Militia in Support of Social Order, 1867–1914," *CHR* 51 (1970).

Business attitudes were affected by contemporary social gospel teachings. A book dealing more with the fall than the rise of the social gospel in Canada is Richard Allen, *The Social Passion: Religion and Social Reform in Canada, 1914–1928* (Toronto: UTP, 1971), chaps. 1 and 2. See also Richard Allen, "The Social Gospel and the Reform Tradition in Canada, 1896–1928," *CHR* 49 (1968). The Grand Trunk strike, treated by Ferns and Ostry, is viewed from another perspective by Hugh Tuck, "Union Authority, Corporate Obstinacy and the Grand Trunk Strike of 1910," *Historical Papers* (1976). The development of Canada's first workers' compensation system is described by Eric Tucker, *Administering Danger in the Workplace: The Law and Politics of Occupational Health and Safety Regulation in Ontario, 1850–1914* (Toronto: UTP, 1990). The steel industry has been studied as an example of new technology and its impact on labour: Craig Heron, "Hamilton's Steelworkers and the Rise of Mass Production," *Historical Papers* (1982) and *Working in Steel*, chap. 3. A group of workers seldom included in working-class history is studied by Greg Marquis, "Working Men in Uniform: The Early Twentieth-Century Toronto Police," *Histoire Sociale/Social History* 20 (1987).

On feminism and labour, see Alice Klein and Wayne Roberts, "Besieged Innocence: The 'Problem' and Problems of Working Women – Toronto, 1896–1914" (among other useful articles) in Janice Acton, Penny Goldsmith and Bonnie Sheppard, *Women at Work: Ontario, 1850–1930* (Toronto: Canadian Women's Educational Press, 1974). See also Bob Russell, "A Fair or a Minimum Wage: Women Workers, the State, and the Origins of Wage Regulation in Western Canada," *L/LT* 28 (1991). See also Ruth Frager, *Sweatshop Strife, Class, Ethnicity and Gender in the Jewish Labour Movement of Toronto, 1900–1939* (Toronto: UTP, 1992).

10. Labour Radicals   For a pioneering look at the roots of socialism in Canada: P.W. Fox, "Early Socialism in Canada," in J.H.G. Aitchison (ed.) *The Political Process in Canada* (Toronto: UTP, 1963); or later works by Norman Penner, *The Canadian Left: A Critical Analysis* (Scarborough: Prentice-Hall, 1977) chap. 3.

On the West: Gerald Friesen, "Years in Revolt: Regionalism, Socialism and the Western Canadian Labour Movement," *L/LT* 1 (1976); David Bercuson, "Labour Radicalism and the Western Frontier, 1897–1919," *CHR* 58 (1977); J.H. Tuck, "The United Brotherhood of Railway Employees in Western Canada, 1898–1905," *L/LT* 11 (1980); also Robin, *Radical Politics*; Phillips, *No Greater Power*, chaps. 3 and 4; Mark Leier, *Where the Fraser River Flows: The Industrial Workers of the World in British Columbia* (Vancouver: New Star Books, 1990); David

J. Bercuson, *Fools and Wise Men: The Rise and Fall of the One Big Union* (Toronto: McGraw-Hill Ryerson, 1978), esp. chap. 4; and A. Ross McCormack, *Reformers, Rebels and Revolutionaries: The Western Canadian Radical Movement, 1899–1919* (Toronto: UTP, 1978).

For the other end of Canada, see David Frank and Nolan Reilly, "The Emergence of the Socialist Movement in the Maritimes, 1899–1916," *L/LT* 4 (1979); Ian McKay, "Strikes in the Maritimes, 1901–1914," *Acadiensis* 13 (1983). On Quebec: Groupe de chercheurs de l'UQAM sur l'histoire des travailleurs québécois, *L'Action politique des ouvriers Québécois, fin du XIXe siècle à 1919* (Montreal: Presses de l'Université du Québec, 1976).

On women and radicalism, see Wayne Roberts, "Rocking the Cradle for the World: The New Woman and Maternal Feminism, Toronto, 1877–1914," in Linda Kealey (ed.) *A Not Unreasonable Claim: Women and Reform in Canada, 1880s-1920s* (Toronto: Women's Press, 1979); Linda Kealey, "Canadian Socialism and the Woman Question, 1900–1914," *L/LT* 13 (1984), and, especially, Janice Newton, *The Feminist Challenge to the Canadian Left, 1900–1918* (Montreal and Kingston: MQUP, 1995).

11. Labour and the First World War   While the war years sowed seeds for the unprecedented postwar explosion of militancy, no single work has focussed on the Canadian labour experience during the war itself, though Craig Heron's *The Workers' Revolt in Canada, 1917–1925* (Toronto: UTP, 1998) is an ambitious synthesis. On the experiences of more than half a million members of the working class who had joined up, see Desmond Morton and Glenn Wright, *Winning the Second Battle: Canadian Veterans and the Return to Civilian Life, 1915–1930* (Toronto: UTP, 1987).

The growth of radicalism is explained by Martin Robin, "Registration, Conscription and Independent Labour Politics, 1916–1917," *CHR* 47 (1966), expanded in *Radical Politics*, chaps. 9 and 10; Bercuson, *Fools and Wise Men*, chaps. 3 and 4; McCormack, *Reformers, Rebels and Revolutionaries*, chaps. 7 and 8. Conscription made Ginger Goodwin a labour martyr. See Susan Mayse, *"Ginger": The Life and Death of Albert Goodwin* (Madeira Park, B.C.: Harbour Publishers, 1990). On other workers, particularly in the munitions industry, see Daphne Read *et al.* (eds.) *The Great War and Canadian Society: An Oral History* (Toronto: New Hogtown Press, 1978), chap. 8; Ceta Ramkhalawasingh, "Women during the Great War" in Acton, Goldsmith and Sheppard, *Women at Work*. A crucial labour dispute is covered by Myer Siemiatcki, "Munitions and Labour Militancy: The 1916 Hamilton Machinists' Strike," *L/LT* 3 (1978). See also Suzanne Morton, "The Halifax Relief Commission and Labour Relations during the Reconstruction of Halifax, 1917–1919," *Acadiensis* 18 (1989); Craig Heron, "The Great War and Nova Scotia Steelworkers," *ibid.* 16 (1987).

Ethnic conflict was a harsh sub-theme of Canada at war. See Stanley Scott, "A Profusion of Issues: Immigrant Labour, the World War and the Cominco Strike of 1917," *L/LT* 2 (1977); Donald Avery, "Ethnic and Class Tensions in Canada, 1918–20: Anglo-Canadians and the Alien Worker" in Frances Swyripa and John H. Thompson (eds.) *Ukrainians in Canada during the Great War* (Edmonton: Institute of Ukrainian Studies, 1983). The war generated a few labour institutions and social programmes: Udo Sautter, "The Origins of the Employment Service of Canada, 1900–1920," *L/LT* 6 (1980); it also launched state surveillance and repression of radical labour movements, a field explored by Greg Kealey, "State Repression of Labour and the Left, 1914–20: The Impact of the First World War," *CHR* 73 (1992); and Stan Horrall, "The Royal North-West Mounted Police and Labour Unrest in Western Canada, 1919," *CHR* 61 (1980).

12. Western Revolt   The Winnipeg General Strike has long been a focus for Canadian labour history and for its historians. See G.S. Kealey, "1919: The Canadian Labour Revolt," *L/LT* 13 (1984). On the struggle in Winnipeg, see Donald Masters' dated but revealing *The Winnipeg General Strike* (Toronto: UTP, 1950); David J. Bercuson, *Confrontation at Winnipeg: Labour, Industrial Relations and the General Strike* (Montreal and Kingston: MQUP, 1974), with a thesis summarised in "The Winnipeg General Strike: Collective Bargaining and the One Big Union Issue," *CHR* 51 (1970). J.M. Bumsted's *The Winnipeg General Strike of 1919: An Illustrated History* (Winnipeg: William Dwyer, 1994), is a more popular account. As a document of the times, Norman Penner published *Winnipeg, 1919; The Strikers' Own History of the Winnipeg General Strike* (Toronto: James, Lewis & Samuel, 1973). For biographies of the Winnipeg leaders and, particularly, what become of them, see Harry Gutkin and Mildred Gutkin, *Profiles in Dissent: The Shaping of Radical Thought in the Canadian West* (Edmonton: NeWest Publishers, 1996).

The events of 1919 spread far beyond Winnipeg. See Heron's *The Workers' Revolt, 1917–1925*; Robin, *Radical Politics*, chaps. 10–12; Donald Avery, "The Radical Alien and the Winnipeg General Strike of 1919" in Carl Berger and Ramsay Cook, *The West and the Nation* (Toronto: M&S, 1976); David Bright, "We Are All Workers: Remembering Labour and Class in Calgary, 1919," *L/LT* 29 (1992); Phillips, *No Power Greater*, chap. 5; Nolan Reilly, "The General Strike in Amherst, Nova Scotia, 1919," *Acadiensis* 9 (1980); James Naylor, *The New Democracy: Challenging the Social Order in Industrial Ontario, 1914–25* (Toronto: UTP, 1991); and Brian Hogan, *Cobalt: Year of the Strike* (Cobalt: Highway Book Shop, 1978). The General Strike was a catalyst for radical politics in Canada. See Kenneth McNaught, *A Prophet in Politics: A Biography of J.S. Woodsworth* (Toronto: UTP, 1959); Allen Mills, *A Fool for Christ: The Political Thought of J.S. Woodsworth* (Toronto: UTP, 1991); Anthony Mardiros, *The Life of a Prairie Radical: William Irvine* (Toronto: James Lorimer, 1979). The labour revolt also helped the career of the Liberal Party's labour expert, W.L. Mackenzie King, whose *Industry and Humanity: A Study in the Principles Underlying Industrial Reconstruction* appeared in 1919 and was reprinted by UTP in 1974. See Reginald Whitaker, "The Liberal Corporatist Ideas of Mackenzie King," *L/LT* 2 (1977).

13. Unroaring Twenties   A decade of setbacks began from a foundation of low incomes: see Michael Piva, "Urban Working Class Incomes and Real Incomes, 1921: A Comparative Analysis," *Histoire Sociale/Social History* 16 (1983). Labour's wartime venture into politics ended with some gains and many failures: Robin, *Radical Politics*, chaps. 14–16 set the stage. For agrarian views, see W.C. Good, *Farmer Citizen: My Fifty Years in the Canadian Farmers' Movement* (Toronto: Ryerson Press, 1958). The decade saw the emergence of the Canadian Communist Party, described sympathetically by William Beeching and Phyllis Clark, *Yours in the Struggle: Reminiscences of Tim Buck* (Toronto: NC Press, 1977), more analytically by William Rodney, *Soldiers of the International: A History of the Communist Party of Canada, 1919–1929* (Toronto: UTP, 1968), and from a more recent, Trotskyite perspective: Ian Angus, *Canadian Bolsheviks: The Early Years of the Communist Party of Canada* (Montreal: Vanguard Publications, 1981). The most recent contribution is by John Manley, "Does the International Labour Movement Need Salvaging?: Communism, Labourism and the Canadian Trade Unions, 1921–1928," *L/LT* 41 (1998). In the West, the One Big Union fought and died, as described by Bercuson, *Fools and Wise Men*, chaps. 7–10, and more lightly by James Gray, *The Roar of the Twenties* (Toronto: Macmillan, 1975), chaps. 1 and 3.

In Quebec, the Catholic syndicates emerged into significance. See Jacques Rouillard, *Histoire de la C.S.N. (1921–1981)* (Montreal: Boréal Express, 1981), chap. 2. See also Alfred Charpentier, *Ma conversion au syndicalisme catholique* (Montreal: Fidès, 1946); Louis Maheu, "Problème social et naissance du syndicalisme catholique" in Fernand Harvey (ed.) *Aspects historiques du mouvement ouvrier au Québec* (Montreal: Boréal Express, 1973). For years the standard work on the CCCL was Alan B. Latham, *The Catholic and National Labor Union of Canada* (Toronto: Macmillan, 1930).

In Nova Scotia, a decade of tragic struggles is described by MacEwan, *Miners and Steelworkers*, pp. 65–168; David Frank, "Class Conflict in the Coal Industry: Cape Breton, 1922" in Kealey and Warrian, *Essays in Canadian Working Class History*; also David Frank, "The Trial of J.B. McLachlan," *Historical Papers* (1983) and David Frank, "The Cape Breton Coal Industry and the Rise and Fall of the British Empire Steel Corporation" in T.W. Acheson *et al.*, *Industrialization and Underdevelopment in the Maritimes, 1880–1930* (Toronto: Garamond, 1985); John Manley, "Preaching the Red Stuff: J.B. McLachlan, Communism and the Cape Breton Miners, 1922–1935," *L/LT* 30 (1992); and "Canadian Communists, Revolutionary Unions and the "Third Period": The Workers Unity League, 1929–1935," *Journal of the Canadian Historical Association* 5 (1994). See also Craig Heron, *Working in Steel*, chap. 4; Donald MacGillivray, "Military Aid to the Civil Power: The Cape Breton Experience in the 1920's," *Acadiensis* 3 (1974). Another coal mining region is depicted by Allen Seager, "Minto, New Brunswick: A Study in Class Relations between the Wars," *L/LT* 5 (1980).

The decade saw social legislation for women and the elderly. See James Struthers, *No Fault of Their Own: Unemployment and the Canadian Welfare State, 1914–1941* (Toronto: UTP, 1983), chap. 1; Margaret E. McCallum, "Keeping Women in Their Place: The Minimum Wage in Canada, 1910–25," *L/LT* 17 (1986); Shirley Tillotson, "Human Rights Law as a Prism: Women's Organizations, Unions and Ontario's Female Employees Fair Remuneration Act of 1921," *CHR* 72 (1991); Veronica Strong-Boag, "Wages for Housework: Mothers' Allowance and the Beginnings of Social Security in Canada," *Journal of Canadian Studies* 14 (1979); Kenneth Bryden, *Old Age Pensions and Policy-Making in*

Canada (Montreal and Kingston: MQUP, 1974), chaps. 4–5. Businesses met labour radicalism with pre-emptive strategies. See Bruce Scott, "A Place in the Sun: The Industrial Council at Massey-Harris, 1919–1929," *L/LT* 1 (1976). See also: Veronica Strong-Boag, "The Girl of the New Day: Canadian Working Women in the 1920's," *ibid.* 4 (1979); Ian Radforth and Joan Sangster, "A Link Between Labour and Learning: The Workers' Educational Association in Ontario, 1917–1951," *ibid.* 8–9 (1981–82); and Hugh Grant, "Solving the Labour Problem at Imperial Oil: Welfare Capitalism in the Canadian Petroleum Industry," *ibid.* 41 (1998).

14. Surviving the Depression   Documents dealing with most aspects of the depression era can be found in Michiel Horn (ed.) *The Dirty Thirties: Canadians in the Great Depression* (Toronto: Copp Clark, 1972). Letters to R.B. Bennett are among the more poignant documents of the period: Linda Grayson and Michael Bliss (eds.) *The Wretched of Canada* (Toronto: UTP, 1971). Among those who did not beg from Bennett were Ronald Liversedge, *Recollections of the On-To-Ottawa Trek* (Toronto: M&S, 1973). See also Victor Howard (ed.) *"We Were the Salt of the Earth": A Narrative of the On-to-Ottawa Trek and the Regina Riot* (Regina: Canadian Plains Research Centre, 1985); Lorne A. Brown, "Unemployment Relief Camps in Saskatchewan, 1933–1936," *Saskatchewan History* 23 (1970); Richard McCandless, "Vancouver's Red Menace of 1935: The Waterfront," *B.C. Studies* (1974) and, on women domestic workers in Quebec, Denyse Baillargeon, *Ménagères au temps de la Crise* (Montréal: Éditions du remue-ménage, 1991).

On the government's way with "troublemakers," see Avery, *Dangerous Foreigners*, chap. 5; and Barbara Roberts, "Shovelling out the Mutinous: Political Deportation from Canada before 1936," *L/LT* 18 (1986). The view that deportation was reserved for labour radicals was corrected by Henry Drystek, "'The Simplest and Cheapest Mode of Dealing with Them...': Deportation from Canada before World War II," *Histoire Sociale/Social History* 15 (1982). The Workers' Unity League still awaits a history. Among the sources are Ivan Avakumovic, *The Communist Party in Canada: A History* (Toronto: M&S, 1975); Myrtle Berggren, *Tough Timber* (Vancouver: n.p., 1966); Tom McEwen, *The Forge Glows Red: From Blacksmith to Revolutionary* (Toronto: Progress Books, 1974); John Manley, "Canadian Communists, Revolutionary Unions and the 'Third Period'"; and several articles in Irving Abella (ed.) *On Strike: Six Key Labour Struggles in Canada, 1919–1949* (Toronto: James, Lewis & Samuel, 1974). See also J. Petryshyn, "Class Conflict and Civil Liberties: The Origins and Activities of the Canadian Labour Defence League, 1925–1940," *L/LT* 10 (1982).

The Left in Quebec has been studied by Andrée Lévesque, *Virage à gauche interdit: les communistes, les socialistes et leurs ennemis au Québec, 1929–1939* (Montreal: Boréal Express, 1984). On another political flank, see Larry Hannant, "The Calgary Working Class and the Social Credit Movement in Alberta, 1932–35," *L/LT* 16 (1985). Labour legislation was part of the rethinking of the Canadian constitution in the period. See A.E. Grauer, *Labour Legislation: A Study Prepared for the Royal Commission on Dominion-Provincial Relations* (Ottawa: King's Printer, 1939); Jacob Finkelman and Bora Laskin, "Labour and

Unionization: Collective Bargaining" in Violet Anderson (ed.) *Problems in Canadian Unity* (Toronto: Thos. Nelson, 1939). On statistical problems of relevance to historians, see Udo Sautter, "Measuring Unemployment in Canada: Federal Efforts Before World War II," *Histoire Sociale/Social History* 15 (1982). The enthusiasm for tax-supported social reform among Canadian businessmen is described by Alvin Finkel, *Business and Social Reform in the Thirties* (Toronto: James Lorimer, 1979), esp. chap. 6. On the long depression-era fight for unemployment insurance, Struthers, *No Fault of Their Own*, chaps. 2–5; and Ruth Roach Pierson, "Gender and the Unemployment Insurance Debates in Canada, 1934–1940," *L/LT* 25 (1990).

15. Industrial Unionism   Through his early works, *Nationalism, Communism and Canadian Labour* (Toronto: UTP, 1973); "Oshawa, 1937" in *On Strike*; "The C.I.O., the Communist Party and the formation of the Canadian Congress of Labour, 1936–1941," *Historical Papers* (1969), Irving Abella has dominated the interpretation of the advent of the CIO and modern industrial unionism in Canada. For another view, see Penner, *The Canadian Left*, chap. 5. On other organizing experiences in the decade, see Duart Snow, "The Holmes Foundry Strike of March, 1937: 'We'll give their jobs to white men,'" *Ontario History* 69 (1977); Kim Adair, Peter Pautler and David Strang, "The U.R.W.A. and the Struggle for Union Recognition, 1937–1939" in J.T. Copp (ed.) *Industrial Unionism in Kitchener, 1937–47* (Elora: Cumnock Press, 1976); and a note on how Winnipeg's garment industry was organized in James Gray, *The Winter Years* (Toronto: Macmillan, 1966), pp. 126–40. Organizing fishermen in British Columbia is described by George North and Harold Griffin, *A Ripple, A Wave: The Story of Union Organization in the B.C. Fishing Industry* (Vancouver: Fishermen's Publishing Society, 1974). A union born in the late 1930s was headed for a short, tumultuous and controversial life. See William Kaplan, *Everything That Floats: Pat Sullivan, Hal Banks and the Seamen's Unions of Canada* (Toronto: UTP, 1987).

Labour struggles in Quebec in the 1930s and 40s were described by Evelyn Dumas, *The Bitter Thirties in Quebec* (Montreal: Black Rose, 1975). See also Denys Chouinard, "Alfred Charpentier face au gouvernement du Quebec, 1935–1946," *RHAF* 31 (1966); Alfred Charpentier, "La conscience syndicale lors des grèves du textile en 1937 et de l'amiante en 1940," *L/LT* 3 (1978); Rouillard, *Syndicalisme Québécois*, chap. 3. A union that barely emerged from the period was the Steelworkers. See Jean Gérin-Lajoie, *Les Métallos (1936–1981)* (Montreal: Boréal Express, 1982), chap. 1. Its struggle in Nova Scotia is recorded in Ron Crawley's article, "What Kind of Unionism: Struggles Among Sydney Steel Workers in the SWOC Years, 1936–1942," *L/LT* 39 (1997). David Frank and John Manley explore a poignant by-product of the Communist switch to a "popular front": "The Sad March to the Right: J.B. McLachlan's Resignation from the Communist Party of Canada, 1936," *L/LT* 30 (1992).

16. Fighting Hitler and Management   The war years were perhaps the most critical period for the development of Canada's industrial relations system. It may be a comment on what labour historians consider important that Laurel Sefton MacDowell has been left almost single-handed to explore the problem. She has been equal to the task. Her signpost article is "The Formation of the Canadian Industrial Relations System During World War Two," *L/LT* 3 (1978) and, in more detail, *'Remember Kirkland Lake': The Gold Miners' Strike of 1941–42* (Toronto: UTP, 1983) and "The 1943 Steel Strike Against Wartime Wage Controls," *L/LT* 10 (1982). See also Jeremy Webber, "The Malaise of Compulsory Conciliation: Strike Prevention in Canada During World War II," *ibid.* 15 (1985). Local experiences are described by Phillips, *No Power Greater,* chap. 8; Paul MacEwan, *Miners and Steelworkers,* chaps. 15–18; Michael Earle, "Down with Hitler and Silby Barrett: The Cape Breton Miners' Slowdown Strike of 1941," *Acadiensis* 18 (1988); Evelyn Dumas, *The Bitter Thirties in Quebec,* chap. 6 (on public service strikes in wartime Montreal); and Bryan Mahn and Ralph Schaffner, "The Packinghouse Workers in Kitchener" in Copp, *Industrial Unionism in Kitchener.* See also J.T. Copp, "The Experience of Industrial Unionism in Four Ontario Towns, 1937–1947," *Bulletin of the Committee on Canadian Labour History* (1978) and "The Rise of Industrial Unions in Montreal, 1935–1945," *Relations industrielles* 37 (1982).

On women workers in the war effort: Ruth R. Pierson, *"They're Still Women After All": The Second World War and Canadian Womanhood* (Toronto: M&S, 1986); and Ellen Scheinberg, "The Tale of Tessa the Textile Worker: Female Textile Workers in Cornwall During World War II," *L/LT* 33 (1994).

A more conventional theme for the period has been the struggle between the Communists and their enemies. The theme is handled, if not to the entire satisfaction of partisans, by Abella, *Nationalism, Communism and Canadian Labour,* Avakumovic, *Communist Party in Canada,* chap. 5; and Gad Horowitz, *Canadian Labour in Politics* (Toronto: UTP, 1968), chaps. 2–3. Communist perspectives are available in Beeching and Clarke, *Tim Buck* and, in a peculiar way, by the CSU's joint founder, J.A. Sullivan, *Red Sails on the Great Lakes* (Toronto: Macmillan, 1955). See also Bill White, *Shipyard at War* (Vancouver: Arsenal Pulp Press, 1983). For defence of Communists interned in the early war years, William Repka and Kathleen Repka, *Dangerous Patriots: Canada's Unknown Prisoners of War* (Vancouver: New Star Books, 1982). See also Reg Whitaker, "Official Repression of Communism During World War II," *L/LT* 17 (1986); and Marcus Klee, "'Hands Off Labour Forum': The Making and Unmaking of National Working-Class Radio Broadcasting in Canada, 1935–1944," *L/LT* 35 (1995).

17. People Coming Into Their Own   Perhaps the obvious is invisible but the history of PC 1003, family allowances and a government commitment to full employment has, with a few exceptions, largely bypassed historians of the working class. H.A. Logan dealt with aspects in *State Intervention and Assistance in Collective Bargaining: The Canadian Experience, 1943–1954* (Toronto: UTP, 1956), chaps. 2–3. Laurel Sefton MacDowell's articles remain basic. See above. David Moulton wrote "Ford Windsor 1945" for Abella, *On Strike.* A romantic view is found in Mark G. Walsh and Mary Baruth-Walsh, *Strike! 99 Days on the Line: The Workers' Own Story of the 1945 Windsor Ford Strike* (Ottawa: Penumbra

Press 1995). See also Herb Collins, *Ninety-Nine Days: The Ford Strike in Windsor in 1945* (Toronto: NC Press, 1995). On the Kaufman strike see "Alone in His Glory" in Copp, *Industrial Unionism*. On King and the welfare state, J.L. Granatstein, *Canada's War: The Wartime Politics of the Mackenzie King Government, 1939–1945* (Toronto: Oxford, 1974), chaps. 7, 10.

18. No Falling Back   The crucial postwar conflicts have also had little more than cursory treatment, but see Heron *et al.*, *All That Our Hands Have Done*; Stuart Jamieson, *Times of Trouble*, chap. 6; Robert England and Del Stewart, "The 1946 Rubber Workers' Strike" in Copp, *Industrial Unionism*. Another, more corporate view of the Stelco strike is William Kilbourn's *The Elements Combined: A History of the Steel Company of Canada* (Toronto: Clarke-Irwin, 1960), chap. 11. On the department store campaign, see Eileen Tallman Sufrin, *The Eaton Drive: The Campaign to Organize Canada's Largest Department Store, 1948–1952* (Toronto: Fitzhenry & Whiteside, 1982). Harold Logan's *Trade Unions in Canada* recorded labour at its postwar high.

On Quebec's most famous strike of the period, see P.E. Trudeau (ed.) *The Asbestos Strike* (Toronto: James, Lewis & Samuel, 1974); Fraser Isbister, "Asbestos, 1949" in Abella, *On Strike*. For a different view of that strike and much else, Gérard Dion (ed.) *Cinquante ans d'action ouvrière: les mémoires d'Alfred Charpentier* (Quebec: Presses de l'Université Laval, 1971). On Quebec from an anti-union perspective, see Conrad Black, *Duplessis* (Toronto: M&S, 1977). See also Rouillard, *Syndicalisme Québécois*, chap. 4; Denyse Baillargeon, "La grève de Lachute (1947)," *RHAF* 37 (1983). On postwar legislation, see Ann Porter, "Women and Income Security in the Post-War Period: The Case of Unemployment Insurance, 1945–1962," *L/LT* 31 (1993).

19. Struggle for Allegiance   Politics have tended to dominate the interpretation of Canadian labour history, with the losers having the most academic admirers. See Abella, *Nationalism Communism and Canadian Labour* and, in a more pointed argument, in "American Unions, Communism and the Canadian Labour Movement: Some Myths and Realities" in R.A. Preston (ed.) *The Influence of the United States on Canadian Development* (Toronto and Durham: UTP, 1972). See also Reg Whitaker and Gary Marcuse, *Cold War Canada: The Making of a National Insecurity State, 1945–1957* (Toronto: UTP, 1995). Less sympathetic to the communist view were Horowitz, *Canadian Labour in Politics*, chaps. 3–4; Walter Young, *The Anatomy of a Party: The National CCF, 1932–61* (Toronto: UTP, 1969), pp. 254–85. J.T. Copp, *The IUE in Canada* (Kitchener: Cumnock Press, 1979) records the story of a break-away anti-Communist union which, on the whole, lost the fight. G.L. Caplan, *The Dilemma of Canadian Socialism* (Toronto: M&S, 1973) deals more directly with the CCF-Communist struggle in Ontario.

A fascinating artifact of the time was J.A. Sullivan's memoir, *Red Sails on the Great Lakes*. A partisan pro-CSU view is in John Stanton, *Life & Death of the Canadian Seamen's Union* (Ottawa: Steel Rail, 1979). For a more objective version, Kaplan, *Everything That Floats*, chaps. 3–5. See also Avakumovic, *Communist Party of Canada*, chap. 7. A version of the IWA fight not recognizable in

Abella's book will be found in Jerry Lembcke and W.M. Tattan, *One Union in Wood: A Political History of the International Woodworkers of America* (Vancouver: Hunter Publishing, 1984). Rick Salutin, *Kent Rowley, the Organizer: A Canadian Union Life* (Toronto: James Lorimer, 1980) provides a eulogy for a significant figure of the period who would re-emerge in the 1970s. See also Howard White, *A Hard Man to Beat: The Story of Bill White: Labour Leader, Historian, Shipyard Worker, Raconteur: An Oral History* (Vancouver: Pulp Press, 1983); and Sue Calhoun, *"Ole Boy": Memories of a Canadian Labour Leader, J.K. Bell* (Halifax: Marine Workers Federation, 1992).

20. The Merger Movement   The best single explanation for the merger movement is provided by E.A. Forsey, "The Movement Toward Labour Unity in Canada: History and Implications," *Canadian Journal of Economics and Political Science* 21 (1958). See also John Tait Montague, "International Unions and the Canadian Trade Union Movement," *ibid.* 20 (1958). For the political aspects, see Horowitz, *Canadian Labour in Politics*, chaps. 5 and 6; Young, *Anatomy of a Party*, chap. 5; Desmond Morton, *The New Democratic Party, 1961–1986: The Politics of Change* (Toronto: Copp Clark Pitman, 1986), chaps. 1–2; Ivan Avakumovic, *Socialism in Canada: A Study of the CCF-NDP in Federal and Provincial Politics* (Toronto: M&S, 1978), chap. 5; Susan Mann Trofimenkoff, *Stanley Knowles: The Man From Winnipeg North Centre* (Saskatoon: Western Producer Prairie Books, 1982), chaps. 12–13. An analysis of Canadian union leadership in the 1950s is found in John Porter, *The Vertical Mosaic: An Analysis of Social Class and Power in Canada* (Toronto: UTP, 1965), chaps. 10–11. On Quebec developments in the Duplessis years see Rouillard, *Syndicalisme Québécois*, chap. 4 and, from another perspective, Jean-Marc Carles and others, *L'Histoire de la FTQ: des tout débuts jusqu'en 1965* (Montréal: Fédération des travailleurs et travailleuses du Québec, 1988). A strike of some significance for the CNTU's evolution is described in Pierre Vadeboncœur, "Histoire de la grève chez Dupuis Frères," *En Grève: l'Histoire de la C.S.N. et des luttes menées par ses militants de 1937 à 1963* (Montreal: Editions du Jour, 1963). Canadian labour's international role is usually overlooked. An exception is Anthony Carew, "Charles Millard: A Canadian in the International Labour Movement: A Case Study of the ICFTU, 1955–1961," *L/LT* 37 (1996).

21. Times of Frustration   Stuart Jamieson, "Labour Unionism and Collective Bargaining" in Michael Oliver (ed.) *Social Purpose for Canada* (Toronto: UTP, 1961) surveyed the goals and problems of a union movement on the verge of new expansion. On the Newfoundland strike: R.J. Hattenhauer, *A Brief Labour History of Newfoundland* (n.p., n.d.), pp. 195–224; H. Landon Ladd, "The Newfoundland Loggers; Strike of 1959" in Cherwinski & Kealey, *Lectures on Labour History*. On the Murdochville strike: Guy Bélanger, "La grève du Murdochville (1957)," *L/LT* 8–9 (1981–82). Industrial relations as they functioned in the early 1960s can be studied in G.F. McDonald's *The Brandon Packers' Strike* (Toronto: UTP, 1971). See also J.C. Cameron and F.J.L. Young, *The Status of Trade Unions in Canada* (Kingston: QU/IRC, 1961). A modern critique of "Fordism," applied to its most characteristic practitioner, is Charlotte Yates,

From Plant to Politics: The Autoworkers Union in Postwar Canada (Philadelphia: Temple University Press, 1993). See also Don Wells, "The Impact of the Postwar Compromise on Canadian Unionism: The Formation of an Auto Worker Local in the 1950s," *L/LT* 36 (1995).

22. Prosperity and Discontent   On the SIU affair, David Kwavnick, *Organized Labour and Pressure Politics: The Canadian Labour Congress, 1956–1968* (Montreal and Kingston: MQUP, 1972); Kaplan, *Everything That Floats*, chaps. 7–11; Robert Laxer, *Canada's Unions* (Toronto: James Lorimer, 1970), pp. 97–107. On the Toronto ITU strike, Walter Stewart, *Strike!* (Toronto: M&S, 1977); Sally Zerker, *Toronto Typographical Union*, chaps. 12–13. On politics and labour in the 1960s: Richard U. Miller, "Organized Labour and Politics in Canada" in R.U. Miller and Fraser Isbister, *Canadian Labour in Transition* (Scarborough: Prentice-Hall, 1971).

A union-based social innovation is described by Jonathan Lomex, *First and Foremost in Community Health Centres: The Centre in Sault Ste. Marie and the PHC Alternatives* (Toronto: UTP, 1985). A less kindly view of another Steelworker initiative is found in Mike Solski and John Smaller, *Mine Mill: The History of the International Union of Mine, Mill and Smelter Workers in Canada Since 1895* (Ottawa: Steel Rail, 1984), with echoes in Dieter K. Buse and Mercedes Steedman, "Reviewing the Past...: Activists Reminisce at the Mine-Mill Centennial Conference, Sudbury, May 1993," *L/LT* 33 (1994).

On industrial relations policy in the 1960s, John Crispo, "Organized Labour and National Planning" and Arthur Kruger, "Public Policy Towards Unions and Collective Bargaining" in Abraham Rotstein (ed.) *The Prospect of Change* (Toronto: McGraw-Hill, 1965) explored roles labour could play in an expansive, reformist decade. See also Joan Sangster, "Women Workers, Employment Policy and the State: The Establishment of the Ontario Women's Bureau, 1963–1970," *L/LT* 36 (1995). As usual, Quebec was different. See Louis-Marie Tremblay, *Le syndicalisme Québécois: Idéologies de la CSN et de la FTQ, 1940–1970* (Montreal: Presses de l'Université de Montréal, 1972). Immigration was both a by-product and a bulwark for postwar prosperity. See Franca Iacovetta, *Such Hardworking People: Italian Immigrants in Postwar Toronto* (Montreal and Kingston: MQUP, 1992).

23. Public Interest, Public Service   On early public-service unionism see Bill Doherty, *Slaves of the Lamp: A History of the Federal Civil Service Organizations, 1865–1924* (Victoria: Orca Books, 1991); Anthony Thomson, "The Large and General View': The Debate on Labour Affiliation in the Canadian Civil Service, 1918–1928," *L/LT* 2 (1977) and also "The Nova Scotia Civil Service Association, 1956–1967," *Acadiensis* 12 (1983). Good recent histories include Wayne Roberts, *Don't Call Me Servant: Government Work and Unions in Ontario, 1911–1984* (North York: OPSEU, 1994); Doug Smith, Jock Bates, Esyllt Jones, *Lives in the Public Service: A History of the Manitoba Government Employees' Union* (Winnipeg: Manitoba Labour Education Centre and MGEU, n.d. [1993]); Maurice Lemelin, *The Public Service Alliance of Canada: A Look at a Union in the Public Sector* (Los Angeles: UCLA Institute of Industrial Relations, 1978); Foster Griezic,

Canadian Union of Public Employees: The First Twenty Years, 1963–1983 (Ottawa: Carleton University Press, 1983); B. MacLean, *"A Union amongst Government Employees": A History of the British Columbia Government Employees' Union* (Vancouver: BCGEU, 1979). Ontario's unique women's teachers' federation persuaded Doris French to write its history, *High Button Bootstraps* (Toronto: Ryerson Press, 1968). A powerful figure in public sector unionism is depicted by Susan Crean, *Grace Hartman: A Documentary Biography* (Vancouver: New Star Books, 1995). See also Joe Davidson and John Deverell, *Joe Davidson* (Toronto: James Lorimer, 1978).

On public sector collective bargaining after the Second World War: Saul Frankel, *Staff Relations in the Civil Service* (Montreal: McGill University Press, 1962). See also J.F. O'Sullivan (ed.) *Collective Bargaining in the Public Service* (Toronto: Institute of Public Administration in Canada, 1973); Allen Ponak and Mark Thompson, "Public Sector Collective Bargaining" in Gunderson and Ponak, *Union-Management Relations.* See Peter Hennessey, *Schools in Jeopardy: Collective Bargaining in Education* (Toronto: M&S, 1979). On the Post Office, Blair Laidlaw and Bruce Curtis, "Inside Postal Workers: The Labor Process, State Policy and the Workers' Response," *L/LT* 18 (1986). For the Woods report, see H.D. Woods *et al., Canadian Industrial Relations* (Ottawa: Privy Council Office, 1968). John Crispo took advantage of his service with the Task Force to provide a snapshot of the system in the wake of the Woods report: see *The Canadian Industrial Relations System* (Toronto: McGraw-Hill Ryerson, 1978).

24. Justice and Nationalism   The radical talk of the era can be sampled in Dimitrios Rossopoulos, *Canada and Radical Social Change* (Montreal: Black Rose, 1973). A more moderate and typical collection of ideas is Trevor Lloyd and Jack McLeod, *Agenda 1970: Proposals for a Creative Politics* (Toronto: UTP, 1968). The arguments for and against international unions were put by John Crispo, *International Unionism: A Study in Canadian-American Relations* (Toronto: McGraw-Hill, 1967) and by Robert Laxer, *Canada's Unions*, esp. chaps. 30–32. On the minor variant from secular unionism, see Edward Vanderkloet, *A Christian Union in Labor's Wasteland* (Toronto: Wedge, 1978), a tract for the CLAC. Labour conflicts of the era are described by Christine Sylvester and Marion Harris, *On Strike* (Toronto: OISE Press, 1973). If strikes were sometimes violent, there was a reason. See Marc Zwelling, *The Strikebreakers* (Toronto: new press, 1972). The story of a union with a lively modern history and much experience of technological change is Elaine Bernard's *The Long Distance Feeling: A History of the Telecommunications Workers' Union* (Vancouver: New Star Books, 1982).

On women and work: Paul Phillips and Erin Phillips, *Women and Work: Inequality in the Labour Market* (Toronto: James Lorimer, 1983). A feminist account of bank organizing is Jackie Ainsworth, *An Account to Settle: The Story of the United Bank Workers (SORWUC)* (Vancouver: Press Gang Publications, 1972).

The organization of east coast fishermen was a feature of the early 1970s. See Silver Donald Cameron, *The Education of Everitt Richardson: the Nova Scotia*

Fishermen's Strike, 1970 (Toronto: M&S, 1977) and David Macdonald, *"Power Begins at the Cod End": The Newfoundland Trawlerman's Strike, 1974–5* (St. John's: MUN, ISER, 1980). Even better is Gordon Inglis, *More Than Just a Union: The Story of the NFFAWU* (St. John's: Jesperson Press, 1985). Illuminating some tough aspects of environmental issues: Lloyd Tataryn, *Dying for a Living: The Politics of Industrial Death* (Ottawa: Deneau & Greenberg, 1979).

25. Quebec and the Common Front   While Rouillard, *Syndicalisme Québécois*, chaps. 5–6, focusses on the 1960–1985 period in some detail, there are many other sources. Jacques Dofny and Paul Bernard, *Le syndicalisme au Québec: Structure et mouvement* (Ottawa: Privy Council Office, 1968) attempted to explain an unfamiliar scene to the Woods Task Force, as did Maurice Pinard, "Working-Class Politics: An Interpretation of the Quebec Case," *Canadian Journal of Sociology and Anthropology* 7 (1970), to a wider audience. Daniel Drache, *Quebec – Only the Beginning: The Manifestos of the Common Front* (Toronto: new press, 1972) was a response to the imminent prospect of revolution. See also B. Solasse, "Les idéologies de la Fédération des travailleurs du Québec et de la Confédération des syndicats nationaux, (1960–1978)" in Fernand Dumont *et al., Idéologies au Canada (1940–1976) vol. II, Les Mouvements sociaux – les syndicats* (Québec: Presses de l'Université Laval, 1981). The QFL carefully laid its claim to history with Louis Fournier's *Histoire de la FTQ, 1965–1992: La plus grande centrale syndicale au Québec* (Montréal: Québec/Amérique, 1994).

James Thwaites foresaw problems in Quebec that would be echoed elsewhere: "Tensions Within the Labour Movement in Quebec: Relations Between the Public and Private Sector: Three Case Studies from 1972 to 1982" in Mark Thompson and Gene Swimmer, *Conflict or Compromise: The Future of Public Sector Industrial Relations* (Montreal: Institute for Research on Public Policy, 1984). Press perceptions of Quebec unions in crisis were studied by Maryse Souchard, *Le discours de presse: l'image des syndicats au Québec [1982–1983]* (Longueuil: la Préambule, 1989). The Cliche commission report was published as *le Rapport de la Commission d'enquête sur l'exercice de la liberté syndicale dans l'industrie de la construction* (Québec: Editeur officiel, 1975). See also Jean Boivin, "Union-Management Relations in Quebec" in Gunderson and Ponak, *Union-Management Relations*, chap. 14. See also Roch Denis and Serge Denis, *Les syndicats face au pouvoir. Syndicalisme et politique au Québec de 1960 à 1992.* (Ottawa: les éditions du Vermillon, 1992).

26. Scapegoat for Inflation   On the AIB, see Allan Maslove and Gene Swimmer, *Wage Controls in Canada, 1975–78: A Study in Public Decision Making* (Montreal: Institute for Research in Public Policy, 1980). On the NDP in and out of power, Morton, *The Politics of Change*, chaps. 7–13. Coherent sources for contemporary history are a challenge to any historian. Guidance can be sought from the *Canadian Annual Review,* at least for the period 1960–79, from the *Labour Gazette,* until wound up in 1978, and from periodical indexes. The CLC published *Labour's Manifesto for Canada* but copies are scarce. Paul Weiler's reforms in B.C.'s labour relations are explained in *Reconcilable Differences* (Toronto: Carswell, 1980). Grain handlers were critical to a resource-based economy and their jobs were in jeopardy in the period. See Joel Novek, Grain Terminal Automation: A Case Study in the Control of Control," *L/LT* 22 (1988). A number of case studies showed how labour law worked in Nova Scotia: see C.H.J. Gilson (ed.) *Strikes in Nova Scotia, 1970–1985* (Hantsport: Lancelot Press, 1986).

27. Recession and Hard Times   During the 1980s, Marc Zwelling's valuable if short-lived *Vector Union Report* provided a central thread of news about the labour movement, especially in English-speaking Canada. On the problems of public-sector bargaining, Jacob Finkelman and Shirley Goldenberg, *Collective Bargaining in the Public Sector: The Canadian Experience* (Montreal: Institute for Research in Public Policy, 1983) offers a cool view. See also Shirley B. Goldenberg, *Canadian Industrial Relations: New Pressures, New Challenges* (Kingston: QU/IRC, 1986). Another review of the Fordist era, predominantly in Quebec, is Rodrigue Blouin *et al.*, *Les relations industrielles au Québec: 50 ans d'évolution* (Québec: Presses de l'Université Laval, 1994).

For a perceptive view of technology and its impact, see Heather Menzies, *Computers on the Job: Surviving Canada's Microcomputer Revolution* (Toronto: James Lorimer, 1982). On the Energy and Chemical Workers, a union that claimed to come to terms with technological change, see Tom Rankin, *New Forms of Work Organization: The Challenge for North American Unions* (Toronto: UTP, 1990).

28. Levelling the Playing Field   In "Towards Permanent Exceptionalism: Coercion and Consent in Canadian Industrial Relations," *L/LT* 13 (1984), Leo Panitch and Donald Swartz argued that Ottawa's Bill C-124 marked the end of conventional collective bargaining as known since 1944, a claim repeated in *From Consent to Coercion: The Assault on Trade Union Freedoms* (Toronto: Garamond, 1985). Bryan D. Palmer, *Solidarity: The Rise and Fall of an Opposition in British Columbia* (Vancouver: New Star Books, 1986) is a fierce attack on those who failed to lead the province to an open revolt in 1983. One of those accused responded. See Jack Munro and Jane O'Hara, *Union Jack* (Vancouver: Douglas & McIntyre, 1988).

A larger, more perceptive view of what was happening is found in Daniel Drache and Meric S. Gertler (eds.) *The New Era of Global Competition: State Policy and Market Power* (Montreal and Kingston: MQUP, 1991). The consequences for labour were evident to Larry Haiven's co-authors in *Regulating Labour: The State, Neo-Conservatism and Industrial Relations* (Toronto: Garamond, 1991) and Tom Rankin, *New Forms of Work Organization: The Challenge for North American Unions* (Toronto: UTP, 1990) (based on Local 800, ECNU). The most fascinating labour book of the 1980s was Bob White's *Hard Bargains: My Life on the Line* (Toronto: M&S, 1987), a highly personal account of the man who created the Canadian Auto Workers. An official version of the story is Sam Gindin's *The Canadian Auto Workers: The Birth and Transformation of a Union* (Toronto: James Lorimer, 1995). Other labour leaders of the decade were interviewed in Pradeep Kumar and Dennis Ryan, *Canadian Union Movement in the 1980s: Perspectives from Union Leaders* (Kingston: QU/IRC, 1988).

For a look at an old faithful, see George Sanderson and Fred Sapenhurst, *Industrial Democracy Today: A New Role for Labour* (Toronto: McGraw-Hill Ryerson, 1979). The subset known as QWL was argued for by J.B. Cunningham and T.H. White (eds.) *Quality of Working Life: Contemporary Cases* (Ottawa: Labour Canada, 1984) and ferociously against by Don Wells, *Soft Sell: "Quality of Working Life" Programs & The Productivity Race* (Ottawa: Canadian Centre for Policy Alternatives, 1986). An iconoclastic view of unionism from an intelligent insider, the president of the NUPGE, is John Fryer's "The State of the Union" in Donna Wilson (ed.) *Democratic Socialism: The Challenge of the Eighties and Beyond* (Vancouver: New Star Books, 1985).

29. Struggling to the Millennium   The present is by definition hard to document, particularly in an era when prevailing ideologies and lack of militancy put the Canadian labour movement on the back-burner. The chief sources, always questionable, become clipping files, overdue government statistics and interviews. Jamie Swift, a Kingston journalist, wrote an excellent account of life for Ontario workers in the 1990's recession: *Wheel of Fortune: Work and Life in the Age of Falling Expectations* (Toronto: Between the Lines, 1995). A shrewd reflection on his times can be found in D'Arcy Martin's *Thinking Union: Activism and Education in Canada's Labour Movement* (Toronto: Between the Lines, 1995).

Two short-lived NDP premiers who faced hostile labour backers described their experiences: Mike Harcourt (with Wayne Skene), *Mike Harcourt: A Measure of Defiance* (Vancouver: Douglas & McIntyre, 1996) and Bob Rae, who challenged the political realism of both labour and the NDP in *From Protest to Power: Personal Reflections on Life in Politics* (Toronto: Viking, 1996). Among Rae's critics was James Laxer, *In Search of a New Left: Canadian Politics After the Neoconservative Assault* (Toronto: Viking, 1996). That matters were different in Quebec seemed evident from Mona-Josée Gagnon, "Le nouveau modèle de relations du travail au Québec et le syndicalisme," *Journal of Canadian Studies* 30 (1995).

30. Unfinished Business   For a personal review of Canadian labour history's achievements and "unfinished business," see Desmond Morton, "Labour and Industrial Relations History in English-speaking Canada" in Gerard Hébert, Hem C. Jain and Noah M. Meltz, *The State of the Art in Industrial Relations* (Kingston and Toronto: Centre for Industrial Relations and QU/IRC, 1988) and, as a balance, James Thwaites, "History and Industrial Relations in Canada," *ibid.*

BIBLIOGRAPHICAL GUIDES

The fullest bibliography of Canadian labour history was compiled by G. Douglas Vaisey, *The Labour Companion: A Bibliography of Canadian Labour History Based on Materials Printed from 1950 to 1975* (Halifax: Committee on Canadian Labour History, 1980) and kept up to date by ample bibliographical articles in *Labour/*

le Travail. A counterpart for French Canada is André Leblanc and James D. Thwaites, *Le Monde ouvrier au Québec: bibliographie retrospective* (Montreal: Presses de l'Université du Québec, 1973). See also Russell G. Hahn, G.S. Kealey, Linda Kealey and Peter Warrian, *Primary Sources in Canadian Working Class History* (Kitchener: Dumont Press, 1973).

Abbreviations

ACCL	All-Canadian Congress of Labour	BRT	Brotherhood of Railroad Trainmen
ACTC	Average Comparability of Total Compensation		
ACTE	Association of Clerical and Technical Employees	CAIMAW	Canadian Association of Industrial, Mechanical and Allied Workers
ACW	Amalgamated Clothing Workers		
AFL	Americal Federation of Labor	CALURA	Corporations and Labour Unions Returns Act
AIB	Anti-Inflation Board		
ASCJ	Amalgamated Society of Carpenters and Joiners	CAW	National Automobile, Aerospace, Transportation and General Workers Union of Canada
ASE	Amalgamated Society of Engineers		
		CBRE	Canadian Brotherhood of Railway Employees
B&SWIU	Boot and Shoe Workers International Union	CBRT&GW	Canadian Brotherhood of Railway, Transport and General Workers
BCFL	British Columbia Federation of Labour	CCCL	Canadian and Catholic Confederation of Labour
BCNI	Business Council on National Issues	CCF	Co-operative Commonwealth Federation
BCT	Bakery, Confectionery and Tobacco Workers Union	CCU	Confederation of Canadian Unions
BESCO	British Empire Steel & Coal Corporation	CECBA	Crown Employees Collective Bargaining Act
BLE	Brotherhood of Locomotive Engineers	CEP	Communications, Energy and Paper Workers of Canada
BLFE	Brotherhood of Locomotive Firemen and Enginemen	CEQ	Corporation des enseignants du Québec
BRAC	Brotherhood of Railroad and Airline Clerks	CFAW	Canadian Food and Allied Workers

CFIB	Canadian Federation of Independent Business		FTQ	Fédération des travailleurs du Québec (QFL)
CFL	Canadian Federation of Labour			
CIO	Congress of Industrial Organizations		GTR	Grand Trunk Railway
			GWR	Great Western Railway
CLAC	Christian Labour Association of Canada		HREIU	Hotel and Restaurant Employees' Union
CLC	Canadian Labour Congress			
CLP	Canadian Labour Party		IAM	International Association of Machinists
CLRB	Canada Labour Relations Board			
CLRC	Canada Labour Relations Council		IBEW	International Brotherhood of Electrical Workers
CLU	Canadian Labour Union		IBT	International Brotherhood of Teamsters
CMA	Canadian Manufacturers' Association		IDIA	Industrial Disputes Investigations Act
CMU	Canadian Maritime Union			
CNR	Canadian National Railway		ILGWU	International Ladies Garment Workers' Union
CNTU	Confederation of National Trade Unions (CSN)			
COLA	cost of living adjustment		ILO	International Labour Organization
CPC	Communist Party of Canada			
CPC(ML)	Communist Party of Canada (Marxist-Leninist)		ILP	Independent Labour Party
			IMB	Imperial Munitions Board
CPR	Canadian Pacific Railway		IMIU	Iron Molders International Union
CPU	Canadian Paperworkers Union			
CPUSA	Communist Party of the United States of America		INCO	International Nickel Company
			IRDIA	Industrial Relations and Disputes Investigations Act
CSD	Centrale des syndicats démocratiques			
			ITU	International Typographical Union
CSN	Confédération des syndicats nationaux (CNTU)			
			IUE	International Union of Electrical Workers
CSU	Canadian Seamen's Union			
CTCU	Canadian Textile & Chemical Union		IUMMSW	International Union of Mine, Mill & Smelter Workers
CUBE	Canadian Union of Bank Employees		IWA	International Woodworkers of America
CUPE	Canadian Union of Public Employees		IWW	Industrial Workers of the World
CUPW	Canadian Union of Postal Workers		LCUC	Letter Carriers' Union of Canada
			LPP	Labour Progressive Party
CWA	Communication Workers of America		LWIU	Lumber Workers' Industrial Union
CWC	Communication Workers of Canada			
			MWUC	Mine Workers' Union of Canada
DOSCO	Dominion Steel and Coal Company		NCCL	National Council of Canadian Labour
ENA	Experimental National Agreement		NDP	New Democratic Party
			NIRA	National Industrial Recovery Act (US)
ESOP	Employee Stock Option Plan			
			NLRA	National Labour Relations Act (US)
FOOTALU	Federation of Organized Trades and Labor Unions			
			NLRB	National Labour Relations Board (US)
FPU	Fishermen's Protective Union		NRA	National Recovery Act (US)

NRMA	National Resources Mobilization Act	SIU	Seafarers' International Union
NTLC	National Trades and Labour Congress	SLP	Social Labor Party
		SORWUC	Service, Office and Retail Workers Union of Canada
NUPGE	National Union of Provincial Government Employees	SPC	Socialist Party of Canada
		STELCO	Steel Company of Canada
NWLB	National War Labour Board	SWOC	Steelworkers Organizing Committee
NWMP	North West Mounted Police		
		TLC	Trades and Labour Congress of Canada
OBU	One Big Union		
OFL	Ontario Federation of Labour	TTA	Toronto Trades Assembly
OPEC	Organization of Petroleum Exporting Countries	TTLC	Toronto Trades and Labour Council
OPP	Ontario Provincial Police	TTU	Toronto Typographical Union
ORT	Order of Railroad Telegraphers	TUC	Trades Union Congress (UK)
PAC	Political Action Committee	UAW	United Auto Workers
PATCO	Professional Air Traffic Controllers' Organization	UBCJ	United Brotherhood of Carpenters & Joiners
PEC	Political Education Committee	UBRE	United Brotherhood of Railroad Employees
PPWC	Pulp and Paper Workers of Canada	UE	United Electrical Workers
PQ	Parti Québécois	UFAW	United Fishermen and Allied Workers
PSAC	Public Service Alliance of Canada	UFCW	United Food and Commercial Workers
PWA	Provincial Workmen's Association	UFO	United Farmers of Ontario
PWOC	Packinghouse Workers Organizing Committee	UMW	United Mine Workers
		UNITE	Union of Needletrades, Industrial and Textile Employees
QFL	Quebec Federation of Labour (FTQ)	UPWA	United Packinghouse Workers
QPP	Quebec Provincial Police	URWA	United Rubber, Cork and Linoleum Workers of America
QWL	Quality of Working Life	USWA	United Steelworkers of America
RCAF	Royal Canadian Air Force	UTWA	United Textile Workers of America
RCMP	Royal Canadian Mounted Police		
RILU	Red International of Labor Unions	VTLC	Vancouver Trades and Labour Council
RNWMP	Royal North West Mounted Police		
RWDSU	Retail, Wholesale and Department Store Union	WCB	Workers' Compensation Board
		WFM	Western Federation of Miners
SEIU	Service Employees International Union	WPTB	Wartime Prices and Trade Board
		WUL	Workers' Unity League

Index

Aberhart, William, 148
Acme Screw & Gear, 296
adversarial bargaining, 309–10
affirmative action, 355
Africa, 330
aging workers, 296, 331
Agnaieff, Michel, 334–5
AIDS testing, 357
Air Canada, 339, 341, strike, 255
air control system, 350
aircraft industry, 170–1, 175, 180, 217
Alberta, 50, 55, 82, 98, 111, 117, 148, 169, 180, 316, 327, 331, 348; civil servants, 263, 301, 348; Depression, 151; labour, 262, 322
Alberta Union of Public Employees, 348
Algoma Steel, 191, 193, 338
Algoma Steel Workers Union, 162; 1943 strike, 261; 1946: 193
Alien Labour Act (Canada), 83
All-Canadian Congress of Labour (ACCL), 76, 132, 141, 146, 148–9, 158–9, 202, 275; formation, 167–9; and Communists, 134
Allan, William, 18
Alma College strike, 331
Alpine Meats strike, 296
Alsbury, Stewart, 210
Aluminum Company of Canada, 17, 289
Amalgamated Association of Street Railway Employees, 71–2

Amalgamated Civil Servants of Canada, 257
Amalgamated Clothing Workers (ACW), 134, 153, 170, 341
Amalgamated Meatcutters and Butcher Workmen, 278, 338
Amalgamated Postal Workers, 257
Amalgamated Sheet Metal Workers, 84
Amalgamated Society of Carpenters and Joiners, 18, 57
Amalgamated Society of Engineers (ASE), 18, 22, 108
Amalgamated Trades Union (Halifax), 6, 59
Amalgamated Transit Workers, 330
ambulance drivers, 297
American Federation of Labor (AFL), 39, 59, 68–9, 73–4, 78, 81–3, 95, 97, 116, 142, 153, 158, 165, 208, 220, 222, 223; and Berlin Convention, 73–4; and First World War, 112; and seamen, 208; merger with CIO, 153–4, 222–4
American Federation of Labor – Congress of Industrial Organizations (AFL-CIO), 223, 233, 277, 293, 320, 321, 331, 340, 349; and building trades, 280; Canadian membership, 333; and building trades, 281–2, 293; and world, 330
American Labor Union, 95
"American Plan," 130
Americanization, 275–6, 320

387